AN AMERICAN ARISTOCRACY

The Livingstons

CLARE BRANDT

Cover Photograph: Honoria and Janèt Livingston with their grandmother, Alice Clarkson, and "Punchie," Clermont, 1910. (Courtesy of Clermont State Historic Site, New York State Office of Parks, Recreation and Historic Preservation, Taconic Region.)

Paperback edition: Poughkeepsie, N.Y., 1990

Originally published by Doubleday & Co., 1986

Library of Congress Cataloging-in-Publication Data
Brandt, Clare.
An American aristocracy.
Bibliography: p. 273
Includes index.
1. Livingston family. 2. Hudson River Valley (N.Y.
and N.J.)—Biography. I. Title.
CT274.L58B73 1986   974.7'3'00992 [B]   82—45475
ISBN: 0-385-15875-0

To Carl

ACKNOWLEDGMENTS

I am grateful to the many members of the Livingston family who shared
with me their recollections and reflections: Richard Aldrich, Susan Aldrich,
Wint Aldrich, Bronson Chanler, Mary Chanler, Frances and Howland Da-
vis, the late Anita and late John Delafield, Libby and Warren Delano, Mad-
die DeMott, the late Olin Dows, Janet Graham, Mary Gray, Emily Harding,
Eliot Hawkins, Benjamin LaFarge, Susannah Lessard, Dorothy Livingston,
Henry Livingston, Mrs. Reginald L. M. McVitty and the late Rex McVitty,
Rosalind Michahelles, the late Roland Redmond, Mary Rosenquest, Alida
Stamm, Margaret Suckley and Alice Van Tuyl.

   Other family members have been helpful in calling my attention to
sources and providing me with materials: Sylvie Griffiths, who permitted me
to read her unpublished biographical sketch of Johnston Livingston; James
Duane Livingston, who shared the products of his research on Robert Cambridge Livingston; Mrs. A. R. Heath, who gave me my first glimpse of Mrs.
Maturin Livingston's letters; Mr. and Mrs. Laurence Walker Livingston Barrington; John C. Claflin; Irene and Victor Livingston; Johnston R. Livingston; and Robert C. L. Timpson.

   A number of other people were generous with their time, thoughts and
observations: Anne and Dick Crowley, Barbara Dupee, Alf Evers, Rose and
Joe Griffin, Allene Hatch, Helen Henderson, Mary Hoffman, Louise and
the late Reamer Kline, Jack Lewis, Elaine Liepshutz, Elliott Lindsley, Stanley
Martin, Eleanor Matthews, Margaret Partridge, Elizabeth Rifenburg, Eleanor and the late Richard Rovere, Henry L. Scott, Margaret Shafer, Andrews
Wanning and Richard Wiles.

   I was extremely fortunate to encounter along the way several scholars
with overlapping fields of interest, who generously shared the fruits of their
labors: Cynthia Philip; Diane L. Zaragoza; Roberta Singer; Kathryn

Lieurance, to whom Hudson Valley historians will be forever grateful for
her translations of the Livingston-Redmond Papers, placed permanently on
deposit at the Roosevelt Library in Hyde Park; Ruth Piwonka, whose
breadth of background saved me days of labor and a number of false conclusions; and most particularly Bruce Naramore, Site Manager at Clermont
State Historic Site, whose relish for historical research and rumination is
matched only by his infinite patience in the face of incessant questions and
demands on his time.

Other members of the staff at Clermont State Historic Site deserve
special thanks for their consistent interest and assistance: former Site Manager Cheryl Gold, Paul Kengla (who also took photographs for the book),
and Jeanne Stalker.

Elaine Liepshutz, Bim Chanler and Anne and Dick Crowley loaned
books, which I often kept for unconscionable lengths of time; and Virginia
Brown, Jack Lewis, Elliott Lindsley and Alice Mathews loaned or gave me
invaluable miscellaneous materials.

I am indebted to Charles Gehring of the New York State Library New
Netherland Project for his exposition concerning "Broek" and "britches"
and other Dutch puns; to Dennis Wentworth and Paul Huey of the New
York State Bureau of Historic Sites for rescuing me from a potential blun-
der concerning George Washington's mysterious coat button; to Carlos
Fuentes for the anecdote of the French aristocrat's nose; to the Marquis and
Marchioness of Linlithgow and the Secretary to the Lord Lyon (Edinburgh)
for information regarding the Livingston Scottish titles; to Marion L. Stock
of the Falls Village-Canaan Historical Society and H. Davis Daboll of the
Salisbury Association for Connecticut Livingston lore; and to Wilma Neyer
and Melodye Kaltz for steering me in various productive directions.

For splendid boating on the mighty Hudson, my thanks to Jack Macrae,
Bob Fennish and Jeff Seiftz; and appreciation to the cordial owners of Grasmere for their hospitality and interest.

I am grateful to the staffs of the following research institutions for their
help:

Clermont State Historic Site
The Columbia County Historical Society
The Franklin D. Roosevelt Library at Hyde Park, particularly William
    Emerson, Director, and Raymond Teichman, Supervisory Archi-
    vist
The New-York Historical Society, particularly Manuscript Curator
    Tom Dunnings
The New York Public Library, Manuscripts and Archives section
The Museum of the City of New York, particularly Steven Miller and
    Valerie Dry-Henich
The New York Genealogical and Biographical Society

The New York State Library, Manuscripts and Special Collections

The Massachusetts Historical Society, particularly Marjorie Gutheim and Virginia Audet

The Adriance Memorial Library in Poughkeepsie, Local History Room, particularly Kevin Gallagher

The Vassar Library, Poughkeepsie, Rare Book Room

The Bard College Library, Annandale-on-Hudson.

Two anonymous members of the Livingston family permitted me to use their family portraits as illustrations for the book, and Elise Barry of Wilderstein Preservation, Inc., helped me search for appropriate photographs. Most of all, Wint Aldrich gave generously of his time and care in recalling, locating and furnishing family photographs from the Rokeby Collection. Other illustrations were provided by:

Paul Kengla

New York State Office of Parks, Recreation and Historic Preservation, Bureau of Historic Sites

Columbia County Historical Society (particular thanks to Sally Bottigi)

Mills Mansion State Historic Site in Staatsburgh (thanks to John Feeny)

Dutchess County Landmarks Association (thanks to Stephanie Mauri)

The New-York Historical Society

The New York Public Library: Astor, Lenox and Tilden Foundations

The Art Commission of the City of New York.

Jennifer Brehl of Doubleday & Co. deserves special thanks for her patience and good humor in initiating me into the mysteries of permissions, captions, photo credits and other esoterica.

Penultimately, I would like to thank five peerless friends/readers/editors, without whose insight, skill and encouragement this book would never have been completed: Kate Medina, whose wisdom and persistence led me out of the trees toward a view of the forest; the late John Cushman, my agent, who gave me confidence when I needed it most; Jane Cushman, his successor, who carries on magnificently; Joe Reed, who informed and energized the final stages with his thoughtful and constructive reading; and Carl Brandt, who—in addition to making life possible in the first place—read and read, listened and talked, and made me believe that it was going to come out right in the end.

Last but not least, I would like to thank Colin and Diana Brandt, who since the beginning of this book, when they were respectively nine and seven years old, have provided stalwart companionship and support. They have tiptoed, taken phone messages, cooked, weeded, cheered up, egged on and never expressed (out loud, at least) the faintest wish to have me stop before I got to the end.

CONTENTS

PROLOGUE

The Indians called it "The River That Flows Two Ways," because it is tidal for its first hundred and fifty miles—all the way from New York Harbor up to Albany. Henry Hudson, who sailed it in 1609 looking for a northwest passage to the Orient, christened it the Mauritius, after the Dutch ruler whom he served. Ruler and sailor were both disappointed: there was no northwest passage. Even so, by the end of the seventeenth century, the river that now bore Hudson's name had become America's busiest commercial and military thoroughfare—and Robert Livingston, the young Scotsman who had managed to possess himself of much of its central valley, was well on his way to establishing the second of the great colonial American aristocracies. Virginia's first families had landed first, by just a few years.

July 22, 1686, is the official date on which Robert Livingston, a thirty-one-year-old immigrant merchant, son of a humble Scottish clergyman, was by royal patent transmogrified into "Robert Livingston, Lord of Livingston Manor," owner of 160,000 acres of the east bank of the Hudson River and master of a potential manorial menage straight out of the Middle Ages. The wording of Robert's royal patent was identical to the standard, centuries-old English baronial grant, complete with vassals and quitrents, days' riding,* courts leet and baron and the right to appoint clergy.

Had Robert Livingston arrived in New York a few years earlier, when

---

* A day's riding, in medieval terminology, consisted of a tenant's labor for a day on manor projects: road repairs, barn building or hauling wood for the manor house.

it was still New Netherland and owned by the Dutch, his title would have been Patroon instead of Manor Lord. (Many of his wife's Dutch relatives still insisted on calling him Patroon.) Patroon or Lord, the title sounded much grander than it was. Livingston Manor in 1686 was nothing more than a vast wilderness, untenanted, unimproved and unprofitable. It took Robert some forty years to remedy that, and in the meantime he matter-of-factly styled himself "Robert Livingston, Merchant." Only on reaching his seventies, after decades of struggle against savage Indians, rapacious royal governors and rebellious tenants, in defense of property, profits and life itself, did he permit himself the indulgence of signing his will "Robert Livingston, Proprietor of Livingston Manor."

But never "Lord"; Robert was a realist.

His children and grandchildren also eschewed the title Lord of the Manor, although they cared deeply for some of the other trappings of gentility. Each of Robert's sons and grandsons inherited at least one of his outstanding traits—charm, acuity, ruthlessness, courage, recklessness, perseverance—but none in a combination to equal their progenitor. Still, these first two generations of American Livingston men managed to consolidate and expand the financial, political and social territory Robert had carved out for them. Livingstons distinguished themselves in the congresses of early America, both colonial and independent, as well as on her battlefields. From the manor house on the Hudson River, Livingston girls were married to the cream of colonial society: Delanos, Beekmans, Schuylers and Van Rensselaers; and Livingston sloops sailed from the manor dock loaded with produce and manufactures for the markets of the world. The family acquired land in the West Indies and pioneered the international trade in rum and sugar.

Most significant of all, at least for the Livingston amour propre, the family landholdings in the Hudson Valley were increased through purchase and marriage from the original 160,000 to nearly a million acres by the end of the second generation. Robert the Founder's grandchildren became—almost overnight, in European terms—a landed aristocracy.

But rapid growth has a tendency to be shallow-rooted and spindly-topped, vulnerable to political winds, social infestations and economic droughts. The Livingston dynasty was no exception. Along with their lands, their family pride and solidarity, and their sense of public responsibility, Robert's children and grandchildren grew up with a set of fixed social assumptions that were doomed to obsolescence. Something over which they had no control—the political destiny of America—created in the late eighteenth century an environment utterly inimical to the manorial attitudes which all the Livingstons had come by then to share. The English model they strove to emulate—that of the landed aristocrat, leisured, cultured and running the country in his spare time—could not be perpetuated here. The budding aristocratic ideals of the Livingstons of the Enlightenment were destined not to flower in America.

Judge Robert R. Livingston, chief justice of the Supreme Court of the province of New York and grandson of the first Robert Livingston, came closest to the ideal; but he never really had a chance. A man of profound erudition, quiet habits, harmonious disposition and distinguished accomplishment, Judge Livingston had the bad luck to be born in 1718 and found himself at the age of forty-seven forced to choose between submitting to the economic strangulation of his family and country on the one hand and committing treason on the other. In 1765, at the request of the New York Committee of Correspondence on which he served, Judge Livingston penned an address to King George III of such felicity of expression, such clarity, conciliation and firmness that it earned him a place at the top of His Majesty's list of colonial traitors.

The Judge's son, also named Robert R. Livingston (in the nomenclaturally maddening manner of the Livingston family), reaped the whirlwind. At the age of twenty-eight he cast his lot with the cause of American independence, not because he was in favor of it or of the democratic principles which it espoused, but because he had no choice. Robert R. Livingston, Jr., served in the Second Continental Congress on the committee to draft the Declaration of Independence and subsequently labored unceasingly, at considerable personal risk, to secure the defenses of New York State—particularly of the Hudson Valley, the military key to the war. He was rewarded for his pains by having his magnificent new Hudson River mansion burned to the ground in 1777, during the British army's only successful foray into the valley. He contributed significantly to New York's first constitution (written for the most part by his best friend, John Jay); and, as Chancellor of New York, he administered the oath of office to George Washington at the first presidential inauguration in 1789. Later, while serving as minister to France, Robert laid the diplomatic groundwork for the 1803 Louisiana Purchase; and privately, during the same period, he designed the financial underpinnings of the first successful steamboat, named the *Clermont* after his Hudson Valley estate.

Robert R. Livingston, Jr., was, by most accounts, the Livingston family star. (The Revolutionary period seemed to bring out the best in many of America's first families.) And yet his career may also be seen as a series of missed opportunities and failed promise. For all his courage, steadfastness and eloquence, Robert the Chancellor—as he is still known, to distinguish him from all the other Livingstons named Robert—was a man utterly unsuited to political democracy. Nothing in his manorial upbringing prepared him to share power with the hoi polloi; and after the success of the Revolution he served so honorably he lived a life in limbo, torn between ambition and repugnance.

His ambivalence was palpable. Failing to receive President George

Washington's appointment as first Chief Justice of the Supreme Court—one of the few jobs in the new administration he deemed commensurate with his abilities and stature—he switched parties and mounted a vicious public attack on the man who had received the coveted appointment, his onetime bosom friend, John Jay. Again, when the Louisiana Purchase was announced in 1803, Robert falsified the dates on his copy of the original agreement in order to take full credit for the negotiations upon himself; but he did it clumsily and was exposed, thereby forfeiting his share of the accolades to the man he was trying to shut out, James Monroe. Finally (and this is a footnote, more emblematic than substantial), he carried on during the spring and summer of 1780, when the Revolutionary War was hanging in the balance, an ardent flirtation with the wife of Benedict Arnold; which is mentioned not to imply any complicity on Robert's part in Arnold's treason —there was none—but only to demonstrate the perpetual susceptibility of Robert R. Livingston's judgment.

In the generation after Robert the Chancellor the social implications of political democracy became crystal clear, and the Livingston family, like many other socially prominent American families, drew up and circled its wagons. Of the eleven Livingstons notable enough to be listed in the Dictionary of American Biography, only one was born after the turn of the nineteenth century. Other members of the clan are listed there under other surnames: for example, William Backhouse Astor, who married Chancellor Robert R. Livingston's niece, and Franklin Delano Roosevelt, whose wife Eleanor was a Livingston. But by and large the family, along with the rest of American society's upper stratum, abandoned politics as ungentlemanly. Its inner life seemed to shrink; and the Livingston consciousness became focused as never before on the Manor of Livingston—which no longer existed —and on the semifeudal society of landlord and tenant, lord and vassal, which did. In the absence of political and intellectual accomplishment outside the Hudson Valley, the Livingston amour propre came to depend almost entirely on the tenants' immutable servitude. The family fought in the nineteenth century to preserve the manorial system and its legal trappings, in defiance of logic, political reality and historical inevitability, long after it had outlived its economic usefulness. Steeped in a manorial tradition that was obsolete at birth, the indomitable Livingstons have often lived their lives and pursued their dreams with one foot in their own century and the other planted firmly in the Middle Ages.

The title, "Lord of Livingston Manor," was not used by the men who had a genuine claim to it—the first three generations of American Livingston landowners. It was first applied to them by their descendants, retroactively, in the aftermath of a mid-nineteenth-century tenant rebellion which finally overturned the rent system of landlord and vassal. When reality becomes unacceptable, the imagination takes over. The first three manor proprietors are still called "Lords of the Manor" today by many people in the Hudson Valley—some of whom aren't even Livingstons.

Inequality is always with us. Class is a fact of life. All men and women are not created, nor do they grow up, equal: there will always be somebody smarter or richer or stronger or more talented or more audacious than his fellows. Since the eighteenth century, American society has consciously strived for equality in education, opportunity and due process of law. But that does not change the fact that social animals always arrange themselves into hierarchies.

America's founding fathers took this for granted, their own grandfathers having carried across the Atlantic a set of remarkably mismatched mental luggage in which the democratic notions of John Locke were packed together with some extremely traditional European assumptions about social organization. This explains, for example, why in early Massachusetts the town meeting existed side by side with a land distribution system based on rank: social rank, that is, in the old country.

"Inequality," said William Dean Howells some three hundred years later, "is as dear to the American heart as liberty itself."

The word "aristocracy" usually implies political as well as social leadership. The original Greek meaning is "rule by the best," and even a contemporary dictionary defines aristocracy as "a hereditary privileged *ruling* class [emphasis added]." In America, however, would-be aristocrats have not ruled, except for a brief moment in the eighteenth century. Earlier, in the colonial period, America's political leaders functioned only under the imperial thumb of their masters across the water. In the process of gaining their independence they also committed themselves to political democracy, thereby effectively disallowing the notion of "a hereditary privileged ruling class." If, in the first generation or two of the Republic, a few members of America's incipient ruling aristocracy still sought to run the country, they were thrown off the track (or perhaps they jumped, just before the train hit them) by the industrial and social upheavals of the nineteenth century. After that, American aristocracy, such as it was, deserted politics for the counting house and the drawing room.

Eliminating the concept of rule, then, what is left to delineate an American aristocracy? Only the outline of a relatively cohesive clan of intermarried families which can trace its development back a number of generations. Two vital elements go into its creation: property and time. The property—preferably a combination of land, goods and cash—must be acquired by the founder, utilizing methods that need be neither honest nor genteel (the first Robert Livingston's methods certainly were not) as long as they are successful. The brew must then be left to mellow for several generations, while the accoutrements of aristocracy are accumulated: elegant surroundings, good manners, decorative daughters, elevated discourse, fine wine and perhaps some horses. During this process the family's sense of its origins begins to fade (who, after all, cares who sired the *first* Duke of Burgundy?), and there emerges a new trait, an immutable one designed to survive even a reversal of fortune: the aristocrat's inner sense of who he is and its concomitant, the secure knowledge that everybody else knows who he is. His name guarantees automatic entrée into society's drawing rooms and also deference on the sidewalks of the local village where, generations ago, his and the local farmer's great-grandfathers worked out the ground rules and drew the invisible lines.

The security of being born into such a well-established set of interlocking relationships produces the aristocrat's social grace and virtuosity—or, in some unhappy cases, his claustrophobia.

American aristocracy, lacking the tradition of rule, becomes as much as anything a state of mind. Theoretically, wherever the aristocrat is, whoever he is with, he knows exactly how to behave and what behavior to expect from others. But this holds true only if the parameters of his society remain constant, which in America they seldom have. The Livingston social equilibrium and security have been consistently undermined: in the seventeenth century by attacks on their sources of income, land titles, and very lives; in the eighteenth century by the imperialistic policies of King and Parliament; in the nineteenth by the challenges of an upstart tenantry; and finally, in the twentieth, by the graduated income tax and the social claims of a middle class on the move.

In the face of pressure from the outside, family solidarity is essential, and the Livingstons have managed to maintain a remarkably unified stance over the years vis-à-vis the outside world. Of course they have quarreled among themselves, sometimes viciously, over property or unsuitable marriages; but at the first sign of threat or intrusion they close ranks.

Hundreds of other surnames have been joined to the clan: the aforementioned Astor, Roosevelt, Schuyler, Beekman and Van Rensselaer; also Schwartz, Duyckink, Wynkoop, Smith, Jones and Brown. But the name that Livingstons have married most often is Livingston. So many Livingstons have married their cousins, and so many of those cousins have borne the name Robert, that even the most devoted family genealogists throw up their hands in despair, and an occasional family wag snickers out loud. The tendency reached its apogee in 1809, when Philip Henry Livingston and his wife and cousin, Maria née Livingston, ran fresh out of invention and named their sixth son Livingston Livingston. A few years later their cousins, John W. Turk and his wife and first cousin, Mary Augusta née Livingston, ran out of forbearance and successfully petitioned the New York State legislature to change their names to Mr. and Mrs. John W. Turk Livingston.

There were once more than forty Livingston houses on the family's vast east-bank holdings. Miraculously, over thirty are still standing, seven of them occupied by direct descendants of the original builders. The rest have been sold over the years to other families, institutions or public agencies, anyone with enough money to keep them going—in these days, a formidable undertaking.

Most of the Livingstons who remain on the old manor lands regard themselves as custodians of the family's past, both its tangible evidence—the houses and the land—and its historical record of accomplishment. They feel, quite accurately, that they are different from most Americans, with their tradition of family and proprietorship going back three hundred years. If they seem to live a great deal in the past, they also live *for* the future, that wonderful Someday when the house will be in perfect repair, the bills paid and their family's place assured. They can conceive no other way to live. Their devotion to both the past and the future is unfailing.

The Manor of Livingston was originally coveted by the first Robert for its potential profit. In the eighteenth century it became the setting for a series of magnificent mansions and experiments in enlightened scientific agriculture. In the nineteenth century both land and houses tended to be devoted to the pursuit of privacy and pleasure. Now in the twentieth century the fraction of the manor lands and houses that are still in the family might be regarded as a liability, requiring enormous annual infusions of tax and repair monies just to keep them intact. Ironically, the only way to make real money on a river estate now is to sell it to a developer, which is precisely what the Livingston sense of proprietorship will not permit.

Of course, for every Livingston who has stayed on the old manor lands, thousands have left, some fleeing as far and as fast as possible from the pressures of Family with a capital F. But wherever they go they seem to carry with them a strong tribal and territorial sensibility. Livingston Manor lives somewhere deep in their souls, vast, spectacular and venerable. Quite tangibly, it is still there, their cousins are still there. No matter how far away a Livingston goes, physically or psychically, there is still a place in the world where he can say he belongs.

A contemporary Livingston who had never been to the Hudson Valley recently referred to it quite unself-consciously as "Livingston Valley." For all its apparent arrogance, his appellation makes perfect sense to his millions of cousins—the ones who live in "Livingston Valley" and the ones who have never seen it.

The upper part of the Hudson Valley, where Robert Livingston staked out his turf in 1686, is remarkably beautiful. The river there is almost a mile wide, lying flat, placid and sparkling blue on an early summer morning, or roiling, boisterous and whitecapped in a November storm. Its surface freezes each December, dead and steely gray, then groans under pressure when thaws of April come. The spring ice floes on the broad avenue of water resemble a Macy's parade of giant, frozen shapes that glide back and forth, upstream and down on the tidal ebb and flow.

To the west, across the river from Robert's manor lands, lie the mighty Catskill Mountains, called by the Indians Ontioras or "Mountains of the Sky." The Catskills are shrouded in mystery: secrets lurk within their forests and around their windy crags, and even on the clearest of autumn days, basking in the sun, they give off an aura of the unfathomable. Bob Chanler, a latter-day Livingston patroon, declared that once a man had lived in the shadow of the Catskills he'd never be sane again; and Uncle Bob knew whereof he spoke.

Two hundred years ago the Livingstons owned most of the Catskill Mountains. From the parlor windows of their river mansions they could survey their half-million-acre alpine asset across a broad river dotted with hundreds of sails, many of them Livingston sails. Their descendants gaze through the same windows at mountains that belong to others and a river that America has passed by. A lone oil tanker making its silent, ponderous way up to Albany is an event, something to call the children to the window for. The Hudson finally looks like what it always was: a dead end.

Dead end or not, "Livingston Valley" is about all the family has to mark its historical place in the world. The Livingstons' territorial sense, rooted in time, is rare nowadays; and modern history has not been benign to such sensibilities. Caught between past and future, the "Lords of the Manor" frequently stumble and fall over the present. But always their goal is the same: preservation of the two vital elements that make them what they are, the Family and the land.

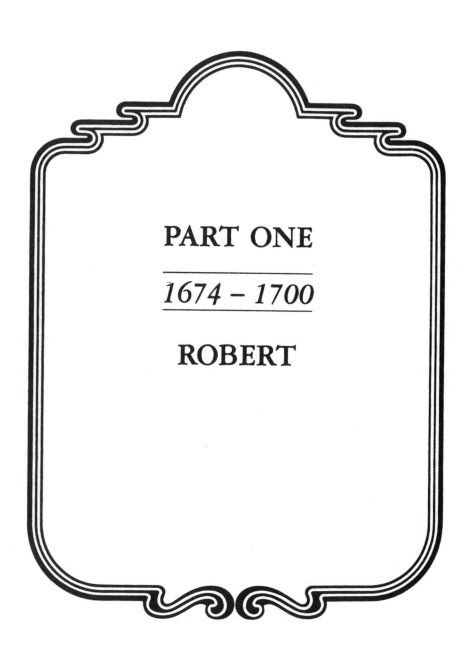

PART ONE

1674 – 1700

ROBERT

1

In the autumn of 1674, twenty-year-old Robert Livingston sailed into the harbor of New York in search of profit and a place to make his mark. Despite his youth, Robert was tough, shrewd and single-minded. His early life in Europe, while teaching him to thrive on crisis, had also inspired him with a strong desire for permanence and a taste for fiscal security.

The New World's unrestrained possibilities were on a scale to suit Robert Livingston's talents and desires. The very sight of New York Harbor itself—its sheer vastness, the wooded wildness of its islands and shoreline, its unfamiliar colors and sounds, its sunsets which, "if seen in England, would persuade the nation that the end of the world was come"—was enough to impress even the most coolheaded of young European adventurers. Robert Livingston, however, with a turn of mind neither aesthetic nor apocalyptic, was far more interested in the town of New York itself and its people.

New York was a tiny settlement nestled around a governor's fort at the southern tip of Manhattan Island, with a wooden stockade as protection along its northern edge. It was home to about three thousand inhabitants: English, Dutch, French, Walloons, Swedes, Norwegians, Germans, Scotch, Irish and Negroes professing over a dozen religions in at least eighteen languages. "Here bee not many of the Church of England; few Roman Catholicks; abundance of Quakers preachers men and Women especially; Singing Quakers; Ranting Quakers, Sabbatarians; Antisabbatarians; Some

Anabaptists some Independents; some Jews; in short of all sorts of opinions there are some and the most part of none at all."

Faith and good works were not the driving force behind the lives of most New Yorkers, however. Money was the mainspring of their lives. New York had been founded as a commercial colony,* and commerce was its main preoccupation. As to the "wealth and disposition" of its citizens, the Dutch were deemed "rich and sparing; the English neither very rich, nor too great husbands; the French are poor, and therefore forced to be penurious. As to their way of trade and dealing, they are all generally cunning and crafty, but many of them not so just to their words as they should be."

In other words, New York Province was materialistic, permissive and freewheeling—a place where young Robert Livingston felt right at home.

Robert lingered in Manhattan only long enough to book passage for the final leg of his journey, the 150-mile voyage by sloop up the Hudson River to Albany, the colony's second population center and his present goal. The river had changed very little since Henry Hudson claimed it for the Dutch sixty years before. Beginning at the southern tip of Manhattan Island, the first sailing reach passes under the precipitous cliffs of the Palisades on the western shore. Soon the river widens into the vastness of Tappan Zee, where Robert may have seen porpoises at play; then abruptly narrows and deepens to enter the Highlands, where the river's tortuous twists and bends, through one ninety-degree turn after another, around and through the mountains—Dunderburg and Buckberg, Bald, Bear, Manitou and Anthony's Nose—have earned the sailors' designation, Martyr's Reach. Suddenly the contortions end, and the ship escapes the "awful solitudes" of the Highlands as the river dilates to a breadth of a mile. From here it is clear, straight sailing all the way to Albany.

About a hundred miles upriver from Manhattan, Robert would have seen his first sign of white civilization, the tiny settlement of Wiltwyck on the west bank. Burned to the ground by Indians only eleven years before, its entire population slaughtered or taken prisoner, Wiltwyck was defiantly coming back to life, with a handful of new houses and barns at water's edge and a little fishing fleet moored in the mouth of the Roundout Creek.†

Beyond Wiltwyck to the west and south stretched the endless, deep forest, and dominating it to the north stood the mighty Catskill Mountains. Directly across from the Catskills on the east bank, Robert could see a vast, forested tract of land, called Taghkanick by its Indian inhabitants, that rose gently from the shoreline in a series of plateaus, mile after mile, from the Hudson all the way to the mountains of Connecticut and Massachusetts some twenty miles to the east. The future Manor of Livingston lay frozen in

* By the Dutch West India Company in 1621. The English seized it in 1664 and changed its name from New Netherland to New York, only ten years before Robert's arrival.
† Wiltwyck was later called Esopus and then Kingston, its present name.

its December sleep as Robert's sloop sailed slowly past; still, it is unlikely that the young man failed to calculate its extent and make a mental note.

Of more pressing interest at the moment, however, was the opposite shore where, about thirty miles north of Wiltwyck, the high escarpment of the Catskills turns abruptly away from the river and the land softens and sinks down into the valley of the Mohawk, where lies the town of Albany.

Albany inhabits a steep slope that rises from the Hudson shore to the summit along the town's main thoroughfare. The brick and clapboard houses that lined the street in Robert's day, their gable ends facing out, Dutch style, were widely spaced, with trees in front and generous gardens behind. It was a charming village—except for the high stockade surrounding its eighty-odd dwellings and the stone fort standing guard at the top, grim reminders of the fate of Wiltwyck and the ever present Indian threat under which Albany lived.

Robert Livingston was accustomed to danger, though, and he had other things on his mind as he stepped ashore at Albany that December day. He had come to engage in the fur trade, and his concern was less with the literal stockade than a figurative one: the solid walls of the Dutch establishment that he would have to breach in order to do business. As representative of a Massachusetts fur trader, Robert had several strikes against him. The Albany Dutch, with official control of all the western fur trade, viewed with jealousy and suspicion any potential interlopers—particularly New Englanders, whom they distrusted almost as much as they did their French and Indian enemies to the north. But this was the kind of challenge Robert relished. It permitted him to exercise his best attributes: charm, persuasiveness, business acumen and the canny ability to measure other people's importance and to exploit their strengths and weaknesses.

Within a year of his arrival Robert had firmly established his financial and political beachheads by gaining three pivotal positions: secretary to the town of Albany (a post of real civic distinction); secretary to Rensselaerwyck, the vast patroonship (manor) that encompassed Albany and dominated its affairs; and secretary to the colonial governor's Board of Indian Commissioners. In addition, Robert had managed to embark on extremely friendly relations with the volatile Iroquois Indians who controlled Albany's supply of beaver skins and was in a position to begin supplying pelts to his Boston principal.

Robert Livingston's astonishing rate of progress was no accident. He had been groomed by his parents—albeit inadvertently—to take advantage of just such a situation. His success may be attributed as much as anything to a set of talents derived directly from his father, John Livingston, a Scottish divine of wide repute and narrow principles.

In an early portrait the Reverend John Livingston smiles winningly at us; bright-eyed, plump and jolly, dressed in black with a wide, white collar,

mindedness that had brought John so much trouble. Both had enormous self-discipline. Finally, the qualities that had preserved John from the dungeon or the block—his quiet charm, the potency of his personality and the "bewichery" of his tongue—belonged to Robert too. The difference was the cause to which these qualities were devoted. John's cause was God; Robert's was himself.

2

Broad acres are a patent of nobility; and no man but feels more of a man in the world if he have a bit of ground that he can call his own. However small it is on the surface, it is four thousand miles deep; and that is a very handsome property.

Charles Dudley Warner
My Summer in a Garden

Robert Livingston was eighteen years old when his father died in 1672, and already he knew exactly what he wanted. The young man had thrived in the Netherlands, where the climate was as favorable to commerce as it was to religion. Robert took to business spontaneously; his temperament and talents flourished best in the marketplace. By the age of sixteen he had, while pursuing his normal studies, built up a modest shipping business, recording his transactions and profits neatly in a ledger and watching his nest egg grow.

After John's death Robert escorted his mother from Rotterdam back to Scotland where she wished to spend her declining years close to her older children and grandchildren. Then, in April 1673, he set sail for the New World, the only place where a person in his position could stretch his luck. Robert wanted two things that his father had never been able to provide—

property and security—and he wanted them more quickly and on a much larger scale than Europe could offer.

He landed first in Charlestown, Massachusetts, in December 1673, and presented himself to the prominent Winthrop family, his father's connection in the Bay Colony. Thanks to them, and to his own contacts from the shipping business, he was soon circulating in the top echelon of the Boston establishment. But it did not take Robert long to determine that Massachusetts wasn't for him. He found its theological orthodoxy all too familiar and its pious ideal of small, independent farming on a rock-ridden freehold utterly unappealing. Robert needed a more unrestrained milieu in which to flourish, and instinctively he waited and maneuvered until he found it.

He became acquainted with John Hull, a respected silversmith and fur trader of Boston, and through Hull was introduced to the glamour of the fur trade. Furs—young America's most profitable trading commodity—occupied the foreground of most of the get-rich-quick fantasies of early New Englanders. Skins were easy and cheap to come by, thanks to a keen appetite for wampum among the skillful, energetic Indians who lived in the great forests of western Massachusetts; and the European craving for beaver pelts appeared insatiable. By the early 1660s fur exports to Europe were valued at over £20,000 annually and a profitable counterfeit wampum ring was operating out of Amsterdam. But by the time Robert got to Boston, a dozen years later, the beaver population of western Massachusetts was close to extinction, and John Hull and his fellow traders were beginning to cast about for fresh sources.

The Canadian forest to the north presented the most tantalizing prospect; but Canada was ruled by Catholic France, implacable enemy to Protestant England and her colonies; and the fierce Canadian Indian tribes that controlled the beaver supply were firmly wedded to France.

The forests on the western frontier, across the Hudson River in the province of New York, were also rich in beaver; but the supply of pelts there was under the control of the mighty Five Nations of the Iroquois, who traded exclusively with the Dutch merchants of the town of Albany, a small trading post situated 150 miles upriver from Manhattan on the edge of the western wilderness. The English, who had seized New York from the Dutch only ten years before Robert Livingston reached the New World, could not govern without the cooperation of the entrenched Albany Dutch; and both Dutch and English depended utterly on the Iroquois for beaver skins and for protection against the Canadian French and Indians. For years the Canadians had harassed Albany and the entire province of New York, raiding isolated settlements, burning and slaughtering. At the same time the French, with economic enticement and Jesuitical skill, mounted perennial assaults on the hearts, minds and military allegiance of the Iroquois.* The Five Nations had so far remained loyal to the English in both trade and war; but they could afford to be demanding, even fickle, in the certain knowledge that the entire province of New York was utterly dependent upon them for both livelihood and protection.

Albany—militarily imperiled but commercially tantalizing—presented still another problem to John Hull and the Boston traders: it was Dutch to its core. In trade, society and day-to-day governance, the life of Albany was dominated by a small, closed, jealous Dutch establishment, whose suspicions of everything English extended to the inhabitants of the New England colonies—all of which had so far discouraged John Hull from attempting to infiltrate the ranks of Albany trade.

Now, however, there appeared on his doorstep a young man, attractive, persuasive, adventurous, with a sharp eye for business, and—most wonderful of all—fluent in Dutch. Thus was born Robert Livingston, Albany agent.

Robert's rapid rise through the Albany financial and social establishments was less solid than it appeared, however, partly because his principal patron was less than solid. During his first few months in Albany, Robert had taken pains to ingratiate himself with the town's most prominent and in many ways most curious personage, Nicholas Van Rensselaer, director of Rensselaerwyck, the greatest of the Dutch patroonships.

The patroonships (which were called manors after the English takeover in 1664) were mammoth land grants given on very easy terms by both the Dutch and English provincial governments in order to promote quick settlement of New York's vast territory. The patroon, or lord, received his enormous parcel of land in exchange for a pledge to import and establish a certain number of settlers within a fixed period of time. He also paid a nominal annual quitrent to the Crown, and in turn collected rents from the settlers who cleared the land and planted crops. These tenant farmers, who signed on for life (or for two or three "lives," or generations), might pay for their modest farms a larger quitrent than their lord's annual fee for his entire fiefdom; yet no tenant was permitted to buy his farm. Title remained perpetually with the lord. Tenant rents were often paid in produce and services: so many "fatt hens," so many days' riding.

Rensselaerwyck, which had been granted to Nicholas's father by the Dutch West India Company in the 1630s, comprised upward of 700,000 acres on both sides of the Hudson, with the town of Albany at its center. The patroon himself had never set foot in America, preferring to run the estate from his counting house in Amsterdam, with his sons serving as over-

---

* The French and Indian bellicosity toward New York was a reflection of the prevailing rivalry between French Catholicism and English Protestantism in Europe, which persisted from the seventeenth century well into the eighteenth. The hostilities which broke out every few years, on one continent or the other, tended to spread rapidly across the water in both directions.

seers on the spot. Of the many brothers, Nicholas was the least likely to succeed in the position, or in any other that demanded prudence and steadiness.

In his youth in Holland, Nicholas Van Rensselaer had fancied himself a mystic. He had quit school early and refused to work in the family business, devoting himself instead to matters of the spirit and the flesh. He interspersed prodigal spending sprees with visionary interludes, and in one of the latter saw the young Charles Stuart (who at the time was still in exile in Belgium) wearing the crown of England. He betook himself to Brussels, wormed his way into the presence of the prince, described his vision and convinced the susceptible Charles that it was a heavenly warranty of success. Two years later, in 1660, when Charles did indeed ascend the throne of England as Charles II, Nicholas was there as chaplain to the Dutch ambassador (having somehow in the meantime gotten himself ordained by an Anglican bishop).

Four years later, in 1664, when Charles's brother, the Duke of York, seized New Netherland for England, the Dutch Van Rensselaers should have been happy to have Nicholas at the English court wielding influence on behalf of their Albany patroonship. But Nicholas's uses were limited, as was his family's patience with his extravagant ways; and in 1674 he was shipped off instead to the province of New York where he landed on October 1, only a few weeks before the arrival of young Robert Livingston. Like Robert, Nicholas immediately set sail upriver to Albany, his family's fiefdom, where he presented the civic leadership with a letter from the Duke of York recommending him as dominie of the Dutch church.

Nothing was better guaranteed to arouse the wrath of the Albany Dutch establishment than a spiritual leader of the Anglican persuasion imposed upon them by an English ruler. But there was little the Albanians could do without offending either the duke, their temporal ruler, or his protégé, whose family owned the town and most of the surrounding countryside. Nicholas wasted no time exploiting their disarray. Within a few months of his arrival he had been invested into the ministry of the Albany church, commenced a campaign to have himself appointed director of Rensselaerwyck and married the reigning belle of Albany society, Alida Schuyler.†

Alida was eighteen years old at the time of the marriage: a handsome Dutch girl with a quick, sharp intelligence and an impeccable family pedigree. The Schuyler and Van Rensselaer families, both early arrivals in the colony, landed and prosperous, together dominated the social life of upriver New York. (Never mind that their *monde*, Albany, was only a primitive trading post on the edge of a savage wilderness; Society is always with us.) The marriage between Nicholas and Alida was very likely arranged. Not

† Emphasis on the first syllable: *A*-lida.

only was Nicholas twenty years older than his bride but he brought her to the altar only three months after his ship docked.

The smoldering resentment of orthodox Albanians at the highhanded method of Nicholas's appointment as minister to their church erupted two years later in 1676, when an influential Albanian merchant, Jacob Leisler—a devil-ridden, doctrinaire, theological purist among purists—filed formal charges of heterodoxy against Nicholas. Van Rensselaer retaliated by suing Leisler for slander, and both cases dragged in and out of civil court for months, with charges and countercharges, hearings and postponements. At one point Nicholas was imprisoned "upon matter of some dubious words spoken by the said Domine in his Sermon or Doctrine"; but the royal governor in Manhattan, fearing the wrath of Nicholas's patron, the Duke of York, ordered his release and arranged for Leisler to be jailed in his place. Jacob Leisler finally had to back down; but he never forgot his treatment at the hands of the English-sponsored landed gentry.

Meanwhile, Nicholas had persuaded his family in Amsterdam to appoint him director of Rensselaerwyck, and he and Alida moved into the patroon's town house at the corner of State and Pearl streets and also occupied the farm at East Greenbush across the river. Having neither the patience nor the inclination to administer his huge holdings, Nicholas immediately set about looking for an able secretary. He didn't have far to look: in the house next door on Pearl Street there lived a lively, able young man, eager for employment, ingratiating, and experienced in business. And so Robert Livingston became secretary to Rensselaerwyck.

Robert had been making his way in Albany just as surely, if not as flamboyantly, as Nicholas had. In the process of setting up a supply of furs for himself and John Hull, he was slowly—very slowly—becoming acquainted with the merchants of the town and, even more crucially, with the Iroquoian sachems (chiefs) whose language he took pains to learn. His efficiency and industry were quickly recognized. Shortly after becoming secretary to Rensselaerwyck he was appointed secretary to the town of Albany and, a few months later, secretary to the newly formed, extremely sensitive Board of Indian Commissioners.

Robert now had fingers in all the choicest pies: Rensselaerwyck, the town of Albany, the colonial government and the Iroquois Council. Singly, any one of these offices was a source of influence and prestige; together they could exert enormous political leverage. Robert was sitting pretty, at least on paper.

The trouble was that all three of his employers had a bad habit of not paying their salaries on time, if at all; so despite his income from the fur trade, Robert was soon in debt. Among his creditors was John Hull, whose original loan Robert had never repaid. Hull tried everything, including emotional blackmail, calling upon Robert to "have some regard of your honored father's steps." But blackmail, emotional or otherwise, never worked on Robert Livingston; he was immune. Hull and the other creditors were kept dangling until an event occurred that transformed Robert in their eyes (and perhaps his own): he married Alida Schuyler Van Rensselaer.

Alida had shared a childless marriage with Nicholas for almost four years when, in November of 1678, her husband was suddenly taken gravely ill. Family legend has it that, on his deathbed, Nicholas, in typical last-minute fashion, called for a clerk to take down his will. The request was passed out to the adjoining room, and a few moments later Robert Livingston slipped through the door of the chamber and approached his employer's bed, pen in hand. The effect on Nicholas was startling. Raising his shoulder from the pillow and pointing a bony finger straight at Robert, he croaked, "No, no, send him away; he's going to marry my widow!" and promptly fell back dead.

The story is really too good to be true; on the other hand, Robert did carry Alida off to the altar within eight months of her husband's death. Whirlwind courtship, or hanky-panky on Pearl Street? Their descendant, Janet Montgomery, writing over a hundred years later, delicately sidesteps: "Whether this prediction made the match or that it was formed in Heaven is a point I undertake not to decide." For the satisfaction of those with precise minds, it may be reported that Robert and Alida's first child, Johannes, was born nine months and seventeen days after the nuptials.

Robert's marriage to Alida changed his life in more ways than one. Naturally, it conferred the Dutch seal of approval, bringing him very close to full-fledged membership in the Albany establishment—as close as a Scotsman could get. Furthermore, Alida's uncles and brothers, all powerful figures in the province, now became his uncles and brothers.‡

A pleasant side effect was that Robert's creditors became, if no less insistent, at least more deferential. Shortly after the marriage one of them airily wrote, "Now you are come into ye Ranke of honest men I am & will be your friend."

The greatest boon of all, however, proved to be Alida herself. Her social attractions were obvious before the wedding. It can't have taken Robert long to recognize her other endowments. Alida had naturally been instructed in the traditional womanly skills—sewing, spinning, gardening, preserving and so forth. But Dutch tradition demanded more of its girls: they were also expected to run thrifty households and to take part in the family business. Albany housewives kept stores and taverns; they traded, signed contracts and appeared in court. Robert soon learned that he could rely not only on Alida's skills but also on her good sense; and throughout their long married life he always sought her advice on matters of politics and business. Finally, and indispensably, she refuted the record of her first

‡ An in-law relationship (affinity) was considered as close as a blood relationship (consanguinity): one's wife's brother became one's own brother. One married, in fact, not an individual but a whole family.

marriage by producing ten children, six of whom lived to maturity. Robert's reference to her in the family Bible on the day of their marriage as "my worthy helpmeet" proved apt, if inadequate.

Nicholas Van Rensselaer had died intestate, so according to a community property arrangement Alida inherited everything, including his debts. She was subjected to a barrage of pleas and threats from creditors on both sides of the Atlantic. Once Robert was installed in the patroon's house, he began to make order in characteristic fashion—by exploiting the confusion to achieve his and Alida's ends.

He orchestrated his moves brilliantly. First, he and Alida sold off some of Nicholas's effects to pay the American debts. This predictably (perhaps deliberately) aroused the wrath of the European creditors who had not been notified, among whom was Nicholas's brother, Richard Van Rensselaer, the head of the family in Amsterdam.

In apparent response to these objections, Robert and Alida petitioned the Albany court for an accounting of Nicholas's estate. The court determined that they had *overpaid* the American debt by 2500 guilders (including a substantial outlay to Alida's father, Peter Schuyler, for unidentified services) and authorized them to recover the sum from Nicholas's share of the patroonship. In other words, Robert and Alida now had a legitimate (or at least legal) claim to part ownership of Rensselaerwyck, which is probably what they were after all along.

The great question was: how could Nicholas's share of Rensselaerwyck be identified and separated out? It couldn't be, a fact which did not prevent Robert Livingston from mounting a vigorous campaign toward that end. The legal battle of Livingston vs. Van Rensselaer raged for five long years. Alida's family, the Schuylers, allied themselves with Robert throughout the struggle. Standard bearer for the Van Rensselaers was Maria Van Cortlandt Van Rensselaer, daughter of another powerful provincial Dutch family (the Van Cortlandts), and widow of Nicholas Van Rensselaer's brother, former director of Rensselaerwyck. Maria, a cripple who went about on crutches, was fixated on securing the directorship for her own son. She had expected him to be appointed in 1675, but Nicholas had been named instead. Now her own brother, Stephen Van Cortlandt, had become director; but Stephen's loyalty in the present controversy was far from assured, thanks to his marriage to Alida Livingston's sister Gertrude.

Maria's fears were aggravated—as was the whole situation—by the fact that Rensselaerwyck itself was under pressure. The English, since taking over the province in 1664, had consistently refused to grant a confirmatory patent to the estate, largely because the Van Rensselaers insisted on retaining title to the town of Albany.

Maria's natural allies, the Amsterdam Van Rensselaers, while strongly supporting her efforts to obtain the English royal patent, were less enthusiastic about her campaign to make her son director. They found her devotion to his cause both offensive and tedious, which is probably why they gave the job to Nicholas in the first place. Poor Maria, alone, besieged and generally unloved, now had to withstand the added harassments of Robert Livingston, who did not flinch at the sight of a lady in distress. He hurled himself through Maria's life much as the Great Comet of 1680 shot through the heavens; both were fiery, implacable and utterly disruptive. The comet spoiled the crops, said the farmers; Robert poisoned Maria's very existence. For five years he kept up a barrage of demands for account books, inventories and copies of family wills; filed a stream of petitions, briefs and claims; and dunned her for Nicholas's share of the income of Rensselaerwyck. He even submitted bills for his own concurrent services as secretary.

The final indignity, the circumstance that really dripped acid into Maria's soul, was Robert and Alida's continued occupancy of the patroon's house in Albany and the Greenbush farm. Her husband, brother and one of her babies were buried in the garden of that farm; and to have "Secretary Livingston" master of it was almost more than she could bear. She came to see him as inexorable, almost crazed: "He cannot be induced to stop. . . . He will not let the matter rest, but insists on seeing it through, even if he should lose by it."

Robert was not about to lose by it—even though at first glance it is difficult to see what he stood to gain. Picking a feud with the province's most powerful family over property rights (rights which themselves were under a cloud, thanks to the withholding of the patent), and in the process causing headaches for the provincial governor and judiciary—these were enormously risky undertakings. But Robert Livingston never took risks without good reason. In this case, his goal was not a piece of Rensselaerwyck; it probably never had been. He wanted, quite specifically, something else, and to gain the leverage necessary in order to obtain it he was not above manipulating the Van Rensselaers or the entire royal government of the province of New York.

Within a year of joining battle with Maria, Robert had started negotiating the purchase of a piece of land south of Albany: 2000 acres on the east bank of the Hudson, directly across from the high peaks of the Catskills— the magnificent tract past which his sloop had sailed on that first voyage to Albany six years before. Its deeply forested hills rose steadily from river's edge toward the mountains in the east, and through its valleys flowed a stream of brave dimensions, the Roeliff Jansen Kill, which boasted a splendid harbor at its mouth.

The property was, of course, uncleared, uncultivated and therefore unproductive; but for the moment Robert would be content with simply owning it. Not that he was ignoring its profit potential—he never did that— but the land represented to him much more than money: it represented dominion and stature.

Robert adhered, quite understandably, to the values of the Old World, where to be prosperous was something but to be landed was everything. European political and social life revolved around the propertied lord, not the rich merchant. Proprietorship conferred position, and position conferred power.

The land meant something very personal to Robert, too. As a man whose youth had been spent in powerless, rootless uncertainty, proprietorship signified permanence and stability. It would revise his very image of himself. Land—lots of it—represented a visible, fixed setting in which to exercise his talents and establish his posterity. It could also provide sanctuary, if needed.

Finding land in the province of New York was one thing, purchasing it another. The problem lay not with the sellers, Indian tribes who were eager for European trade goods; nor with the English government in London, which was anxious to settle the colony. It lay rather in the fact that the patent of ownership had to pass through the hands of the colonial governor in Manhattan. The office of royal provincial governor was typically filled by the second-rate courtier, the backsliding aristocrat or the politician on the make who—foolish and incompetent at best, venal and corrupt at worst—expended his energy and ingenuity on lining his own pockets. Every petition, every patent, every transaction between the citizens of New York and the government in London was funneled through the governor's office; and a prospective colonial lord in pursuit of a manor patent needed leverage, patience and deft reflexes under the counter.

Robert Livingston had all three—his leverage deriving from the influence he wielded over the Five Nations of the Iroquois—so his progress from first petition to final patent was relatively quick, only four years. On November 4, 1684, Robert received a patent for a 2000-acre "Tract or Parcell of Land together with all and Singular woods underwoods Waters Runnes Streames Ponds Creeks Meadow Marshes Fishing Hawking Hunting and Fowling . . . in ffree and Comon Soccage. . . ." The sellers were listed as the Indians Ottonowaw, Tataemsheet, Oothoot, Maneetpoo, Tamaranachquae and Wawanitsawaw, and the purchase price consisted of "Three hundred guilders in zewant, eight blankets and two child's blankets, five and twenty ells of duffels, and four garments of strouds, ten large shirts and ten small ditto, ten pairs of large stockings and ten small pairs, six guns, fifty pounds of powder, fifty staves of lead, four caps, ten kettles, ten axes, ten adzes, two pounds of paint, twenty little scissors, twenty little looking glasses, one hundred fish-hooks, awls and nails of each one hundred, four rolls of tobacco, one hundred pipes, ten bottles, three kegs of rum, one barrel of strong beer, twenty knives, four stroud coats and two duffel coats, and four tin kettles."

One year later, in 1685, Robert filed a petition to purchase an additional 300 acres far to the east of his river-front property, "in the territory called by the Indians Tachkanick"—300 acres which mysteriously doubled into "about 600" by the time the patent was officially recorded a few months later.

Which was nothing compared to what happened the following year: on July 22, 1686, Robert Livingston was issued a patent uniting his holdings into the Manor of Livingston—a patent which describes his two parcels of land as *adjacent*. The 2000 acres along the river and the 600 acres far inland had, as it were, gobbled up the 157,000 acres in between. A dash of the gubernatorial pen added 250 square miles to Robert's possessions without so much as a blanket, fishhook or tin kettle changing hands. It also imposed the manorial tenant system on his holding and created him Lord of Livingston Manor—all in exchange for twenty-eight shillings annual quitrent to the Crown of England.

This miracle, like most miracles, didn't occur without careful preparation. For a number of years Robert had been quietly gathering in all the high cards and storing them up his sleeve, and when the time came he played them with exquisite finesse. The Van Rensselaers represented his trump suit. As long as Robert and Alida persisted in their suit for a partitioning of Rensselaerwyck, the huge patroonship could not be issued an English patent—a patent the royal governor was eager to bestow and the Van Rensselaers desperate to receive. After five years of stalemate, all parties were ready to find a compromise.

The ensuing chronology (masterminded, no doubt, by the indispensable Livingston) is revealing. Shortly after Robert received his first patent for 2000 acres along the river he signed a settlement withdrawing his objections to the Rensselaerwyck patent in exchange for exoneration from Nicholas's debts. One month later his second 600-acre patent was issued. The ensuing year saw the London Board of Trade issuing two manorial patents: first to Rensselaerwyck (without Albany) and then to the miraculously engorged Livingston Manor. Robert and Alida gave the patroon's farm back to Maria Van Rensselaer and kept the house on the corner of State and Pearl.

Everybody was happy and everybody gained, including, presumably, the royal governor and even Maria Van Rensselaer, whose daughter was married a few years later to Alida Schuyler Livingston's brother. In retrospect the only losers would appear to have been Ottonawaw, Tataemsheet, Oothoot, Maneetpoo, Tamaranachquae and Wawanitsawaw, and, of course, their heirs and assigns forever.

3

At the time of their elevation to manor lord- and ladyship, Robert and Alida had been married seven years. Their eldest child, Johannes (John, after his grandfather Livingston), was six years old. Next came four-year-old Margaret (named for Alida's mother); then Johanna Phillippina (for both grandfathers); and finally Philip, who was born on July 9, 1686, just thirteen days before the Manor of Livingston was granted its patent.

The vast, empty manor was of no use whatsoever in feeding all those mouths; and until a sufficient number of tenants could be established to clear and cultivate the land, grow wheat, plant orchards, raise poultry and pay rents—a slow process at best—the manor lord and lady had to earn a living. With typical energy and resourcefulness, Robert and Alida ignored their titles and went to work. Robert retained his two government posts (secretary to the town of Albany and to the Board of Indian Commissioners) and received a further appointment as Collector of the Excise at Albany. Alida ran a store (probably on the ground floor of the patroon's house) and also acted as her husband's Albany agent in their principal business: that of merchants and traders.

New York and Albany, in the late 1680s, lived "wholly upon trade." To England were shipped "Beaver Peltry, Oile and Tobacco. . . . To the West Indies we send Flower, Bread, Pease, pork and sometimes horses; the return from thence for the most part is rumm which pays the King a considerable excise." Ocean-going vessels on the New York run numbered about three dozen, while "six or seven sloops . . . use the river trade to Albany."

Colonial trade was an uncertain line of work, however, subject to market and currency fluctuations, the depredations of weather and pirates, the regulatory whims of the Board of Trade in London and, of course, the favor of the royal governor. In order to keep an eye on all the variables and oversee the transfer of their goods in the port of New York, Robert found himself spending more and more time in Manhattan, while Alida remained in Albany filling his orders for lard, flour and beaver pelts, placing her own orders in return, minding her store and raising the children.

Meanwhile the manor sat, waiting. Although Robert sailed past it each time he traveled between Albany and Manhattan, he never went ashore. There was no need. The land was empty and profitless without tenants—and able tenants were, for a variety of reasons, difficult to find.

The primary stumbling block was the tenant system itself—a system whereby no tenant farmer, however industrious and ambitious, however faithful in payment of rent, "fatt hens" and days' riding to his landlord, could ever receive title to his farm. Naturally, the most enterprising and able immigrant farmers—men whose desire for independence and proprietorship ran just as deep as Robert Livingston's—chose instead to settle in the neighboring colonies of Massachusetts and Connecticut, where sizable freeholds were plentiful.

New York manor lords had to settle for newcomers with no capital and no prospects. Desperate to people their fiefdoms, the manor proprietors often ransomed whole families out of indentured servitude and then offered them attractive lease terms: an initial rent-free period of a year or more, free provisions for the first year, and seed gifts of livestock and fruit trees. To the down and out, the tenant system offered a chance of getting started, for which many were willing to sacrifice their independence.

From the proprietors' point of view, settlement was agonizingly slow: during its first three decades of existence Livingston Manor attracted only about thirty tenant families. At that rate it takes a long time to turn 160,000 acres to profit, and meanwhile the lord and lady of the manor lived in town and worked, just like everybody else. To a large degree, Robert and Alida lived on credit and their wits, borrowing here, lending there, never letting their creditors compare notes. Robert was extremely proficient at these elaborate financial balancing acts. He always seemed to live well—and he was always short of cash.

In those days, however, living well in Albany didn't necessarily depend on cash. Food was plentiful the year around, at least for the resourceful. The Hudson teemed with shad, salmon, bass, perch, pike, trout, eel and sturgeon, and the surrounding forests with deer and wild turkey. In autumn clouds of migratory duck, geese and pigeon obscured the sun; and Albany housewives were as famous for their pigeon pies as they were for Dutch pastries, doughnuts, crullers, breads and cakes. (The recipe for Schuyler wedding cake, probably served at Alida and Robert's marriage, calls for twelve dozen eggs, forty-five pounds of raisins, twenty-four pounds of currants, four quarts of brandy and one quart of rum all mixed together in a washtub.)

Most families had a vegetable garden behind the house and another in the town plot outside the stockade, where even women "in very easy circumstances and abundantly gentle in form and manners, would sow, and plant, and rake incessantly." The autumn fruit harvest was a busy season, with jam kettles and cider presses working overtime. (The old apple varieties, alas, are lost to us, except for their names: Newtown pippin, Double Paradise, Swaar-apple, Red-streak, Spitzenburgh and Guelderleng.) Pig slaughtering in late autumn was a cooperative venture, with all the neighbors taking home a share of chops, sausage meat and head cheese. Every family kept ducks, chickens and at least one cow which, after grazing all day on the common at the end of town, found her own plodding way home alone through the streets at evening milking time.

Luxuries consisted of oysters, lobster and fine French wines obtained by barter from connections in New York. Not many Albanians drank wine— but drink they did. The high per capita consumption of rum, cider and homemade beer kept the constabulary constantly alert. For the most part, though, the food was fresh and the cooking plain but excellent. Even in winter a resourceful Albany family could survive very nicely on salt beef, pork or fish; root vegetables from the cellar; preserved fruits; and cornmeal porridges made from Indian recipes.

The housewives who masterminded this year-round effort naturally required well-trained, industrious troops. Some had black slaves, perhaps two or three in a prosperous family; and a Dutch youngster might have a slave child of the same age and sex attached to him for life. But the Dutch boys and girls were brought up to work, too. Divided by sex for specific training —many of the boys went out in late adolescence to live with the Indians and become traders, while their sisters at home learned spinning, weaving, sewing and gardening—all learned to keep good account books and to read and write in Dutch (most also spoke English, though few could read it).

The pleasures of childhood varied with the seasons. In winter the young people went skating, sleigh riding and—most thrilling of all—sledding down the steep and icy length of State Street, a careening, dizzying, clattering quarter of a mile from fort to river. In April the whole town gathered for its favorite spectator sport: watching the ice break up in the Hudson. Whenever the first thunderous crack was heard, day or night, wet or dry, the town's inhabitants dropped everything and ran, in aprons, nightcaps or party gowns, to the river shore to witness in concert the first magnificent stirrings of spring.

Later in the season berry picking provided the excuse for a picnic. Wild strawberries grew "in such abundance in June, that the Fields and Woods are died [sic] red: Which the Countrey-people perceiving, instantly arm themselves with bottles of Wine, Cream, and Sugar and instead of a Coat of Male, every one takes a Female upon his Horse behind him, and so rushing violently into the fields, never leave till they have disrob'd them of their red colours, and turned them into the old habit." As summer's heat descended on the town, the family's front stoop became the parlor where, every evening under a ceiling of leaves, parents and grandparents hashed over the day's business with every passer-by.

Robert and Alida lived comfortably in their house on the corner of State and Pearl streets, building up their business and minding the children. Like all provident parents, they planned each son's future with one eye toward his individual advancement and the other on his usefulness to the family. The family's role as an economic unit was extremely important, and every member was trained to make his contribution toward the good of the whole. John, the eldest, was destined to become the second proprietor of Livingston Manor; however, since the manor's productive potential would be realized only in the distant future, John was sent out in his teens to live with the Iroquois and learn the fur trade. Philip, the second son, was designated a merchant. The next slot to be filled was that of family lawyer; and on July 24, 1688 (two days after the second anniversary of Livingston Manor), at five o'clock in the afternoon, Alida obliged by giving birth to a boy who was christened Robert.

The Livingstons now had three healthy sons and two daughters: a fine crop, a good beginning. But if, in those warm August days of 1688 following Alida's confinement, she and Robert enjoyed an interval of tranquil complacency, it was short-lived. Within weeks another birth far away in England, that of a son to King James II, rocked the mother country to its foundations and split the colony of New York right to its core.

James II was a Catholic whose rule was tolerated by the Protestant English only because the heir to the throne, James's grown daughter, Mary, wife of William of Orange, was Protestant. When, in 1688, James's queen produced a Catholic heir—a male, with precedence over Mary in line of succession—his English subjects, disinclined to fight their bloody religious wars all over again, staged what is known as the "Glorious Revolution."

The backwash of this revolution in the American colonies was somewhat less than glorious, and it very nearly swept away the Manor of Livingston, its lord and lady, and their burgeoning dynasty. Baby Robert's lullaby might well have been the sinister little verse written about the birth of King James's son:

> Rockabye, baby, in the treetop,
> When the wind blows the cradle will rock.
> When the bough breaks the cradle will fall,
> And down will come baby, cradle and all.

4

News of the royal birth, which reached New York in August 1688 (when baby Robert Livingston was a month old), immediately catalyzed the colony's long-held fears of James and his religion. Living under the shadow of Catholic Canada and its fierce Indian allies, New Yorkers had always suspected their English monarch of brewing an alliance that could spell an end to their trade, their property and perhaps their very lives.

Unfortunately, on the day the news was received, the royal governor, Sir Edmund Andros, was absent in Boston, and his deputy was in charge. Francis Nicholson was unintelligent and tactless at the best of times; under pressure, he succumbed to fits. (An Indian who once witnessed Nicholson's behavior in a crisis observed that he was drunk; on being informed that the man didn't drink he replied, "I do not mean that he is drunk with rum. He was born drunk.") Thrown into a paroxysm of delight over the infant prince's birth, Nicholson decided to celebrate with a party at the governor's fort. The sounds of revelry that wafted over the walls and through the streets of the town were naturally interpreted by the citizens of New York as an answer to their question: official policy favored the Catholic succession and alliance with French Canada.

But for the next seven interminable months, while Governor Andros lingered in Boston and London remained silent, New Yorkers were forced to wait—and watch for fearful signs of activity in the Indian villages across the northern frontier. Finally, in March 1689, there came the electrifying news that William and Mary had successfully invaded England and King James had fled. The colonials' delight was tempered by uncertainty: was William firmly on the throne or was he not? And who now wielded royal authority in the province of New York?

Up in Boston the citizenry quickly arrived at a collective conclusion and acted on it: in the name of William and Mary, they seized Governor Andros and clapped him in jail. New Yorkers, typically, were incapable of such concerted, decisive action and probably would have remained so without the inspired bumbling of Lieutenant Governor Nicholson. News of Andros' incarceration coincided with alarming reports of an enormous force of French Canadian troops and Indians massed on the border ready to move south. Manhattanites, seeing no preparations for defense, became convinced that Nicholson was going to surrender the town without a fight. They took to the streets, and a series of small, nervous clashes occurred between the citizenry and English troops.

Nicholson was completely out of his depth. As tension mounted, he greeted each citizens' petition and deputation with increasing contempt and even flippancy. Finally, when a member of a delegation was actually manhandled in front of witnesses, the pot boiled over. The populace of Manhattan came together in sufficient strength and for just long enough to storm the fort and throw Nicholson out.

Having gained this splendid victory—and duly celebrated it—the "rebellion" immediately began to waver. The people held the fort, to be sure, but what were they to do with it? Out of their floundering emerged a leader in the person of Jacob Leisler, wealthy merchant and militia captain—the very same Jacob Leisler who thirteen years before had arraigned Nicholas Van Rensselaer for heterodoxy and been brought down by the combined muscle of the royal government and the Albany establishment.

Leisler tried hard to make order and secure the province's defenses, but his efforts were doomed, not because of what he stood for but because of what he was. In order to carry out his policies—policies everyone agreed on: support for William and Mary and strong defense against the French—he needed the cooperation of the colonial establishment, the landed gentry which, practically to a man, regarded him as "ye vulgar sort." Leisler was rich, to be sure; but he had no land and no graces. His flagrant Dutch provincialism repelled the English; his militant religious bigotry offended even the Dutch; and his rigidity, tactlessness and lack of humor appalled almost everyone. The colonial leadership (including Robert Livingston of Livingston Manor) could not bring itself to cooperate with him, even under imminent, dire threat from the Canadian French and Indians. Quite the contrary, it did everything it could to undermine and bring him down.

Leisler, for his part, seemed eager to offend. His first political action after declaring himself lieutenant governor in the name of William and Mary was to dismiss the entire New York City Council, which was composed exclusively of wealthy and distinguished Dutch names (including Alida Livingston's brother-in-law, Stephen Van Cortlandt). Leisler justified the measure in legal terms: the Council, having been appointed by a king who was now deposed, no longer had official sanction. But it was also quite clear that he relished the opportunity to thumb his nose at the gentry. Van Cortlandt and his colleagues retired in a huff to Albany, where they joined with Robert Livingston and the rest of the colonial establishment to plot the downfall of Jacob Leisler, the "Dutch boor."

Albany was by this time in a state of acute nerves. Although the April invasion rumors had proven false, the French and Indians from Canada could not be expected to wait forever to take advantage of the emerging divisions within the province of New York. In October, therefore, Leisler dispatched troops upriver to Albany, the colony's first line of defense. But by now Robert Livingston and his friends had improvised a makeshift organization called the Albany Convention, which claimed jurisdiction over the town until the new regime in London could send representatives. The Albany Convention refused to garrison Leisler's troops, which were forced to withdraw downriver, leaving the outpost virtually defenseless.

The citizens of Albany panicked, and within months over one quarter of them had fled. Their leaders moved quickly to raise a militia and hire reinforcements from New England, with the members of the Convention themselves, led by Robert Livingston, subscribing the necessary funds.

Next the Convention drafted and signed an oath of allegiance to William and Mary—too late to satisfy Jacob Leisler, who accused them, with ample justification, of hedging their bets. (Robert Livingston, Stephen Van Cortlandt and a number of the others were indeed in communication with Governor Andros in his Boston jail and with Lieutenant Governor Nicholson, who had removed to England.) In turn, the members of the Convention mounted a vicious propaganda campaign against Leisler, filling the mail pouches and the ears of the people with anti-Leislerian facts, innuendos and rumors. In January 1690 the Convention adopted an official letter denouncing Leisler's regime; and when a copy fell into the "Dutch boor's" hands, the name of its author—Robert Livingston—went to the top of his enemies list.

The colony's two principal towns, Albany and New York, thus became warring camps, and its leadership irrevocably split along lines of social class.

That same January 1690 little Johanna Phillippina Livingston died, one month short of her sixth birthday—a private prefiguration of the public tragedy that struck the colony a month later. On the bitter cold night of February 9 a force made up of French and Indians attacked the town of Schenectady, only a few miles northwest of Albany, and over a period of several hours massacred sixty-two men, women and children, took twenty-seven others captive, and burned the town to the ground.

Thus was Albany's vulnerability—and that of the whole colony—palpably and horribly displayed. In the weeks following the Schenectady Massacre, Albany's evacuation rate escalated alarmingly as citizens by the hundreds deserted their homes and crammed themselves aboard every available conveyance to New York. The Albany Convention reluctantly concluded that it could no longer afford to snub Jacob Leisler's offer of troops. When the defenders, led by a Leisler lieutenant, reached Albany from New York a few weeks later, the garrison was turned over without a murmur and the town was theirs.

Robert and Alida (who was eight months pregnant) had remained in Albany with the children. The arrival of Leisler's troop of soldiers may have alleviated their danger from the French and Indians, but it also intensified Robert's exposure to Leisler's vengeance. Indeed, Leisler wasted no time in moving against his enemies, many of whom were arrested on trumped-up charges and chained to the walls of their prison cells for months on end. Robert was officially accused of defaming King William, as attested to by his next-door neighbor, Sheriff Richard Pretty, who swore that "Ro. Livingston towld me that there was a plott of robbery gon out of Holland into England, and the Prince of Orringe was the hed of them, and he . . . should come again to the same end as Monmouth did, this I can testify." (The Duke of Monmouth had been beheaded for challenging King James's succession.)

But the "Dutch boor" was slated for disappointment: when officers appeared at Robert's door to serve their warrant (which, in a typically Leislerian touch, further charged that Robert had acted at "the instigation of the Devill") their prey had vanished. Robert had gotten himself appointed by the Albany Convention as commissioner to Connecticut where he was, even then, busy raising additional troops for Albany's defense against the French.

Alida, who gave birth to a son, Gilbert, on the very day her husband received his commission to Connecticut, was shortly submitted to a series of harassments by Lieutenant Governor Leisler's minions. A troop of constables appeared at her door and in the course of searching the house turned up a piece of solid evidence against her husband: ". . . a case belonging to a french Jesuite of Canada, & some Indian Categismes, & the lesson to learne to make their God before they eit them, with crucifix." Robert Livingston may have been called many things in his life, but traitor and Catholic sympathizer were not among them. There are two possible explanations for the appearance of the case in his house: either it was a souvenir of his fur trading days among the Iroquois (a rather ghoulish one, to be sure) or it was planted by Leisler's constables. In either case, it failed to serve its purpose. Robert remained safely out of reach in Connecticut, raising troops for an invasion of Canada and, at the same time, waging a thoroughly nasty epistolary counterattack against Jacob Leisler. It was no holds barred—Robert even accused his enemy of responsibility for the Schenectady Massacre: "We have all Leisler's seditious letters . . . which was the occasion of the destruction of Synedhtade, miraculously found in the streets, all embrued with blood the morning after the massacre was committed." Miraculously found indeed. It appears that Robert knew how to turn up evidence too.

But of course he was hamstrung by the fact that Alida and the children remained under Leisler's authority; and during his four months of exile in Connecticut, Robert devised an elegant plan of rescue. He had renewed his acquaintance with Connecticut's prominent Winthrop family, and after the Connecticut governor agreed with New York's Lieutenant Governor Jacob Leisler to mount a joint military expedition against Canada, Robert managed to have Fitz-John Winthrop of New London appointed commander. When the expeditionary force, marching north in July of 1690, arrived in Albany to regroup for the assault, Robert Livingston entered the town with it, under the unassailable protection of Winthrop. By the time the army departed for Canada, Robert had spirited Alida, the children and himself to safety back in Connecticut.

There they waited while the expeditionary force marched north to meet the enemy. Jacob Leisler was in charge of supplying the campaign from New York; and when supplies failed, the army foundered and turned back. Leisler's motives were murky at best, but anger at Robert Livingston's subversion of the campaign's leadership may have been among them. In any case, Leisler tried to vent his frustration by seizing Fitz-John Winthrop during the retreat and placing him under arrest. This, too, backfired: Winthrop was rescued from prison by a troop of Mohawk Indians and escorted to Connecticut, where he swelled the ranks of the anti-Leislerian refugees. Meanwhile, Albany remained just as exposed as ever, and its citizens continued to flee.

Finally in January 1691—over a year and a half after the seizure of the fort of New York—a fleet of royal ships appeared in the harbor. Its commander, Major Richard Ingoldsby, landed with a smart troop and marched to the gates of the fort where he was halted by Leisler's sentries and asked to state his business. Ingoldsby, momentarily nonplussed, replied that he was simply reporting for duty, as ordered by his sovereigns, William and Mary, to New York's new royal governor, Colonel Henry Sloughter. But Lieutenant Governor Captain Jacob Leisler had never heard of Governor Colonel Henry Sloughter, nor had anyone else in New York. Ingoldsby, surmising correctly that Sloughter's ship had been delayed, decided to carry out the rest of his orders while awaiting his chief's arrival, which included taking military command of the town and fort. Unfortunately, he did not have the orders in writing; and Jacob Leisler, who by now trusted no one, refused to turn over the fort.

Negotiations failed, blandishments failed, even threats failed to budge Jacob Leisler. Ingoldsby wisely decided to wait it out. For two long months the opposing forces surveyed each other uneasily over the walls of the fort. By the time Governor Sloughter appeared in March the town was in a virtual state of war. Amazingly, Jacob Leisler, whose stubbornness had apparently petrified into total paranoia, refused to concede the fort even to the new governor in person. Sloughter, with no other choice, ordered Ingoldsby to mount an assault by land and sea. During the action two bullets fired from the fort found their way into the hearts of two English troopers, and that, if nothing else, sealed Jacob Leisler's fate. Upon the fort's capitulation he and several of his lieutenants were placed under arrest and charged with treason.

Almost immediately Leisler's enemies began to appear out of the woodwork—including, of course, Robert Livingston, who journeyed posthaste from Connecticut to pay his respects to the new governor and offer his services.* (Sloughter was Robert's third royal governor, and the courting ritual must have become pretty routine.) The colonial elite, on whom Governor Sloughter must rely to establish his authority and consolidate the colony's defenses, was implacably anti-Leislerian; and so it necessarily became the governor's first order of business to bring Jacob Leisler to trial.

Had Leisler been less recalcitrant, had he at least surrendered the fort to Major Ingoldsby in January, Sloughter might have tried to protect him from his enemies in March. But now the governor offered nothing. The trial proceedings were efficient, the outcome inevitable.† Leisler, with several others, was sentenced to be hanged, disemboweled and beheaded. Governor Sloughter managed to commute the sentences of all but Leisler and his principal lieutenant (Jacob Milborne, who was also Leisler's son-in-law). He would no doubt have liked to do the same for them, but his indispensable political allies, the colonial landed gentry, demanded blood. Leisler and Milborne were publicly hanged and beheaded (the disemboweling was omitted) on May 16, 1691, in the presence of Governor Sloughter and his party, which included Robert Livingston. The governor was observed on the occasion to appear unwell; and immediately rumors flew through the town that his newly appointed Council had gotten him drunk and tricked him into signing the death warrants. The stories became uglier still when, a few days later, the colonial Assembly, dominated by the anti-Leislerian party, voted Sloughter a substantial gift of money.

None of these rumors has ever been proven; but their persistence through the centuries is typical of the whole Leisler interlude. The hostility between Leisler and his enemies was not political, it was personal, hatched from snobbery and envy and force-fed with insinuation and calumny. The two parties fought—and in their fighting almost brought about the destruction of the colony of New York—not because they disagreed about policy

---

* It is not known exactly when Robert learned that his distant noble Scottish cousins, Lord Livingston and his brother, the Earl of Callendar, had fought in the Glorious Revolution on the losing side.

† But jury tampering and bribery were whispered, particularly after one of the defendants, Peterse Delanoy, was acquitted on evidence virtually identical to that which condemned several others. One of Delanoy's descendants dropped the final *y*, and the family became Delano.

but because they hated each other. One does not forgive being dubbed a "Dutch boor."

One of the participants' descendants has written a history that treats the whole affair as a simple misunderstanding due to errors in translation between Dutch and English. Nonsense: it was a nasty little class war—intense, personal and dirty—that brought out the worst in everyone. Only luck prevented it from tearing the province of New York apart and surrendering it to the French. The battle left social and political scars that persisted for generations; and its stench is clearly discernible even at a historical distance of three hundred years.

5

A few days after Leisler's execution, Governor Sloughter embarked by sloop for Albany to attend to his next most pressing duty, securing the northern frontier. He must have been thoroughly briefed on the sober facts of life in the Hudson Valley; still, it is doubtful that he was prepared for the sheer scale of the landscape—river, mountains and endless forest—or that he ever fathomed the mentality of the settlers whose houses and barns he saw as his sloop glided past the tiny, brand-new settlement of Poughkeepsie on the Hudson's eastern shore.

Sloughter's specific object in Albany was to meet with the Iroquois sachems, exchange gifts and assure them of the high regard in which they were held by their new White Father in London. As liaison and translator, Robert Livingston was indispensable, and he enhanced the obligation by acting as the governor's host in Albany. Sloughter responded handsomely, publicly confirming Robert in all his former government offices (which Leisler had naturally removed) and adding a new plum, the post of victualer to the garrisons of Albany and New York.

The victualing system of the English colonial army was rife with possibilities for profit—and knavery. The system itself was simple: the victualer received a set fee from the government (Robert got fivepence per day per man), and if he could feed the soldiers for less he kept the difference. It goes without saying that the typical English colonial trooper did not eat very well and that Robert Livingston was pleased to have the job.

But, in the typically convulsive manner of New York politics, Robert's fortunes reversed themselves again when, after only four months in office, Governor Sloughter took sick and died. Robert, with his government loans now virtually uncollectable* and his tenure in government office uncertain, watched while, under Sloughter's successor, his victualing payments slowed to a trickle and then stopped completely. He had to continue victualing the troops in Albany lest they depart and "the enemy finds an open door." Lingering in Manhattan, courting the new governor and trying to get his money, he heard from Alida in Albany that "the homesteads above Schaneghtade and Kinderhoek have been abandoned" and that Albany itself was becoming deserted, as families continued to flee by every sloop. Typically, though, she expressed no personal fear and ended the letter with her own special mixture of the lofty and the mundane:

> I long for you to come up   greetings to all the friends   send a wheelbarrow and a whitewash brush
>> your loving wife till death do us part
>> Alida Livingston

Robert, with no real choice, continued to victual the Albany garrison out of his own pocket.

Meanwhile the new royal governor, Benjamin Fletcher, undertook to mine all the known veins of gubernatorial graft and to stake claim on some new ones. He made a specialty of pirates, a species which New York Province boasted in at least four varieties. First was the genuine, out-and-out pirate, who swaggered through the streets of Manhattan and dined at all the best houses—including the governor's. A less obvious variety was the privateer, commissioned by European governments to seek out and capture outlaw ships, who turned outlaw himself. Next came the respectable New York merchant who doubled as a secret backer of pirate voyages; and finally there was the governor himself, who was handsomely rewarded by all for looking the other way.

Governor Fletcher, being no fool, took care to balance his image by periodic spasms of law enforcement, during one of which he irretrievably alienated Robert Livingston. Robert was part owner of a brigantine which returned in 1694 from a Caribbean voyage with a cargo representing a 500% return on investment—an extraordinary profit, even in 1694. Governor Fletcher ordered the ship seized and the owners charged with violation of the English Navigation Acts (i.e., trading with the French). His prosecution was foiled, however, when the grand jury, whose foreman was Robert Livingston's good friend, William Kidd, refused to indict.

---

* Government loans were signed for *personally* by the colonial governor, and when an individual governor died the government in London often refused to honor the debts incurred during his tenure. Lending was therefore an enormous risk to be undertaken only in defense of the colony or to curry favor with the governor. Robert's loans usually did both.

Exonerated or not, guilty or not (500% says he probably was), for Robert it was the last straw. For the first time in his life he openly turned on an English governor and tried to withdraw completely from politics and government contracting. Of course it was impossible, he was in too deep. Robert could not afford to write off his loans any more than he could afford to lose the political leverage they provided. Most urgently, he could not afford to stop victualing the garrison of Albany, whether or not he ever got paid back.

As Fletcher's hostility became more and more evident, Robert's cash position became more and more precarious, until he was finally driven to undertake a lengthy, perilous voyage to England to seek restitution directly from Their Majesties' Government—and, at the same time, if possible to cut the ground out from under Benjamin Fletcher's feet. Robert sailed on the ship *Charity* on December 10, 1694, accompanied by a cargo of pelts for sale in England and his eldest son, John. Alida, in Albany, marked the hour of his ship's weighing anchor by giving birth to a baby daughter, a second Joanna.† She was getting used to being left alone in the half-deserted town; but this time she could not expect to see her husband for well over a year. She had plenty to keep her busy, of course, with the children and the store. Robert had left his power of attorney so that she could run their trading and shipping enterprises and handle affairs on the manor during his absence. But it remained to be seen what power she could draw on to guard his political flanks from Governor Benjamin Fletcher and to fight off the French and Indians hammering at the gates of Albany.

Robert's voyage was horrendous, worse than the one his father had endured half a century before. Vicious gales ripped the *Charity*'s sails and snapped her masts; finally adrift, her rudder smashed, she began to leak. All able-bodied men took turns at the pumps, and cargo was jettisoned (including some of Robert's beaver pelts) to lighten her in the water. Food supplies began to give out; and the captain and passengers—who had separate stores from the crew—armed themselves. Sickness ravaged passengers and crew alike. Young John Livingston could not rise from his bed, and a sailor was found dead in the gunner's room, "having perished from exposure and being eaten by vermin."

Even Robert—silver-tongued Robert, the great persuader and negotiator—was confounded. Like his father in similar circumstances, he offered a compact to God: "O, what is there in this world, riches, honors, land, houses, property, all vanity. O Christ is the only pearl"—the specific terms of the contract being that Robert, if rescued, promised to serve God "as a true Christian" and keep Thursday as a day of fasting and thanksgiving in

† Named after her sister, who had died in 1690. The names of dead children were frequently given to next-born siblings of the same sex.

perpetuity. Characteristically he made no mention of tithing, which the Lord seems to have overlooked: on April 26, John's fifteenth birthday and the one hundred and thirty-eighth day out of New York, the *Charity* drifted within sight of the Portuguese coast.

Food and medical supplies were brought aboard, and a few days later the crippled ship touched land. Robert removed his son to the house of the consul in Lisbon and then set about landing his goods. A snag developed when Robert balked at paying the £15 balance for his passage, on the grounds that nobody should have to pay in full for such a voyage; but when the captain refused to release his beaver pelts, he consented to a £10 compromise. Robert's crates were carried up to the consul's attic where he spent the days of John's convalescence laying out the skins to dry and repacking for the trip to London.

They continued their journey overland (with Robert complaining about prices: "the Spanish are a jealous nation") and reached London on July 25, 1695, seven and a half months after leaving home. Robert placed John in school and immediately set about his own business, principally the recovery of the money owed him by the English government.

Two major stumbling blocks quickly appeared. First was the considerable influence exercised long distance by Robert's enemy, New York Governor Benjamin Fletcher. Fletcher had been barraging London officialdom with a litany of weighty charges against Livingston, which served not only to undermine Robert but also to deflect attention from Fletcher's own fiscal abuses: "[Livingston] has made a considerable fortune by his employments in the Government, never disbursing six pence but with the expectation of twelve pence, his beginning being a little Book keeper, he has screwed himself into one of the most considerable estates in the province. . . . [I] hope you'll endevour to keep a man of such vile principles from sucking any more the blood of the Province, for he has been a very spunge to it . . . he is known by all men here, to have neither Religion nor morality, his whole thirst being at any rate and by any ways to inrich himself . . . he had rather be called knave Livingston than poor Livingston."

Robert had perhaps expected something of the sort, being an old hand at that game himself. But the second obstacle standing between him and the recovery of his debts must have come as a nasty surprise: the Whig Party, searching for an issue on which to challenge the incumbent Tories, had latched on to the case of Jacob Leisler. During the previous winter of 1695, while Robert was bobbing around on the Atlantic Ocean in the *Charity*, an inquiry had been held; and the parliamentary Whigs, Leislerians to a man (only because the Tories were anti-Leislerian), had managed to have Leisler's conviction reversed. Now it became Robert's unenviable task to convince the Whig leadership (which had the full support of King William) that he—a lifelong Tory and prominent anti-Leislerian—was to be credited contrary to the testimony of the royal governor of the province of New York.

There was one glimmer of hope: rumor said that the Tory Fletcher was about to be replaced as governor by a Whig, one Richard Coote, Earl of Bellomont. Robert wasted no time in making the earl's acquaintance. They found they had a lot in common. Bellomont coveted the governorship ardently and was therefore predisposed to help Robert dig the incumbent Fletcher's grave. Robert, for his part, would not have hesitated to apprise the earl of his prominent position in the colony, his influence with the Iroquois, and all the various ways in which he would be useful to a new governor. The upshot was that Bellomont found Robert's version of the Leisler affair quite acceptable while Robert began to appreciate the merits of Whigdom.

Within a fortnight of their first meeting Robert obtained a hearing before the Lords of Trade, where he testified that most of the money due him for victualing and back salaries (primarily as Secretary for Indian Affairs, a post he had fulfilled for twenty years with only sporadic recompense) had gone instead into Governor Fletcher's pocket. While the Lords spent weeks scrutinizing every shred of Robert's evidence and investigating his conduct during the Leisler affair, Robert orchestrated a skillful defense, calling witnesses to testify to his loyalty and even attempting to tug at their lordships' heartstrings: "My Lords this hard treatment together with the disasters of my voyage and the melancholick consideration of haveing left a wife and numberous family of young helplesse children, under streights, have almost broken my spirits."

The business was finally concluded in the spring of 1696, mostly to Robert's satisfaction. His financial claims were declared valid, and part of the cash was paid him on the spot. He invested it in goods to ship to Alida for sale in New York and also went on a modest shopping spree for clothes and books. His choice of reading matter included the works of Livy, Tacitus, Plutarch and—perhaps superfluously—Machiavelli. Robert also received assurances of Fletcher's ultimate removal from the post of governor, but unfortunately without a precise timetable. Meanwhile he would have to rely on Fletcher for the recovery of the rest of his government debt, a doubtful prospect at best.

During the long and trying weeks of the Board of Trade's deliberations, Robert had been keeping busy with another scheme, one that stood to make him a great deal of money and, at the same time, ingratiate him with the Whig leadership. It all revolved around Robert's good friend from New York, William Kidd. Both Robert and Kidd were the sons of Scottish clergymen, and both were men of conspicuous, if varied, talents. Kidd had been known as a "mighty man" for his exploits against the French in the West Indies, and in 1691, in response to a call for aid from Governor Sloughter, had brought his ship into the action that ousted Jacob Leisler from the fort of New York, for which he was rewarded with £150 voted by the provincial Council. A onetime merchant, Kidd now dealt in New York City real estate based on the property of his wife, a respectable widow. The couple lived in considerable comfort in a large town house on Hanover Square, Manhattan, and on their country estate in Haarlem. Just before leaving New York for his current business trip to London, Kidd had sold an elegant house on Dock Street to his friend Robert Livingston (who, quite coincidentally, was also on the verge of departure for England). The two friends naturally saw each other in London, and when Robert needed a character witness in the hearings before the Lords of Trade, William Kidd enthusiastically obliged. Now Robert was hatching a scheme that appealed enormously to Kidd's restless nature.

The plan was for Kidd to serve as captain of a privateer outfitted to fight and seize pirate vessels in the Red Sea. He and Robert between them were to raise one fifth of the outfitting money; the rest would be the responsibility of Lord Bellomont, who would also obtain the official documents—including a royal commission empowering Kidd to seize enemy (i.e., French) vessels as well as pirates. The profits of the voyage, potentially enormous, were to be divided as follows: one quarter to the crew (which was hired on a strictly commission basis—no captures, no pay) and the rest to Kidd, Livingston and Bellomont in the same proportion as their original investments. Captain Kidd would receive the ship itself as a bonus if the total profits exceeded £100,000.

Once the terms were laid out and Kidd's participation assured, Lord Bellomont went about raising his share of the outfitting money from among his friends. The five gentlemen who became his partners constituted a Who's Who of Whigdom. They were: Henry Sidney, Earl of Romney, Secretary of State and Master-General of the Ordinance (later a Lord Justice); Edward Russell, Earl of Orford, First Lord of Admiralty; Charles Talbot, Duke of Shrewsbury, a Secretary of State and Lord Justice; Sir John Somers, later Lord Chancellor; and Edward Harrison, director of the East India Company. King William himself almost certainly gave the enterprise his blessing in exchange for the customary royal perquisite, ten percent off the top.

Kidd and Robert also brought in other investors to make up their share, among whom, unfortunately, was one Richard Blackham, a merchant who subscribed a one-fifteenth share of the voyage and was guaranteed full repayment of his investment in the event of failure. Shortly after signing the agreement with Kidd and Livingston, Blackham was imprisoned on charges of bribery and later convicted for currency manipulation. An unsavory character at best, his membership in the syndicate cast a shadow on the whole enterprise and made it difficult later to deny that its intent had been felonious from the start.

But all that was in the future on the April day in 1696 when Kidd and his crew set sail from Plymouth in the *Adventure Galley*. The following month Robert himself set sail for New York, having dispatched the remainder of his business and collected John and a nephew, Robert, the son of his brother James. For once the voyage went smoothly, and on August 2, 1696, Robert and the boys sailed through the Narrows and across the broad harbor to Manhattan Island.

Robert stepped ashore to find himself sinking in political quicksand. His old political and business associates—friends, neighbors and relations, all staunch Tories—quickly let him know that his conversion to Whiggery was unacceptable. Within a month the provincial Council, in direct contradiction of the Board of Trade's written confirmation of Robert's official titles, stripped him of all government offices on the grounds that he was, of all things, "aliene born." This gave Governor Fletcher the perfect excuse to withhold the balance of Robert's victualing money and to leave him out of a session of important negotiations with the Iroquois—a deliberate snub, and a dangerous one. Robert could not justifiably blame his friends; he had, after all, committed political apostasy and must accept his term in limbo. His place in the sun could be restored only by the accession of Bellomont, an event for which he had to wait a very long year and a half.

6

"Spero Meliora [I hope for better things]." Robert Livingston, usually more of a doer than a hoper, submitted reluctantly to his role as a political pariah. He had never been ambitious politically for its own sake; what was the point, when the highest position a colonial could aspire to was membership on an advisory council to the English governor? But, like all New York businessmen and landowners, he knew that political leverage was the *sine qua non* of economic prosperity, and his term in political limbo represented a genuine threat to his and his family's survival. This is perhaps why, shortly after his return from England, Robert wrote to his brother William in Edinburgh, inquiring after the Livingston coat of arms and, in adapting it for his family's use, replaced the demisavage on the crest with a ship in distress and changed the motto to "Spero Meliora." (The original Scottish motto, *"Si Je Puis* [If I Can]," was clearly supererogatory for Robert, who could and did at every opportunity.)

John Livingston, considered ready at sixteen to enter the family business, began traveling extensively among the Iroquois and shuttling with his father back and forth between Albany and New York. It was in personal affairs, however, that John proved most precocious. During the unusually cold winter of 1697–98 he began to spend his time in Albany "courting after Jacob Rutsen's daughter who is 28 years old and has a mouth as if she has followed the army all her life." Alida told her son in no uncertain terms "what he should expect," but the eighteen-year-old blandly ignored her.

His father was, as usual, far from home in New York, and a frustrated Alida entreated Robert to "write [John] about that and give him a reprimand and enclose his letter in mine and see to it that you now get those 20 [shillings?] from Jacob Rutsen for I hate to hear his name and don't care to have any dealings with him."

John gave up Miss Rutsen in the face of his father's wrath; but poor Alida, who at forty-two had just lost another baby and was herself "weak of the burning fever and sick out of my head," began to worry about her husband, whose temper was apparently beginning to fray. She heard a rumor from New York that Robert, in a violent quarrel with a Mr. Broek, had been thrown down a flight of stairs and threatened with "a sword and cane." Robert, in turn, had called Mr. Broek "the son of a pair of pants [broek in Dutch means britches, so, "son of a britches"] and . . . a foundling.* I think," Alida expostulated, "that you would be wiser than to say such things even if it was true." But underneath the energy and spirit, she was worried and—perhaps for the first time—frightened. She accused him of neglect and took to signing her letters, "your loving and lonesome wife."

In April of 1698 the Earl of Bellomont finally replaced Benjamin Fletcher as governor of New York, and Robert moved back into the limelight. His relations and former allies, observing his personal influence with the new governor, lifted his political quarantine and permitted themselves to be persuaded to join a coalition of Leislerians and anti-Leislerians being formed by Robert at Bellomont's request. The new Whig governor, in a fervent effort to consolidate his power, tolerated as allies even rabid Tories like Stephen Van Cortlandt and Peter Schuyler (Robert's brothers-in-law) because of their enthusiastic denunciation of his predecessor, Benjamin Fletcher (who, once upon a time, had been their ally).

Most significantly for Robert, Bellomont's gratitude was expressed concretely: by appointment to the highest political office in the colonial administration, membership on the Governor's Council. Unfortunately, one of the perquisites of Council membership was that Robert was expected to resume victualing the Albany garrison. For the moment, however, thanks to Bellomont, victualing money from London was flowing into his pocket. Robert and the governor were thick as thieves, and Alida sent Lady Bellomont six marten skins from Albany to make a tippet.

Then, within a few weeks of Bellomont's accession to office, a piece of startling news arrived from London: William Kidd had turned pirate, and a warrant was out for his arrest.

Kidd's two-year passage in the *Adventure Galley* had been long on incident and short on profit. Whether or not it actually included piracy is still an unanswered question. He had certainly chosen his acquaintances unwisely

* Foundling is probably a translator's euphemism for bastard. All the quotations from Alida's letters are translated from the Dutch. She was bilingual in Dutch and English, as were all the Livingston children, but she apparently felt more comfortable writing in Dutch.

and spent far too much time in the port of Madagascar, a notorious pirate den. But he had also had extremely bad luck: cholera hit his crew at about the same time his ship contracted terminal leakage, and he went for over a year without a capture. The surviving crew members no doubt put murderous pressure on him to earn them their pay in any way he could. In the process of so doing, he captured two "French" ships which turned out to belong to an ally of England, and the Whig government was both embarrassed and incensed. Shortly thereafter the crying-out against Captain Kidd began.

The Whig leadership in Parliament was up to its ears in Kidd's enterprise, so of course its moral indignation and demands for swift justice were all the more strident. In order to save themselves, the Whigs would have to throw Kidd to the Tory wolves—together with any dispensable confederates, who might or might not include Robert Livingston and the Earl of Bellomont.

But first Kidd had to be captured. For the first few months after the warrants were issued he managed to stay out of sight. Then, in June of 1699, his ship materialized briefly in Long Island Sound and a few days later quietly dropped anchor in Boston Harbor. Governor Bellomont was in Boston on business, and Kidd had apparently decided to seek his protection. Instead, Bellomont, reading correctly the barometric indicators from London, arrested him, took possession of all his logs and papers and announced that he would be sent to England to stand trial.

Robert Livingston was in a terrible fix. As the man who had engineered the whole enterprise and introduced Kidd to Bellomont and the other Whigs, he stood in deadly peril of becoming the next sacrificial lamb, should one be required. He was far from confident of the governor's good will. Things were in the wind, and their relationship had begun to cool even before the advent of pirate Kidd. Bellomont had for months been busy vacating large land grants, and although Robert and his friends were not yet touched they were apprehensive—quite correctly, as it turned out. Bellomont had made specific plans to vacate all grants over 2000 acres and requested that the Board of Trade send him "a good Judge or two and a smart active Atturney General" for the purpose. Robert also observed that his victualing money was once again drying up. In fact London had cut off all victualing funds but Bellomont, unwilling to see the northern frontier undefended, had neglected to tell Robert and the others. One of Robert's friends, having tried for months to collect, wrote, "His Lordship has beene kind to mee in words but . . . that will butter no Parsnips."

Parsnips were suddenly the least of Robert's worries: Captain Kidd could cost him his life. He rose to the occasion magnificently. Speeding to Boston, he marched into Governor Bellomont's presence and, instead of defending himself or pleading, demanded the prompt return of his £10,000 bond which, according to the original agreement, was forfeit if Kidd turned pirate. Bellomont, a practiced politician, was completely thrown off stride. Having seriously considered tossing Robert to the wolves—he had already written London that the "honest" owners of the *Adventure Galley,* including himself, were "perswaded by Mr. Livingston to put the Ship under the command of a most abandon'd Villain, for we were, all of us, strangers to Kidd . . ."—he now changed his mind in the face of Robert's boldness, and also, perhaps, at the thought of trying to govern and defend New York without him. He had Robert examined, briefly, under oath, and then recommended to London that he be exonerated and his bond be refunded.

Robert returned quickly to New York and retired upriver. He was still unsure of Bellomont's support and of what might come out at the trial of Kidd, so he decided to lie low. He remained in Albany most of the winter, 1699–1700, mourning with Alida the death of their youngest baby, Catherine, and planning the construction of a house—their first—on the Manor of Livingston.

In midwinter Robert received an urgent summons from Governor Bellomont which he could not afford to ignore. An important Iroquois council was to be held in April at Onondaga, and rumor had it that the Five Nations planned to debate a French alliance. Bellomont wanted Robert to undertake the 540-mile journey to present His Majesty's case to the sachems. Robert had no choice but to comply. Paying all expenses out of his own pocket (including gifts for the Iroquois chiefs), he made the wilderness trek and returned triumphant. The Indians had reaffirmed their allegiance to the English and agreed to the relocation of three tribes nearer Albany and the construction of several new forts on their land.

Even this did not earn Governor Bellomont's loyalty. The governor, still holding Robert in reserve as an offering on the Kidd funeral pyre, continued to undermine Robert's reputation with the Lords of Trade: ". . . at Albany the soldiers have been worse used than here, to Mr. Livingston's only satisfaction and profit; he haveing pinch'd an estate out of the poor soldiers bellies." Robert, ever sensitive to the humors of governors, did not linger in New York but returned upriver to his family and their nearly completed manor home.

The house, constructed during a period when Alida averred they were "without a nickel or a quarter," did not conform to the latter-day notion of a manor house. What Robert and Alida called "our homestead" fulfilled a number of functions: residence, trading post, fortress, meeting house and manor bakery. It stood on a point of land overlooking the harbor where the Roeliff Jansen Kill flows into the Hudson. Today that harbor has filled up with tiny islands, but in 1700 it was wide and deep enough to accommodate large trading sloops. Beyond the harbor lies a magnificent sweep of mile-wide river, with the Catskill Mountains rising on the far shore. The house was completed toward the end of 1700, and it was there on December 20 that Robert and Alida celebrated the marriage of their oldest daughter, Margaret, to the glamorous young Scotsman, Samuel Vetch.

Vetch had entered the Livingstons' lives the year before, when he appeared in New York with a shipload of goods rescued (he said) from the abandoned Scottish colony of Darien in the Caribbean. The Vetch family in Scotland was intimately connected to the Edinburgh Livingstons: the Reverend John Livingston had guided Sam's father's entry into the Presbyterian ministry; and William Livingston, Robert's older brother, had stood witness at Sam's baptism and later married into the Vetch family. So the very first marriage of an American Livingston girl was to a man whom her father called "cousin."

Unbeknownst to Robert and Alida, however, Sam was in deep political trouble at home, under accusation of responsibility for the Darien disaster and of illegally appropriating goods from the site (goods which, once they reached New York in Sam's ship, were probably disposed of by his helpful cousin, Robert Livingston). On the very day of the wedding Robert's niece wrote to him from Edinburgh that she would be "ashamed to let any hier know that your Daughter should entertain such a man whoe is haeted by al his country and that for his evil deeds." But the warning came too late. The marriage was performed; and the bride's father, short of cash, gave the couple as dowry instead an imposing and elegant house in New York—the very house which he had purchased seven years before from William Kidd.

Captain Kidd was not, of course, invited to the wedding. Instead he was holding center stage in the London legal extravaganza stage-managed by a Whig parliamentary leadership desperate to demonstrate to the world —and the Tories—the depths of its astonishment and revulsion at Kidd's betrayal of trust. In his first examination in the House of Commons, Kidd did his best to implicate the "others who knew better, and made me the Tool of their Ambition and Avarice, and who now perhaps think it their interest that I should be removed out of the world." He swore that he was "partly Cajold, and partly menac'd into [the enterprise] by the Lord Bellomont, and one Robert Livingston of New York, who was the projector, promoter, and Chief Manager of that designe. . . . He was the man admitted into [the owners'] Closets, and received their private Instruction, which he kept in his own hands, and who encouraged me in their names to do more than I ever did, and to act without regard to my Commission."

But the juggernaut of Whig justice was not to be stopped. In Kidd's trial at Newgate, the only piece of evidence that could conceivably have cleared him—a document from one of the captured French ships—turned out to have been "lost" by Governor Bellomont. Kidd was convicted and hanged on May 23, 1701. His property, valued at £6471, was forfeit to the Crown. In a gesture of royal philanthropy Queen Anne donated the sum for the founding of Greenwich Hospital.

So Kidd went to his fate, and so the grand lords of Whigdom once again rested easy in their chairs of state. As for Robert, we may never know to what degree Kidd's testimony was true. But his extended stay at the manor during this period did give rise to a certain amount of speculation concerning, among other things, Kidd's supposed pirate treasure. Rumor had it that Robert had spirited the gold off Kidd's ship in Long Island Sound and buried it at various locations on the manor. Rumors die hard, particularly rumors of buried treasure; and I understand that to this day an unfamiliar figure may occasionally be seen on the old manor lands armed with map, pick and shovel, earnestly searching the earth of Columbia County, New York, for the hidden gold of Captain Kidd.

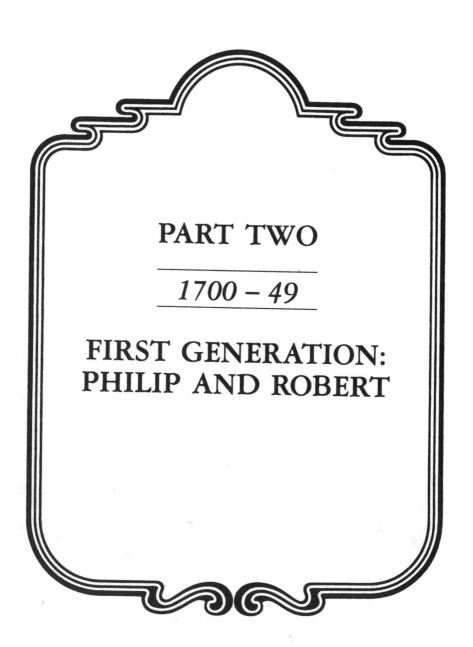

PART TWO

1700 – 49

FIRST GENERATION:
PHILIP AND ROBERT

7

Robert Livingston was forty-six years old in 1700 when his daughter Margaret was married. The marriage proclaimed the coming of age of the first American-born generation of Livingstons. Robert and Alida were far from ready to retire from active life, however, which was just as well: having survived savage Indians, rapacious royal governors and vengeful politicians, the Livingston parents now found themselves in their declining years fighting off a new threat, the irresponsible adventurism of their male offspring.

In general health and numbers, Robert and Alida's six children represented a solid dynastic foundation. But the individual characters of at least three of the four boys sadly lacked solidity. Each of the four young men inherited one of his father's outstanding traits: John and Gilbert the seductive charm, Philip the cool head for business, and young Robert the graceful flair. But, in each, the salient trait seemed to overshadow any others, and the boys' personalities lacked balance and proportion. Their strong differences in style and outlook surfaced early, and they tended to grow apart as they matured. Their parents' dynastic ambitions—which the boys all shared—demanded that they operate as a family unit; but it was quite clear that, as adults, they didn't like each other very much.

John, the oldest boy, turned twenty in 1700, the year of his sister's wedding; but John had "survived to maturity" (as the genealogists put it) in the physical sense only. His romance with Miss Rutsen was a single interlude in an adolescence of unusual restlessness and profligacy—an adolescence John showed no sign whatsoever of outgrowing. The future proprietor of Livingston Manor had all his father's style without the substance. He was irresponsible, willful and arrogant; and his parents were beginning to realize that the less he bestirred himself the better for the family.

Mercifully, their second son, Philip, appeared to be John's opposite. Slated for a career as a merchant, Philip at fourteen was diligent, obedient and—except where business was concerned—utterly unimaginative. Having mastered mathematics and French (all New York merchants learned French, although trading with French Canada was against the law), Philip was already embarked on a business apprenticeship with his Uncle Schuyler in Albany.

Twelve-year-old Robert had sailed for Edinburgh two years previously, in 1698, to live with his Aunt Barbara and attend the Latin School in preparation for a career in the law. As a younger son who would inherit neither the family estates nor the family business, Robert required more elegant schooling than either of his older brothers. An attractive youth, he struck his Aunt Barbara as "very like" his father: "comely and fond of being fine."

Gilbert, at ten, was hardly old enough to bustle in the world; still his character already seemed more to resemble that of his oldest brother, John, than any of the others. Handsome and indolent, Gilbert had so far failed to distinguish himself at his studies or to exhibit any enthusiasm for the profession his parents had chosen for him at birth, the ministry.

As for the girls, Margaret and six-year-old Joanna, they simply did not figure dynastically. After marriage, girls were considered members of their husbands' families; so in a way Margaret and Joanna did not count as Livingstons. Their own mother, strong and independent though she was, had always functioned strictly within the context of her marriage. Unfortunately, however, Margaret's husband, Sam Vetch, was considered part of the Livingston family (perhaps because his own family was so far away in Scotland), and his every action reflected on the family's reputation.

John Livingston did not attend his sister Margaret's wedding, being busy instead in Connecticut pursuing matrimonial ambitions of his own, as usual to the discomfiture of his parents. His object was Mary Winthrop, the only daughter of Robert's old friend, Fitz-John Winthrop. Robert and Alida took exception to Mary because her mother and Fitz-John had not been married at the time of her birth, twenty years before—nor, rumor had it, were they wedded yet, except by common law.*

Their son's pleading ("to be parted asunder . . . wou'd certainly break both our hearts") did not soften the Livingstons' position nor did assurances from the Winthrops' minister that the couple "were as certainly married as God was in heaven." But finally a letter from an old mutual New

* The Winthrops were apparently married officially when Mary was six years old, after the death of Fitz-John's father. The elder Winthrop had no doubt objected to an innkeeper's child as his daughter-in-law.

London friend, Duncan Campbell, forced them to reconsider. Campbell, shrewdly observing that "Miss Mary" was an only child, transmitted Fitz-John's specific promise of a handsome dowry and assurances that Mary was his sole heir; and, in a telling aside, submitted that the Livingstons "need not screwple giving your consent to your son to marry so worthious and sober young lady." Robert and Alida underwent an abrupt change of heart. The financial argument cannot have failed to move them—but equally appealing may have been the good influence that "so worthious and sober young lady" might have on their feckless son. The marriage was performed in April of 1701 in New London, and the young couple promptly journeyed to New York, where Mary's gentle firmness and "good humor" quickly captured the hearts of her formidable Livingston in-laws, who were "extremely taken with her."

Unfortunately, Mary's influence did not prevent John and his new brother-in-law, Sam Vetch, from striking up a friendship and deciding to go into business together. John and Sam were extremely compatible in style, character and aspirations, which simply meant that they managed to get into far more trouble together than either might have done alone. They purchased a sloop, romantically christened the *Mary*, loaded her with trade goods and, with Sam at the helm, took her to Newfoundland. The return cargo—illegal French wines and brandy from Canada—sold so well in New York that John and Sam decided to repeat the exercise. While John remained in New York managing sales, Captain Vetch sailed north again, this time directly to Quebec.

A few weeks later, in late November 1701, Margaret Vetch, waiting at Livingston Manor for her husband's return and the birth of her first child, learned with horror that the *Mary* had drifted ashore, unmanned, at Montauk Point on the tip of Long Island. The sloop was intact, her cargo still aboard—amazingly, also still aboard were the *Mary*'s logs and papers, furnishing every detail of her illegal voyage; but of captain and crew there was not a trace.

They turned up after a few days: Sam always turned up. He and the crew had disembarked to seek help when the *Mary* ran aground on Block Island. During their overnight absence the tide had come in, lifted the sloop, carried her across Long Island Sound and gently deposited her on the beach at Montauk—illegal cargo, damning papers, logs and all.

Sam was promptly placed on trial for trading with the enemy. In the midst of the proceedings, on Christmas Day, 1701, Margaret gave birth to a daughter whom she named Alida. Sam's trial ended with the confiscation of the *Mary* and her cargo—an expensive penalty. He and John each lost approximately £2000, which the lackadaisical John greeted philosophically: "I hope that wee are all Sensebell that the Almighty God gives and takes."

Robert Livingston had almost certainly been aware of the nature of his son's and son-in-law's business; but their debacle came at the worst possible moment for him. A few months previously, Governor Bellomont had finally turned against Robert openly and, citing "great frauds," removed him as Collector of the Albany Excise. Robert's old Leislerian enemies, taking their cue from the governor, fell in behind in full cry. They passed an Assembly bill subpoenaing Robert's accounts for his entire twenty-one-year term as excise collector and, after he failed to appear in person to explain £20,000 in unattributed expenses, passed a bill of confiscation on his entire property, including the Manor of Livingston.

Everything Robert had worked for all his life—land, livelihood, dignity, his children's future—would be swept away if the bill were to be carried out. It was at this moment, as he was waiting to see how far his enemies actually dared to go, that that irrepressible duo, John Livingston and Sam Vetch, managed to land their sloop on Montauk Point and expose the Livingston family in a blatant felony.

The Leislerians, of course, adored it and fed like vultures on every detail of the proceedings against John and Sam. In such a climate they were able to proceed with impunity against Robert, removing him from the Governor's Council and commencing the confiscation process by taking away his house in New York.

Robert and his manor were saved in the nick of time by two persons (or parties): first his old friends, the Iroquois sachems, who met in conference to insist that Robert, and only Robert, be sent forthwith as their emissary to London to plead with the King for reinforcements against the Canadian French and Indians; and secondly by Governor Bellomont, who chose this propitious moment to die. His replacement, Edward Hyde, Lord Cornbury, an ardent Tory (and, therefore, ardently anti-Leislerian), promptly reinstated Livingston in all his offices, acquitted him of all charges, purged the Council and Assembly of their Leislerian majorities and—to Robert's infinite satisfaction—brought about Assembly repeal of the confiscation bill against the Livingston property.

As icing on the cake, Governor Cornbury also stopped the sale at auction of the sloop *Mary* and returned her to the owners, John Livingston and Sam Vetch—an action which one doubts he performed out of the kindness of his heart. In fact Cornbury proved to be the quintessential colonial governor, carrying the arts of bribery, peculation and mismanagement to new heights during his six-year term. Most unsettling of all, perhaps, was his habit of appearing at parties rigged out in the latest female fashions, a practice which disconcerted almost everyone except his wife, who was his helpmeet in all things. Lady Cornbury "borrowed coats and gowns and never returned them . . . whatever she admired on her visit she was sure to send for the next day. . . . As her's was the only carriage in the city and the rolling of the wheels was easily distinguished, the cry in the house was 'hide this and take away that.' " However, Lord Cornbury did manage, through negative influence, to accomplish what three successive New York royal governors before him had failed to do: he united the colony. Leislerians and anti-Leislerians, loathing him with equal fervor, buried the hatchet for a time to plot his downfall.

Robert Livingston did not participate, however. Instead, he prudently judged the time propitious for his voyage to England to plead the Iroquois' cause and his own—the Crown was in debt to him for over £2000 by now. Leaving his affairs once again in Alida's capable hands (ever frugal, he renewed her power of attorney by scribbling a note at the bottom of the 1694 document), he set sail on June 2, 1703, and arrived in London the following month.

A single incident marred the voyage: Robert's ship was boarded by French privateers who were in the process of divesting the passengers of money and possessions when they were frightened off by the appearance of a British man-of-war. It was only by the sheerest good fortune, then, that they failed to realize that one of the men at their mercy was the principal angel of that onetime nemesis of French shipping, Captain William Kidd.

Kidd's ghost rose up again one last time to haunt Robert, at the very end of his English sojourn. Before that happened, however, Robert spent three long years threading the London bureaucratic labyrinth on behalf of the Five Nations and himself. His primary goal—the mounting of a full-fledged English military campaign against Canada, which would destroy forever the French and Indian threat against the province of New York and the Iroquois lands—was not forthcoming. During the months of petitioning, soliciting, paying court and waiting—endlessly waiting—for satisfaction, Robert's energy seemed for the first time to flag. In October of 1704, just before his fiftieth birthday, he wrote to the Lord High Treasurer that all he wished for, after collecting his money and paying his debts, was to "Sitt down quietly & end my days in Some ease after a 30 years fateague & Hurry of publik Businesse." And to Alida, who also seemed weary, he confessed, "Now, my love, I cannot but do my best. I am so tired every night from walking that I cannot sleep well."

Perhaps his happiest moments were those spent in reunion with his son Robert, whom he had not seen for over seven years. The elegant seventeen-year-old, who was nearing the end of his Edinburgh schooling, stayed several weeks in London with his father, during which time they arranged his legal apprenticeship with a London attorney aptly named Mr. Wordford. Beginning his three-year stint in 1708, young Robert Livingston was the first American to be apprenticed at the Middle Temple of the Inns of Court.

In the spring of 1706, Robert received a grant for most of his money and royal confirmation of all his official positions. For the Iroquois he succeeded only in obtaining the services of two additional missionaries, in lieu of troops and guns. Satisfied nonetheless, he packed his goods for home—a "chest with provisions, a desk in the shape of a chest of drawers, and a wig box with 5 wigs . . . 13 bales of goods, amounting to more than £940

. . . also a box with clothes for my sweetheart and Annatie [Joanna], and a box with 3 veils, 2 for my sweetheart and 1 for Natie . . . [and] 120 dozen [quarts of] claret"—and booked passage on the ship *Unity*, which lay at Gravesend with Captain William Patience in command.

Taking a final stroll on the dock prior to embarking, Robert was abruptly seized and taken into custody on a complaint brought by his old cohort in the Kidd venture, Richard Blackham. Blackham (whose shady career has been previously outlined) had waited ten years to sue for the return of his original investment in the *Adventure Galley*, which, with interest, now amounted to £850. Believing that he finally had Robert Livingston over a barrel, he chose this moment to press charges. Robert was taken to jail while the *Unity* sailed, with all his goods aboard. From prison he penned a letter to Alida: "Now, my dear sweetheart, if it pleases God to chastise me in such a way as not to let me return to you, you must try to sell the goods as best you can. . . ." Fortunately, bail was arranged a few days later by Robert's cousin William, who traveled down from Edinburgh. Robert boarded the next ship for home and landed in New York on September 16, 1706.

Three years later, in the spring of 1709, the long-awaited campaign against Canada was announced—the campaign for which Robert had argued so eloquently in London—and, to the astonishment of the entire colony, its commander was to be none other than Robert's son-in-law, Samuel Vetch. Sam had been in London on a fence-mending trip, his reputation being in shreds thanks to the *Mary* scandal on top of the Darien disaster. With an uncanny capacity for turning ruin into triumph (almost rivaling that of Robert Livingston), Sam managed to return to New York as a newly fledged adjutant general, with responsibility for the entire invasion and the governorship of Canada promised as a reward for success. Sam moved his family —Margaret and baby Alida—to Boston where he established his campaign headquarters. There they were met by John Livingston, who could not resist leaving his gravely ill wife with her family in New London and marching off to war.

The campaign went swimmingly at first. Port Royal, in Nova Scotia, fell to Sam's troop, and he promptly renamed the settlement Annapolis Royal, in honor of Queen Anne. John was dispatched to Quebec under a flag of truce to negotiate an exchange of prisoners. During his stay he managed to make a careful mental survey of the fortifications of Quebec City which, on his return to Boston, he committed to paper for the benefit of his brother-in-law's army.

The grand assault against Quebec was launched by land and sea in September 1711. As ships of the British navy, carrying heavy guns and thousands of troops, advanced up the St. Lawrence River, they were engulfed in dense fog. Many ran aground and their occupants drowned; others withdrew in confusion. To attack without them was out of the question. Sam had to order a retreat to Annapolis Royal, where he spent the winter nursing his frustration.

The disaster was a blow to the Livingstons personally and to the whole province of New York, now left more vulnerable than ever. Philip Livingston, an established merchant in Albany, suspected that the Five Nations would finally "fall on us"; and Alida, alone on the manor, recounted a bizarre incident in which "senecas and coyouges . . . have beaten to death several farmers' pigs."

Robert was in New York tending to business and to the terrible afflictions of his daughter-in-law, Mary. On September 7 he wrote to Alida, "Your daughter Mary has been operated upon for cancer in the breast this forenoon, but the nipple has been saved. . . . She is still full of pain." Robert sat up with Mary several nights after the operation. Finally, sixteen-year-old Joanna Livingston came down from the manor to escort her sister-in-law home to New London. John Livingston joined his wife and sister there for the winter; but in spring he was off again to Annapolis Royal with a troop of fresh Indian reinforcements, leaving Mary to face her illness without him. Mary had three more operations during the ensuing year, with faithful Joanna in attendance.

Robert, meanwhile, was up to his ears in a new scheme: one that promised at last to turn Livingston Manor into a paying proposition.

8

In 1710, while the Canadian campaign was under way, New York had the satisfaction of receiving as governor a man who actually knew how to govern. Robert Hunter was honest, intelligent and politically skillful, a paragon among royal appointees. Robert Livingston, paying his usual prompt call on the new administrator, immediately found a way to make himself useful.

Hunter's ship had crossed the Atlantic with a convoy of refugee boats containing 3000 men, women and children of the German Palatinate, fleeing their homeland in the wake of the War of the Spanish Succession. Enticed to New York by promises from Queen Anne of land and religious freedom, they had contracted to repay the Crown for their passage by manufacturing naval stores, principally tar. Governor Hunter's chore was to find land for them—good farming land, with the right kind of pine trees for tar-making—and a supervisor to settle them, feed them for the first season and oversee their work for the British navy.

In the quarter century since becoming proprietor of Livingston Manor, Robert Livingston had been able to attract only a dozen or so tenant families to the manor. He was proprietor of nothing but an undeveloped tract, lord over virtually no one—a situation he was desperate to remedy. Tenants were vital, both to the manor's financial development and to Robert's sense of proprietorship and sovereignty. Now, perceiving a windfall, he made a deal with the governor: in exchange for selling back to the Crown a 6000-acre plot of Livingston Manor—whose pine trees he vouched for as suitable for tar-making—he undertook the victualing and supervision of the 1800 refugees who were to be settled there.

Hunter's relief was so enormous that he ignored all the warnings that came to him from both sides of the Atlantic. In London, Lord Clarendon confided in Lord Dartmouth, "I think it is unhappy that Col. Hunter . . . fell into so ill hands, for this Levingston [sic] has been known many years in that Province for a very ill man, he formerly Victualled the forces at Albany in which he was guilty of most notorious frauds by which he greatly improv'd his Estate . . . if he can get the Victualling of those Palatines who are so conveniently posted for his purpose, he will make a very good addition to his Estate, and I am persuaded the hopes he had of such a Subsistence to be allow'd by Her Majesty were the Chief if not the only Inducements that prevailed with him to propose to Col. Hunter to settle them upon his Land, which is not the best Place of Pine Trees."

Even in England they knew about the pine trees. If Robert knew, he kept it to himself. He and Alida began construction on the manor of a bakery, brewery, gristmill and sawmill to service and victual the Palatine communities.

Things quickly turned sour for all parties. The Queen's government in London lost interest in the Palatine project within a few months, after it became apparent that the promised tar was not forthcoming; but Governor Hunter did not inform Robert of this until much later, and Robert's victualing account rapidly slid into arrears. He and Alida had to absorb the costs of constructing the new facilities and feeding the hungry Palatines.

As for the refugees, they soon fell behind in their obligations to the British navy—thanks to Robert Livingston's wretchedly unsuitable pine trees—and found themselves devoting all their time to catching up and none to raising their own crops and planting orchards. The Queen, contrary to her promise, had retained title to their farms and to the houses they had built on them. Even more urgently, they and their families, utterly dependent on the lord and lady of Livingston Manor for provisions, were going hungry.

Desperate after a winter of spoiled meat and short rations, the Palatines broke into open rebellion in the spring of 1711. The ringleaders were promptly caught and prosecuted; and by midsummer naval stores were being produced under the watchful eyes of an armed detachment of British troops.

Alida was alone at the manor during most of this period, while Robert tended to business in New York. At the height of the crisis she did get the support—or at least the company—of young Robert, who had returned from London a few months before, his apprenticeship in the law completed. Very much the polished gentleman, twenty-three-year-old Robert was more interested in the pursuit of good-fellowship, sartorial splendor and the ladies than in gainful employ. Alida, in the midst of her troubles with the

Palatines, found time to grumble about his boarding arrangements in New York "at Aryaentje Verplanck I fear he is not in the right house for she has older daughters in the house and seamstresses if he minds his business then all will go well." With no business to mind, the young man was shipped instead upriver to help his mother; and on the manor, during the summer of 1711, he is supposed to have performed the feat of "intrepidity" that so pleased his father that he changed his will to leave Robert "the lower end of the Manor—a tract consisting of about thirteen thousand acres."

According to a version of the story written in the nineteenth century by one of young Robert's descendants, his "attention was attracted one afternoon by what seemed to him an unusual number of Indians skulking around and keeping within the shadow of the woods. That night, after he was in bed, he heard a noise in the chimney. He lay quite still and watched; presently a pair of legs descended upon the hearth. Robert sprang from his bed, seized the fellow before he could extricate himself, exclaiming at the same time; 'Villain confess!' The man, utterly confounded, confessed that he was one of a gang who had fixed upon that night to rob and murder the whites."

If anyone was plotting to murder the Livingston family in the summer of 1711, it was just as likely Palatine Germans as Indians.* Alida had no money to purchase wheat for baking, and her husband in New York reported "the melancholy news that there is no money for us here because of all that we have advanced for the Palatines, so that it is high time to stop baking." Governor Hunter's secretary candidly regretted that Robert asked "for money at this time when 'tis scarcer to be met with if possible than truth and honesty."

Alida continued to feed the Palatines, because (she confessed to Robert) "I can not stand the crying of the people so they call for bread and beer." Robert was adamant, long distance: "My love, don't be faint-hearted. . . . Be careful not to advance a single stuiver nor to give credit to any one of these people. . . . Keep brave, and tell the Palatines with gentleness how things are. . . ." With gentleness indeed. Alida, fed up with worry lest she be murdered in her bed and, at the same time, trying to ship bread to her husband to sell in New York, reproached him, "You won't do for your children as other fathers you prefer another to have it," which was almost—but not quite—fair.

Robert spent Christmas on the manor and in January witnessed firsthand an armed raid on the manor storehouse by the hapless Palatines. His incessant appeals to Governor Hunter for victualing funds had all gone unanswered. Hunter had no money to give him; in addition, the governor had done a complete about-face with regard to Robert Livingston.

Hunter, like most royal governors before him, had initially fallen head

---

* Actually, the author of the account changed "Indians" to "Negroes" in an Erratum at the end of her book, published in 1877.

over heels for the Livingston charm. But as the first rush of infatuation slowed the charm began to wear thin. Robert's formidable seductive powers had little stamina, it seems. People saw through him quickly and thoroughly. Perhaps they simply didn't have as great a capacity for cynicism as he did. In any case, Robert always ended by alienating people in power; and Governor Hunter was no exception. Determining that Robert Livingston was guilty of "base and Villainous practice," Hunter deemed him "ye most selfish man alive" and withdrew all his support.

The governor was finally forced to concede publicly in the autumn of 1712 that subsidization of the Palatines had come to an end. The hapless refugees were left on their own, as of that moment. The proclamation, coming just a few days before the first killing frost could be expected, was unbelievably cruel. It was also foolish, since it declared officially that the refugees, still under obligation to Her Majesty's navy, were expected to resume tar-making in the spring and were therefore forbidden to leave their settlements to take up freeholding on the west bank of the Hudson River.

Naturally, many of the Palatines, facing a winter of starvation, defied the order, crossed the river and never returned. Another number moved south into Dutchess County, where there was no tenant system, and became independent farmers on land belonging to the Beekman family. Others stayed where they were, eventually assuming title to their farms from the Crown and creating the settlement of Germantown.

The last group—and one cannot help surmising that they were the least resourceful and most wretched of the lot—crossed into the Manor of Livingston and signed themselves into tenancy under Robert and Alida.

From Robert's point of view, they constituted a bonanza: his first significant number of tenants. God knows he had paid dearly for them—the vast victualing account still owed him by the British government—and had risked his own (or rather his wife's) personal safety to get and keep them. That they were indigent and desperate only bound them to him more irrevocably. That they had been brought to that state under his stewardship could be forgotten now that they were his.

Or could it? By Robert, of course, it could, and very easily. By the Palatines—and by their children and their children's children—it never has been.

9

Home, to Robert, was always where the profits were; so he spent the winter of 1712–13 at the manor, helping Alida to settle the Palatine families. They supervised the building of farmhouses and barns, the clearing of land, planting of orchards and sowing of wheat. Their gristmill, bakery, brewery and store, which had been operating in the red for three years, now had a monopoly on all the tenants' business and would soon begin to pay off.

The Livingston children were scattered: Margaret, Sam and their infant son at Annapolis Royal (while their daughter Alida wintered on the manor with her grandparents); young Robert living with Philip in Albany, trying to establish himself in the legal profession; Gilbert in Esopus, where his new wife's family, the Beekmans,* had their headquarters; John in Boston on urgent business (he said) for the army; and Joanna attending the deathbed of John's wife, Mary, in New London. Mary's release finally came in January. In tribute to her goodness, over three hundred people braved a severe blizzard to follow her coffin to the graveyard, the pallbearers wearing snowshoes.

---

* Robert and Alida had objected at first to Gilbert's marriage to Cornelia Beekman, despite the fact that her father, Colonel Henry Beekman, was a considerable landowner and public personage. In addition to his property in Esopus, the colonel owned some 240,000 acres on the east bank of the Hudson, south of Livingston Manor; but he had a number of children, and the Livingstons were concerned about the size of the bride's dowry. Once satisfied, they sent Gilbert off to be married in "a good garment," probably purchased on credit, since they were broke at the time. Still, one must keep up with the Beekmans.

Mary's death was a release for Joanna, too. Barely eighteen, she had devoted the past year and a half to nursing her sister-in-law, most of the time in New London. She longed to see her mother and the manor—but how was she to get there? John, finding it imperative to return to Boston immediately after his wife's funeral, declined to accompany her. Robert and Alida, preoccupied with their own problems, sent no one to fetch her and even forgot to forward spending money. Joanna stayed in New London until the spring, when she journeyed to Boston to meet Margaret and attend the birth of another Vetch baby.

Once both his sisters got to town, the reason for John's fascination with Boston became quickly apparent: her name was Elizabeth Knight, and she was the only child of the widow Madam Sarah Knight, a renowned schoolmistress, successful businesswoman, wit, woman of the world and intimate friend of the Reverends Increase and Cotton Mather. Nevertheless, Joanna wrote her parents, the daughter was "a woman of a very Stained Character"; and Margaret expressed "abhorrance" at Elizabeth's encouragement of John while his wife was still alive and the talk of "unlawful familiarityes which is best known to himself." John, she added, was furious at his sisters' interference and "told mee hee Values it not whether you leave him any of your Estate or not."

Madam Sarah Knight was a match for the Livingston daughters. She penned Robert an elegant letter in which, after acknowledging that both "decency and good manors [sic]" prevented her from approving the marriage until she knew his wishes, she carefully made note of the fact that Elizabeth was her only heir. Satisfied as to the lady's fortune but not her reputation, Robert and Alida temporized, while John fulminated against their foot-dragging, reminding them that he was "past ye years of an unthinking boy" (which is debatable). Finally, after receiving his parents' grudging consent, John Livingston and Elizabeth Knight were married on October 1, 1713, in a ceremony presided over by the Reverend Increase Mather. The couple repaired to John's home in New London accompanied by Madam Sarah, who opened a business there and prospered. The same cannot be said of her son-in-law, whom she began to bail out financially at the time of the marriage and apparently continued to do so for the rest of his life. Elizabeth took several months to summon up courage to write to her new in-laws, whom she dutifully addressed as "Hond Parents." Her penmanship was graceful and her sentiments sublime; but none of her efforts, either then or later, ever gained her acceptance in the family.

Joanna Livingston, her duties finally at an end, made her way home where, at the age of twenty-three, she fell in love with young Henry Beekman, her brother Gilbert's brother-in-law. For reasons which remain obscure, the entire Livingston family was adamantly opposed to the match. Her brother Philip, whose mind always ran in pecuniary channels, said that he would "be sorry if she should not light on a better match, or a good

young man without any such publick blott and as much Estate as this has."
("Publick blott" suggests a scandal, but there is no evidence of one.) Her
brother Robert, more fastidious than financial, objected to Henry as "disfigured," which may be nearer the mark—Henry Beekman, Jr., did have a
facial blemish, attested to later by his granddaughter. It seems extraordinary
that the Livingstons should have refused so fitting a man on such trivial
grounds, but refuse they did. Young Beekman, deeply in love, begged that
"the Gratious God who is the manager of all things will yet Convert your
Harts . . . and will not make that vertious Dear Lady your Daughter be
Gulty of Cruelty to a man who never deserved such." But the Livingstons
stood firm, and young Mr. Beekman had to go courting elsewhere.

Ironically, he eventually married a Livingston: the daughter of Robert's
nephew, Robert, who had come to America with his uncle in 1696, settled
in Albany, and shortly thereafter married Alida Livingston's niece, Margaretta Schuyler (who was, in turn, the granddaughter of Maria Van Rensselaer). Their daughter, Janet Livingston, became young Mr. Beekman's bride
in 1721; and *their* daughter, Margaret Beekman, eventually married Robert
and Alida's grandson, Robert, bringing with her as dowry some quarter of a
million acres of Beekman property. Turning down Henry Beekman, Jr., for
Joanna was one of Robert and Alida Livingston's few miscalculations; but
the family ended up with his property in the long run.

This propensity toward intermarriage, by the way, was not exclusive to
the Livingston family. It was a practical answer to limited choice. The population of the colony of New York in the seventeenth and eighteenth centuries was extremely small, and there could be only a few individuals within it
whom a Livingston or a Van Cortlandt or a Van Rensselaer or a Schuyler
would find compatible in terms of goals, culture, wealth and education.
Under such circumstances, marrying a cousin was not only desirable, it was
practically inevitable. The Livingston family, however, pursued the practice
(and the practice of recycling family given names) with uncommon devotion, to the chagrin of family genealogists and each other.

The tenant families of Livingston Manor—who in 1713 numbered
about thirty-three—had not yet begun to produce a profit for either themselves or their landlord. It takes time to clear land and cultivate it, to establish productive orchards and raise mature livestock. Meanwhile, the tenants'
debts to the manor store (which had a monopoly on their trade) grew
alarmingly. Robert, leaving Alida as usual in charge of the manor's financial
details, nevertheless let his impatience show: "As regards the Palatines: it
has been told to you a thousand times, that they are rascals, and that you
must not give them credit, for they are worse than northern savages, if you
pay them in advance."

His deep anxiety—for himself, his property, his old age and his children's patrimony—clearly warped his perception of the collective Palatine

character. All his frustration and impatience fell on the heads of the hapless tenants, and they became, in Robert's eyes, nothing more than shiftless parasites, out to bleed the Livingston family and its resources to death. "Worse than northern savages"—which meant something quite specific to seventeenth-century New Yorkers—was probably the worst thing he could think of to say about his tenants.

This attitude of profound suspicion, mixed with overwhelming contempt, was inevitably passed along to the next generation of Livingstons. They, and their children, and their children's children, grew up equating Palatine with parasite, tenant with scoundrel. It is an attitude that appears over and over, in generation after generation of the family, and exists even to the present day.

In 1715, Robert was given the opportunity to obtain a royal confirmatory patent from the British Crown for the Manor of Livingston. Believing that the new patent would finally confirm his family's title in perpetuity, free of any future whims of royal governors and the London Board of Trade, he spared no effort on behalf of it. The primary task was to make a new survey of the manor boundaries, which immediately resulted in his being sued by the Van Rensselaer family over the line dividing the two patroonships (Rensselaerwyck bounded Livingston Manor on the north). The original Indian deeds described the boundary as a place called "Wawanaquassik," and Robert invited the judge, jury, attorneys and his Van Rensselaer opponent to accompany him on a trudge through the woods to see the place. Van Rensselaer took one look at Robert's Wawanaquassik—a large heap of stones—and strenuously protested. He then slogged the whole group another three miles south through the deep woods, where he pointed to a fallen, half-rotted tree and declared that *it* was Wawanaquassik. The jury scratched its head, hiked back to the courtroom and effected a compromise.

The Manor of Livingston received its confirmatory patent on October 1, 1715, just a few weeks before its owner's sixty-first birthday. Robert's relief and gratification are easily imagined. The patent conferred on him the two rewards for which he had come to America over forty years before and for which he had labored so hard ever since: property and security.

It also conferred a new privilege: the manor's right to send its own representative to the colonial Assembly. Robert had his own pocket borough, and in 1716 he took his place in the Assembly chamber as representative from Livingston Manor. His first priority was to maneuver the Assembly into voting him the funds still owed him by the British government, and his son Philip wrote, "I wish you heartily Joy with the fruits of your Labour and I hope you may be so happy to gett your just demand allowed by the assembly."

To nobody's great surprise, the Livingston tenantry continued through this generation and the next—until the manor itself ceased to exist—to elect their proprietor or one of his close relatives as assemblyman from the manor.

The year 1715 was significant for the Livingston family in Scotland as well. In the Jacobite rebellion of that year the Livingston Earl of Linlithgow took up arms in the cause of the Stuart pretender. When the rebellion failed, seven hundred years of Livingston advancement were wiped out in a single day. The earl escaped with his life to France; but his family's estates were forfeit and their titles allowed to lapse.† If Robert Livingston of New York was aware of it—and almost certainly he was, being in constant communication with his Edinburgh kin—he seems to have been unconcerned. His sense of the Livingston dignity extended only so far as it affected himself. His adoption of the family coat of arms indicates that he cared. But once he had what he wanted, the fate of the family title and its bearer, cousin or not, was apparently irrelevant.

† The family of the present Marquis of Linlithgow received the title in the 1920s.

10

On May 27, 1718, Robert was elected Speaker of the provincial Assembly. He was sixty-three years old and ready for honors. The position gave him greater political leverage than ever, which he used to seize some succulent political plums for his offspring. Philip Livingston became his father's successor as Secretary for Indian Affairs; young Robert was appointed Clerk of the Chancellery; Gilbert became escheator-general; and Robert's nephew, Robert, was named mayor of Albany. (When Peter Schuyler succeeded in maneuvering the latter out of office in order to replace him with a Schuyler cousin, Robert Livingston demonstrated his clout with London by getting the decision reversed.)

The speakership demanded Robert's presence in New York for much of the year. Alida remained on the manor, of course, and under her guidance it slowly but surely began to show a modest profit. Philip held down the Albany end of the family business; and the three of them developed their own private version of the triangle trade. Alida shipped flour, bread, pelts, butter and lard to Albany and New York for her husband and son to sell, and also provided them with fresh fruit and vegetables from the manor gardens. Robert sent her manufactured and imported goods: linseed oil and paintbrushes, sugar and rum, spectacles, teakettles, pins and ribbons. (In 1717 she asked him to send "your shoes that you don't wear. Our people [Palatines and slaves] are walking around without shoes.") Robert also provided Philip with imports, such as garlic and daffodil bulbs and, on one occasion, "a likely negro girl of about 16 year of age" for which he was authorized by his son to spend up to £30.

The harbor in the Roeliff Jansen Kill became a sloop-building yard for the family's active West Indies trade, and Alida's bakery and gristmill worked full time. The arrangement was both efficient and profitable—but, for both Alida and her husband, increasingly lonely. Robert began sending constant little gifts to the manor: "A veil . . . for [you] my little heart, of the best silk; and Natie's [Joanna's] coat is being lined with white"; and he longed for home. "My body is here but my soul is with you." Alida responded, "My longing is so strong that I can not write of your arrival here." Still, the demands of business and the Assembly kept them apart for months at a time.

Alida wore glasses now and suffered periodic attacks in which she was "seiz'd with an extreme pain all over her Body as if her Blood was stop'd in its circulation." Between attacks, her legs swelled up, bringing further torment.

In 1720, Robert had his first attack of kidney stones, that painful and debilitating ailment that was to plague him for the rest of his life. When the stones passed, his agony was so great that he "had to be carried in cousin Bayard's chair. . . . I have lost much sand; I hope that it will relieve me." His youngest daughter, Joanna, recently established in New York as the wife of the merchant Cornelius Van Horne, moved her father into her house to look after him and also, as Robert carefully pointed out, to save money. Joanna's presence was a blessing; but her absence was sorely felt by Alida on the manor, who wrote her husband, "I want you to come home again, for it is very sad for me to be so lonely, and have nobody to talk to."

Robert sent a doctor to take up residence on the manor, ostensibly to serve the tenantry. Alida was furious: "You sent me a doctor. You must be thinking I have no work but looking after strangers! . . . today I was at the smith's to get his room, but all walls have to be plastered before he can come in there and we are in the hay-harvest now, so it may take a long time yet before I get rid of the queer fish." When Robert wrote that he had given up spirits in favor of almond oil and "tea from the ash-tree seed," she chided, "Please do not take too much doctor's stuff lest you convert your body into a pharmacy!" And when he sent pills for her swelling, she scolded, "You know, don't you, that I cannot take any pills? I got [the swelling] down with sour buttermilk, and every time it occurs I put my feet in milk and I get ease that way."

For both of them, the sharpest pain of old age was their children's collective failure to measure up. As Alida put it, "It seems we can never get any service from our children." Gilbert's only talents seemed to be for fathering children (he had six by now, out of an eventual fourteen) and losing money. In 1720, while still serving as escheator-general, Gilbert went into tax farming. Posting bond with funds borrowed from his brother

Robert and brother-in-law Henry Beekman, he purchased the excise on hard liquor. The enterprise was virtually foolproof—except that this was Gilbert, who managed to go bankrupt within two years. His father despaired: "He is less worried about it than I, so it seems. . . . The debts he has are inexpressible, and what he has done with the money is unimaginable." Gilbert was imprisoned for debt but managed to buy his way out by selling all his wife's New York properties. Another creditor filed a complaint, but by this time Gilbert was safe in Esopus and the complainant, a friend of his father's, did not pursue the case. Nevertheless, Gilbert dared not show his face in New York, "for as soon as he comes here he will be put into prison." Robert's tolerance for the failings of his youngest son had long since run out, and he persisted "in my intended resolution to do nothing more than I have done, in no way."

The failings of his oldest son, John, were still as obvious as ever—but in 1720, at the age of forty, John provided his final diversion by dying. He left a wife, no children, and a multitude of debts. Robert and Alida displayed no more sympathy for the widow Elizabeth than they had for the wife, ignoring her pleas for John's records and a power of attorney and even pressing her for the money John had owed to them.

John's death caused a major dynastic reshuffling: the next proprietor of Livingston Manor would now be Philip, the eldest, who at thirty-eight was a well-established, highly respected, prosperous Albany merchant and trader. Philip was the only one of his parents' children who in any way fulfilled their expectations. His wife of fourteen years was the former Catrina Van Brugh, whose father had been mayor of Albany. They had five children (of an eventual nine), the eldest named Robert. Philip and Catrina, firmly and comfortably entrenched in Albany's upper social stratum, privately found the prospect of life in an isolated manor "homestead" far from appealing. But duty outweighed personal inclinations, and Philip accepted his new responsibilities with his usual chilly aplomb. Catrina, whose aplomb was generally overwhelmed by a violent temper, was less compliant, at least in private.

Robert's new will left Gilbert some land near Saratoga and elsewhere in New York; but a deep-seated fear of Gilbert's improvidence led his father to cut him completely out of the manor. Conversely, young Robert, whose dandified, spendthrift ways had given his parents much grief, was bequeathed (as already noted) a 13,000-acre plot carved out of the manor's southern end—a fact which cannot have failed to gall both Gilbert and the dutiful Philip.

Young Robert had spent a great deal of his parents' money on clothes and other forms of good living, while failing to establish himself in his profession of the law. He was not above exploiting Alida and Robert's solicitude for family appearances, to the point where his father finally complained that "Our son has cost a lot here, but accomplished little or nothing.

A seven pound wig in these times is unbearable." Despite his protestations, however, Robert, Sr., seemed unable to resist the charms of his namesake. While refusing to help his other son, Gilbert, when he faced imprisonment, he shrugged at young Robert's escapades: "It's a shame, but what shall one say? Being silent is best, but it goes to my heart, frankly." Apparently it did go to the heart of even this most cool-headed and undemonstrative of men. Robert was unmistakably partial to this foppish, foolish son and preferred him even to the irreproachable but colorless Philip.

Robert's kidney complaint continued to intensify; he was in more or less constant pain and confessed to Alida, "I always walk here with a wet sail." Nevertheless he continued to show flashes of his old style. At an Iroquois conference held in Albany in 1722 and attended by the governors of three British colonies, the Livingston family reigned socially supreme: Governor William Burnet of New York was a guest at Robert and Alida's house on Pearl Street; the governor of Virginia stayed with Robert's nephew, the mayor of Albany; and Sir William Keith of Pennsylvania was housed with Philip Livingston's father-in-law, Peter Van Brugh.

Robert continued to serve in the Assembly despite his advancing illness. He saw Joanna's first child, a "beautiful daughter" named Alida (he christened a new sloop in 1724 the *Alida,* too), and secured Philip's appointment to the powerful Governor's Council. His last appearance in the Assembly took place in May of 1726, and it was vintage Livingston. Robert had been confined to his room for four days in intense pain; but hearing that a bill to tax untenanted property was being brought up for debate, he roused himself, got to the hall, launched a vigorous attack, pulled a few strings and defeated the measure. Shortly thereafter he retired from the Assembly and made the long, familiar sloop voyage up the magnificent Hudson for the last time. At the Assembly session the following autumn Livingston Manor was represented by his son Robert.

He and his "faithful dear Sweetheart" spent a relatively quiet year on the manor, settling new tenants and overseeing the construction of a new gristmill and cider press. Alida died in the autumn of 1727, at the age of seventy-one. Robert remained secluded on the manor throughout the following year. When summer came Philip wrote of the birth of a new daughter named Alida; but Robert never saw her. In August he rewrote his will for the last time and two months later, on October 1, 1728, he died.

Robert signed his last will "Robert Livingston, Proprietor of Livingston Manor"—a departure from his habitual "Robert Livingston, Merchant of New York." The change was certainly justified by the shift toward the manor of the Livingston family finances. But one hopes he also took some pleasure in the writing of it. He had done what he set out to do: Livingston Manor was his. It did not matter that he had barely had time to enjoy it. What mattered was the taking and holding of it against all odds—and the passing of it, inviolate and secure, to his posterity.

11

The death of Robert, first proprietor of Livingston Manor, in 1728 ushered in an interlude of peace for the province of New York and the family of Livingston. For the next fifteen years no French and Indian wars threatened the town of Albany, and New York City's streets were quiet. (Even the founding of the Sons of Liberty, in 1734, failed to cause a ripple.) Robert's three sons also managed to keep the peace for a few years after his death, with some difficulty.

Philip, Robert and Gilbert Livingston were not only utterly lacking in mutual congeniality; they had also been raised—as most children were, at the time—without regard for what we would call natural family affection. The emotional ties that bind were far less important to parents in the seventeenth and early eighteenth centuries than the economic and dynastic bonds that held a family together. Group values transcended the individual value of any family member, and personal feelings were quite irrelevant. The Livingston children, therefore, grew up utterly devoted to the Livingston Family—its position, its economic health and its prerogatives—but not necessarily to one another personally.

The three brothers, incompatible, uncongenial and disputatious as they were (snarling sometimes, like bulldogs in a pit), invariably presented a solid front to the outside world. Each of them entertained his own sense of what it meant to be a Livingston; each, in his own way, cared deeply; and on this ground at least they unfailingly found common cause. This sense of overriding unity is cherished in all great families; it is perhaps the *sine qua non* of their greatness. It also tends to persist long after the greatness is gone.

It was, therefore, perfectly natural that young Robert, on giving up the manor seat in the colonial Assembly in 1729, the year after their father's death, turned it over to Gilbert. (Elections for manor representative tended to be a mere formality, since all the voters were Livingston dependents.) Never mind that Gilbert was a bankrupt, short on talent and long on shift-lessness; and never mind that he owned not a shred of the manor nor lived anywhere near it. Philip, already a member of the Governor's Council, was not available, so Gilbert it had to be. He kept the seat warm for nine years until Philip's oldest son, crown prince Robert, was ready to assume it.

With the Livingstons, *e pluribus unum* did not extend to the girls. Joanna Van Horne, with her husband and son, fell (or was pushed) out of the family orbit after her parents' deaths. Margaret Vetch, who had followed her husband to England in 1717—slipping aboard a ship without a word to Robert and Alida and leaving her sixteen-year-old daughter behind—was not welcomed by her brothers on her return to New York in the 1730s, after Sam Vetch's death in a London debtors' prison.*

Gilbert Livingston, cut off from the manor by his father's will, remained nestled in the bosom of his wife's family at Esopus, giving comfort to his relations by the simple (but for him formidable) achievement of staying out of trouble. The income Gilbert received from his Saratoga farm had been earmarked in Robert, Sr.'s will for the settlement of his debts, under the trusteeship of his older brother Philip. Gilbert's income, in other words, was subject to Philip's discretion—a circumstance that effectively squelched any possibility of rapprochement between the two.

Philip himself became the new proprietor of Livingston Manor; a somewhat reduced manor thanks to the excision of the 13,000-acre section south of the Roeliff Jansen Kill, which was bequeathed to his brother Robert and entailed to Robert's "heirs male . . . of ye name of Livingston, and not to be disposed of to a Stranger." Once again their father had fashioned circumstances that seemed guaranteed to keep his sons at each other's throats: not only had he reduced Philip's inheritance for Robert's benefit, but in the process he had made Robert forever liable to Philip for the sum of eight shillings in annual quitrent. Philip may never have bothered to collect; but the role of liege lord was no doubt as agreeable to him as the role of vassal was disagreeable to his elegant younger brother.

Philip was forty-two when he succeeded to the manor proprietorship, but then Philip had been born forty-two: he was levelheaded, upstanding, industrious and stodgy. Business was his first (and, given the personality of

* Margaret Vetch survived all her children. Her grandsons were Loyalists in the American Revolution and left the country after the war was over.

his wife, probably his only) love. On it he lavished all his talent and energy, and he made of it a great success. As expected, Philip took his new roles as head of the family and proprietor of the manor very seriously. His social, political and financial duties were discharged with distinction and his fraternal ones with ponderous severity. While his imperious personal style won him no friends at home, it did serve well in the world of business. So did the long apprenticeship under his parents. With a firm grasp on the family trade, Philip was able to expand and diversify it until, at the time of his death twenty years later, it stretched from Oswego on Lake Ontario across forests, mountains and oceans to Lisbon, the British Isles and south into the Caribbean. Livingston Dock in Manhattan's East River hummed with activity, and the manor's role as producer of trade goods loomed more important than ever.

Philip governed his empire primarily from Albany, obviously preferring (or was it the starchy Catrina who preferred?) the Dutchness of Pearl Street to the rustic isolation of the manor or the English governor's "court" in New York. Philip perforce spent a great deal of time in New York, however, where he occupied an elegant house on Broad Street. He grew positively sleek, living well because he wished to and also because, as a Livingston, it was expected of him.

Robert, two years younger, had always harbored a self-image as potent as Philip's but lacking in definition. If, metaphorically speaking, Philip's ambition and imagination did not extend beyond "a good warm room & fire and also a good trade," Robert's fantasies were much more highly embellished. Loathing the marketplace and all its commercial bustle, he longed instead for a life of ease and cultivation. He craved, in his rather unfocused, scatterbrained way, what are known as the finer things of life. He was squeamish only when it came to earning the income to support them.

His extravagance and indolence had more than once brought his parents' anger down on his head, and his superciliousness had precipitated a family crisis during his stay in Albany a number of years before. Young Robert had naturally taken up residence in Albany in Philip's house, and much of the blame for the fracas must be laid at the door of that worthy gentleman and his redoubtable wife. Catrina Van Brugh Livingston ruled her roost with a fine Dutch hand; she was ramrod stiff and pudding plain. She was also, unfortunately, given to matchmaking, and she concocted a romance between Robert and his cousin, the daughter of Myndert Schuyler. Robert would have none of it: "Myndt must not think to catch old Birds with chaff for I should take myself to be a greater ffool than his Daughter if I should marry her. . . . I . . . cant perswade myself," he wrote to his father, "you would advise me to marry a Woman for whose silliness [I] should be obliged to blush as often as she was in Company."

Catrina was furious and retaliated by refusing to allow her brother-in-law a fire in his room against the January cold. Robert "told very modestly that if I could not be oblig'd with a fire there, that she would not take it ill if I supply'd myself elsewhere, and she told me that I might do that when I pleased." Robert moved to other lodgings, after which Catrina refused to "so much as look or speak to me. I thought [Philip] had more sense than to take so much notion of his Wife's imprudence as to espouse it."

Without Philip's wholehearted support (perhaps even with it), Robert failed to prosper in Albany, and he soon retreated to New York. There, in 1717, he fell in love with Miss Mary Howardon and married her over his parents' objections. (Alida disdained even to refer to the young lady's mother by name. On the other hand, mindful of her son's long string of broken hearts, she allowed, "if that is how it is he should not break it off again.") Within a year of the marriage Robert had fathered his first and only child, a son named Robert R. Livingston (the "R" stood for Robert but was never spelled out). Thereafter he seems to have virtually ignored his wife's existence. The only historical glimpse we have of her character came many years later in reminiscences by her granddaughter, who described "a melancholy but a sensible woman," crying over stories in the Bible. Whether Mary's melancholy was congenital or developed after years of neglect at the hands of her bon vivant husband is unknown. She performed her function of perpetuating the Roberts, sat for one portrait, and then disappeared from sight.

Despite marriage and paternity, forty-year-old Robert was, at the time of his father's death, still floundering. He had a few legal clients and a minor role in the family trade; but there was no center, financial or otherwise, to his life. His older brother Philip looked with scorn on Robert's indetermination; Robert, in turn, continued to despise Philip's marketplace mentality; and the two remained on very cool terms.

What galvanized Robert was the assumption of his Hudson River estate. Suddenly the future leapt into focus, and he knew that he wanted to become, as quickly and painlessly as possible, a country gentleman. The vision transformed this lackadaisical and indolent creature into a man of vitality and purpose. Ascertaining that his law practice was paying out too slowly, he abandoned it to become a full-time merchant. It soon became apparent that he had inherited his father's eye for a shrewd investment and his acute sense of timing: a new round of French wars broke out, Robert launched himself into privateering and within a few short years had become positively prosperous.

Meanwhile, long before he could afford it, he began constructing a fine house on his upriver estate. The brick mansion, built in the elegant Georgian style, was sited atop a fifty-foot bluff commanding a vast sweep of the Hudson—three quarters of a mile wide at this point—with the mighty peaks of the Catskills forming a dramatic backdrop. According to one of his descendants, Robert decided to name his house Callendar, after the Livingston title and estates in Scotland; but Philip, his liege lord, found this unacceptable: "Callendar was an historical name, and therefore ought to belong to the estate of the elder brother. Robert yielded and changed the name to Ancram after the parish where their grandfather, John Livingston, had labored so long and so successfully. This name was also found fault with as too ambitious for the second son. Robert . . . yielded again. This time he made all further difficulty impossible by going to France for the name of his estate."

The house became Clermont, the name by which it is still known today; and its owner became, at least to later generations of the family, "Robert of Clermont." The appellation was devised to distinguish this Robert from all the other Roberts, and for that reason we will employ it too. (Already in 1730, when Clermont was built, Robert shared his name with at least five other members of the family.)

Philip was acting the spoiler; he had no intention of naming his manor "homestead" Callendar or anything else. One imagines that the little victory gave him a twinge of satisfaction, sweetened no doubt by anticipation of his flighty younger brother's imminent financial collapse.

Philip's complacency may also have been bolstered by the procreative record: his six sons to Robert's one. Totemically gratifying though this was, it was also awkward in that the five younger boys, none of whom would share in the manor inheritance (Philip's adherence to the rule of primogeniture was predictably fervent), must be educated to fend for themselves. Philip rigorously determined not to "bring any of my Sons up for Idleness but to mind some Imployment or another, or Else youth are deluded & brought over to bad Company & begett ill vices from which I pray God to preserve them." Four of the younger boys (the fifth, Henry, was apparently never a star and after a few years of elementary schooling was apprenticed to a Boston merchant) attended Yale where they achieved either first or second ranking in their respective classes. This breathtaking statistic is not a reflection of scholarly achievement, however. Yale ranked its students in the early eighteenth century according to social position, and in that sphere the Livingston boys yielded first place only to the sons of Connecticut families of equal substance.

For his oldest son, Robert, Philip replicated his own preparation for manor proprietorship. The young man attended school at New Rochelle just long enough to master the basics (including business French) and then, in his early twenties, became his father's agent in New York. Young Robert quickly earned his parents' praise for his business acumen as well as his choice of a marriage partner. His bride, Maria Tong, forthwith confirmed their confidence by producing, in gratifyingly rapid order, a string of healthy male offspring.

Meanwhile, Robert "of Clermont"—another college-educated younger son—was bringing up his only child "to keep an Estate not to get one." In his teens, Robert R. Livingston commenced the study of law and, unlike his father, showed signs of great promise. He had a gift for the word, a taste for erudition, strong religious principles and a profound capacity to enjoy life and love his fellow man.

The careers of the nine sons of Gilbert Livingston, on the other hand, present a lamentable chronicle; they range from the undistinguished to the unsavory. The eldest son, Robert Gilbert, seems to have had an extraordinarily rigid personality, in reaction perhaps to his father's inveterate laxity. The most repulsive side of Robert Gilbert was his craven treatment of tenants and slaves; he had the soul of a Legree without the guts. On one occasion, finding himself saddled with a drunken, "obstrepolous" slave woman who was six months' pregnant and had an infant daughter and six-year-old son, he decided to sell her with her baby—but to keep the boy for himself. Unable to contend with the woman's frantic pleadings, he shipped her and her children off to his brother Henry in Poughkeepsie with instructions to sober her up and then sell her. "As to the boy hope you have resirved [him]. You can (to assure her) persuade her to believe you Intend him for yr Self & hope by that means she may consent. But if she don't you can try another method Selling her by force without the boy. Threten to have him wipd [whipped] &c." In other words, Henry was pleased to lie, use force and apply torture if necessary to get his brother's dirty work done. (Unfortunately, no record has been found of how Henry actually dealt with the slave family.)

The Henry to whom Robert Gilbert applied in his hour of need was the second oldest of Gilbert's brood. He had started out on the wrong foot at twenty-six by falling in love with fifteen-year-old Susannah Conklin, a Poughkeepsie farmer's daughter. The Conklin farm was circumscribed by the lands of Livingston, and Papa Conklin viewed the match with alarm as great as that of Henry's parents. But "Love laughs at bolts and bars and parents and difficulties . . . [and] there finally came a Sunday when Henry thought he would not go to church with the family, but thought he *would* take a canter, and quite naturally to Poughkeepsie. Being a fine day farmer Conklin and wife went a few miles away to visit some friends, so Susannah and her governess walked up to church in the village. When the Domine was well under way and the congregation getting comfortably drowsy our young maiden told her companion she wished to go out for a few minutes— which of course was not to be objected to—a few minutes—a good many minutes passed and no return—then Miss Governess, fearing her charge might be ill went out too, but nowhere could she be found. At the close of the service others joined in the search without success. At last, when apprehension was at its height, some lounger who had not been to church, said he saw a young girl lifted up on a horse by young Mr. Henry Livingston and they rode off up the north road. Sure enough . . . a few miles ride and a domine was found who tied the knot and bestowed his blessing, then they demurely ambled home to supper."

Henry and Susannah's luck continued to hold. They produced a healthy brood of children, one of whom carved out a reputable career in the Church and another who may—or may not—have been robbed of his reputation as a popular poet. (His family's contention that he wrote "A Visit from St. Nicholas" is discussed in a later chapter.) Henry himself was elected to the provincial Assembly and served as lifelong Clerk of Dutchess County—not exactly a career to set the world on fire (compared with those of his cousins at Clermont and the manor, its little light shines rather dimly), but at least a respectable one.

The same cannot, alas, be said of two of his younger brothers, Samuel and Cornelius. Sam shipped off to sea at the age of fifteen and lived to regret it: "Dear brother . . . I do repent very much my coming in a man of war for here is nothing Else but Cursing and Swaring Everyday. . . . I wish I was now with you at home out of this miserable place." The experience brutalized Sam sufficiently that he became a drunk and disappeared from sight. Brother Cornelius at the age of twenty-two stood trial with three other youths for raping a fourteen-year-old girl. His cousin William Livingston of the manor (Philip's youngest son), serving as the boys' attorney, managed to frame the girl's mother for stealing in order to discredit her testimony (at least the Attorney General said later that she was framed). The mother was publicly whipped for absconding with a petticoat; Cornelius and his friends were acquitted. He later joined his brother Sam at sea, and rumor has it that they ended their days in an alcoholic haze somewhere in the Far East.

12

During Philip Livingston's lifetime, political influence remained a vital ingredient of financial security in the province of New York; so, like his father, Philip found himself practicing the politics of necessity. As a member of the Governor's Council, he exerted a great deal of political power, of which he was as much the slave as the master.

Philip and his political allies, the party of landowners, were challenged in the 1730s by a strong rival faction representing the increasingly powerful merchant class of New York City. The disagreement between the two parties was ostensibly over economic policy: the merchant faction favored commercial and political accommodation with the French and Canadians, whereas the Livingstons and their landed allies did not. But since this was the province of New York, political differences could be explained only in part by disagreements over policy.

In fact, Philip and his landed allies all had extensive commercial interests that were just as vital to their financial well-being as their broad acres. They were merchants, just like the members of the "merchant" party; but they opposed a trade agreement with the French because the leaders of the pro-French party were the sons of men who had supported Jacob Leisler, the "Dutch boor," over forty years before. At the core of all the economic debate and political deliberation there festered a social ulcer, kept open by the old distrust and rancor between urban merchant and upriver patroon, while jealousy and snobbery dripped the acid in. It is impossible to explain otherwise the depth and duration of the struggle between the two factions, which lasted into and beyond the American Revolution.

At the same time, members of either party were perfectly capable of shifting ground for the sake of expedience. As Philip Livingston put it, "We Change Sides as Serves our Interest best." (Among the Livingstons, blood usually remained thicker than water, but not always.) At various times during the protracted conflict the policies of the parties themselves veered and swerved from one end of the political spectrum to the other, with yesterday's credo becoming today's abomination. It was difficult to follow, then or now—which is only typical in New York politics.

The man who led the "merchant" party to power in the late 1730s was James DeLancey, an English-trained lawyer and gifted politician whose mother, Anne née Van Cortlandt, was Alida Livingston's niece. James's father, Stephen DeLancey, a substantial New York merchant, had come to the colony in the 1680s in a wave of French Huguenot immigration and had been a political ally of Jacob Leisler.

Now, the DeLancey faction and the Livingston faction surveyed each other over the political barricades, their antipathy for one another infinitely greater than their antipathy for each other's beliefs and policies.

Philip, like his father, found occasional respite from politics by shifting his focus upriver to the Manor of Livingston, where the economic picture grew brighter every day. Each year more land was cleared for cultivation, more marketable goods were produced, more quitrents collected and more business done by the manor stores and mills. A large influx of new tenants had been attracted by the size of the leaseholds Philip was offering—about 170 acres on the average, far larger than the corresponding New England freehold. An enterprising farmer on this amount of land could handily fulfill his commitments to the lord for wheat and "fatt hens," and turn a good profit for himself on the surplus.

As some tenant families grew more prosperous, tenant society, like society everywhere, became stratified. A select group of tenants on the manor eventually banded together in the Private Club of Claverack Manor and the Roeliff Jansen Kill. Members of this exclusive fellowship met every three weeks at a different member's house for supper, discreet quaffing and card playing. Rules of decorum were strictly observed: disputes arising over the cards were to be immediately reconciled by a majority of those present, and any member who suggested continuing the game after midnight was automatically fined eight shillings on the spot.

All the tenants benefited from the manorial policies of their feudal lord, Philip Livingston, who expanded the manor's services and diversified its trading goods. Philip even concerned himself with the community's spiritual welfare, building a church in each new tenant village and causing them all to be painted bright red.

But paternalism is not the same as benevolence, and of the latter Philip Livingston had not a shred. It would have been surprising if he had. Raised from the cradle to regard tenants as "worse than northern savages," he viewed his vassals' motives and characters with the deepest suspicion and disdain. They existed in his eyes solely to serve the manor's interests, and he provided for them only insofar as his provision assured their ability to do so. It never occurred to Philip to take heed of their humanity. His attitude remained dispassionate and objective—as long as they did their work, paid their rents and held their tongues. But the slightest murmur of dissent or hint of recalcitrance provoked his deep-felt scorn. "Our people," he wrote his son, "are hoggish and brutish. They must be humbl'd."

In 1740, Philip broke ground for his most ambitious project to date, an iron forge near the eastern boundary of the manor. As the first forge in New York, positioned to capitalize on the newly opened ore beds in nearby Connecticut, it stood to make an enormous profit, and Philip's preoccupation with it verged on obsession. The furnace took three years to construct. In a stunning display of Philippian tactlessness, he chose to christen the forge and its little community of workers' houses Ancram—the very name he had disallowed for his brother Robert's mansion a few years before.

If Robert was offended, he swallowed it for the moment, permitting himself to be distracted by an engaging financial project of his own: buying up the Catskill Mountains. The immense Hardenbergh Patent across the river from the manor had come on the market, and between 1740 and 1743 Robert purchased close to half a million acres of its prime woodland and choice scenery. Robert's plans for the tract were a typical combination of the practical and the romantic: they consisted of a grand Panglossian sweep of hills and valleys, dotted with pretty little model farms on which happy and prosperous tenants would live in harmony with each other and with their benevolent lord, himself. In addition to farming their fertile acres, this eager band would carry out the mining and timbering projects designed to bestow everlasting security on themselves and vast riches on their master. In a final burst of enthusiasm Robert determined to change the name of the mountains from Catskills to "Lothian Hills" in honor of his Scottish origins —and also, perhaps, to get back at Philip for Ancram. With this project as lure, and another round of privateers as security, Robert in 1743 finally turned his back on New York and took up full-time residence at Clermont— his dream come true.

Philip's dream, on the other hand, was faltering badly. His beloved iron forge, while engrossing more and more of his time, energy and resources, had failed so far to show a profit. His absorption in it was so great, however, that he too was lured from the city to establish his base of operations (and his family) on the manor.

Predictably, the brothers' relationship did not benefit from living in close proximity. Their first squabble arose over water rights to the Roeliff

Jansen Kill, the stream that formed the boundary between their two estates. Robert wished to build a gristmill on the kill, but Philip said the kill belonged to him. Consanguinity, as everyone knows, tends to turn skirmishes into all-out war, and this little spat grew into a legal battle that persisted over three generations.

By now the proprietor of Livingston Manor had more than one reason to feel testy toward his younger brother. Robert, having failed to conform to everybody's dire predictions, had amassed a comfortable fortune and was supporting himself, at Clermont, in the style to which he had always wished to become accustomed. Adding insult to injury, the amplitude of his new acreage across the river made Livingston Manor seem positively puny. Robert's Hardenbergh land engrossed the whole of Philip's view: every time he looked out his west windows toward the mighty Catskills, everything he saw belonged to Robert. Finally, Robert—or rather his twenty-four-year-old only son, Robert R.—had brought off the greatest coup of all: marriage to not just an heiress but *the* heiress.

She was eighteen-year-old Margaret Beekman, daughter of Colonel Henry Beekman of Esopus—the very same Henry Beekman whose suit to Philip and Robert's sister Joanna had been rejected by their parents twenty-five years before—and his wife, Janet née Livingston; which meant that the bride and bridegroom were second cousins, once removed.

Margaret Beekman, as her father's only surviving child, stood to inherit his portion of the immense Beekman Patent, which lay to the south of Clermont in Dutchess County. This meant that her children, in turn—Robert of Clermont's grandchildren—would eventually go shares in a total of 753,000 acres: Clermont's 13,000, plus the 500,000 Hardenbergh tract, plus their Beekman mother's 240,000. It was a mathematical calculation designed to gall the mind and poison the dreams of Philip, second proprietor of Livingston Manor.

The population of New York in the 1740s was still overwhelmingly Dutch, although the English minority had by now assumed economic and social primacy. British influence was particularly strong in Manhattan where the English, gathered in the city's newest and most fashionable section, Dock Ward, imposed their language and styles on society. "Women of the upper class adopted the Stuart dress as soon as it was imported. The short gown and petticoat of the vrouw were exchanged for the English printed bodice and hoop, the Dutch cap for one of the new bonnets."

Even in Dutch Albany, where a solid phalanx of gable-ended houses stood guard against intrusion, the modern modes began to gain a foothold. In the parlors of the newer mansions (built front to the street) Delft was giving way to Lowestoft, pewter to silver, and linen to damask. Gilt mirrors appeared on the walls and Turkey carpets on the floors.

Most disquieting of all, the young people of Albany became subverted in 1746 by the arrival of a company of British troopers and "seemed resolved to assume a lighter style of dress and manners, and to borrow their taste in those respects from their new friends." They flocked to balls and parties given by the officers and even attended performances at a private theater in which the young men performed such scandalous frivolity as *The Beaux' Stratagem* and *The Recruiting Officer.* The Dutch establishment, in the person of its dominie, did everything it could to stem the tide, "[but] what, alas, could Dominie Freylinghausen do but preach! This he did earnestly, and even angrily, but in vain. Many were exasperated but none reclaimed. . . . M. Freylinghausen . . . invoked heaven and earth to witness and avenge this contempt, not only of his authority, but, as he expressed it, of the source from which it was derived."

The occasion that prompted the arrival of the British troops was far from frivolous: a French and Indian attack in 1745 on the fort at Saratoga, which ushered in a new era of colonial warfare. A raid on Schenectady brought the war very close to the Livingstons at the manor and Clermont; and the fall of Oswego plunged it right into their pocketbooks. Philip, convinced that Albany would fall and the valley be exposed to the enemy, made plans to move his family down to New York. His son Henry raised a company of militia from the manor and marched north to join the line of defense. Camped near Saratoga in March of 1747, he wrote that more than two thirds of his men were desperately ill, and "if the French knew this they would soon make a visit."

But the Canadians left Albany untouched—perhaps to reciprocate a new policy of neutrality on the part of the Iroquois, or possibly to signal approval of the appointment of James DeLancey, who favored accommodation with the French, as lieutenant governor of New York. Turning their attention elsewhere, they staged a series of vicious raids on New England, and the settlements there suffered horribly. The contrast between their own blood-soaked landscape and the peaceful countryside of New York did not escape the New Englanders; rather it reawakened all the ancient hatred and distrust of their Dutch neighbors. Angrily, passionately, they accused the town and citizens of Albany of trading with the enemy and of actually encouraging the slaughter by purchasing goods plundered from murdered New Englanders. Wildly exaggerated though the charges became, they had some basis in fact, and the agonized vituperation of those years left deep scars on both sides of the provincial border.

DeLancey's appointment as lieutenant governor aggravated Philip Livingston's attack of nerves. Sitting on the manor, with the military and commercial situation steadily deteriorating around him, he cannot have been much cheered at the spectacle of his younger brother raking in proceeds from the war. Robert, together with three of Philip's own sons, had ventured once again into privateering and all were realizing huge profits. Although as responsible citizens they naturally desired the restoration of peace, it is still possible that they viewed the actual cessation of hostilities in late 1748 with somewhat mixed emotions.

Philip's anxiety about the war and the DeLanceys, exacerbated by the unmerited good fortune of his insufferable younger brother, had taken its toll, and no sooner had the peace treaty been signed than he died at the age of sixty-two—young, by Livingston standards. Two funerals were held, the first in New York where his death occurred and another on the manor at his interment. Both were very much in the Philippian mode: sumptuous, pompous and no doubt long-winded. In colonial tradition, the mourners received gifts and an exquisite banquet, and every tenant on Livingston Manor was given a pair of gloves and a black handkerchief.

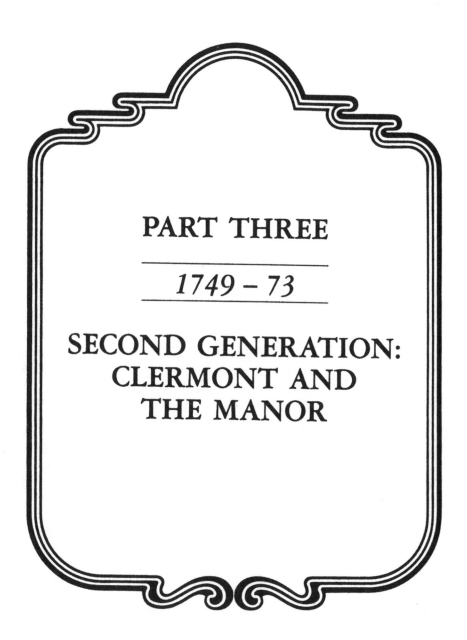

PART THREE

1749 – 73

SECOND GENERATION: CLERMONT AND THE MANOR

13

Chief mourner at Philip's funeral was his oldest son, forty-year-old Robert Livingston, now third proprietor of Livingston Manor. Robert and his wife, with their four sons and five daughters (including the infant Margaretta, born just a few days after her grandfather's death), moved from New York upriver to the manor; while Robert's mother, the redoubtable Catrina, decamped for New York, obviously preferring the comforts of her younger sons' city firesides to a manor house presided over by the new lord and lady.

The new proprietor's character was an unfortunate mixture of traits from both his parents. Robert had his father's finely tuned sense of position, privilege and duty and replicated Philip's elegance as a public figure and heavy-handedness as head of the family. But he also had his mother's volatile temper and appeared moody, unpredictable and irascible.

He also suffered incredibly bad luck, beginning with his very first winter on the manor, one of the most severe ever recorded there. An economic slump, brought on by the end of the war, spread its effects throughout the Livingston financial empire. Robert's New York merchant brothers were appalled: "If trade continues so much longer, we must turn farmers." But hard times were soon overshadowed by a more immediate threat to the very existence of Livingston Manor and the life of its proprietor.

It began in 1751 as a minor nuisance: a tenants' rent strike on the eastern end of the manor, near the Massachusetts border. William Livingston, Robert's brother and lawyer for the manor, counseled patience, reminding his prickly older brother that Providence "wisely orders a perpetual vicissitude in human affairs to prevent our too great Attachment to the World." Events quickly engulfed both William's advice and Robert's equanimity.

The governor of Massachusetts officially recognized a group of petitions from Livingston Manor tenants for Massachusetts title to their farms. A boundary dispute had existed between New York and Massachusetts for decades, and Massachusetts officialdom saw no reason why discontent among the Livingston Manor tenantry should not be exploited to further the cause of the Commonwealth. (There is evidence that the rent strike was instigated in the first place by agitators from Massachusetts and Connecticut.) The disputed border had been drawn and redrawn by the contending governments many times—at one point in the seventeenth century, Massachusetts claimed everything westward from Boston as far as the Pacific Ocean—but by 1751 the border claimed by New York was the Connecticut River and by Massachusetts a north-south line just twelve miles east of the Hudson. If the latter should prevail, Livingston Manor would be reduced by half.

William Livingston filed a formal request with the government of New York for support of the manor's legal position. But the provincial governor was very much under the influence of his lieutenant governor, James De-Lancey, implacable foe of the landed gentry in general and the Livingston family in particular. Robert Livingston had to plead directly to his father's old foe, and his chagrin was nearly palpable: "I find myself Obliged to address your Honour for assistance and protection as an Inhabitant of this Province, which from the Long personal acquaintance I have had of your honour, and your Love for Justice, to protect the Inosent, and punish the Guilty, leaves me no room to doubt of your Honours readiness to defend me against the Incroachments of these restless people. . . ." But DeLancey turned a deaf ear. As far as the provincial government was concerned, the Livingstons could stew in their own juice.

The juice came rapidly to a boil. Agents of the Massachusetts General Court appeared on the manor and proceeded to lay out farms on which Commonwealth citizens were installed as proprietors. When Robert Livingston sent men to pull down the houses and eject the interlopers, the New Englanders returned with reinforcements. A group of Livingston tenants, sensing potential advantage to themselves, joined with the Massachusetters in harassing the manor. As each new incident added to the anger and frustration of both sides, the stealing of beehives quickly escalated into the kidnapping of sheriffs, destruction of dams and—in a particularly vicious action—the girdling of something like twelve hundred trees in the forest near Ancram.

Robert Livingston's own makeshift army was finally reinforced by a detachment of colonial militia, grudgingly dispatched by the governor when things threatened to get out of hand; and by 1753 a state of war existed in the eastern manor. "You are not unacquainted," wrote Robert Noble, a tenant leader of the insurrection, to a Massachusetts friend, "how our Houses have been torn down about our Ears, burnt before our Eyes, our Fences thrown Down, our Corn Fields laid waste. . . . Husbands and heads of Families Carried to Gaol without Law or the Form of It. Wives and Children left in the Wilderness unprovided for as the Ostrich's young. . . . You won't wonder if our hearts faint. . . . They seem to be at their last Gasp one and all ready to Despair and give up all hopes. . . ."

Not to question Mr. Noble's veracity, and with all due respect to his horror and despair, one must still recognize a fine example of insurrection rhetoric, in which the righteous tenant (white hat) struggles to free himself from the yoke of the cruel master (black hat). In fact the situation was a great deal more complicated. The majority of Livingston tenants, intensely distrustful of the pivotal role of New Englanders in the insurrection, refused to take part. Naturally, the insurgents attempted to recruit them; and when they resisted, there erupted a collateral, and equally vicious, war of tenant against tenant.

Perhaps if the third manor proprietor had been a more imaginative man—or even more humane, or kindly disposed, or simply imperturbable— the personal intensity of the rebellion might have been avoided. But Robert was none of these. From his point of view, the entire tenantry, "hoggish and brutish," was suspect. The tenants, for their part, were requiting three generations' worth of manipulation and contempt. So it is not surprising that Robert, learning that a reward had been posted for his capture, "Dad or Alife," withdrew into the fortress of his manor house for weeks at a time; or that one of his tenants, in escaping capture, hurled over his shoulder a colorful adieu to Robert's minions: *"Robert Livingston: Kiss his ass!"*

In the spring of 1754 war broke out against the French and Indians in the Ohio Valley and spread quickly eastward to threaten the Hudson. The danger to Livingston Manor was great, but as usual not without advantage to its proprietor. Robert Livingston became a principal provisioner of the colonial troops; and by threatening Lieutenant Governor DeLancey with summary withdrawal of supplies, he could demand—and get—military reinforcements for his own private war on the manor. An added blessing was that the governments of Massachusetts and New York, facing a common enemy, could no longer afford to offend and finally began to negotiate the border dispute in earnest.*

The common enemy had no effect whatsoever on the dispute between Robert Livingston and his tenants, however. On the contrary, forts built on the manor and in western Massachusetts to defend against the Canadians

---

* At the Albany Congress of 1754 the Pennsylvania delegate, Benjamin Franklin, introduced a plan for unification of the American colonies, which was adopted by the Congress but subsequently rejected in the assemblies of the several colonies.

became strongholds in the tenant war, and militias raised on both sides to fight the French began instead to fight each other. The tenant forces took to wearing Indian disguise in order to conceal their identities, adding a new and sinister tone to the conflict. In early 1755 the first deaths occurred, and May of that year witnessed an attack on the Livingston ironworks at Ancram in which the furnace was laid in ruins and eight senior workmen were kidnapped and taken to Springfield (Massachusetts) jail as hostages for a group of tenants incarcerated at Albany. Robert's cousin, Robert R. Livingston of Clermont, traveled to Springfield to arrange bail but, finding it impossible, negotiated instead a formal exchange of prisoners which took place the following month.

Surfeited with public woes, the third proprietor of Livingston Manor now suffered a series of private tragedies: the deaths, in rapid succession, of his nephew (his sister Alida's child, to whom he was particularly close), his brother-in-law (Alida's husband), and then his mother and oldest son.

Twenty-two-year-old Philip Livingston was attending college with his younger brother in Boston when, in the autumn of 1755, he was taken so ill with a painful "Ulcer in his Bladder or Kidnes" that both boys had to return to the manor. During the long and anxious winter, while British redcoats camped in the valley to deter a Canadian invasion and dangerous rioting recurred on the manor, young Philip suffered the agonies of his illness— while his brother Peter played at his German flute and penned complaints to his Boston friends on the tedium of country living.

In February came the unexpected news of the death of the boys' grandmother in New York. Catrina, her son Robert consoled himself, had been "prepared for this very great change." Her "dear Remains" were placed in a vault in the city until spring, when Robert could send his sloop downriver to fetch them for burial on the manor. The sloop pulled into the manor dock on April 15, within hours of the death of young Philip, and Catrina and her grandson were buried in a double funeral.

Peter R. Livingston, now heir apparent to the manor, was a jaunty nineteen-year-old of bonny good looks and grace. Not noticeably cut up by his older brother's death, he viewed the prospect of proprietorship—and its income—with some pleasure, while contemplating with horror the thought of actually living on the manor. For the moment he was spared when his father shipped him off, with his two younger brothers, Walter and Robert, to Newark College in New Jersey (later Princeton).

Their father may have been partially motivated by fear for the boys' safety. In May of 1757 there occurred a riot on the manor "in which one man was killed and several wounded. . . . Mr. Livingston represents that the Rioters have lately purchased a considerable part of His Manor of the Stockbridge Indians, who have undertaken to assist them in Settling the Lands." At the same time, to the south near Minisink, the Delaware Indians went on the warpath and butchered seventeen people in one week. When

Oswego to the west and Fort William Henry to the north fell to the French, the manor's encirclement was complete.

The border dispute with Massachusetts was settled later that year, at least on paper, when the Lords of Trade in London drew a straight north-south line on the map twenty miles east of the Hudson River and instructed their two warring colonies to accept it as their mutual border. The line, coinciding precisely with the eastern border of Livingston Manor, suited Robert Livingston just fine. But his recalcitrant tenants and their New England allies were less amenable, and five years later Robert still had ample cause to fear that if his tenants "get the least encouragement [from Massachusetts] I shall not be able to live here as my life will be in danger."

The French and Indian conflict was also resistant to closure. The capture of Montreal by the British in 1760 under the leadership of Lord Jeffrey Amherst brought the French to the bargaining table; but during the three years it took to negotiate a treaty the American frontier remained a dangerous place, even for young British gentlemen armed with an independent income: "We have heard lately from Detroit—the Indians have taken Sir Robert Davers a young gentleman of £3000 a year who two years ago came over from England & out of mere curiosity went to the Lakes. It is said that they have cut [him] to pieces & boiled & eaten [him]."

The French and Indian Wars had one final spasm yet to visit upon the exhausted colonies. The peace treaty of 1763 called for an exchange of prisoners—Indians for captured white children—which took place in front of the fort at Albany in 1766:

> Poor women, who had traveled some hundred miles from the back settlements of Pennsylvania and New England, appeared here, with anxious looks and aching hearts, not knowing whether their children were alive, or how exactly to identify them if they should meet them. . . .
> The joy of even the happy mothers was overpowering and found vent in tears; but not like the bitter tears of those who, after long travel, found not what they sought. It was affecting to see the deep and silent sorrow of the Indian women, and of the children, who knew no other mother, and clung fondly to their bosoms, from whence they were not torn without the most piercing shrieks; while their own fond mothers were distressed beyond measure at the shyness and aversion with which these long-lost objects of their love received their caresses. I shall never forget the grotesque figures and wild looks of these young savages; nor the trembling haste with which their mothers arrayed them in the new clothes they had brought for them, as hoping that, with the Indian dress, they would throw off their habits and attachments. It was, in short, a scene impossible to describe, but most affecting to behold.

14

Robert of the Manor's sea of troubles was all the stormier in comparison to the smooth sailing of his uncle, Robert of Clermont. The old man turned seventy-five the year the French treaty was signed. His tenantry remained at peace, and only a small contingent of British troops, billeted at Clermont during the winter of 1760, disturbed his composure: ". . . my kitchen wore out and broke the floor and closets broke in sundry places, all my drinking glasses broke or carried away with them. . . . As to the Major's religion I have not seen the least spark but presume he left it in Scotland."

On the other hand, Robert of Clermont was reaping enormous profits from the war. Military depredations aside, he was a happy man. The life of country gentleman suited him perfectly; it brought out the best in him. Emancipated from the countinghouse mentality of his father and older brother, his personality blossomed. The onetime dabbler became a scholar, who read—mostly the classics—each morning beginning at five o'clock. The feckless youth became the energetic architect of a Catskill utopia; and the fickle swain mellowed into an attentive, but harmless, cavalier. He took delight in discovering diverting ways to spend his handsome income, and his choices were remarkably lacking in self-indulgence—except of course for keeping Clermont up in fine style. Once so ready to squander his parents' money, he now spent his own indulging his grandchildren in little extravagances. Even his old "fondness for being fine" that so outraged his father had transmogrified into a mild, rather endearing sartorial eccentricity whereby he persisted in retaining the fashions of the year in which he retired to Clermont: "the flowing well powdered wig, the bright brown coat, with large cuffs, and square shirts, the cut velvet waistcoat, with ample flaps, and the breeches scarcely covering the knee, the silk stockings, rolled over them with embroidered clocks, and shining squared-toed shoes, fastened near the ankle with small embossed gold buckles. These were retained in his service," explained a fond grandson later, "not to effect a singularity, but because he thought it ridiculous, at his time of life, to allow the quick succession of fashion."

After the death of his wife in 1748 (which was apparently as unremarkable as her life) he lived alone. The ladies never tired of his attentions and gallantries, but none was invited to share the busy, prosperous, happy life of the squire of Clermont.

Every spring Robert's solitude was delightfully interrupted by the advent of his grandchildren making their annual sojourn at Clermont to escape the New York summer's heat and pestilence. There were nine in the brood by 1763 and another on the way. Their mother, Margaret Beekman Livingston, stayed with them the whole summer at Clermont, while their father, Robert R. Livingston, commuted back and forth to the city on business.

Now in his mid-forties, Robert R. Livingston was a universally esteemed member of New York's legal and political fraternity. As Dutchess County representative in the provincial Assembly, he joined with his cousin William (representing the manor, even though he lived in New York City), his cousin Philip (who lived in Brooklyn and represented the city and county of New York) and his cousin Henry of Poughkeepsie (also for Dutchess County) in presenting a formidable challenge to the DeLancey-merchant faction. One of Robert R.'s finest moments in the Assembly was his argument against a proposed tax on undeveloped land—the very issue that had roused his grandfather from a sickbed twenty-five years before. Arguing that "to oblige Persons to sell their Estates in order to Pay their Taxes is not prudently sharing, but flea[c]ing," Robert proposed instead that "all taxes must be paid out of an Income." This raised a howl of protest from the merchant interests, and the feud went on.

Robert R. Livingston's legal talents and reputation were such that even the DeLancey opposition could not prevent his appointment to the Admiralty Court in 1759 or his elevation to the Supreme Court of the province four years later. These appointments were agreeable not only to him and to his family at the time but also to his descendants, who, in order to distinguish him from all the other Robert Livingstons, have always styled him simply "the Judge."

Being a Livingston cannot have hindered Judge Livingston's rise, but neither did it accomplish it. He was richly deserving of his honors, on both intellectual and human grounds. His formidable erudition was tempered by gentle humor, and his political polemicism by piety. "[His expression] was dignified and singularly benign, his smile was one of uncommon sweetness." A fellow lawyer, William Smith, avowed, "If I were to be placed on a desert island with but one book and one friend, that book would be the Bible and that friend Robert R. Livingston," and even a political rival once told him, "I do not believe you have an enemy in the world."

The Judge's greatest joy and source of strength was unquestionably his wife. Margaret Beekman Livingston's assets transcended real estate, even 240,000 acres of it: she had an affectionate nature, an amiable disposition and a strong character tempered by childhood sorrow. Having lost her mother while still an infant, Margaret had been sent to live with a maternal aunt, with whom she remained after her father remarried. This was just as well; Margaret's stepmother, Gertrude Van Cortlandt,* rapidly transmogrified after the nuptials from a great beauty into a great shrew. She had (according to a grandchild's memoir) "in Pope's words 'all the little pilfering temper of a wife' . . . and all the cunning of intrigue that her weak intellect would allow." Her stepdaughter remained untainted, however, growing instead into the affectionate, intelligent and deeply principled young woman who at the age of eighteen "was made the happy wife of Robert R. Livingston." It was a love match and remained so through thirty-three years of married life.

During their frequent separations in the summer the Judge in New York wrote to his wife at Clermont, keeping her minutely informed on every aspect of his business and political life and soliciting her advice at every turn. Invariably the private Robert peeped through: "[If] upon reading what I have said you find me either too Serious or Dull remember you have taken me for better & for worse. I for my part have pleased myself in Conversing with her who is my greatest Happiness on Earth." He chided her gently when she did not write (which was seldom); and when she did, declared that her letters "bring me back to such a train of thinking as is most comfortable to a Christian." And, in the midst of a particularly "hot, tedious & disagreeable" summer, in the thirteenth year of their marriage, he wrote:

> I have for a long time been generally sad, except when your presence & idea enliven my spirits. . . . You are the cordial drop with which Heaven has graciously thought fit to sweeten my cup. . . . My imagination paints you with all your lovliness, with all the charms my soul has for so many years doated [sic] on, with all the sweet endearments past & those which I flatter myself I shall still experience. I may truly say I have not a pleasant thought (abstracted from those of an hereafter) with which your idea is not connected, & even those of future happiness, give me a prospect of a closer union with you. . . .
>
> May the God of Heaven preserve you & grant us a happy meeting, for without you I am nothing.
>
> > Yours most affectionately,
> > R. R. Livingston
>
> Remember me to all the little ones Providence has committed to our charge & kiss them for me.

* She was Alida Livingston I's niece and the sister of James DeLancey's mother, Anne.

In 1764 the ten little ones ranged in age from twenty-one to infancy (Edward was born May 28, a few months after his mother's fortieth birthday). They were a lively and affectionate group, devotedly attached to their parents and to each other. The oldest son, Robert R., Jr., attended King's College in New York (later Columbia) where, at the age of eighteen, he pursued the study of Greek, Latin and "natural and moral philosophy" in preparation for a career in the law. He pursued pleasure as well: vivacious and sociable, he was known as "a very Proteus in Love." His oration at the commencement exercises in 1765 (he was one of a class of eight) was roundly applauded by the press for its "choice of . . . subject"—*Liberty* was an extremely newsworthy topic in 1765—the "justice and sublimity of his sentiments, the elegance of his style, and the graceful propriety of his pronunciation and gesture." Young Robert R. Livingston, Jr., had clearly inherited his father's intellectualism and eloquence. Finishing his legal apprenticeship in record time,† he quickly took his place in the forefront of that profession.

In the Clermont branch of the family, even young girls pursued erudition for its own sake. While Robert R. Livingston, Jr., was studying at King's College, his fifteen-year-old sister Margaret attended school in "Nouvelle Rochelle" where she became entranced with the French language. Their great-grandmother Alida, living in a more rigorous time, would no doubt have considered French wasted on a girl; French was for business. But somehow Alida's son, Robert "of Clermont," had developed an appetite for the pleasures of learning and passed it along to his progeny. What to the founding generation of the family would have seemed fruitless vanity, to the third-generation Clermont Livingstons had become lifeblood.

Humanist education was not solely responsible for Clermont becoming "a house [of] peace and love": the phrase is Margaret Beekman Livingston's, and it is to her and her husband's characters that much of the credit must be given. But the fact remains that the Clermont branch of the family was beginning to deviate from the Livingston pattern by developing strong emotional ties to one another. It was a new trend which lasted only two generations; but during that time it was the governing principle of Clermont life.

The mutual devotion and cohesion of the Clermont Livingstons is all the more startling in contrast to the fragmentation of their cousins' family at the manor. The sons of Philip were of course estranged physically by the rule of primogeniture: Robert, the third proprietor, owned and operated the entire manor, while his five brothers had to seek their fortunes elsewhere. With the single exception of Henry, they proved extremely good at it, although their success did not bring the family closer together. The three older boys, Peter Van Brugh, John and Philip, upon graduating from Yale,

† Apprenticeship was the standard route to the bar. Law school as we know it did not exist.

repaired to New York where they devoted their considerable talents and energies to artful trading and timely privateering, eventually achieving the comfortable status of merchant princes. But it was William, the baby of the brood, who became this generation's star.

William Livingston, born in 1723, was a man of many parts. He practiced law, wrote poetry, edited a weekly paper, the *Independent Reflector,* and was founding president of an exclusive lawyers' social club called The Moot. His public sobriquet was "the whipping post," in honor of his wiry frame and caustic tongue.

William was opinionated and resolute, often quite stylishly so. At twenty-one he fell in love with Susannah French, the daughter of a New Jersey gentleman with impeccable social credentials and an empty bank account. William's father did not approve but, counting on the passage of time to do his work for him, he permitted the engagement to be announced while insisting on a three-year delay in the marriage itself. During this period William decided to travel to England to further his studies, but this time his mother forbade it. The parents had underestimated their son. Angry and restless, he and Miss Susannah simply went and got themselves pregnant, and the lord and lady of Livingston Manor had to give belated though grudging consent. William went on to an extremely distinguished public career in politics and the law, eventually achieving fame as the "War Governor of New Jersey."

Meanwhile, as William and his merchant brethren waxed elegant and prosperous in New York, their brother Robert, third proprietor of Livingston Manor, was finding primogeniture something other than a blessing. Tenant riots, Indian attacks and a perpetual cash crisis continued to dog his existence. His own sons were no comfort: all three seemed doomed to perennial failure in one business enterprise after another. None of these young men—Peter R., the heir apparent, Walter, or Robert Cambridge‡— shared their uncles' aptitude for business. At a deeper level, they seemed utterly void of determination and purpose. While floundering in various degrees of financial embarrassment they were also mired in irresolution; and their bafflement eventually turned to rancor at the notion, which all seemed to share, that success was automatically due them because their name was Livingston.

But carrying the name inevitably meant that their performances were (and still are) viewed in comparison with the brilliant showing of their contemporary cousin from Clermont. Young Robert R. Livingston, Jr., ful- filling the promise of his graduation oration, "In Praise of Liberty," was slowly emerging as a leader in the movement of resistance to the repressive trade policies being imposed on the American colonies by Parliament. The ensuing conflict became a crucible in which the whole family—individually and collectively—was severely tested.

‡ He adopted the middle name after attending Cambridge University, England.

15

In April of 1764 the British Parliament in London passed the first of a series of reform measures designed to clarify and codify the Crown's relationship with its American colonies—which is, at least, the way the Currency and Sugar Acts were regarded in London. In America, as we all know, they were viewed quite differently. Indignation against what Americans saw as unprecedented incursions on their traditional colonial rights spread throughout the thirteen colonies, crossing social and economic barriers and bringing together individuals who otherwise had nothing in common, from the lowest "mechanic" to the patrician Judge Robert R. Livingston, who wrote to his father, "The ministry appears to have run mad. . . . I cannot possibly describe to you the manner in which people here are affected on this occasion. One will wear nothing but homespun; another will drink no wine because it must pay a duty; another proposes to dress in sheepskin. . . . All express their resentment in the warmest manner."

Resentment grew warmer still the following year in response to the Stamp and Quartering Acts; and there began to emerge an organized, vocal, radical leadership, recruited largely from the city's lower and middle classes, which—for the first time since the days of Jacob Leisler—was able to harness and focus the restless political energy of the New York populace. These Sons of Liberty, as they were known, were hardly the sort of people with whom the Judge and his political friends were used to rubbing elbows. Furthermore, they posed a dire threat to all the standards of order and enlightenment that the Judge and his fellow conservatives so fervently espoused.

In Judge Livingston's view the mob by its very nature was shortsighted, narrow-minded and reckless. He felt it incumbent on him and his peers—men qualified by erudition, culture and substance—to govern for the good of all. Government must be conducted serenely, justly and providently, *for* the many *by* the few. Everything in the Judge's upbringing, experience and education cried out a warning against the ascendancy of the mob. Nevertheless, in the present circumstances, he and his friends found themselves, willy-nilly, on the same side of the colonial fence as the unsavory newcomers, and despite their qualms they had to make a connection or risk losing control of the resistance.

As the date drew near on which the Stamp Act was to take effect (November 1, 1765) the streets of the city seemed about to explode. Thoroughly alarmed, the Judge and his political allies came together with the popular leadership to organize the Stamp Act Congress, which met in New York in October. Attended by delegates from nine of the thirteen colonies, the Congress had no legal standing in the eyes of Great Britain. Still, its impeccable parliamentary conduct—achieved by the conservative majority—and the elevated style of its address to the King—penned largely by Judge Livingston—lent a modicum of legitimacy. The Judge, throwing himself wholeheartedly into the business, commented wryly on his unfamiliar adventurism: "Every man amongst us that can contribute anything to this grand work stands on tiptoes & calls himself a Patriot."

Any optimism he may have felt about the work of the Congress was dispelled within the month by the outbreak of the Stamp Act Riots, the very thing the Congress had been designed to forestall. As street mobs rampaged through Manhattan and other colonial cities, destroying property and burning in effigy selected functionaries of the British ministry, the Judge saw his hopes for peaceful accommodation with Parliament go up in smoke.

Rioting became almost a way of life in New York during the following months, even years, as each new piece of parliamentary legislation was proclaimed; and the Judge's personal popularity with the citizenry made his house a regular stopping place for the mob. The spectacle must have dismayed him, but he never lost his composure and tact. One evening, shortly after the duty on tea had been imposed, the procession arrived as the family was sitting down to dinner. The Judge appeared at the window holding a cup—of coffee, as it happened—and the crowd shouted, "No tea, Judge! No tea!" whereupon that amiable gentleman declared, "No tea!" and emptied his cup out the window.

While the attention of the colony was focused on these engrossing events, the tenantry of the Hudson Valley—with its habitually exquisite timing—reared up and delivered its masters a solid kick from behind. Prompted by the Stamp Act mobs in New York, whom they regarded as their brothers in oppression, and abetted once again by land-hungry New Englanders, the tenants on Philipse Manor in Westchester broke into open rebellion in early 1766. Under the inspired leadership of William Prendergast, a Philipse tenant, the movement quickly spread north to Livingston Manor and south to the gates of the city.

Prendergast unquestionably had a gift for pungent rhetoric: "If any Person or persons offended us, the Sons of Liberty . . . we should take them to the first convenient Place of mud and water, and there duck them as long as we think proper from thence we should take them to a white oak tree, and there whip them as long as we think proper, and thence take them out of the County and there kick their Arses as long as we think fit." He was also an organizational genius, able to inspire his motley army to acts of great courage and self-discipline.

In April of 1766, Prendergast's forces, confidently expecting the support of their urban counterparts, staged a mass march on New York City to free several of their number from jail. What the tenant leaders failed to realize was that the urban Sons of Liberty now boasted a fair number of patrician members—radicals from either conviction or whim—whose fathers, brothers and cousins held title as Hudson Valley manor lords. To Prendergast's great surprise, the Sons of Liberty (New York) served in the vanguard of the troops which beat the Sons of Liberty (rural) back from the city gates. As one British observer put it, "The [New York City] Sons of Liberty . . . are of the opinion that no one is entitled to Riot but themselves."

Prendergast and his men returned to the countryside where, for a number of months, they roamed at will, raiding, burning, vandalizing and forcibly ejecting from their farms tenants who refused to collaborate. On Livingston Manor an armed band marched on the manor house, threatening to kill the proprietor, Robert Livingston, but was turned back in the nick of time by Robert's son Walter and a hastily formed armed troop. The entire Livingston family was badly shaken; and Robert's cousin, Judge Robert R., who by now had seen more than he wanted of the puissance of mobs, advised the proprietor to "give up nothing, for if you give anything by compultions of this sort you must give up everything. I would . . . get a Warrant & take up those that are most dangerous and guilty & carry them to Albany Goal [sic]. I can't think they dare offer any Insults to your Person . . . if you have a few armed Men to defend you [the Judge underestimated his cousin's capacity to provoke], & if they should chance to kill any Person in the Fray every Man of them is guilty of murder & then the Government must interpose. . . ."

The government had thus far deliberately failed to interpose. King George, always jealous of the manor lords' hegemony, was now further alienated by the prominence of many landlords in the Stamp Act Congress; and he saw no reason to come to their aid in the present tenant crisis. But in the early summer of 1766—after the Prendergast army had gained firm control of the entire eastern end of Dutchess County, and after the landlords' Whiggery had been toned down by repeal of the Stamp Act—British troops were sent into the field against the tenant forces. The rebel leaders were quickly captured and their insurrection crumbled.

Prendergast was found guilty of high treason and sentenced to be hanged, drawn and quartered.* The sentence was to be carried out by Dutchess County Sheriff James Livingston (of the Poughkeepsie branch of the family), but when that gentleman advertised for assistants not a single soul came forward. During the delay Prendergast's wife rushed to New York and obtained a stay of execution from Governor Sir Henry Moore, pending an appeal.

Judge Robert R. Livingston may have permitted himself a guarded sigh of relief: the crisis in the Hudson Valley was over. (Not quite yet on Livingston Manor, however: the Judge's cousin, Robert the proprietor, decided to punish his vassals' latest folly by imposing harsher lease terms and serving eviction notices on the ringleaders, with the result that many of "those Pests of Society" remained at large and continued to harass him.) Even more gratifyingly, the Stamp Act had been repealed, vindicating to all the world —including the Sons of Liberty—the conservative, conciliatory approach of the Stamp Act Congress. But the Judge was too wise to relax vigilance entirely, and he took great care to warn London that "some little time of calm seems necessary before government can regain its authority & the lower sort can be reduced to a due submission." And just so there could be no mistake, he added that, apropos of the notion of American independence, "nothing is more foreign from the thoughts of every man of property amongst us."

Repeal of the Stamp Act set off days of celebration in the colonies. Solemn services of thanksgiving were interposed with military festivals and less inhibited merrymaking in the streets, and the New York provincial Assembly voted funds to erect new statues of George III and Prime Minister Pitt. The jubilation was short-lived, however. Parliament, ignoring the plea of men like Judge Livingston for a "time of calm," quickly replaced the Stamp Act with a series of equally repugnant measures—the Townshend Acts, the Tea Act and a new Quartering Act, all lumped together in colonial parlance as the "Intolerable Acts"—and the American mood plunged from euphoria to bitter anger. Resentment and frustration drove many into the arms of the radicals. Judge Livingston, his moderate, conciliatory approach now discredited, became ill, and his doctor diagnosed "intense thinking [as] the original Cause."

In December of 1766, when Judge Livingston and his fellow conserva-

---

* During the trial Prendergast's favorite issue in the insurrection—that the annual quitrent for his small farm exceeded the Philipses' quitrent for their entire manor—was addressed, and Prendergast admitted that he had never actually been called upon by the landlord to *pay* it.

tives were at their most dejected, King George delivered them yet another royal slap in the face: he pardoned William Prendergast. The gesture served two princely purposes. First, it punished the landlords for the trouble they'd given their sovereign over the Stamp Act; and second, it revealed to a surprised and ecstatic Hudson Valley tenantry the uses of a king's favor—a seed which eventually bore fruit.

As for the landlords, they naturally felt that King George, whom they had always regarded as a natural ally against the forces of radicalism, had slammed the door in their faces. When they turned to look for new allies among their own countrymen, they discovered an unpleasant truth: while they had been preoccupied with their congresses, committees and addresses to the King, the opposition had been busy in the streets of New York. The DeLancey party, recognizing the political potential of the newly aroused masses, had successfully wooed the radical leaders and manipulated their followers in order to control votes. It was all quite cynical; the DeLanceys were no more dedicated to the radical cause than were the Livingstons (even less, as it turned out). But they did recognize an electoral bonanza when they saw one, and they mined it with ruthless ingenuity.

In a series of stunning electoral victories between 1767 and 1770, the DeLancey party assumed political control of the province of New York, and in the process confirmed all the conservatives' fears about the baseness of popular politics. In pursuit of votes, they used all the time-honored political techniques: inflammatory catchwords, oversimplification of issues, concoction of scapegoats, not to mention intimidation, bribery and titillation. Exploiting their party's merchant origins and urban orientation, they depicted the Livingstons as aloof highbrows and would-be intellectuals lolling on their vast country acres. They maligned the entire legal profession (because of the prominence of the Judge and William Livingston) as a source of social evil—an appealingly plausible notion under any circumstances:

> Beware my good Friends of the Wolf's gripping Paw,
> And the man who will rob, under Sanction of Law;
> Nor trust your dear Rights in the Hands of a Knave,
> Who will sell them for Gold, and your Persons enslave—
> Consider before—Hand, mark well his Intent,
> Or you'll find it—perhaps, when too late to repent.

They turned religion into an issue, in which Anglicans were depicted as snobs and royalists and Presbyterians as men of the people. They even tried to defame a Livingston political ally, John Morin Scott, as a homosexual: "[He] dances with, and *kisses (filthy beast!)* those of his own sex."

The Livingstons and their allies naturally fought back, indulging in a little mudslinging of their own. But their squeamishness, their scruples and their basic conservatism made them no match for the DeLanceys. They simply could not bring themselves to play the game of crowd politics. So the humbuggery rushed on unchecked until, by the end of the campaign of 1770, the DeLancey's were firmly established as the political darlings of the crowd and undisputed masters of the provincial Assembly.

For the Livingstons, the dilemma was particularly poignant: their admirable reluctance to debase the electoral process to the lowest level was undergirded by a keenly felt, deeply personal disdain for the masses, bred into them as part of the manorial experience. To them, the *hoi polloi* were not only politically unreliable but personally repellent. Unable to cast their lot with the people, and spurned by their King, they stood and watched their hard-earned political power slip away.

Both Judge Robert R. Livingston and his cousin Philip were unseated from the provincial Assembly during this period. This left family representation solely in the incompetent hands of the manor assemblyman, Peter R. Livingston, eldest son of the manor proprietor. When his Uncle Philip was turned out by the voters, Peter R. had to bow to family discipline and resign the manor seat in favor of his politically potent kinsman; but the DeLanceys, in turn, passed an unprecedented bill in the Assembly requiring assemblymen to reside in their districts and Philip, who lived in Brooklyn, was refused the manor seat. At the next election Judge Robert R. Livingston stood for the manor and gained an overwhelming victory (tenant votes, at least, could still be delivered), whereupon the Assembly passed a bill disqualifying judges from sitting in the chamber. The Livingstons, finally confounded, proceeded for the next four years to reelect the Judge to the manor seat; and the Judge, appearing at each opening session, was perennially denied his seat.

Within the bosom of his own family Judge Livingston attempted to laugh it off, describing the yearly ritual in joking terms. But his humiliation and anxiety for the welfare of his native province were great. "Madness seems to prevail on the other side of the water; melancholy and dejection on this," he pronounced in a low moment, and added, "This country appears to have seen its best days."

But politics, as we have seen, makes for strange bedfellows—King George locked in the embrace of the Hudson River tenantry, the elegant DeLanceys couple with the radical mob. Because the mob was fickle, the game of musical beds soon started up again, an event precipitated by the death in 1769 of Governor Sir Henry Moore. The removal of Moore, who had always been a staunch advocate for the upriver landlords, might have further eroded the Livingston party's already ravaged political power. Instead, it inadvertently shored it up, in a preposterous sequence that went roughly as follows.

The new acting governor, Cadwallader Colden, in an attempt to ape his sovereign, withdrew gubernatorial support from the landlords and, in the process, allied himself with the DeLancey opposition. In order to capitalize on his support, the DeLanceys found themselves having to deliver votes in the Assembly on unpopular measures like the £2000 appropriation bill to provision British troops stationed in New York City. The Livingstons naturally exploited these issues to wean the populace away from the DeLancey party and then, in order to solidify their gains, found themselves toeing the popular line on almost every issue.

This is, of course, an oversimplified description of a very complex shift. Suffice it to say that, once the political seesaw had tilted again, the Livingston and DeLancey parties found themselves at the opposite ends of the political spectrum from where they had started, with the Livingstons, perhaps to their own surprise as much as anyone else's, holding down the left. If this seems unlikely, just remember that this was New York, where politics was practiced with mirrors, and logic, loyalty and principle stood regularly on end in obeisance to power.

Judge Livingston was as active during this period as his lack of an Assembly seat would allow. In addition to his judicial duties, he, together with his cousin Philip and other family members, represented the Livingston interests and the conservative position in a series of extra-legal congresses and committees that met throughout the late 1760s and early '70s: the New York Committee of Correspondence, the Committees of 60 and 100, and the First Continental Congress. As time went by, and the voters responded to further affronts from King and Parliament, these bodies came to exhibit an increasingly radical complexion. The Judge and his moderate friends, trying to keep at least a modicum of control, swallowed their misgivings, made common cause with the radical leadership, and desperately sought to forge a feasible, rational response to the growing threat of runaway imperialism.

16

The measured tone of Judge Robert R. Livingston's response to the political drama unfolding in New York was not emulated by some of his kinsmen. The Judge was a subtle and sagacious man who could appreciate the complexity of the issues dividing the colonies from the mother country and see both good and bad in any course of action. He must have known that, whatever the outcome, great damage had already been done and that life in the province of New York would never be the same. Nevertheless, he declined to stand down and maintained instead that most difficult of postures, firm moderation.

Other members of the family achieved a less balanced stance. There were Livingstons who became radical Whigs, Livingstons who remained Tory Loyalists, and Livingstons of every possible political complexion in between. Robert of Clermont, for instance, the Judge's own father, quixotic as ever, converted to radicalism at an early stage and espoused the cause of American "independency" long before his son had accepted its necessity. Still spry in his early eighties, Robert spent the months of New York's greatest political turmoil dabbling in a new financial scheme for his beloved Catskills: large-scale timbering. His son warned, "You have a parcel of People about you who are endeavoring . . . to fatten themselves on your Spoils. . . . He that had the consumate Impudence to tell you that you might make money by making Oars carried the abuse of the confidence you place in him to the greatest Height. He might as well have put you on making Brooms. . . ."

The timbering project fizzled (fortunately, before the Judge's patrimony had vanished), and Robert of Clermont retired from business. But he missed the stimulation and began learning German "so that he might have something new to read." Suffering occasional insomnia, he took to singing the Psalms at the top of his lungs in the middle of the night, either to assay communication with the Lord or perhaps, during his grandchildren's summer sojourn, to cajole a sleepy-eyed toddler into keeping him company.

Another Livingston adherent to the cause of radicalism was thirty-year-old Peter R. Livingston, eldest son of Robert, the manor proprietor. Peter R. had served as manor representative in the provincial Assembly before the DeLancey ascendancy, and he adored the hurly-burly of the new street politics: "We are hott and pepper on both Sides . . . and if there is not fair play shewn there will be blood shead as we have by far the best part of the Brusers on our side."

Peter R. jumped on the radical bandwagon about 1766, perhaps because the rest of his immediate family deplored radicalism or maybe just because he was bored. (With Peter, the ideology didn't matter, only the enthusiasm.) Flaunting his Livingston-ness as a badge of immunity, he joined the Sons of Liberty and donated land for the erection of a new Liberty Pole, after the old one was destroyed by British troops. Meanwhile he fended off bankruptcy, mostly through loans from his father, and jealously guarded the Livingston social prerogatives. In a letter to his father in 1766, written to ask for an extension of the latest loan, he pleaded to be given the new family carriage for his use in the city: "As to the Old Chariot Beg you'll not send it to me to make me appear more Ridiculous." Heaven forbid that a Son of Liberty should be seen conducting a revolution in last year's model.

Peter R.'s business sense was no better considered than his political impulses. Handsome, impetuous and lazy, he had managed to go under in a whole series of financial ventures, including dry goods. Like his Great-uncle John (Robert and Alida Livingston's oldest), Peter R. seemed embedded in a particularly trying adolescence. He was improvident, arrogant, charming and inclined to self-dramatization. He also had a galloping case of family hubris, little regard for other people's feelings, a faulty sense of proportion and no scruples.

Peter R. was no callow youth whose indiscretions could be charged to inexperience; he was in his thirties and had a family to support. (His wife was his distant cousin, Margaret née Livingston, granddaughter of "The Nephew" and first cousin to Margaret Beekman Livingston.) Nevertheless, he continued to flit from one financial and political adventure to another, causing a perennial drain on his father's revenue and patience. By 1771 the proprietor had had enough. Peter R. was summoned home, with his pregnant wife and six children.* The trip upriver brought on a sea change in which this Livingston Son of Liberty underwent a conversion to ultraconservatism. Robert the proprietor was not fooled. Before his son was allowed through the door he had to sign, on behalf of himself and his heirs, a bond to his father for £26,000. Robert then combined with Peter's wife in financing construction of a house for the growing family; but the proprietor prudently retained title in his own name. Perhaps he was also responsible for christening the house The Hermitage, in the fervent hope that its feckless master would now retire from mischief-making in the great world.

Another of the proprietor's grandchildren received shelter at the manor house in 1771 as well: the young son of Alida Livingston Gardiner and her husband, Valentine Gardiner, who had recently taken ship for England. Valentine Gardiner was an Englishman and a Tory—as was the husband of another of the proprietor's daughters, Catherine Paterson. The sisters' marriages, occurring at a time when anti-British feeling was running high, constituted political and social faux pas that deeply wounded their father in principle as well as person. Still, Robert took his young grandson in and raised him at the manor; and when John Paterson's politics made life in New York City impossible for him and Catherine, the proprietor gave them both a home upriver.

At Clermont, too, a new generation of children, the Judge and Margaret Beekman Livingston's brood, was beginning to reach marriageable age. The oldest son, Robert R. Livingston, Jr., was wed in 1770 to Mary Stevens, daughter of a wealthy New Jersey landowner.

Young Robert, who turned twenty-four the year of his marriage, was already well established in the legal profession in New York in partnership with John Jay. Jay and Robert, best friends since college, had completely antithetical personalities: Jay was quiet, introspective and somewhat humorless; while Robert was sociable, pleasure-loving and amorously inclined. Each was the other's equal, however, in ambition and pride. In addition to their legal activities, both young men found colonial politics unavoidable if not irresistible, and were well on their way to leadership in the new generation of young Whig intellectuals.

Robert's bride was also quite his opposite, being "very quiet in her manner and domestic in her habits." It is likely that the marriage was arranged, particularly given the size of Miss Stevens's inheritance. If so, Robert accepted it with good grace. He may even have found a stay-at-home wife a great convenience: ladies' men frequently do; and Robert, although never demonstrably unfaithful to his "Polly," was also never known to dodge the shaft of Cupid.

---

* Out of an eventual ten. After the birth of the fourth son Peter R. had written his father, "We are at a loss what to call the child as we want some New Names in the family." It was only a whim, however, and the child was christened James William.

Once married, Robert began to build a house just south of his grandfather's Clermont, sharing its magnificent view. The mansion was appropriately christened Belvedere, and Robert and Polly decided to spend the winter there, tête-à-tête. John Jay, knowing Robert's predilection for society, gently teased, "You are now in the Country, separated from Temptations, your Passions are reduced to their usual calm, and your Spirits; like a silent Stream whose woods defend it from the Winds that rage on Shoars more exposed to Storms, again unruffled flow and glide with Ease. Reason has resumed her Seat." Urbane, gregarious Robert naturally viewed the delights of Clermont differently: "I hardly know whether the quiet of a country life compensates for its insipidity—for my own part I love to have my passions agitated; and if it was not for a little spice of melancholy in my composition, which I love to indulge . . . I should half wish to bustle in town again—my round of amusements are very small, I read till my head aches . . . and ride till I am froze. It is true indeed we have some other sublime pleasures, such as a walk in the mud, or a slip on the Ice, but these we do not experience so often as to make them any part of our Routine."

Given the political situation in the province of New York, restless Robert soon found a number of excuses to return and "bustle in town"—in fact, a few more than he had bargained for.

The Boston Tea Party of December 1773 was replicated four months later by the citizens of New York. On April 22, "The *Mohawks* were prepared to do their duty at a proper hour; but the body of the people were so impatient that before it arrived a number of them entered the ship, about 8 P.M., took out the tea, which was at hand, broke the cases, and started their contents into the river, without doing any damage to the ship or cargo. Several persons of reputation were placed below to keep tally, and about the companion to prevent ill-disposed persons from going below the deck."

Exactly ten years had passed since the promulgation of the Currency and Sugar Acts of 1764: a decade in which New York's political parties had expended almost as much energy and rhetoric fighting each other as they had spent resisting the incursions of King and Parliament; a decade in which the Hudson Valley tenantry had once again risen to challenge its masters' suzerainty; and a decade in which the people of New York City had taken to the streets and discovered their political voice and muscle. All parties, regardless of political stripe, had heretofore exploited the imperial issue quite cynically for their own ends.

Nevertheless, ten years of rioting, of addresses to the King, of burnings in effigy, of parliamentary bumbling and of misunderstanding had taken their toll. By 1774 positions in the struggle had hardened on both sides of the Atlantic. As open conflict with the mother country appeared more and more inevitable, the infighting among the political parties of New York became less and less relevant. The time had come when every person, Livingston or DeLancey, radical or conservative, Judge or mechanic, had to make a public choice for or against the British Crown.

The DeLanceys, being at this moment—almost by accident—politically bound to the imperialist policies of Lieutenant Governor Cadwallader Colden, came down on the side of the King; they remained Loyalists and thus lost their place of honor in American history books. The Livingstons stood firmly for colonial rights and became our heroes. Perhaps their motives were less elevated than one might wish: acting primarily in defense of their own political and economic prerogatives, they remained highly skeptical of the great democratic ideals of Thomas Jefferson and Tom Paine. They were not alone in this, or in their stated preference for accomplishing their aims as citizens of the British Empire. They were, in fact, very reluctant revolutionaries who, only when the imperial door was firmly slammed in their faces, turned to address the proposition of an independent, democratic America.

In 1769, at the height of New York's political turbulence, Peter Van Brugh Livingston—brother of the manor proprietor, wealthy New York merchant and prominent member of the radical branch of the Whig Party†—sat down to write a Livingston family genealogy, the first such effort by an American Livingston. It seems a strange moment for an active politician to take the time for such a project; but it is not difficult to understand. Two of Peter Van Brugh Livingston's sons were out-and-out Tories, and evidence indicates he was conducting a poignant search in the past for congruity.

Peter Van Brugh's genealogy takes only brief note of the family's noble connections in Scotland (unlike the pedigrees written by some of his descendants, which dwell on them obsessively); he was much more interested in the American Livingstons and their immediate progenitor, the Reverend John Livingston (whose autobiographical notes reside today with his papers at the New York Public Library). Peter Van Brugh's grandparents, Robert Livingston and Alida Schuyler, and all the Schuyler-Livingston-Van Rensselaer intermarrying throughout the intervening generations fascinated him: the genealogical maze explored in order to thread his own political and paternal labyrinth.

Peter Van Brugh Livingston did not find what he was looking for. After his son "Gentleman Phil's" emigration to England at the height of the Revolutionary War in 1775, he resigned his position as chairman of the First Provincial Congress, ostensibly for reasons of health, and lived in retirement in New Jersey until his death, seventeen years later.

The Livingstons were not the only colonial American family with members on opposite sides of the Revolutionary fence. Even the family's most

† Unlike his nephew, Peter R. Livingston, Peter Van Brugh's radicalism was a well-considered and serious commitment.

celebrated Whigs, Judge Robert R. Livingston and his son Robert R., Jr., tried to straddle that fence for as long as possible, and when they did jump, it was with great reluctance and profound misgivings.

But despite their misgivings, despite division within the family ranks, despite eventual fear for their very lives, the Livingstons who took their stand stood tall. We have already seen the Judge and his cousin Philip laboring over the months and years to modulate and legitimize the course of the resistance. Now, approaching their sixth decade of life, they watched, advised and cheered on the next generation.

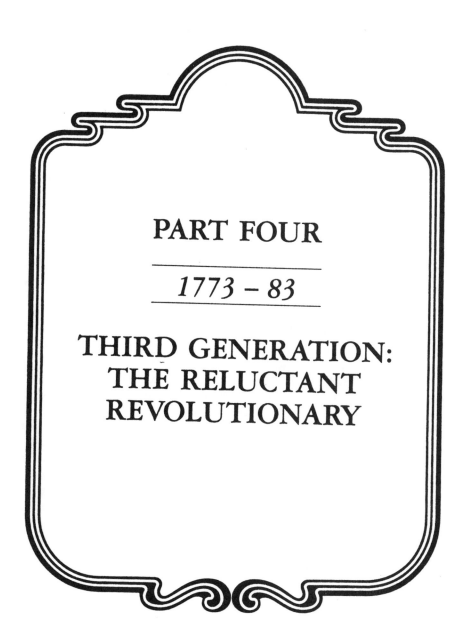

PART FOUR

1773 – 83

THIRD GENERATION: THE RELUCTANT REVOLUTIONARY

17

On the nineteenth of April 1775 British troops exchanged fire with Massachusetts Minutemen at Concord and Lexington, men died on both sides, and the war was on.

The news reached New York four days later, and Judge Robert R. Livingston wrote to his wife (who was at Clermont with the younger children) that the town was "in a continual Bustle," adding wryly that "People here are perfectly Fearless I mean the Wigs, and the Tories turn Wigg so fast that they will soon be as much united as they are in the Massachusetts Bay."

The latter was the Judge's little joke: New Yorkers would never be as united as the citizens of Boston; in fact the news had caught the city in the throes of a typical political imbroglio. The Loyalist/DeLancey interests in the colonial Assembly had managed to block the appointment of New York delegates to the Second Continental Congress, which was scheduled to convene in Philadelphia within the month; so the Whigs bypassed the Assembly (not for the first time) and invented yet another extralegal body to serve its purposes. The New York Provincial Convention went into session on the morning of April 21, selected twelve congressional delegates, and dissolved itself by afternoon. Three of the twelve chosen to go to Philadelphia were Philip Livingston, the manor proprietor's brother; James Duane, the proprietor's son-in-law; and their young cousin of Clermont, Robert R. Livingston, Jr., the Judge's son.

All three Livingston delegates entered Congress with extreme ambivalence concerning its crucial topic, American independence. Their confusion was mirrored by their Hudson Valley relations, in both branches of the family. Robert, the manor proprietor, wrote to Duane his fervent hope that God would "turn the hearts [of King and Parliament] to prevent them the destruction of this my native & already oppressed & bleeding country," and Duane responded, "I sincerely join with you in dreading a separation from Great Britain, which can be acceptable to very few." Even Judge Livingston, writing to his son at Congress, lapsed into uncustomary vagueness: "Every good man wishes that America may remain free: in this I join heartily; at the same time I do not desire, she should be wholly independent of the mother country. How to reconcile their jarring principles, I profess I am altogether at a loss."

But if the manor and Clermont Livingstons were equally ambivalent at this stage concerning independence, they diverged dramatically in their expectations for the immediate future. In 1775 both the manor proprietor and the Judge constructed new mills: the manor's was for grain, Clermont's for gunpowder.

The colonies' capacity for waging war was practically nonexistent, so the gunpowder was going to be needed. Command of the Continental Army was placed in the hands of George Washington, a Virginia delegate to the Continental Congress who had earned his reputation for skill and courage under fire during the last round of French and Indian wars. Washington's "army" was only a figment of Congress' hopeful imagination; and it became his unenviable task to create something out of nothing. With only a motley collection of independent local militias to build on, Washington's greatest need was for experienced officers. One of his first appointments was that of the Judge's son-in-law, Richard Montgomery, as brigadier general—an action which, as much as any other, drew the Livingston family into the fight for independence.

Richard Montgomery, the younger son of an Anglo-Irish landowning family, had joined the British army at the age of fifteen but resigned years later "in disgust" after military politics blocked his well-deserved promotion. Emigrating to America in 1771, he met and fell in love with Janet Livingston, oldest daughter of the Judge and Margaret Beekman Livingston. Janet was nearly thirty, with a forceful personality and a set of extremely exacting standards regarding the male of the species. It was difficult to please Janet, standing there on her Livingston pedestal, wielding her wit to skewer the inadequate, the overweening, the unwary. Richard, who was handsome, amiable, witty and affluent, apparently broke down her defenses. Janet fell swiftly and deeply in love, and the couple were married in the parlor at Clermont in July of 1773.

Two years later, when the call to arms came, the Montgomerys were just preparing to move into a fine new brick house on their large farm near Rhinebeck. A quiet country life was their hearts' desire; nevertheless, Richard's sense of devotion to his adopted country demanded that he accept the "melancholy honor." Janet's reluctance turned to outright terror after she had a dream in which she saw her husband die of wounds inflicted by his own brother.

When recruiting began in the Hudson Valley, the proprietor of Livingston Manor naturally expected to furnish his own company of militia. His tenants thought otherwise. Still under the spell of the King's pardon of William Prendergast, and now subjected to intense propaganda by British agents promising land in exchange for loyalty, many tenants refused to enlist in the Continental Army. One outspoken vassal, threatened with coercion, declared that if armed "the first person he would shoot would be his captain." In fact Livingston Manor was, in the words of one historian, "the most Tory-ridden part of the county." When meetings were held at Clermont to collect signatures on the Articles of Association,* Robert R. Livingston, Jr., reported to John Jay that "many of our Tenants refused to sign . . . [but] since troops have been raised in the province & two of my Brothers have got commissions they have been frighted & changed their battery." Over a hundred Clermont tenants signed a petition to Congress demanding land; and Robert's mother, Margaret Beekman Livingston, informed him, ". . . they boast that in less than a fortnight they shall have what they want—I think the powder mill in danger Your father says he will write for a guard when the powder comes."

The Battle of Bunker Hill, in June of 1775, proved the undoing of Robert of Clermont. At the beginning of the war in April the old man (whose birth had heralded another revolution, eighty-seven years before) was "in raptures. . . . He seemed to begin life again; his eye had all the fire of youth, and I verily believe," his granddaughter reported, "that the Battle of Bunker Hill (of which such a false and disastrous report was made) was his death. He took to his bed immediately, lay there a week without pain, and died. The last words he uttered were, 'What news from Boston?' "

Judge Livingston was holding court at Albany when his father died and- "only arrived [at Clermont] to close his eyes." The rest of the family gathered quickly, and Robert—the last of the children of Alida and Robert, the first proprietors—was laid to rest at his beloved Clermont.

Bunker Hill had quite the contrary effect on Brigadier General Richard Montgomery, who confided in his wife, "What I feared has not happened. The Americans will fight." Janet was in New York during the week following Bunker Hill, and she witnessed General George Washington's triumphal progress through the town on his way to Boston. Unfortunately, on that very day, a British ship dropped anchor in the harbor bearing royal

* A kind of loyalty oath, commonly known as "The Pledge." Refusal to sign could result in imprisonment.

Governor William Tryon back to his duties after a yearlong absence in London. The city fathers were in a quandary: which of the two dignitaries should receive the official welcome? Debate over protocol soon became irrelevant as the people of New York took matters into their own hands. Janet reported, "All the militia were paraded—bells ringing, drums beating —and in that moment Tryon arrived. As he landed he looked with delight at this commotion, and on a company covered with gold lace which he had commissioned and called the Governor's guards. As he landed he said, 'Is this all for me?' when two of his councillors took him by the hand mournfully and led him to a house in Broadway, where he nearly fainted when he saw the great Washington pass, attended by a crowd of patriots. . . . He drove a sulkey, with a pair of white horses. His dress was blue, with purple ribbon sash, a long plume of feathers in his hat. What a mortifying sight to Governor Tryon."

But soon more than a hundred British warships had taken up positions in New York Harbor, and by the end of summer the city was under incessant bombardment, its citizens fleeing in droves.

Taking and holding New York City was crucial to the British, not only because of its excellent harbor. New York was the key to the military strategy on which the whole war would turn: the campaign to seize control of the Hudson Valley and split the colonies in two. The attack on the valley was to come from two directions. British troops based in New York would march north, accompanied by warships in the river and reinforced along the way by a fifth column of tenant Loyalists. At the same time another British army would fight its way down from Canada. When the two linked up, somewhere midway, the colonies would be irretrievably divided and British victory only a matter of time. It was a grand plan on paper, simple and practically foolproof; and lying right at its geographical center were Clermont and Livingston Manor.

General Washington proposed to preempt the northern invasion by sending a continental expeditionary force into Canada. In the autumn of 1775 this troop was gathered at Albany, with Richard Montgomery as second in command and his two young brothers-in-law, Henry and John Livingston, serving as junior officers. (Montgomery reassured their father, the Judge, "I will if possible put them in separate regiments.") A family party came to see them off: Janet, her father, and two of the younger children, Catherine and eleven-year-old Edward.

Montgomery had grave reservations about the leader of the Canadian expedition, his commanding officer, Philip Schuyler: "His consequence in the province makes him a fit subject for an important trust—but has he *strong nerves?*" Nevertheless, during those final days in Albany, for the benefit of his wife and the rest of the family, he maintained a cheerful, almost bantering tone. On one particularly low afternoon, with Janet sighing her regret that they did not have a son, Montgomery gently teased, "Be contented, Janet. Suppose we had a son and he was a fool. Think of that!" On another occasion he apparently made her laugh by hopping around the room on one leg, holding the other up behind him, asking, "Janet, how would you like [it]?" But in a more sober moment he was heard to muse, " 'Tis a mad world, my masters"; and his parting words to his wife were, "You shall never have cause to blush for your Montgomery."

By early November, General Montgomery's troops had seized St. John's and were marching on Montreal. The Second Continental Congress, galvanized by the news, proposed to send a civilian commission to Canada to operate behind enemy lines, inciting the citizenry to join the American Revolution; and its appointment as chairman—an unenviable job—was Robert R. Livingston, Jr., congressional delegate and brother-in-law to the triumphant General Montgomery.

During the two years since Montgomery's marriage to Janet Livingston he and Robert had become close friends. Sharing a passion for scientific agriculture and a yearning for the life of gentleman farmer, they also saw eye to eye on the political and military issues facing the colonies; and their frequent letters provided a direct, if unofficial, link between Congress and the northern campaign. In one letter from Canada, Montgomery expressed his conviction that the key to the defense of the Hudson Valley was the promontory of West Point in the Highlands. Ironically, in the same missive, he called to Robert's attention the name of an unknown officer in his command whose ability and courage he found noteworthy: Benedict Arnold. "He is very active intelligent and enterprising—I think he should have rank given him." But the private Montgomery, too, appeared in these letters, one of which closed, "O fortunate Agricolae! would I were at my plough again!"

Robert and his congressional committee headed north in mid-November 1775 and reached Fort Ticonderoga at the head of Lake George by the end of the month. By this time the Continental Army had taken Montreal and was marching on Quebec. General Montgomery had orders directing him, on his way through the Canadian countryside, to attempt to persuade the citizenry to support the Revolution by sending delegates to the Continental Congress, a replication of Robert's commission. But Montgomery quickly realized that the Canadians would never undertake such a perilous commitment until the American army had proven itself in the field, by taking Quebec. Robert, reading his brother-in-law's dispatches in the chilly, windswept fort at Ticonderoga, agreed, and he and his delegation decided to withdraw forthwith. It was in Albany, then, that the tidings of fresh family tragedy reached him.

While Robert was en route from Ticonderoga to Albany his mother, Margaret Beekman Livingston, had been summoned from Clermont to Rhinebeck to the bedside of her eighty-eight-year-old father, who was gravely ill. She left Clermont somewhat reluctantly, since her dear Judge was suffering from a "cold & small feavor." At the end of her third day in Rhinebeck the old gentleman rallied and she gratefully turned her face toward home, "pleasing myself with the thought of meeting him . . . my dearest friend & Husband." Her carriage was intercepted by a messenger on horseback who brought from Clermont the inconceivable, staggering news that her husband was dead. A "fit of apoplexy" had taken him at the age of fifty-seven, barely six months after his own father's death.

The blow to his wife—confidante, soul mate, lover—was severe. For days she wandered through the house in confusion and despair, wrestling with her grief. ". . . when painful remembrence brings to my mind past tenderness (for every object I turn to presents me with some instances), I strive to put it out of my mind for fear I should sin—I give him up to God—but oh how soon I do take back. . . ."

Nine days after burying her husband Margaret was once again summoned to Rhinebeck to attend her father, who died peacefully a few days later, on January 3, 1776. His housekeeper, who had been with him for twenty-three years, died the same day; and it took Margaret several weeks to deal with all his personal and household affairs. She returned to Clermont —a Clermont empty of her Judge—at the end of January, and twenty-four hours later the family received the news that Richard Montgomery had been killed under the walls of Quebec. General Schuyler broke the news in a letter to Robert R. Livingston, Jr.: "I weep, my Dear Sir, and shall long weep; and never forget that I had a friend, the affectionate the gallant Montgomery, he is no more. Heaven was pleased to crown him with Laurels and to suffer him to make his Exit in the Cause of his Country; he was Slain in an unsuccessful attack on Quebec the night between the 30 & 31st [of December]; my grief for the distress of your family is too poignant to be declared, yet a kind like yours will bear up against it. Consider my Dear Sir how many you have to Console and when you weep let it be in your Closet."

Robert, obliged to inform Montgomery's British relatives—a family steeped for generations in fidelity and service to the British Army—felt some awkwardness in writing to Richard's brother: "As, Sir, I have not the pleasure of knowing your political sentiments, I am unable to say whether you will derive any consolation from the manner of General Montgomery's death."

Thus "the shot heard 'round the world," fired from a British musket at Lexington Green, spent itself in the bosom of the Livingston family of Clermont. Titular leadership of that branch of the family (an honorific seriously taken) now devolved upon the shifting personage of Robert R. Livingston, Jr.—bon vivant, muted husband and reluctant revolutionary. He was twenty-nine years old.

18

Robert R. Livingston, Jr., shared the political conviction of his father, the Judge, that the interests of *all* the people were best served by a government of the qualified elite. He had also inherited a number of the Judge's finest talents and traits: charm, eloquence and an intellectual bent. But Robert's charm, unlike his father's, was only skin deep; and too often his pride of family, impatience with fools and deep disdain for the lower orders came glaring through.

Unfortunately for his own peace of mind, Robert R. Livingston, Jr., was also vastly ambitious for political power. Finally, and this must be remembered, he was heir to a political tradition—which his great-grandfather had helped create—in which self-interest always came before the public interest. It is not surprising, therefore, that at the Second Continental Congress, and throughout the rest of his long political life, Robert's motives, loyalties and goals were badly muddled; a fact which eventually escaped neither his colleagues nor his constituents. It was perhaps Nature's little joke to have given him one blue eye and one brown eye.

Livingston-like, Robert found the day-to-day maneuverings and intrigues of the Second Continental Congress repugnant and the radicalism of some of his fellow delegates appalling. In the winter of 1776 the deaths of his grandfather, father and brother-in-law provided the excuse to linger at Clermont, avoiding both the congressional sessions in Philadelphia and the meetings in New York City of the newly formed New York provincial

Congress, to which he and his cousin Philip had been elected. Philip and Robert had already established a system of taking turns attending the two congresses, to ensure continuous family representation at both. Now, in the early months of 1776, Philip Livingston had to cover both New York and Philadelphia. Under the pressure of unfolding events, he and his fellow conservatives were finally, reluctantly, beginning to abandon their hopes for reconciliation with Britain and to commit themselves to an all-out fight for "independency."

The discomfiture of New York's delegates at the Continental Congress was intensified by the absence of instructions from home. The provincial Congress, apparently unable to agree on anything, stranded its delegation in Philadelphia month after month without instructions while the Continental Congress debated the great issues of independence and self-governance. It was for this reason that Robert, on his return to Philadelphia in May of 1776, was appointed to the committee to draft a declaration justifying America's independence in the eyes of the world. He was chosen not for his eloquence or rhetorical skill (which he had in good measure) but because his direct participation might draw the province of New York into a firm commitment on independence.

For a man whose talents and training were honed for such a task, Robert's lack of involvement in the actual writing of the Declaration of Independence must have been very frustrating. Overshadowed by Jefferson, Adams and Franklin, he contributed not a single word to the document that was submitted to Congress. Furthermore, on July 2, when Congress finally voted to declare American independence, it did so without the assenting vote of the delegation from the state of New York, which was forced to abstain.*

New York had declared itself a state the previous week; and its provincial Congress, after fleeing New York City to avoid imminent capture by the British, reconvened at White Plains as the New York Convention. Convention approval of the Declaration of Independence was vital—Congress correctly insisting that so perilous a step be taken by all thirteen colonies together or not at all—so Robert traveled posthaste to White Plains in early July to steer ratification through the faction-ridden body. Poor Robert, he always underestimated his fellow creatures' capacity to do without him: the Convention approved the Declaration of Independence on the first day of debate, a week before he got there. He was permitted to contribute nothing, not even his vote. Having thus forfeited this mark of distinction in the history books of his home state, he proceeded to lose his rightful place on his country's most exclusive roll of honor. Becoming engrossed in urgent business at home, he was unable to return to Philadelphia in time to sign the Declaration, a ceremony which took place (popular legend notwithstand-

* Congress spent two days debating and amending Jefferson's text. July 4 is the date on which it went to the printer. After the New York Convention ratified the Declaration two weeks later, the vote was retroactively ruled unanimous.

ing) on August 2. His cousin Philip was there to give the Livingston seal of approval, and he is known in the family to this day as "Philip the Signer."

Robert's posterity, on the other hand, has had to be content with the inadvertent, but devastatingly accurate, designation on a plaque in the town of Rhinebeck, where he is memorialized as

Robert R. Livingston
Draftee of the Declaration of Independence

Robert's failure to return to Philadelphia was more than justified by the dire predicament of his native state. On Long Island (where his younger brother, Henry Beekman Livingston, was making a name for himself in the army), enemy troops had advanced until they stood poised in Brooklyn, just across the river from New York City. With the harbor completely under British control, the city's capitulation was obviously only a matter of days.

On the very day that the Declaration of Independence was being signed in Philadelphia, Robert was at Poughkeepsie at the behest of the New York Convention, organizing a secret committee to coordinate the state's defenses. The following day he traveled at considerable risk into New York City to confer with General Washington, and a few days later was back in Poughkeepsie to take his place on the committee to draft a constitution for New York State.

His mother, Margaret Beekman Livingston, alone at Clermont with her younger children and servants, pleaded with him not "to expose your self needlessly. You are in the Civil Department let others be in the Military . . . oh my Dear Child consider your Situation with Respect to my Self, and my other Children. . . ." The danger at Clermont was acute: Indians in the Mohawk Valley, allying themselves with the British, had gone on the warpath and "massacreed about 20, some they drown'd some they burnt"; and right in Margaret's backyard was a band of tenant Tories, "Some say their number is 4000 . . . they have taken a Congress Member . . . and carried him off to no one knows where, they have three boxes of gun powder that has been sent to them by some as bad as themselves."

The greatest threat of all, of course, came from the British, whose troops were massing both to south and north for their mighty thrust into the Hudson Valley.

Margaret's younger son, twenty-six-year-old Henry Beekman Livingston, was meanwhile having himself a fine time in the army. Henry was completely devoid of the Livingston intellectualism, political dedication or scruples; in fact from the day of his birth his nature had been utterly intemperate and lawless—the black sheep in an otherwise fair-haired flock. Before the war broke out Henry had taken to plowing the fields of Clermont wearing his court uniform to show "his contempt for King George III." Now he threw himself wholeheartedly into the fray; and the wilder it got the better he liked it. On the eve of the Battle of Long Island he sailed for Huntington "in order to Harrass and distress our Enemies all in my power. I have a spy amongst them and have almost daily intelligence of their motions. . . . I shall now if possible cut off all Communication between the Enemy and Suffolk County. I have taken Col. Gardiner and some other Prisoners. . . ."

Henry's courage and resourcefulness were commendable. But, as his brother-in-law, General Montgomery, had observed during the Canadian campaign the previous year, "He is brave—but so imprudent in his conduct that I have been made very uneasy by his disputes, and often wished him at home—for my own part I by no means think him fit for a field officer—I would rather advise him to quit his present corps, and get into a genteeler regiment, should such a one be established." The warning came as no surprise to Henry's mother, who had long ago been forced to concede the immutability of her son's vicious temper, licentious appetites and runaway case of Livingston family pride.

War gave Henry license to display his only gifts, and in battle he was superb. But in the context of army discipline he was predictably a disaster. In the thick of the desperate fighting on Long Island his commanding officer, General Alexander McDougal, found it necessary to issue an official reprimand for insubordination, to which Henry responded that the general's "Cowardice has rendered him unworthy of my Notice . . . he has in many instances Besides that which Particularly Affect me behaved unbecoming the Character of a Gentleman and an Officer which I believe will be sufficient to Reduce him to that Rank which will make it excusable in me to Cain him which I shall certainly do the first opportunity that offers—He has also endeavored to make a Party against our Family . . . [and] has formed a Party against me even in my own Regiment. . . ."

Henry decided to trade on his family's personal friendship with General Washington to appeal the case directly to the continental high command. His mother and brother, Robert R., Jr., were acutely embarrassed. Washington directed Henry, tactfully but firmly, to "lodge [your] complaint to General Putnam and desire a Court of Inquiry. This is the Proper Mode of Proceeding when an Inferior Officer thinks himself aggrieved by his superior." It was excellent advice, which Henry proceeded to ignore. Within six months he was court-martialed for using disrespectful language to McDougal but escaped with a reprimand when the court noted that, "though the colonel [Henry] appears to this Court to be guilty of great imprudence and indiscretion in some parts of his language and conduct towards the general, yet his conduct was not such as will warrant the appellation of being unbecoming a gentleman and an officer." Colonel Livingston was sufficiently mollified—for the moment—to withdraw his threat of resigning from the army.

On September 12, 1776, the British took New York City; and the New York Convention, with the enemy once again breathing down its neck, removed farther north, this time to Fishkill. There Robert R. Livingston, Jr., spent much of the ensuing winter—between military inspection trips up and down the Hudson Valley—laboring with the committee to draft a state constitution. If the disunity and motleyness of the Philadelphia Congress had appalled him, Fishkill was even worse: "In this state we are to form a government under which we are to spend the remainder of our lives, without that influence that is derived from respect to old families wealth age &c —we are to contend with the envy of some, the love of power in others who would debase the government as the only means of exalting themselves and above all with that mixture of jealousy and cunning into which Genius long occupied in trifles generally degenerates when unimproved by education and unrefined by honor—hitherto," he cautioned his friend Edward Rutledge, "you have seen mankind but partially—come here and I will show you the whole human heart: believe me there is a greater mixture of intrigue, artifice and address in the [government] of N.Y. than in a conclave of cardinals.

"I am sick of politics and power, I long for more refined pleasures, conversation and friendship. I am weary of crowds and pine for solitude nor would in my present humor give one scene of Shakespeare for one thousand Harringtons, Lockes, Sidneys and Adams to boot. If without injuring my country I could once return to my own farm and fireside, I aver, I would not change any situation to be Great Mogul or President of the Congress." Sadly, the latter was not true: Robert hungered for recognition, fame and power; so, despite his revulsion, he stayed on.

The New York State constitution was submitted to the Convention in March of 1777. A predictably conservative document (penned largely by John Jay, with Robert's assistance), it won almost unanimous approval—but only after considerable emendation from the floor, engineered by a large group of delegates from the new political class: mechanics, small farmers and country lawyers, "unimproved by education and unrefined by honor." Robert accepted the final version of the constitution with qualms—"[one must swim] with a stream it is impossible to stem"—but the document was far too radical for his cousin, Peter R. of the manor, whose new-fledged ultraconservatism led him to cast the only Nay vote.

Robert was appointed Chancellor of New York, the state's highest legal office, second in precedence only to the governorship. The title of Chancellor pleased him enormously; he employed it to the end of his life (even after resigning in 1801 to become minister to France) and is known by it still. On the same day as his appointment his old friend and now cousin-in-law, John Jay (who was married in 1774 to Sarah Livingston, the daughter of New Jersey Governor William Livingston) was made chief justice of the state Supreme Court.

The dire threat under which the infant state of New York struggled to survive came not only from the British army but also from a large armed contingent of its own citizens. In May of 1777 bands of Tory tenants in the Hudson Valley staged an uprising against their landlords and the state. The timing was disastrous—for the instigators themselves. The rebellion was intended to coordinate with the great British thrust into the valley, but the tenants' intelligence was poor and they moved prematurely. When the British army failed to materialize, the rebellion was easily quashed. Many of the ringleaders were arrested; some were executed as traitors; and the bad blood between tenant and landlord ran thicker than ever.

Tenant despair found immediate vent in the June gubernatorial election. Instead of delivering votes for their landlords' candidate as they had always done (open balloting had left them no real choice), they simply stayed away from the polls. To the landowners' astonishment and dejection, the winner—over the patrician Philip Schuyler—and first governor of New York State was George Clinton, a country lawyer and the son of a farmer.

A month after the election, news reached the valley that General John Burgoyne's British army from Canada had taken Fort Ticonderoga and was marching south. Margaret Beekman Livingston, alone at Clermont with her daughters and house servants, prepared for possible retreat. The house was stripped: silver and porcelain were buried in the woods, books lowered into a dry well and camouflaged with rubbish, and French mirrors concealed in the false wall of an outside shed. Then, throughout the long summer, the family waited for developments.

Their single diversion was a guest, a wounded officer of the British army, distantly related to Richard Montgomery, who had been captured at Ticonderoga and assigned to spend his convalescence at Clermont. The fireside chats between him and his widowed cousin-in-law, the outspoken Janet Montgomery, would have been worth hearing. One can be sure, however, that—heartbreak and political loyalties aside—Mrs. Montgomery and her mother would have received their enemy and kinsman with the utmost courtesy, respect and solicitude.

Finally, in early October, the British fleet in New York Harbor weighed anchor and headed north up the Hudson for its rendezvous with Burgoyne. Thirty strong—men-of-war and transports carrying three regiments of redcoats—the armada sailed through Tappan Zee and Haverstraw Bay, surprised and overran two American forts in the Highlands and progressed unimpeded into the lower valley. Under the command of General John Vaughn in his flagship *Friendship,* the flotilla made its stately way past Newburgh and Fishkill, paused off Poughkeepsie to shell the continental shipyard (which stood on Livingston land), then turned toward the opposite bank and its first real objective, Kingston, where the New York State legislature sat. Robert R. Livingston, Jr., was not in Kingston; but his friend Gouverneur Morris wrote to him, "We are hellishly frightened but don't say a Word of that for we shall get our spirits again and then perhaps be so full of Valor as to smite the air for blowing in our faces."

At this juncture a rumor reached the valley that a decisive battle had been fought to the north at Saratoga, between a hastily improvised Continental Army and the advancing forces of General Burgoyne. The outcome of the battle was unknown. General Vaughn, surveying the town of Kingston from the deck of the *Friendship*, was not inclined to await developments; and citing Kingston as "a Nursery for almost every Villain in the Country," he put the town to the torch. Before the fires died, however, Vaughn received the startling news that Burgoyne was defeated and his entire army surrendered to the enemy. With one more call to pay, Vaughn refused to be deflected. Crossing to the east bank, at Rhinebeck, he put troops ashore with orders to march north, burning and looting patriot property as they went, and to rendezvous with the ships at his next target: Clermont.

Margaret Beekman Livingston was under no illusions as to Vaughn's purpose, especially after the fate of Kingston became known. Declining the offer of protection extended by her British guest, she and her household hastily gathered the rest of their belongings, piled them into farm carts and carriages, and set off eastward toward Salisbury, Connecticut, where they had been offered the shelter of a house belonging to the manor proprietor. It is said that amidst the hurry and confusion young Gertrude Livingston, climbing into her carriage, burst out laughing at the sight of an overladen cart with a plump old slave woman perched on top of the swaying bundles, holding on for dear life. Merriment soon came to an end, though; within a mile, Gertrude, her sisters and her mother, looking back, could observe the first few curls of smoke from their burning home rising over the treetops and disappearing into the October sky.

The British land party burned both Clermont and Chancellor Livingston's Belvedere, the latter to the ground. Only Clermont's outer walls survived. Before General Vaughn had time to gloat, his own plans and hopes went up in smoke as well. Burgoyne's surrender at Saratoga was finally confirmed, and within twenty-four hours of destroying Clermont, Vaughn was on his way downriver in retreat.

Chancellor Robert R. Livingston, owner of the ruined Belvedere, perhaps took some comfort from the significant Livingston presence at the Battle of Saratoga: eight men of the family saw action there (seven with commissions and one humble foot soldier, first name unrecorded), including his brother Henry, who fought with distinction under the hero of the day, Benedict Arnold.

But the measure of the Chancellor's deep despair is that he put up his Clermont property for sale, excepting only "two acres adjoining my mother's garden"—a gesture of hopelessness that ran counter to all of his and his family's most cherished principles. The sale never took place—Robert withdrew the offer—but he didn't have the heart to rebuild his house. Gouverneur Morris suggested instead that a memorial column be placed on the site, for which he submitted the following inscription:

> When the King of Great Britain attempted to establish
> Tyranny over the extensive regions of America
> > The Roof of Hospitality
> Sacred to Friendship to Science & to Love
> > Was violated by the Hand of War
> To perpetuate the Pleasure he received from British
> Barbarity this Pillar is erected by
> > Robert R. Livingston
> Who would have blushed to be exempted
> > From the calamities of his country.

19

Christmas of 1777 was a dark season for the homeless and separated Clermont Livingstons. Margaret Beekman Livingston was in Salisbury with her
daughters and young Edward; Henry was with the army at Valley Forge;
and Chancellor Robert R. Livingston and his wife took their Christmas
dinner at the manor house with their cousin Robert, the manor proprietor,
and his family.

The manor Livingstons, together in body for the holiday, were as separated as ever in spirit and sympathy. Two of the proprietor's sons were
present at the feast, both in retreat from financial failure in the city: the
feckless Peter R., over for the day from The Hermitage with his wife, and
his brother Walter, who was building a fine new house called Teviotdale
next door. The proprietor's daughter and son-in-law, the James Duanes,
were present as well as several guests.

Robert the proprietor, who had recently marked his sixty-ninth birthday, was a staunch but troubled patriot. The iron furnace built by his father
in the 1740s had been operating at full force throughout the war, turning
out iron bars, ball chain and grapeshot for the Continental Army. The proprietor's principal problem was lack of cash: paid only sporadically in continental currency, whose value fell every day, the manor was in dire financial
straits. Still, he stood firm for the continental cause and General Washington
("God bless him, and all his undertakings"), and he kept the furnace fired.

At least two of his sons, Walter and Henry, had been having a good war. During the previous autumn, while General Vaughn was indulging his pyromania at Clermont a few miles to the south, they had enjoyed a "flutter in rum." When they learned at the Christmas dinner table that in Boston the Chancellor's brother John was reaping great profits from the war, they eagerly planned a Massachusetts sojourn for themselves to see what they could accomplish—which only serves to illustrate that the Livingston clan, like many other politically prominent Whig families, had its share of apolitical opportunists.

The table conversation that Christmas Day, 1777, also turned on the danger to local property and lives from bands of roving Tory renegades operating in the valley. "Robert R. Livingston said retaliating burning for burning would ruin the Country & that the true Mode of acting was instantly hanging every Man who had been concerned in such Work. . . . Mrs. Robert R. Livingston instantly took Fire & said [they] deserved to be hanged & Quartered." The final member of the feast demurred: he was William Smith, a former law partner of William Livingston, married to a Livingston,* who, having been adjudged a Tory at the beginning of the war, had been placed in a kind of house arrest at his wife's sister's home on Livingston Manor, The Hermitage. Smith apparently took offense at his cousins' fulminations against the Tory guerrillas, and, according to his own account, put an abrupt end to them with the pointed observation that "the Consequences of a War should have been considered before it was begun."

The manor proprietor's invitation for Christmas Day and the Chancellor's acceptance were prompted by family obligation rather than family affection. Like their progenitors, the children of Alida and Robert the First, they didn't like each other very much. But Livingstons invariably stand together when the going gets rough, as any powerful clan does if it wants to stay powerful. Personal antipathy may render the obligation onerous, but the advantages more than balance the inconvenience; which is why it never occurred to Robert of the manor not to offer Margaret Beekman Livingston his house in Salisbury and to invite the Chancellor and his wife for Christmas, just as it never occurred to them not to accept.

The two Robert Livingstons did have one thing in common: the desperate state of their personal finances, subject to rampant inflation, currency devaluations and skyrocketing taxes and exacerbated by "a disaffection of [the] tenants who have during this controversy very generally withheld their rents." This included not only the tenants on the manor and Clermont but also the farmers of the vast Hardenbergh lands across the river, and a great deal of money was involved. The manor proprietor's grandchildren went barefoot while taxes on the manor totaled nearly $400,000 in one

---

* His wife, Janet, was Peter R. Livingston's wife's sister. Both women were granddaughters of Robert Livingston "the Nephew" and first cousins to Margaret Beekman Livingston, who visited them at The Hermitage later in the war with her daughter, Mrs. General Richard Montgomery.

calendar year. "I well know," the proprietor conceded, that "it is necessary in time of war that taxes should be laid to carry it on, but more time for breathing ought to be given, and the burdens made more equal. This might be done by our legislatures, but alas! I fear they have but little judgment in these matters. They are all new raw hands, and we must submit and wait with patience for better times. If these do but come before we are ruined it is well." Nevertheless, he chastised his brother, Peter Van Brugh Livingston, for complaining about taxes: "We must defend ourselves like men and fight it out to the last, we surely can hold it out longer than they. . . . You still enjoy the necessaryes and many Conveniencys of Life which is a great Blessing and injoy a large landed Property . . . we must be thankful to Kind Providence and patiently wate his time."

The Chancellor, too, had to sell off a fair number of worldly goods— including his beloved carriage horses—to pay his taxes; still, he managed to send a contribution, together with an offer of 5000 acres of land, toward the rebuilding of the town of Kingston. His mother, Margaret Beekman Livingston—who returned to Clermont in the spring of 1778 and began rebuilding her house, war or no war—was also heavily burdened with taxes; but, she informed her son, "I would not have you think that I am uneasy because I give you a state of my affairs. I assure you I am not one way or another I shall Rub through."

Despite the war and their continuing exigencies, the manor proprietor and his Clermont cousin managed to find time and energy for a recreation the Livingstons have always found irresistible: family squabbling. In October of 1779, Robert the Chancellor airily informed Robert the proprietor of his plans for a new gristmill on the Roeliff Jansen Kill, which stream, he claimed, forming the border between their two estates, belonged to both of them. Hackles rising, Robert the proprietor—son of Philip—tartly pointed out that the will of Robert the First had bequeathed to Robert of Clermont all the land lying *south* of the kill, "which surely cannot be construed with the least propriety to be the Center of the Stream." The Chancellor, after months of arguing the legal fine points with his cousin, lost patience and built his mill. Robert the proprietor fumed and stewed; and the battle raged between the two branches of the family for another sixteen years, well into the next generation.

Robert R. Livingston, Jr., resumed his itinerant existence, traveling up and down the Hudson Valley, regardless of weather and Tory guerrillas, to examine and evaluate New York State's military capabilities. His unqualified recommendation to General Washington that the Hudson Valley's defenses be concentrated at West Point in the Highlands, where the river makes a sharp S-curve under high cliffs on both sides, was promptly acted on. The small fort at West Point was enlarged and hardened, and an iron chain was stretched across the river just below water level, under the fortress's guns. The new chain was much heavier than the one General

Vaughn's ships had broken on their foray upriver in 1777, and the links were forged at Livingston Manor.

Between trips Robert attended sessions of the New York State legislature at Poughkeepsie. The parliamentary deportment of farmer-delegates and mechanic-delegates still repelled him, and he confided to John Jay, ". . . from habit & passion I love and pity my fellow creatures would to God I could esteem them." His fellow creatures confirmed his worst fears by passing the series of escalating tax bills on undeveloped property that put Robert, his mother and his manor cousins on the financial ropes.

While Robert labored in Poughkeepsie, that "dirty village where no society can be maintained," his friend John Jay was elevated to the presidency of the Continental Congress in Philadelphia. Jay and his wife, Sarah née Livingston—whose beauty, vivacity and social acuity complemented perfectly her husband's intellectual and political skills—were entering the limelight at the national level. Robert Livingston felt outclassed, a dangerous situation for so oversensitive a man. He began to find fault with Jay, carping about his public and private demeanor to all their mutual friends. To Gouverneur Morris he complained, "I have found myself sometimes a little hurt by his dogmatical manner and incommunicableness," which sounds like nothing more than the usual Jay, only Robert's perception had changed. Morris, who loved them both, attempted mollification:

> . . . your Tempers are so different that you will make the best Friends in the world. You are too lazy, he is too proud. He is too hasty, you too inattentive to the public affairs. Shall I go on. No. With all the faults both of you have, I have as many as both of you together. You both pardon me therefore you must pardon each other. And do you hear none of your stomaching—Tell the women they must all love me for I love them all. And tell yourself and make yourself believe it too that I am,
>
> most sincerely & sacredly
> Your friend
> Gouverneur Morris

Robert's chagrin was further nourished when, during 1779, he waited months for an appointment as American minister to France which never materialized, while Jay sailed away to Madrid as ambassador, accompanied by the lovely Sarah and, as secretary, her brother Brockholst Livingston. Jay, who was just as haughty as Robert, naturally responded to the growing coolness from his friend, and the rift eventually widened into a chasm.

In the autumn of 1779, Robert was again summoned as delegate to the Continental Congress, "drawn . . . from domestick peace, to bustle in the great world. I am to have the supreme felicity of making them a second sacrifice of my health, fortune & enjoyments at Congress: to this I submit, but with the reluctance of the shipwrecked wretch who embarks again after having once safely landed." His wife's first successful pregnancy after nine years of marriage was perhaps more gratifying. Polly made the journey to Philadelphia with him and settled into one of her father's houses in nearby Lebanon, New Jersey, to await her confinement. The Chancellor's mother, Margaret Beekman Livingston, looking forward to the new grandchild, concluded her New Year's letter to him: "May the Almighty pour out his best Blessings upon you & Polly give you wisdom Grace and Health and as much fortitude as the Times require—May he give us Peace and Independence and deliverance from the persecutions of the Lower Class."

Robert, leading a bachelor life in Philadelphia, celebrated the new year (1780) with a bit of a flirtation—which was nothing unusual for this perennial ladies' man, except that this time he was playing with fire, his object being Peggy Shippen Arnold, the wife of General Benedict Arnold.

Arnold was acquainted with the Clermont family, having served with Richard Montgomery at Quebec and witnessed Montgomery's will the night before he died. A brave and able soldier, Arnold had nonetheless conceived a notion that he was being passed over for promotion and honors; and his wife, an intelligent, vivacious and extremely political animal, decided during his absence in the field to go to work on his behalf. As the daughter of a prominent Philadelphia family, Peggy moved in all the right circles, and naturally her path crossed that of the susceptible Chancellor Livingston. Under the glow of Peggy's attentiveness and charm, Robert soon found himself penning a letter to General Washington strongly recommending Benedict Arnold as commander of the newly fortified bastion at West Point.†

The recommendation was more than justified by Arnold's demonstrated ability, and it was not the only one Washington received. Coming from such a source, however, it carried great weight, and Washington acted forthwith, handing over to Arnold the fortress of West Point, key to the Hudson Valley and perhaps to the entire war.

Arnold's sister Hannah wrote to him from Philadelphia, "As you have neither purling streams nor sighing swains at West Point, 'tis no place for me; nor do I think Mrs. Arnold will be long pleased with it. Though I expect it may be rendered dear to her for a few hours by the presence of a certain chancellor; who, by the by, is a dangerous companion for a particular lady in the absence of her husband. . . . I could say more than prudence will permit. I could tell you of frequent private assignations and of numberless *billets doux,* if I had an inclination to make mischief." Hannah's inclination to mischief is quite clear, as is her antipathy toward Peggy. For the record, Robert's biographer, George Dangerfield, avers that all the Chancellor's flirtations were absolutely chaste. It doesn't really matter in this instance; degrees of chastity are irrelevant in the light of ensuing events.

† Historians still debate whether or not Mrs. Arnold consciously committed treason. Some contend that the whole plot was her idea, others that she was merely her husband's pawn.

By the time Arnold got Hannah's letter his treasonous plans were already far advanced. A final meeting with his British liaison, Major John André—a distinguished and gifted officer and, not incidentally, a former suitor of Peggy Shippen Arnold—was scheduled for September 21, 1780, at which time Arnold was to turn over the plans of West Point's fortifications. André's ship, the *Vulture,* carried him upriver from New York into the Highlands and put him secretly ashore on the west bank, just across from Verplanck's Point, for his appointed rendezvous with Arnold. The *Vulture* then stood off in mid-river to await his return. André, having concluded his meeting with Arnold, returned to the riverbank carrying the precious plans only to discover that the *Vulture* had disappeared.

During his absence the continental commander at Verplanck's Point— one Colonel James Livingston, grandson (as fate would have it) of the prolific "Nephew," and the Chancellor's third cousin—had grown uneasy at the sight of the British ship lingering hour after hour in the river opposite his battery. His own small guns were powerless against her, so he dispatched an urgent request to General Arnold at West Point for a larger piece. Refused his cannon, the intrepid Livingston persevered anyway, lobbing a couple of ineffectual shots in the *Vulture*'s direction—a gallant if futile gesture. Except that it worked: the *Vulture*'s captain actually conceived a danger and, weighing anchor, withdrew his ship to safety downriver.

The stranded Major André was forced to return to New York overland, in disguise. He was detained and questioned by three suspicious American irregulars (Paulding, Williams and van Wart), the incriminating documents were discovered and the plot was revealed, including the role of Benedict Arnold. General Arnold found out in time to make his escape. André was not so fortunate, and he was hanged as a spy within the week.

Patriotic Americans throughout the colonies were horrified at the near miss (Margaret Livingston bristled from Clermont, "Had Arnold's treachery taken effect what must have been my situation!"); and the general's legion of admirers staggered with shock and surprise. Robert R. Livingston, Jr., simply took to his heels. Gathering up his wife and infant daughter, he turned his back on Philadelphia and withdrew, as so many Livingstons in discomfiture have done before and since, into the fastness of Livingston country, where he spent most of the ensuing twelve months lying low.

Thanks to the intrepidity of General Washington, the reinforcements of the French and the exhaustion of the British, the war was finally winding to a close. In Philadelphia political progress was made as well. The Articles of Confederation passed, a new government was formed, and in August of 1781 Chancellor Livingston was invited to become its first Secretary for Foreign Affairs.

As Robert's pride was by now legendary, the invitation was carefully worded: "The Office of Secretary for foreign affairs is one of the most honorable in the gift of Congress, and will not . . . be attended with much drudgery." Robert could not refuse, and his return to Philadelphia in October coincided with the celebration of Cornwallis' surrender at Yorktown.

Robert was thirty-five years old and, some would say, at the peak of his powers (despite an advancing case of premature deafness). He no doubt felt a certain expansiveness in his new position, a fact which did not escape the eagle eye of his mother, who chided from Clermont: "I have heard of the gay life yr family lead . . . is it not . . . necessary my dearest son that people in yr rank of life should stem the torrent of luxury and dissapation which must end in the ruin of these infant States . . . to dare to be singular when yr countrys well being is at stake shows an elevated mind such I wish yours to be—You have been invited round. I suppose you have returned it —there Stop at least by degrees."

The war was won, but negotiating the peace required more than a year. On April 19, 1783—eight years to the day after the battles of Concord and Lexington—the Treaty of Paris was officially proclaimed; and Chancellor Robert R. Livingston, as Secretary for Foreign Affairs, had the honor of imparting it to General Washington and the governors of the several states. It was his last official act. Having adjudged the Foreign Affairs office not commensurate with his political abilities and social standing, he resigned. With his wife and two daughters (the infant Margaret Maria was born the month the treaty was proclaimed), he made his way once more to Clermont where, Robert wrote, "I hope . . . to repair the waste (of fortune time & health) that the War has occasioned and to live the rest of my life for my friends, my family, myself." He spent the rest of the summer submitting to a series of electric shock treatments for deafness.

In November 1783 the last British military units withdrew from New York City. The British occupation of New York had commenced in 1776 with a devastating fire; seven years later debris from the fire still choked the streets, and many of New York's returning citizens found nothing left of their homes but burnt-out shells.

Margaret Beekman Livingston was fortunate: her house, surviving the fire, had been spared further depredation by a British officer who appropriated it. She and her unmarried daughters spent most of the winter in the city celebrating, in perhaps a more subdued and recollective fashion than many, the end of the war and the birth of their new nation.

PART FIVE

1783 – 1836

THIRD GENERATION:
AUT MORS VITA DECORA

"My son Robert [R. Livingston, Jr.] must not live in the country, he has talents, if he will use them, to make a figure at the head of his profession, a farm would ruin him."

Judge Robert R. Livingston

20

Mrs. Livingston's unmarried daughters, Catherine, Joanna and Alida, burst from their wartime cocoons and fluttered happily onto the social scene. The girls were heartily glad to be quit of Clermont, which the long war years had rendered "insupportably dull and irksome." They and their married sisters, Mesdames Montgomery, Tillotson and Lewis,* spent the first peacetime winter showering the Livingston charm on Boston (where they visited brother John), Philadelphia, Baltimore, and of course New York, where their mother held court in her house on Pearl Street.

Their brother, Robert R. Livingston, Jr., felt quite the reverse. Having seen enough of the perilous highroads—both political and actual—of Revolutionary New York, he determinedly narrowed his sights to his Hudson Valley estate. (Clermont technically belonged to him, although his mother still lived there and reigned supreme.) As Chancellor, Robert was still obliged to engage regularly in the public business; but whenever possible he conducted chancery court at Clermont. The principal focus for his considerable energies now became the estate and its restoration to a peacetime footing.

* Both Gertrude and Margaret had been married in 1779, the former to Morgan Lewis, son of a prosperous furrier and tanner and military aide during the war to General Horatio Gates; the latter to Dr. Thomas Tillotson of Maryland, who was described by the waggish Gouverneur Morris as "*not* of any distinguished Family, *not* of great and distinguished Abilities . . . *not* eminent in [the field of medicine] . . . neither above or below the common Map of Men Brilliant in Nothing."

But the footing was precarious, as Robert and his fellow landlords soon discovered. Underneath, the ground had shifted: the rent system on which was based their social and financial way of life was severely modified by legislatures and judges in the democratic aftermath of the War of Independence. Entail and primogeniture were abolished; tenants were given written guarantees of equal rights under the law; the last vestiges of feudal privilege ("days' riding," for example) were stricken from lease terms; and the secret ballot was instituted for all elections.

The bestowal of the fruits of democracy on the tenants of the Hudson Valley was a cruel irony to their landlords, considering how many of those same tenants had fought tooth and nail against the Revolution. Nevertheless, "fatt hens" and "courts leet and baron" had no place in the new America, and they disappeared from the books. But the landownership system of New York, in which no tenant could purchase his land, remained intact with all its ingrown animosities. Fewer reminders of personal servility might be demanded of the tenants—but landlord was still landlord, tenant remained tenant, and not an acre of land or an ounce of fellow feeling passed easily between them.

Tenant Toryism more or less evaporated after the war (or rather, it condensed back into simple straightforward tenant disaffection). Most of New York State's more prominent Loyalists, however, went into exile after their estates were confiscated. Chancellor Robert R. Livingston was opposed to the confiscation laws, viewing any citizen of substance who had not committed out-and-out treason as a potential ally of postwar conservatism. In a rare lighthearted exchange with John Jay, he expressed his hope that "the race of Tories will not, after all, be totally extinct in America. Perhaps by good training, and by crossing the breed frequently (as they are very tame), they may be rendered useful animals, in a few generations." (Jay, who was in Paris negotiating the peace treaty with Great Britain, sent Robert a set of commemorative medals with the quip, "I send you a box of plaster copies of medals if Mrs. Livingston will permit you to keep so many mistresses." Both men were still trying.)

Once the confiscation laws were passed, however, Robert and his family apparently felt no compunction about buying up Loyalist property—finding particularly sweet the acquisition of extensive holdings in New York City formerly belonging to the DeLancey family, including Oliver De-Lancey's old pew at St. Paul's Church.

Robert R. Livingston, Jr., naturally assumed a position of leadership at the convention held in Poughkeepsie in 1788 to ratify the Constitution of the United States of America. Ratification by New York was far from assured, thanks to deep divisions between the state's Federalist and anti-Federalist parties. (In Rhinebeck, Dominie Romeyn balked one Sunday at the baptismal font and, instead of blessing his parishioner's baby with the name "Thomas Jefferson [Smith]" as requested, substituted "John Adams

[Smith]," to the dismay of the babe's parents.) Robert R. Livingston, Jr., was staunchly Federalist and pro-Constitution, while his fellow delegate and distant cousin, Gilbert Livingston of Poughkeepsie, was just as staunchly anti- on both counts. Debate went on for six long, hot weeks—at which time, ten other states having ratified, New York City went ahead with its celebration of the Constitution, including parades, fireworks and *tableaux vivants*. When the Poughkeepsie convention finally assented, six days later and by only three votes, it was almost an anticlimax in Manhattan.

New York was designated capital of the United States, and the following March the city laid on another gala in honor of the first United States Congress. Alas, on the appointed day too few members showed up to constitute a quorum, and the official convening had to be postponed for another three weeks. Meanwhile the first presidential election was in progress. Margaret Beekman Livingston, horrified to realize that her tenants' votes were no longer hers to command ("I was so unsuccessful in my application . . . that I have given up all thoughts of going among them"), was relieved when her friend George Washington was elected anyway.

His inauguration took place on April 30, 1789, on the steps of Federal Hall in Manhattan with Chancellor Robert R. Livingston, Jr., as New York's highest legal official, administering the oath. As Washington bowed to kiss the Bible, Robert was heard to murmur, "It is done." Turning to the crowd, he raised his hand and cried out, "Long live George Washington, President of the United States!" and—together with most of the other onlookers— burst into tears. The new President spent the evening at Livingston's house watching the fireworks, returning to his own lodgings on foot when his carriage could not get through the crowd.

Unfortunately the whole experience went to Robert's head, and he conceived a burning notion that a major post in Washington's first cabinet was his due. Ignoring the implications of his voluntary resignation from his last national post, Secretary of Foreign Affairs, five years before, Robert determined to become the first United States Secretary of the Treasury, or, failing that, Chief Justice of the Supreme Court. His composure and indolence deserted him and, together with his sister Janet, he waged a strenuous, behind-the-scenes campaign during the early weeks of the new administration to secure one of the coveted places.

But although President Washington solicited Robert's advice on several matters, including presidential etiquette,† the expected offer of a cabinet position did not ensue. Finally Robert swallowed his pride and applied to Washington directly. The President's reply was swift, tactful and devastating: "When I accepted of the important trust committed to my charge by my Country, I gave up every idea of personal gratification that I did not

† The form of presidential address was a thorny issue. While the Senate debated "Excellency" and "Highness," the House stood firm for "Mister." Washington himself was said to prefer the title used by the Stadtholder of the Netherlands: "High Mightiness."

think was compatible with the public good . . . however strong my personal attachment might be to anyone—however desirous I might be of giving a proof of my friendship—and whatever might be his expectations, grounded upon the amity, which had subsisted between us, I was fully determined to keep myself free from every engagement that could embarrass me in discharging this part of my administration. I have therefore, uniformly declined giving any decisive answer to the numerous applications which have been made to me. . . ."

Decisive answers came soon enough, however, and it became immediately apparent why Mr. and Mrs. Jay's behavior toward Janet had become "very formal": Jay had received one of the coveted appointments, Chief Justice of the Supreme Court. Secretary of the Treasury was to be Alexander Hamilton.

The depths of Robert's disappointment and humiliation are easily measured: within a year he had turned on the President, Secretary Hamilton, Chief Justice Jay, the Federalist Party, and all of his former political allies and taken himself—and the entire Clermont branch of the family—out of the Federalist Party into a political alliance with its former foes.

In the New York gubernatorial election of 1792, Chancellor Livingston actively supported the anti-Federalist candidate, incumbent George Clinton, not because of personal enthusiasm for the farmer's son but because his opponent, the Federalist candidate, was John Jay. A sixteen-page diatribe, "John Jay Exposed for What He Is," appeared over Robert's name. But the Clinton victory (a highly questionable one, after the votes from two large Federalist districts were invalidated on a technicality) must have been a bittersweet triumph for the Chancellor of New York.

The manor branch of the Livingston family remained by and large loyal to the Federalists, for reasons not entirely political: "I should be very warm for Clinton," wrote the proprietor's son John to his brother, "was not the Chancellor in his favor." John abruptly reversed himself two years later, after his branch of the family had compromised with the Chancellor on the Roeliff Jansen Kill dispute, and came out strongly against Jay. In fine New York tradition, where expediency ranked on a par with principle, a manor lordling might reasonably expect to work out in the public arena his deepest cravings for private, patrilineal revenge.

In 1785, William Livingston, a son of the manor, now governor of New Jersey, decided to change the Livingston family motto for his branch of the family. *Spero Meliora* (I hope for better things), the esteemed and prosperous William said, no longer applied to him. "Not being able, without ingratitude to providence, to wish for more than I [have]," William announced that he would live henceforth under the motto *Aut Mors Vita Decora* (Either death or a life of honor).

Society in New York City in the immediate postwar period was extremely gay, and its acknowledged queen was Sarah Livingston Jay, daughter of William Livingston of New Jersey. On her exclusive Invitation List (from which she composed all her dinners and soirées) were Chancellor Robert R. Livingston and Mrs. Chancellor, Mrs. Judge Livingston, Mrs. Richard Montgomery, Mr. and Mrs. Morgan Lewis (the Chancellor's sister Gertrude), Mr. and Mrs. Walter Livingston, Mr. and Mrs. James Duane, and no fewer than four unattached Livingston spinsters and bachelors.

A Frenchman visiting New York during the season 1787–88 commented on the "ravages of luxury. . . . In the dress of the women you will see the most brilliant silks, gauzes, hats and borrowed hair. . . . The men have more simplicity in their dress; they distain gewgaws, but they take their revenge in the delicacies of the table." He also bemoaned the American vogue for cigars, "which come from the Spanish islands . . . and are smoked without the aid of any instrument. This usage is revolting to the French. It must be disagreeable to the women, by destroying the purity of the breath. . . . It has, however, one advantage: it accustoms to meditation and prevents loquacity. The smoker is asked a question: the answer comes two minutes after, and is well founded."

Mrs. Judge Livingston (née Margaret Beekman), the matriarch of the Clermont family, spent every winter at her Manhattan house on Pearl Street, where she maintained an elegant salon. All her children, married or unmarried, gathered there on evenings when they were not otherwise engaged, including Chancellor Robert R. Livingston and his wife, who kept their own elegant establishment nearby, at No. 3 Broadway.

None of the Chancellor's six sisters was beautiful but, being rich, all were accounted "extremely graceful." Gertrude (Mrs. Morgan Lewis) and Joanna, the best-looking of the brood, "greatly enjoyed each other's society, and when they sat together on one of Mrs. Livingston's little red morocco sofas, just large enough to hold the two, they were so perfectly contented it was a pleasure to look at them."

The oldest sister's, Janet Montgomery's, eyes "had the peculiarity of being always half shut. The lid was probably too long." But Janet—who once announced firmly, "I don't like stupid people; I have never been accustomed to them"—added spice to the evening with her razor-edged repartee. Janet made a visit in 1789 to Ireland to meet her late husband's sister, Viscountess Ranelagh—a woman whose haughtiness equaled Janet's but whose temper was a good deal viler. The two spent weeks locked in verbal combat when Janet, losing her appetite for the exercise, abruptly quit the Ranelagh household without saying good-bye. Her ladyship fired a letter after Janet which, since it cast aspersions on both Mrs. Montgomery's manners and motives, she felt obliged to answer before her ship sailed:

From the letter I received last night, I have again to thank your Ladyship for wounding my feelings and affronting my understanding. . . .

I am neither a Courtier nor a Lady of Quality—but a Proud Republican who cannot suffer herself to be insulted even by the Sister of General Montgomery. . . .

One thing further and I end gladly a correspondence so painful. Had pleasure been my Motive I need not have left my own happy Country—for however great the sphere in which your Ladyship moves Mine be assured is a little less contracted.

The feud with her ladyship did not prevent Janet from forming an affectionate friendship with the Ranelagh family's sixth son, William Jones, who came to America at her behest and eventually assumed the role of the son she and Richard never had.

Janet's youngest sister, Alida, with "large, dark, expressive eyes" and extremely high principles, was married in 1789 to John Armstrong of Pennsylvania, a former major in the Continental Army and anonymous author of the controversial Newburgh Addresses.‡ Armstrong was a man of enormous talent and vast insecurity, who papered over the gap with haughtiness and pugnacity. During his courtship of Alida he wrote to a friend, "I'm too poor to marry a woman without some fortune & too proud to marry any woman, that I know, who possesses one." His pride eventually succumbed to Alida's charms, or her fortune. Shortly after the nuptials Armstrong, on a visit to his home state of Pennsylvania, sent a message to his bride that he would return to New York only if her mother, Margaret Beekman Livingston, made an immediate transferral of her property to her children. Poor Alida: Livingstonlike, she had never faced the possibility of living anywhere except New York. Margaret made the transfer within the year, placing Alida's portion of the vast estate—about 25,000 acres—in her husband's name.

Margaret Beekman Livingston had even more reason to worry about the fortune of her third daughter, Catherine, who in 1787 underwent a religious epiphany while praying, " 'By thine agony and Bloody sweat, by thy cross and passion, by thy glorious Resurrection and Ascension and by the coming of the Holy Ghost.' Scarce had I pronounced those words, when I was received and made unspeakably happy. A song of praise and thanksgiving was put in my mouth—my sins were pardoned and my state was changed. My soul was happy—In a transport of Joy I sprang from knees, and happening to see myself as I passed the L Glass I could not but look with surprize at the change in my countenance all things were become new." Catherine was introduced by her mother's housekeeper to the teachings of

‡ About which one historian remarked, "Better English has seldom been wasted in a worse cause." The Addresses were written to protest Congress' refusal to pay the officers of the Continental Army who served during the period between the British surrender and the signing of the peace treaty.

John Wesley and converted overnight to Methodism. The Methodists—regarded as a dangerously radical, renegade sect by most orthodox Protestants, including Margaret Beekman Livingston—were the objects of consistent abuse and persecution; so Catherine's conversion was understandably greeted by her family with dismay. Her attendance at Methodist services was tolerated, however, until she conceived a strong romantic attachment to the Methodist circuit-riding preacher, Freeborn Garrettson, whereupon her mother lost her equanimity and demanded that Catherine stay away from both the man and his church.

Margaret viewed Garrettson as a fortune hunter, pure and simple. Her daughter, however—thirty-five years old and decidedly plain—saw instead a man who loved her and whom she deeply loved. The two women locked horns; and the ensuing contest endured for four long years. In 1791, Catherine fled Clermont when the strain became unbearable, taking refuge with her sister, Margaret Tillotson. She wrote to Garrettson, "I do not think I can write [my mother] on the subject. . . . If you knew what I suffered last winter, you would not be surprised at my declining a thing that may be attended with such painful consequences." The couple swore that it was not "the loss of property" that prevented their eloping; nevertheless, they were understandably reluctant to marry without Margaret's blessing. It came, grudgingly, a year and a half later, and Catherine became Mrs. Freeborn Garrettson on June 30, 1793.

Another star of Margaret Beekman Livingston's New York salon was her youngest son, Edward, who, having graduated from Princeton toward the end of the war, was launched on a legal career in the city. Edward's sharp, angular looks nearly succeeded in making a virtue of the elongated Livingston nose. His erudition and wit (which ran to puns) were assets in the drawing room, and his sartorial dash earned him the nickname "Beau Ned." But Edward also had a profoundly intellectual and philosophical turn of mind and a high, if remote, regard for his fellow man. Even the dour John Jay had acknowledged Edward's precocity, in sending the medals to the Chancellor with instructions to "reserve the Ladies for yourself and give the Philosophers & poets to Edward."

Edward was married in 1788 to Mary McEvers, who had made her mark in society early that season at an evening reception at Mrs. Washington's when her ostrich feather headdress caught fire from the chandelier. The following year, Mary's sister Eliza was married to Edward's brother, John R. Livingston.

The black sheep of Margaret's flock, Henry Beekman Livingston, had also been active in the matrimonial line, with disastrous consequences. Henry's career in the Continental Army had continued its established pattern, with magnificent displays of courage and fortitude—at Saratoga, Monmouth, Quaker Hill and Newport, and during the terrible winter at Valley Forge—punctuated by outbreaks of unbridled rage and hubris. Henry resigned from the army at the height of the war in 1779, in a fit of pique at being passed over for promotion by other officers he considered "my inferiors." Throwing himself into civilian life with characteristic willfulness and drive, Henry cut a wide swath through the female population of Dutchess County, resulting in a staggering number of bastard Livingston babies of a variety of hues, religious persuasions and social classes. Henry financed his profligacies by selling off land, an action which was deeply resented by his brothers and sisters, who deemed it "rather low and the money seems to be going to nothing very fast."

Then, on a visit to Philadelphia toward the end of 1780, Henry at the age of thirty fell in love with eighteen-year-old Nancy Shippen (a first cousin of Peggy Shippen Arnold, whose husband's treason had come to light only the month before). Nancy was pretty, vivacious, pleasure-loving —and spoiled, high-strung and unconscionably coquettish. Underneath all the girlishness ran a deep vein of morbidity—an unstable mixture under any circumstances, guaranteed to explode in combination with Henry's seething obsessiveness.

When she met Henry Livingston, Nancy had been in love for a year with a young French diplomat, Louis Otto. Otto was not in a position to marry immediately, but Henry was; and patience was not among Nancy's virtues: "On Monday she likes L[ivingston] & his fortune. On Tuesday evening when O[tto] comes he is the angel. . . . L has 12 or 15,000 hard O has nothing now, but honorable expectations hereafter. A Bird in hand is worth 2 in a bush." Compared with the elegant Otto, Henry's wooing was coarse; ". . . to divert myself will Scrall a few Lines; the writing, which at Best Bad, is now worse, from the Dimness of a Lonesome Taper, emblematical of your Lovers Situation with this Difference that it Burns at one End, I all over." Nancy succumbed to Henry's importunity—and to enormous pressure from her parents, whose eagerness for an alliance with the powerful Livingston clan rendered them blind to Henry's shortcomings and their daughter's true feelings—and the marriage was solemnized in Philadelphia on March 14, 1781.

The couple repaired to Henry's home near Rhinebeck: the old Dutch farmhouse of his Grandfather Beekman, which, compared to the elegant Shippen house in Philadelphia, must have seemed to Nancy very dark, constricted and primitive. Here were no doting parents to indulge her every whim; only the cold, windy Hudson Valley and her husband's powerful family among whom she was on probation. She fulfilled a primary obligation within the first month, by becoming pregnant; but it proved her only triumph. Nancy—girlish, pampered Nancy—was utterly unable to deal with her husband's fits of vicious rage or with his reckless licentiousness. Her only confidante was her mother-in-law, Margaret Beekman Livingston, who understood all too well her son's true character and pitied his hapless wife.

Using her approaching confinement as an excuse, Nancy fled to Philadelphia where her daughter, Margaret Beekman Livingston, was born in December of 1781. But at the insistence of her parents, who feared more than anything giving offense to the Livingstons, she made plans to return as soon as she could travel. Henry, smarting from wounded pride at her departure, refused to have her back and accused her publicly, and most unjustifiably, of infidelity. Nancy was forced by her parents to plead. When Henry finally relented she returned to Rhinebeck, only to learn (secretly, from her mother-in-law) that her husband was hatching a plan to bring together under one roof—her roof—all his illegitimate children to be raised alongside her child. Nancy fled once again with little Peggy to Philadelphia and the implacably unsympathetic arms of her parents.

Three months later she was invited by her mother-in-law to come to Clermont, the "Old Lady" (as Nancy affectionately referred to her) having resolved to take personal charge of little Peggy's upbringing. Margaret, in her wisdom, may have recognized Nancy's instability and feared for her granddaughter. She could also have been motivated by guilt over her own failure with her son; or perhaps she simply thought that Livingstons should be raised by Livingstons. The only thing certain is her genuine desire to protect Nancy and Peggy from Henry, a protection which Nancy's abject parents were clearly unwilling to provide.

But Nancy's position at Clermont became untenable after Henry, whose rage and suspicion had by now blossomed into full-blown paranoia, refused to recognize her as his wife and continued to level public accusations of infidelity. She returned once again to her parents' home; but this time, utterly heartbroken, she left her baby at Clermont.

Sixteen-month-old Peggy and her grandmother were among the first Americans to reenter New York City after the British withdrawal in November 1783. Nancy visited from Philadelphia in the spring, but little Peggy did not recognize her mother, running instead to her Aunt Kitty (Catherine) who was her "friend and favorite," or seeking refuge in the arms of her Uncle Robert and Mrs. Chancellor, whom she had taken to calling Mama and Papa. Nancy returned to Philadelphia suffering from severe depression, which she called "fogs in the moral as well as the natural world." She was not angry at her in-laws, quite the contrary. Badly in need of a family, she felt fondly attached to them and regretted deeply the circumstances that kept her from them.

Henry took to skulking around her house in Philadelphia in disguise, which unnerved her profoundly. When she refused to meet him alone in his lodgings to discuss a reconciliation, he returned to Rhinebeck and plunged back into his former dissolution with renewed vigor. His anguished mother reported to Nancy, "I have seen him only three times in about a year. He never comes here nor I at his house. . . . I am a Mother and every Misconduct every Sin and Immorality recoils upon my heart and makes it Vibrate with ten fold force. . . . He has seen his Daughter only once and that by accident at Mr. Tillotsons. His behaviour was so cool to her that I felt the utmost pain. It has convinced me that she must not be often with [him] and she shall not."

When little Peggy was four, her grandmother proposed that she spend the winter with her mother. Nancy was ecstatic and showered her daughter with pent-up love and attention. When Peggy returned to Clermont in the spring, her grandmother was so pleased with the results that she proposed returning her regularly to Philadelphia every winter.

In 1787, Nancy's former suitor, Louis Otto, was married to Eliza Livingston, the daughter of Peter Van Brugh Livingston, Nancy's own husband's second cousin. But within the year Eliza Otto had died in childbirth, Louis Otto had revived his correspondence with Nancy, and Nancy decided to sue Henry for divorce. Her father refused to give his support, siding instead with Henry and insisting that little Peggy, who was on her annual sojourn in Philadelphia, be sent immediately back to her grandmother. But Margaret Beekman Livingston warned her daughter-in-law not to comply: "Were I to take her tomorrow [Henry] would take her from me the next day till I give up her Estate to him. When that is accomplished I suppose he will never care a straw where she is. . . . Do not be Secure. . . . Everybody [in the family] admires your firmness, prudence & maternal affection and applauds your conduct." Ironically, Henry's family was the only source of support and encouragement Nancy had; her mother-in-law even sent money for her legal expenses.

The following summer, while little Peggy was at Clermont, during the family's absence from the house one day Henry appeared and, over the housekeeper's protestations, kidnapped his daughter. His sisters, Catherine and Joanna, were dispatched in the coach to his house to fetch her back, but Henry "refused. They wished to see her but were refused except they would go in his house. This Kitty & Joanna did not chuse to do, and came away without her." Henry was finally prevailed upon to return the child, but only after exacting from his mother an absolute promise not to permit her to return to Philadelphia.

Instead, Margaret spirited the child away to a secret hiding place beyond Henry's reach. From there the eight-year-old conspirator, using the alias "Louisa Ann Lewis," penned comfort to her mother: "I will find out a way to see you without putting myself in danger don't be affraid. You must not make any attempts. I beg you wont. I'll manage it never fear. You must not know where I am. I am safe & comfortable." Henry filed suit in federal court against his mother for custody of the child. Although Margaret's "heart [was] sore, very, very Sore," her head remained clear. Reasoning that her son's suit released her from her promise to him, she packed little Peggy hastily into a closed coach and saw her off on the road to Philadelphia. "Y^e next day I wished to avoid him and left home . . . a strategim which succeeded beyond my expectation. He . . . came to Genl Armstrongs [the home of Henry's sister and brother-in-law near Clermont] in the morning Saying he came to fetch P . . . & asked me where she was. I was Silent, and he remained there till night. I had then gained a whole day & a night. He left us at dark expecting to get intelligence from ye Chancellor & family, but in vain. My Servants were then asked. Money was offered but not one of the number could be tempted to betray the trust. He then returned to [the Armstrongs'] expecting I suppose to find her, but not seeing her he attacked me most violently affecting [illegible] passion Spoke of his feelings, his heart torn &c but as I knew he had many times disowned her to be his child and that it was all Duplicity I remained silent & left the room." Margaret managed to stall Henry for four more days. Then, secure in the knowledge that little Peggy "was safe in the embraces of her Mother & friends in Philada.," she wrote to inform him of her action, explaining that it was "impossible to permit a child of one of the first families in the United States to be in a family without a white woman in it."

Henry's wrath was formidable, but there was little he could do—except revenge himself on Nancy. If he could not have his child, he could at least destroy her mother, and his weapon would be Louis Otto. Henry offered to consent to a divorce on one condition: that Peggy be given up to his exclusive custody. Nancy, forced to choose between her daughter and Otto, capitulated and dropped the divorce suit. The elegant but elusive Monsieur Otto promptly remarried and disappeared forever from Nancy's life. She and her daughter continued to see each other every winter, and summers Peggy spent with her grandmother at Clermont while Nancy brooded alone in Philadelphia.*

As for Henry, he retreated once again into his own realm of anarchy and chaos, becoming forever alienated from mother, brothers and sisters— in perpetual exile from Clermont.

In the late winter of 1790, Margaret Beekman Livingston received an inquiry from a distant cousin about the Beekman family tree, and she took the opportunity to air her views on pride of pedigree: "Is the subject of Genealogy often the source of pride and ostentation alas why should it be so, when we are led to reflect on the unstability of all human affairs. . . . It is true none who possess family despise it neither ought we to do it but look upon [it] as a particular favor to have derived our being from men and women fearing God, and respected in their day for virtue and goodness."

---

* Peggy lived exclusively with her mother after the age of sixteen. As the years went by, both women became increasingly reclusive, hypochondriacal and devout, the prey of quacks and self-appointed messiahs. They both lived into extreme old age and were buried in a single grave.

21

Every spring, when the forests lining the Brooklyn and New Jersey shorelines began to leaf out, and "Staten Island rose gradually from the sea in which it seemed to float, and was so covered with innumerable fruit-trees in full bloom that it looked like some enchanted forest," Margaret Beekman Livingston moved her household upriver from New York City to Clermont. Her granddaughter Peggy, who turned nine in 1790, was invariably of the party, as were her son, Chancellor Robert R. Livingston, Jr., and his family.

In 1793, Robert began to build a new mansion at Clermont, a few hundred yards to the south of the ruined Belvedere and linked to his mother's house by an *allée* of acacia trees. The two-story structure was in the shape of an H with a riverfront facade over a hundred feet long. One of the four corner pavilions contained Robert's library, some 4000 volumes. A greenhouse ran the length of the south front, outside of which, in the "pleasure grounds," plantings of flowering trees and orchards were laid out. Along a two-mile path paralleling the river, "the natural features [were] everywhere preserved, though softened and harmonised by the happiest efforts of art." Robert, Polly and their two teen-age daughters moved into the new mansion in the spring of 1794.

The move coincided with an offer from President Washington for Robert to become United States minister to France—a gesture of reconciliation to the anti-Federalists, whose support Washington needed for a new trade treaty with Great Britain currently being negotiated in London by John Jay.

Robert was eminently suited for the post; yet he declined it, against the advice of most of his friends including Edward Livingston, his younger brother and closest confidant. Instead he tendered Washington, in a presidential gesture of his own, a gift which clearly indicated his present mood: a transcript of the recent proceedings of the Society for the Promotion of Agriculture, Arts and Manufactures, over which he presided. Washington was delighted; the role of enlightened gentleman farmer was just as dear to him as it was to Robert. He reciprocated with a cordial note of thanks, enclosing a pamphlet on the scientific cultivation of potatoes.

In October of the same year Robert was honored by a visit from William Strickland, the celebrated British agriculturalist. It was an occasion of intense satisfaction: Robert conducted Strickland over his domain, demonstrating all his pet projects, and the two passed a long evening before the fire in contented discourse on the breeding of oxen and the fertilizing effects of gypsum.

Genteel husbandry was a flourishing intellectual movement in the eighteenth century. The members of this elite transatlantic fraternity, espousing their own particular brand of *noblesse oblige,* determined to contribute to the "happiness of man" by making their discoveries "known into the common stock . . . by which," as Robert Livingston expounded in a letter to Arthur Young, "the friends of the earth are increased." Among other things, however, this estimable crusade permitted Robert Livingston to rest intellectually easy in his manorial seat. William Strickland, on the other hand, was shocked by the Hudson Valley tenant system, which he found—in comparison to the more highly evolved English system—appallingly feudal and primitive.

The eighteenth-century model of enlightened gentility toward which Robert Livingston so admirably strived encompassed more than scientific farming. The ideal gentleman was also a classical scholar, a student of mechanics and of botany, a connoisseur of the arts, a fashion plate and a statesman. Chancellor Livingston excelled in almost every area. The volume and variety of his literary output during this period of his life included: "Reflections on Peace, War and Trade"; "Thoughts on Lime and Gypsum"; "Reflections on the Site of the National Capital"; "Complaint on the Postal Service"; "The Use of Ashes and Pyrite as Manure"; "Reflections on Monarchy" (written in 1793, in response to the guillotining of Louis XVI); "Notes on Alkali"; "Thoughts on Coinage and the Establishment of a Mint"; "Oration on the Fine Arts"; a plan regarding "the discovery of the Interior parts of this Continent & establishing the Indian trade in that Quarter"; "Notes on Winds"; and many, many others. He also maintained a voluminous correspondence with his peers throughout America and Europe and conducted a series of scientific experiments of his own.

His consort in a number of projects was a newcomer to the Hudson Valley, the French émigré Pierre Delabigarre. Delabigarre, having escaped

Paris and the Terror with only his life and a set of highly utopian notions, proposed to construct on the eastern shore of the Hudson River, just south of Clermont, an ideal community called Tivoli whose streets, laid out in a perfectly symmetrical grid, would be known as Peace, Plenty, Friendship, Laws—and Chancellor, in honor of Robert R. Livingston, Jr., its principal patron. Delabigarre took to addressing Robert as

> Maecenas: . . . Continue, dear Sir, to immortalize yourself through your dis-
> coveries & your researches, while our days fly toward the temple of oblivion!
>   Happiness and fraternity,
>   Pierre Delabigarre

Delabigarre got Robert's backing for a dubious venture that involved the conversion of a river weed called conserva (popularly known as "frog spit") into paper. Lengthy experiments were conducted and a patent obtained, all at Robert's expense. When the project failed and Delabigarre landed in debtors' prison in Poughkeepsie, Robert had to bail him out.

Occasional setbacks never daunt a scientific spirit, however, and Robert continued to devote vast amounts of time and energy to research and writing in a variety of specialized agricultural and technical fields. His name was known and esteemed in the fraternity of learned men—Strickland's visit alone attests to it—as well as in legal and judicial circles, where his performance on the bench drew continued regard. He also found time to supervise his estate, adorn his mansion, pursue the wily woodcock (his favorite recreation) and pay country calls in an elegant carriage with matched team.

It was not, of course, enough—not for a spirit in which inner contentment was so dependent on outward acclaim. Living the private life that he professed to find ideal, Robert burned when others' public lives outshone it. In a sense, "the farm" had ruined him, just as his father had predicted, by leading him to demand deference but giving him a demeanor that prevented his receiving it. Robert habitually expected, as a Livingston of Clermont, automatic primacy in every undertaking; at the same time the powers which bestow such primacy sensed his manorial disdain, so utterly out of place in the new America, and denied him his heart's desire. "The farm" also provided a safe refuge and a beguiling distraction from inevitable failure. Robert, as the son of manor lords, both expected more than was perhaps his due and ended by settling for less. The son of the manor was also its victim.

Robert's new house was part of a postwar Livingston building boom. In the decades following the War of Independence more than a dozen mansions were built by members of the family along a twenty-mile stretch of the Hudson's eastern shore, over half of them by Robert's sisters and brothers. "There was not one of them," a grandchild recalled later, "who did not think, and sometimes say, that his or her country-seat was the choicest spot on the Hudson River; and that if there was nothing like it on the Hudson River, there was nothing like it in the world, for there was no river to compare with the Hudson." Strung like pearls on a chain, these houses bespeak the solidarity, self-confidence and self-satisfaction of the Livingstons of the Hudson Valley in the postwar period.

Robert's siblings' houses stretched south from Clermont into Dutchess County. First in line, about four miles from Clermont itself, was Alida and John Armstrong's The Meadows, built in 1790 but sold shortly thereafter by the restless Armstrong, who constructed another new mansion just to the south called Mill Hill. Next came Château de Montgomery, erected about 1800 by the widowed Janet Montgomery. Janet sold her former mansion, Grasmere—which she and General Montgomery had been finishing on their Rhinebeck farm at the time of his death—to her sister Joanna, now married to their cousin, Peter R. Livingston (another Peter R., not the manor proprietor's eldest son). Château de Montgomery's imposing scale was nicely counterpoised by the elegance of Massena, next door, which was built in 1797 by Janet's brother, John R. Livingston, and became justly famous for its lofty, glass-domed library ceiling. Farther south, on a point of land facing downriver just west of Grasmere, Catherine and Freeborn Garrettson constructed the charming clapboard Wildercliff, which they turned into a retreat for persecuted Methodists—one of organized Protestantism's more elegant asylums. Less than a mile farther was Margaret and Thomas Tillotson's Linwood; and last but not least came the Staatsburgh mansion of Gertrude and Morgan Lewis, "a capacious brick house . . . as ugly as it was comfortable," set atop one of the best sledding hills in Dutchess County.

Eight of Margaret Beekman Livingston's ten children now lived along the same stretch of the Hudson River's east bank, within a few miles of one another.* These men and women, affectionate and closely knit, shared the same outlook and prospects, in every sense of the words. Their houses proclaimed not only their substantiality as individuals but their solidarity as a family. Unfortunately, the same cannot be said of the new houses of their manor cousins, which became instead rival fortresses in the manor's running internecine battle and issues in the conflict itself.

Before turning to the manor it is worth noting parenthetically the building of three fine mansions in the valley during this period by Livingstons who bought their way in from the outside—outside the valley, that is. One of these distant cousins "came home" from New Jersey: Henry Brockholst Livingston, son of New Jersey Governor William Livingston, who purchased in 1797 a piece of property between the Tillotsons' Lin-

* Henry Beekman Livingston was by now effectively exiled from the family circle, never to return. Edward, on the other hand, was extremely close to his mother and siblings and visited them in the valley frequently.

wood and the Lewises' Staatsburgh and constructed a grand house which he called The Locusts.†

From even farther away, proprietarily speaking, came members of the Gilbert branch of the family in search of their roots. It will be remembered that Gilbert Livingston, alone among the first manor proprietor's sons, did not receive a portion of Livingston Manor as part of his inheritance. About 1790, Gilbert's granddaughter, Catharine Livingston Reade, and her husband bought a piece of land just south of Clermont, on the outskirts of the burgeoning village of Tivoli, and built a house overlooking the river which they called Green Hill. Four years later Reade sold Green Hill to his brother-in-law, Henry Gilbert Livingston (who, just for the record, had two brothers named Robert Gilbert and Gilbert Robert). Henry Gilbert constructed a second grand mansion on the property called Sunning Hill, which he sold to his distant cousin, Philip Henry Livingston, scion of a branch of the manor Livingstons who had emigrated to the West Indies before the war. (Also for the record, Philip Henry was married to Maria Livingston, a granddaughter of the third manor proprietor; and his brother, Edward P. Livingston, was shortly to become the husband of Chancellor Robert R. Livingston, Jr.'s daughter Betsey, from Clermont next door.)

Perhaps a remark made in 1797 to Henry Brockholst Livingston's brother by a cousin in New Hampshire is apt: "Permit a distant relative to enjoy the pleasing reflection of an Old Adage, that the Blood can *crawl* where it cannot run."

During the War of Independence three of the manor proprietor's sons had built houses on Livingston Manor. The mansion of the oldest, Peter R. Livingston, was named The Hermitage. His brother Walter—who, like Peter R., had come slinking back to the manor after a series of business failures in the city—constructed the graceful Teviotdale next door, on the same high inland plateau with a magnificent sweep of fields and forests and the Catskills rising blue and misty in the background. A third brother, John, erected the noble Forth House, named after Scotland's Firth of Forth, adjacent to the nearby Post Road.

Right after the war the enterprising John Livingston began buying up large tracts of undeveloped land across the river for speculation. He and his partners built roads, established towns and then sold the land piecemeal to independent farmers—a lucrative undertaking which permitted John to construct a magnificent new riverfront villa atop a wooded bluff just north of the old manor house. Family legend says that he chose the site by climbing a tall oak tree to determine the best view, in commemoration of which the house is still known as Oak Hill.

† Henry Brockholst was quite sensitive about having the elongated Livingston nose. He fought a duel against a man who had ridiculed it, in which the other was killed while Brockholst was wounded—in the nose. His *nom de plume* in the newspapers was "Aquiline Nimble-chops."

The showplace of the manor was constructed in 1800 by one of Walter Livingston's sons. The Hill, home of Mr. and Mrs. Henry Walter Livingston, with its tall white columns and twin octagonal wings, was, in the words of the renowned designer Andrew Jackson Downing, "one of the chastest specimins of the Grecian style" in America. The mansion "stands in the midst of a fine park, rising gradually from the level of a rich inland country, and commanding prospects for sixty miles around [including the entire Catskill range]. The park is, perhaps, the most remarkable in America, for the noble simplicity of its character, and the perfect order in which it is kept." There Henry Walter and his wife, who was known as "Lady Mary," raised their seven children, supervised their tenantry and lived a life of cultivation and elegance unrivaled by any other establishment in this branch of the family.

When the old manor proprietor died in 1790, at the age of eighty-two, the terms of his will precipitated a devastating clash among his already antipathetical sons—a clash in which both the manor house and The Hermitage became pawns and eventually victims. Peter R. Livingston, as eldest son, had fully expected to receive the manor, intact. Instead his father, in a major break with family tradition, divided the property more or less equally among Peter and his four brothers. Peter R. received the manor house, his share of the manor land and tenant farms, a house in Albany, and the now hollow title, "Fourth Lord of Livingston Manor." The final indignity was the entail placed on the property by the third proprietor: Peter R. was required to pass his estate, intact, to his eldest son; he could sell not a single acre, farm, barn, orchard or house to satisfy his many creditors.

These terms had been conceived by Peter R.'s father in full knowledge of his eldest's profligate tendencies. But they had also been urged on him by his younger sons, who for years had resented the claims made on their father's estate by Peter R.'s perennial bankruptcies. The new manor "lord" was well aware of his brothers' role and blamed them for his disappointment.

His own eldest son was a source of resentment as well. Young Robert Tong Livingston, with his cousin/wife Margaret née Livingston, had been living at The Hermitage for a number of months, to the discomfiture of his parents: "It is impossible for us to live under same roof with them she continues as bad as ever and his temper is such as tenders it impossible for his poor mother to live with him." Now, Peter R. and his wife had to vacate the elegant, relatively new Hermitage, leaving it for their son and daughter-in-law, and move into that "untenantable old house," the manor headquarters.

Little wonder that Margaret Beekman Livingston of Clermont, paying a call on Mr. and Mrs. Peter R. after the third proprietor's funeral, should come away sighing with relief that "heaven has preserved my children from yᵉ hatred [I] see in them. . . . God Bless [us] all and keep us all from avarice and Injustice."

In the weeks immediately following the third proprietor's death, before the house switching commenced, the manor house was occupied by Peter R.'s younger brother, Henry, who had attended their father during his last illness and who now served as self-appointed guardian of his effects. It was Henry who first felt the brunt of Peter's bile when he and his son came to look the place over: "All is not well in the State of Denmark as Othello says," reported Henry to Walter. "Peter & his Son Robert were down here yesterday to renew his reiterated demands for the wearing apparell." Henry, justifiably suspicious that Peter intended to "plunder" the estate if he could, refused to hand over their father's clothing and jewelery without an inventory. He finally sent them to The Hermitage—with an itemized receipt which Peter R. refused to sign. A few days later, learning that Peter R. planned to return to the house, Henry prepared himself by hiding the family silver.

Peter R. announced that, since his brothers were responsible for disinheriting him, they were morally obligated to pay his debts, and he billed them $1000 apiece. When they failed to respond he paid calls on each in turn, but not a single brother could be found at home. Peter took to dropping in at the manor house to harass Henry and throw his weight around: ". . . in going away he stop'd at the Barn and scolded at George for feeding an oxen which came down from Ancram . . . he told George that we had no *right* to keep them here and if we did he would also send down his cattle, he also said the hay at Ancram was not ours (and *I suppose if George had condescended to have heard him, he would have explained the whole will to him*)." On his next visit Peter R. was accompanied by his wife and eldest son, "who after dinner," Henry reported, "did in a most unwarrantable manner, abuse me, Charging me with Cheating them out of their Estate and our oldest Executor (as he calls himself) told me several times that I was a Lyar . . . made use of Billingsgate language, and cast many severe reflections upon the memory of our ever Blessed Father . . . the rest is too bad to be told."

Abruptly, Peter R. seemed to realize he had gone too far. He attempted to pay a conciliatory call on Henry at the manor house but was turned away at the door—"our late *Frolic*," Henry explained to Walter, "will forever prevent me from any conversation or connection with him." Nevertheless, when Peter came cringing back—having failed in an attempt to drive a wedge between Henry and their other brothers—he relented and forgave Peter "all the expressions which you made use of to me at our unhappy altercation on the 16 Inst. in my Room"—but only on condition that Peter and his son never again "by word or act reflect upon the memory or last act of our Blessed Father."

It was at this moment that the term "Lord of the Manor" was first used by a member of the family: by Henry, referring sarcastically to his brother Peter R.

One of Peter R.'s younger sons, Walter Tryon Livingston, had spent the months of the third proprietor's final illness behaving "in a very gross manner to his parents . . . [he] is going to be married to . . . Blatner's daughter, who is in a pregnant situation, & the Boy swears he will marry her let the consequence be what it will, and I am sure the girl is so common she cannot tell who the father is—." After the wedding, Peter R. "sent [Walter] his things and forbid him the house," refusing to be mollified when the baby boy was named for him.

Walter T.'s Uncle John Livingston took to calling him "Walter Tryon Blatner"; and his cousin Peter Schuyler Livingston (Walter's son), peering down from an Olympian perch at Harvard College, positively squeaked with pious indignation: "Was not so much startled at hearing that my cousin Walter T. was travelling on to *Poverty, wretchedness* and *distress* as I should have been had I not known that he was a young man void of all taste for Literature, moving in no particular sphere, nor preparing himself to act in any capacity on the great Theatre of Life." Peter Schuyler righteously noted his own continued devotion to "the study of History—than which no study is better calculated to infuse the mind with noble sentiments, or cause it to despise the foibles of the present world . . . this proof of the inconstancy of the Populace is an instructing lesson to me and all young candidates for glory."

Peter R. Livingston, "Fourth Lord of Livingston Manor," died in 1794, only four years after his father's death; whereupon the game of musical houses set in motion by the third proprietor's will commenced again. Peter's widow vacated the manor house in favor of her oldest son, the vile-tempered Robert T., and moved back to The Hermitage. After her death a few years later, The Hermitage became the joint property of her younger children; but none of them wanted to live there, so they rented it out to a series of relatives, including "Walter Tryon Blatner," and the poor Hermitage began to run down.

As for the manor house, Robert T. Livingston had it pulled down (after removing the firebacks, door frames, mantelpieces and anything else of value) and built a new and grander house up the bank. His Great-great-grandmother Alida would have hooted—and moved it back down to the dock where it belonged. Robert T.'s new house no doubt afforded him a loftier view; but unfortunately it failed to bestow on him or his immediate progeny any distinction whatsoever.

The signs of disintegration in the manor clan after the death of the third proprietor were hardly surprising, given the fact that property divisions often bring out the worst in siblings, even those who once liked each other. In that sense, "the farm" ruins everybody. More noteworthy, perhaps, is that the damage seems to have been confined to Peter R. and his immediate family: Walter, Henry and John remained friends, and Walter's children at least felt considerable affection for their father, as in this enduring testimonial written by his younger son from Yale:

> I acknowledge that you are my best and dearest friend, and that paternal affection is the strongest of all human ties, and consequently shall prefer your advice before any other person, and shall not be swayed by the opinions of those who wish to palliate my extravagance.
> I have no money.
> Your affectionate son
> Walter T. Livingston

The three brothers, Walter, Henry and John, also had to close ranks against an outside threat. A few weeks after their father's death a rent strike was instigated by a group of manor tenants, no doubt to test the mettle of the third proprietor's boys. Columbia County Sheriff Hageboom, serving eviction notices in the eastern end of the manor, was shot and killed by a band of tenants dressed in Indian disguise. The twelve men brought to trial for the murder were all acquitted—a sinister mark of changing times. Four years later more than two hundred tenants signed a petition (many with X's) to the New York State legislature to vacate the Livingston title to Livingston Manor, basing their appeal on the claim that the original Robert Livingston in 1686 "did falsely and fraudulently suggest and represent to [Governor] Thomas Dongan that the Lands Granted to him [in the patents of 1684 and 1685] were lying together"—Robert the Founder's real estate "miracle" returned to haunt his great-grandsons. The petition further stated that the tenants of Livingston Manor held their farms "upon terms & conditions oppressive & burdensome to the last degree . . . & tending to degrade your Petitioners from the ranks the God of Nature destined all mankind to move in. . . ." The level of discourse had certainly elevated since the days of "Robert Livingston kiss his ass." Nevertheless, the legislature dismissed the petition: the time had not quite come when New York State was ready to void the land patent of the Hudson Valley's first family. The underlying issue—ownership of the tenants' farms—was not so easily dismissed, of course. Walter, John and Henry Livingston knew enough not to practice retaliation against the tenant ringleaders; but their leniency, while commendable, was not enough to square the account.

Margaret Beekman Livingston attended the funeral of the third manor proprietor and paid condolence calls on his children, despite the fact that the "Old Gent," virtually to the day of his death, perpetuated the feud with her son, Robert R. Livingston, Jr., over water rights to the Roeliff Jansen Kill. Family courtesy demanded her attendance; but in addition she and the Clermont family would always be grateful to the proprietor for his aid and comfort during the darkest days of the war.

The manor-Clermont feud was finally called off in the summer of 1794, after a case involving Walter Livingston of Teviotdale was favorably concluded in the chancery courtroom of his cousin, Chancellor Robert R. Livingston, Jr., of Clermont. Walter's case won on its merits, not because of favoritism. Still, he was grateful and seized on this excuse to make up. He and his brothers reached a compromise with the Chancellor on the Roeliff Jansen Kill dispute, and the thaw was on. Within five years the alliance was cemented in true dynastic fashion: Walter's son, Robert L. Livingston, became the husband of the Chancellor's fifteen-year-old daughter, Margaret Maria Livingston; and his cousin Edward P. Livingston was married to Margaret Maria's sister Betsey.

22

The weddings of Chancellor Robert R. Livingston's two daughters took place within eighteen months of each other in the parlor of their grand-mother's house at Clermont. Margaret Beekman Livingston, vigorous at seventy-five, still held the center of the Clermont family. But on July 1 of the following summer, 1800, "The old Lady of Clermont took her leave of this world with great éclat she walked about the Gardens and did business all the morning, had several of her friends to dinner of which she amply partook. In taking a glass of wine she found her right hand failing changed it to her left soon fell in a fit and expired without a groan."

Margaret's death cut out the core of the Clermont family; but its heart continued to beat. Her children—Robert, his brothers John and Edward, and their sisters Montgomery, Tillotson, Garrettson, Lewis and Armstrong —drew, if anything, closer than before. Their affectionate solidarity was their mother's greatest legacy.

But about the time of Margaret Beekman Livingston's death the beams in the ceiling of Clermont's dining room began to crack. Shoddy construction work during the War of Independence was probably to blame. The damage was not at first apparent on the surface; but eventually, little by little, hairline cracks began to appear in the plaster ceiling and walls, and the floorboards in the room above began to buckle. Over the ensuing decades cosmetic repairs were made—a little shimming here, a bit of spackle there— but no one looked behind the plaster or beneath the floorboards for the essential cause. Decade after decade, in infinitesimal progression, Clermont creaked, and splintered, and sagged; until, a hundred years later, it joined the twentieth century, sprung and slightly cockeyed, but by some miracle still standing.

A painful irony of Chancellor Robert R. Livingston's backwater existence was John Jay's spectacular progress in the mainstream—up Robert's own Hudson River. In 1795, while Jay was abroad negotiating the treaty with Great Britain, he was elected, *in absentia,* governor of New York, an office ardently coveted by his old friend, the Chancellor. Three years later the Republicans nominated Robert to run against Jay's second term. The political barometers all pointed to victory for the incumbent, and Robert R. Livingston, Jr., declined to put up a fight. Waging only the most perfunctory of campaigns, he lost by the largest majority in the state's history.

Robert professed complete indifference to the outcome, but his nonchalance is difficult to credit: he wanted the governorship badly and had always wanted it. The years of disappointment, of being passed over, of failing to achieve the public eminence he thought was his by right, had apparently taken their toll. It is understandable that he should undergo a crisis of confidence in his public self. And it is a measure of his character that he should refocus his energies and talents so fiercely and to such good effect in the private area.

The steamboat became his new passion. As a scientist he was enthralled with the conceptual possibilities of steam propulsion; as a gentleman of expensive tastes he warmed to its profit potential. In partnership with his brother-in-law, John Stevens, he built a prototype vessel in the North Bay near Tivoli and obtained a monopoly from the state of New York to operate steamboats on the Hudson. The prototype failed and the monopoly lapsed; but Robert's enthusiasm never flagged. His family and friends—who regarded steam propulsion in the same category as making paper from frog spit—thought he was crazy; and the more doggedly Robert persevered, the louder they laughed. For once, however, he seemed neither to hear nor care.

After the presidential election of 1800, in which Thomas Jefferson narrowly defeated Aaron Burr on the thirty-sixth ballot in the House of Representatives, Robert and the rest of the Clermont family were back in politics. Robert's youngest brother, Edward (who, as congressman from New York, had supported Jefferson consistently, if somewhat passively, throughout the balloting in the House), was appointed both federal district attorney for New York and mayor of New York City. His and Robert's brother-in-law, Thomas Tillotson, was appointed New York Secretary of State; another brother-in-law, Morgan Lewis, was made state chief justice; and a third, John Armstrong, was appointed United States senator. Their cousin, Henry Brockholst Livingston of The Locusts, was promised the first vacant seat on the state Supreme Court; and Robert R. Livingston, Jr., received the lushest plum of all: the post of American minister to France.

He and Polly, accompanied by both their daughters and sons-in-law (who also received official appointments) and an infant grandchild, set sail from New York in October of 1801. Within days of their arrival in Paris, Robert and the two young men were summoned by First Consul Napoleon Bonaparte to an official reception. Their dress for the occasion was in accordance with American republican standards: formal and elegant—they were, after all, Livingstons—but somewhat somber in contrast to the dazzling peacock display of the First Consul and his courtiers. Napoleon took note and, according to the observant Madame de Staël, "paid [Robert], through an interpreter, a number of compliments on the purity of morals in America, and added: 'The old world is very corrupt.' Then, turning to M. de Talleyrand he repeated twice: 'Explain to him that the old world is very corrupt. You know something about that, don't you?' "

Monsieur de Talleyrand's corruption probably didn't surprise Robert; but it certainly complicated and frustrated his pursuit of a primary diplomatic objective, the purchase by the United States Government of West Florida and the port of New Orleans. Months of negotiation only served to bog the enterprise down in bureaucratic red tape, Monsieur de Talleyrand's venality and the whims of the "Wary Corsican," as Janet Montgomery dubbed him. Robert complained, "Nothing is done here because it is right, because it is just, or because it is politick but because the Consul wills it"—and the Consul's will seemed to reverse itself every other day.

Even France itself—long the object of Robert's intense admiration—was something of a disappointment. After a few months of "intimate acquaintance with this people," Robert satisfied himself "that they never had the smallest idea of Liberty, at least in our sense of the word. I am also convinced that there was never a people better formed to do without it. 'I begin to think (says I yesterday to one of the Ministers) that Liberty was formed for the Americans & the arts & pleasure for you Europeans.' You are perfectly right says he, & I am sure we have no reason to complain of the partition."

At least one of his sons-in-law agreed with him: Margaret Maria's husband, writing home to announce the birth of a second daughter ("I cannot say much for her beauty *Spero meliora* being our motto"), expressed the opinion that the French must have received "from our maker . . . a blow on the head which cracked the brain—if this is true my next shall be born in America."

But Robert R. Livingston, Jr., refused to let his sojourn in Paris be spoiled, and he offset diplomatic frustration with three of his favorite pursuits: house adornment, agriculture and mechanics. He purchased an impressive array of furniture, chandeliers, porcelain and *objets d'art* for his mansion at Clermont; he made a study of the merino sheep, shipping home two rams and two ewes from the famous Rambouillet flock; and finally, to his eternal credit, he enlisted the services of a young American inventor, Robert Fulton, for the next round in his struggle to unlock the mysteries of steam propulsion.

Fulton, a handsome six-footer in his mid-thirties, was in Paris at the behest of the French government to build an experimental submarine in the Seine. He and Robert quickly discovered their mutual interests and decided to form a partnership. Robert, ignoring the fact that he already had a formal steamboat compact with his brother-in-law, John Stevens (he told neither Stevens nor Fulton about the other), wrote to another brother-in-law, New York Secretary of State Thomas Tillotson, requesting him to file an application for a new monopoly to operate steam vessels on the Hudson. "I fear you will laugh at me," he admitted, "but I give you leave to do so, provided you by no means neglect to execute it this session of the Legislature through some of my friends."

In the spring of 1803, Robert's diplomatic mission took a dramatic leap forward, after President Jefferson dispatched special envoy James Monroe to Paris in order to get the New Orleans purchase negotiations back on track. Robert barely had time to resent the intrusion: forty-eight hours after Monroe's arrival, Napoleon stunned the two Americans by offering to sell not only New Orleans but the whole of the Louisiana Territory, a tract of some 825,000 square miles, whose acquisition would double the size of the United States. Livingston and Monroe, with no instructions, took a deep breath and accepted, and the formal agreement was drafted and signed within a fortnight.

It was a diplomatic coup of major dimensions, a political jewel to fit nicely into Robert's well-earned crown—except that his cursed pride rose up and knocked it away. After all his months of patient toil behind the scenes, Robert felt upstaged by Monroe's dramatic entrance just before the dénouement—and so he altered the dates in his official record book to indicate that Napoleon had offered to sell Louisiana three days earlier than he actually did, the morning *before* Monroe's arrival in Paris. To drive the point home, he leaked a "secret" memorandum to the same effect to the New York press.

The government in Washington not only issued a vigorous denial, it published Robert's own official correspondence, which clearly revealed the true timetable. Robert's bungled lie cost him whatever credit he rightly deserved for the negotiation of the Louisiana Purchase, and it tarnished his reputation irreparably. It also cost him the New York governorship. A few weeks before, with George Clinton on the verge of resignation, the party had promised the accession to Robert. Now the offer was withdrawn, this time for good.

The public uproar was slow to die down; and Robert and his family lingered in Europe for a year and a half, long after the arrival of his replacement as minister to France—his brother-in-law, John Armstrong. Robert spent the winter in Italy with Margaret Maria and her husband, then made his leisurely way back to Paris to collect Polly and the grandchildren, and finally sailed for home in early summer of 1805. Once back at Clermont, it was easy for Robert to become embroiled in domestic details: his daughter Betsey was already ensconced with her husband and baby in his mother's former house; now Margaret Maria and her family, along with Polly and himself, had to be accommodated in the new mansion. The furniture and fittings from Europe arrived, and plans were drawn up for an enlarged greenhouse and a new ballroom. The merino sheep herd, now satisfactorily established, required attention and study. And there was always Robert Fulton and the steamboat.

Still, one would like to know how often his thoughts turned to the New York governorship, a post which he had fully expected to occupy by now, and to its new incumbent, a man of distinctly inferior intellect and attainments, his own brother-in-law, Morgan Lewis.

Robert R. Livingston, Jr.'s youngest brother, Edward, had also spent the winter of 1803–4 in voluntary exile, at the outer reaches of the civilized world, New Orleans.

Edward was Robert's physical opposite: where the older brother was endomorphic, plumpish, jowly and soft, his body at war with the long, pointed Livingston nose, Edward was all sharpness and angles, lean and erect, with the nose as hallmark looking quite at home. But the two were equal in elegance, erudition, eloquence—and ambition. Edward had financed his first political campaign by mortgaging his vast Hardenbergh acreage (a step he would later regret) and served three terms in Congress. After Thomas Jefferson's election as President in 1800 he received the two distinguished appointments of federal district attorney of New York and mayor of New York City.

From the outset, Edward's tenure in office was dogged by tragedy and mischance, beginning with the death of his young wife of "a malignant Sore Throat & Scarlet Fever" only days after his inauguration. Placing his three small children primarily in the care of his brother John (who was married to his late wife's sister), he threw himself into the duties of office, becoming one of the most progressive, popular and effective mayors the city has ever known.

But in June of 1803, during a routine audit of the accounts of the district attorney's office, a shortfall of almost $50,000 was discovered. The money had been embezzled—and lost—by one of Edward's clerks. Edward insisted on taking complete responsibility: he refused to prosecute the larcenous clerk and assumed the burden of repaying the government personally, out of his own pocket. Since his own private debts totaled nearly $200,000 at the time, this was a formidable undertaking. The terms of his indemnity to the government would obviously be crucial, and Edward set out for Washington to negotiate with the Treasury Department the timetable and rate of interest. But virtually on the eve of his arrival, his brother Robert R. Livingston's "secret" memorandum concerning the Louisiana Purchase appeared in the papers, followed by the government's devastating refutation. Edward arrived in Washington paralyzed and tongue-tied, impaled on his own chagrin. During his two-day sojourn in the capital he called on neither the President nor Treasury Secretary Albert Gallatin, and during a social evening at the Gallatin house he failed even to raise the subject of his indemnity.

Within days of his return to New York, yellow fever broke out in the city. Edward, who still served as mayor, submerged all personal and financial troubles in a sea of benefactions. Throughout the terrible weeks of the epidemic he traversed the city tirelessly, visiting the sick, setting up medical centers and arranging supplies. In September, Edward contracted yellow fever. But by the time cool weather came and the epidemic subsided he had recovered sufficiently to address himself to the United States Government's judgment against him in the amount of nearly $100,000.

With outstanding debts now in excess of a quarter of a million dollars, Edward realized that he could never free himself by clinging to a conventional political or legal career. So he took a flyer. Leaving his children in the care of John Livingston and his wife, and borrowing money from John for the trip, he set sail in December of 1803 for New Orleans, the new frontier —and, ironically, the subject of his brother's recent disgrace. He arrived in the city in January 1804, a complete stranger, armed with only a thousand dollars in cash and a somewhat subdued ambition.

Robert R. Livingston, Jr., far away in Paris, knew nothing of Edward's vicissitudes until February. His shock and disbelief were directed more at the solution than the problem: cautioning Edward, "You are not formed for the acquisition of fortune by speculation," he begged him to end his wild "excursion" to the back side of the moon. But Edward refused to be daunted; and in the tradition of his great-grandfather Robert, the first proprietor, trained his sights on the new world and the main chance.

Edward's personal wounds were soonest mended. Eighteen months after arriving in New Orleans, in June of 1805, he took to wife Louise D'Avezac de Castera Moreau de Lassy, a nineteen-year-old widow, daughter of a French planter, in flight from the Haitian insurrection in which two of her brothers had recently been massacred. Louise's fragile beauty belied her strength of character, and although she was less than half Edward's age she proved a sterling companion. Edward spent the first year of his marriage happily awaiting the birth of a child and teaching his bride to speak English.

But the same month as his marriage, Edward's financial doom was inadvertently sealed by the arrival in New Orleans of his old political associate, Aaron Burr, fresh from the scandal of his fatal duel with Alexander

Hamilton. Burr, still under suspicion for the alleged treason that had given occasion for the duel, was now shrouded in a miasma of rumor wherever he went; and his arrival set the New Orleans grapevine humming with speculation, all of it extravagant and some of it true. One gossip spoke of an unnamed foreign power which had paid half a million dollars to Burr and two fellow conspirators—the financier Samuel Swartwout, Burr's traveling companion; and the notoriously quirky, hotheaded General James Wilkinson, American military commander for Louisiana—to separate Louisiana and the American western provinces from the Union. Another rumor gave details of the size and disposition of an army being raised by the trio to invade Mexico and set Burr up as Emperor. All the speculation and innuendo, swirling around the heads of the actual conspirators, misted finely over the persons of their innocent acquaintance, including Edward Livingston.

That gentleman was thoroughly preoccupied elsewhere, with a new baby daughter and a scheme to make a financial killing at last—the latter in partnership with another recent arrival in New Orleans, none other than Pierre Delabigarre, the founder of Tivoli, New York, and champion of Hudson River frog spit. Edward and Delabigarre, investigating opportunities in New Orleans real estate, discovered that a sizable section of the city's Mississippi River frontage was without an owner. Known as the Batture, this natural landing, formed by the river's silting action, was put to constant use by the public, free of charge. Edward approached the families who owned the property immediately inland from the Batture and in October of 1805 filed claim to a section of the waterfront on behalf of one of them, the Gravier family. Identical suits were soon filed by the adjacent titleholders, and a major legal battle began to take shape between the private owners—with Edward as their champion—and the citizens of New Orleans.

At this juncture the city received the startling news that Aaron Burr had been captured on his way down the Ohio River with an army of sixty men in flatboats and was under arrest for treason. His erstwhile coconspirator, General James Wilkinson, had informed on Burr and now led the crying-out against his confederates. While the city throbbed with excitement, uncertainty and suspicion, Wilkinson imposed virtual martial law and instituted a policy of wholesale arrest and incarceration. Samuel Swartwout, among others, was scooped up in the net. Edward Livingston, appalled at Wilkinson's tactics, instituted a public campaign to obtain the prisoners' release, whereupon Wilkinson lashed out with a vicious lie: that Edward had been a party to the Burr conspiracy. It was utterly untrue; but in the manner of all public rumors, no matter how bizarre or mendacious, it stuck. Edward, already tarnished by the scandal of the New York district attorney's office embezzlement, and under a public cloud in New Orleans because of the Batture controversy, had to live with the stigma of Wilkinson's calumny which, in some circles, was never entirely discounted or forgotten.*

In May of 1807 the court awarded title to the Batture to the Gravier family and its adjacent neighbors. Edward Livingston promptly purchased from his former client—unquestionably by prearrangement—a large section of the Batture and announced plans for a private, commercial landing. The profit potential was enormous—but the people of New Orleans were furious. On the opening day of construction an angry mob battered down the fence that separated them from Edward's work crew and raged through the site, inflicting and sustaining considerable injury. They showed up the next day, and the next. Edward was in a terrible bind; but he could not back down, he had too much at stake. Only by realizing profits from the Batture could he begin to pay off his huge government debt—already, after only three years, hopelessly in arrears. But after weeks of disruption and injury at the work site, Louisiana Governor William Claiborne intervened. Sending in troops to separate the combatants, he ordered the case turned over to the federal government for judicial resolution.

Unluckily for Edward, President Jefferson decided to take a personal interest in the case as a means of punishing Edward for crimes past: his failure to speak out strongly enough in Jefferson's favor in the election of 1800; the embarrassment of the New York district attorney's office scandal; his brother's attempt to defraud the public concerning the Louisiana Purchase; and—no doubt weightiest of all—Edward's protracted friendship with the President's sworn enemy, Aaron Burr. Without even waiting for the judicial process to commence, Jefferson issued a peremptory executive order prohibiting any further construction on Edward's Batture property and thus spelled his financial ruin.† When Edward made the long and arduous trip to Washington to lodge a protest, the President refused to receive him; and he had to journey back to New Orleans, to Louise and baby Coralie, empty-handed.

The summer of Edward's Batture disaster, 1807, was a season of triumph for his brother, Robert R. Livingston, Jr. On August 18 the *North River Steam Boat* (later renamed the *Clermont)* set out from New York City for her maiden voyage upriver to Albany. An outlandish-looking craft—130 feet long, only 16 feet wide, with a 16-foot paddlewheel—she was the object of considerable jocularity on the part of the spectators who lined the dock in Manhattan that August morning. Confidently expecting first a good laugh and then a spectacular midriver explosion as the ship got up her first full head of steam, they were doomed to disappointment. Twenty-four

* Burr and Samuel Swartwout stood trial for treason but were acquitted for lack of evidence. Afterward, the two traveled together to England.
† Jefferson's gesture was unquestionably aimed at Edward personally; none of the other Batture property owners was so enjoined.

hours later Robert R. Livingston, Jr., watched his ship pull into the dock at Clermont for her only intermediate stop, and eight hours later she landed safely in Albany.

The *North River Steam Boat* was in business, to the delight of Robert Livingston and Robert Fulton. Quickly undertaking a regular schedule between New York and Albany, the ship was still slow to show a profit, and Fulton traveled to Washington to pursue government contracts for additional vessels: "The Next president is to be either Mr. Madison or General Clinton *god Willing* if War the General will have it—In either case Steam boats and Torpedoes will Succeed—Nil deperandum [sic]."

War or no war, the steamboat altered forever the quality of life in the Hudson Valley. Heretofore the pace of living and of commerce along the river had been dictated by the stately progress of the tall-masted, broadsailed Hudson River sloop, which took anywhere from a week to ten days (depending on tides, wind and weather) to complete the journey from Manhattan to Albany. Now the steamboat made the same trip in little more than twenty-four hours. But with the passing of the sloop's lofty grace and silence there vanished also much of the mellowness and tranquillity of river life. Robert R. Livingston did not perhaps foresee this as he drew plans for a fleet of bigger and better steamboats. The mechanical monsters, roaring and belching their way upriver and down, transporting greater numbers of passengers, goods and produce, would undoubtedly bring prosperity to the valley—together with noise, disruption and a sense of hurry. Robert, who thirsted so for the quiet, contemplative life of Clermont, became inadvertently one of the instruments of its destruction.

Robert was sixty years old the summer of the *North River Steam Boat.* Ironically—in a life beset with irony—his triumph with the steamboat brought little more than vexation to the remaining six years of his life, and it poisoned the legacy he left behind. This did not happen by accident; it happened because Robert's behavior toward the steamboat company he founded with Robert Fulton was just as ambivalent and equivocal as his behavior had always been toward the things he cared about. Shortly after the company started operating commercially Livingston fell behind in his financial obligations and began to play pecuniary cat and mouse with Robert Fulton. He also kept his heirs completely in the dark about the partnership arrangements and made no provision in his will for the disposition of his steamboat shares.

Robert found himself in the middle of a quarrel between his brother John and Fulton, after John bought into the company. He was also called on to mediate on behalf of Fulton's wife, Harriet née Livingston, the daughter of Walter Livingston of Teviotdale and therefore Robert's cousin. Harriet complained to Robert that her husband had sold some of her steamboat shares without her knowledge and that, since Robert was "involved in the horrible sin against a defenseless woman, I must appeal to you for justice."

There was an additional fly in the ointment, as Robert learned from steamboat Captain Andrew Bartholomew during the summer of 1811: "With respect to Bugs . . . we have taken all the Beding out and scalded the bottoms this we have found to keep them down the best but the Boat is full and I do not believe they can be got rid of without burning the Boat to Ashes."

Robert typically detached himself from all of it, focusing his attention instead on his library, his hunting, his horses, his estate and his latest intellectual passion: *Ovis aries,* otherwise known as the domestic sheep. After long labor he brought forth in 1809 his "Essay on Sheep," a 186-page treatise on the housing, feeding, birthing, doctoring and shearing of the species, together with its history, variety and civilizing effects on the human race: "That we are not at this moment fierce, savage, and brutal, little superior to the beasts that roam in the wilderness . . . is probably owing to the domestication of granivorous animals, and first of all, to that of the sheep." He sent a copy of the book to his old colleague, Thomas Jefferson, now retired from public life, and received a cordial if ruminative note of thanks: "Being a farmer myself I write to you as a farmer, leaving politics to those who are not worn down by them. I reduce myself to the reading 3 or 4 newspapers a week only and shall soon I believe give up them also. I mark with a white bean the days on which I hear from my old friends and shall always be happy to learn from yourself particularly that you enjoy health and quiet with all the comforts which can cheer the evening of our days."

Within six months of receiving the letter, Robert R. Livingston was bedridden, suffering the effects both of apoplexy and of the prescribed treatments, which included bleeding, purging and sweating. He was mercifully taken on February 25, 1813. According to his sister, he murmured, just before the end, "I have always shared what I had with my friends, there is one thing that I wish I could share." On being asked what that was, he declared, with his last breath, "The peace that I feel."

One hopes that he meant it: that at the end all the old frustrations, disappointments, mistakes and mortifications faded from mind, leaving only the glow of his very real accomplishments. Robert R. Livingston, Jr., had failed to achieve the eminence he expected because his own profound ambivalence had rendered him unreliable. Had he been born into a time of peace and to a society with stable institutions and social structure, perhaps Robert the politician, Robert the scholar, Robert the man of fashion and Robert the farmer would have blended together harmoniously. Instead he was born into a family whose aristocratic appurtenances were scarcely in place when a democratic revolution swept away the props on which they rested. Robert's inbred sense of disdain for those who were socially, intellectually and financially his inferiors made it impossible for him to serve in political harness with democratically elected politicians from the middle and lower classes. Lacking the Jeffersonian faith in the virtue and wisdom of the common people, Robert was utterly unable to reconcile his patrician instincts with the new democracy. His admirable qualities—erudition, cultivation, breadth of vision, and a taste for public service—had not earned him the crown he sought. His ambition had festered on the farm. But perhaps at the end his thoughts dwelt instead on his fellowship with William Strickland, on the "Essay on Sheep," on Clermont, his library, his sleek horses, and his faithful Polly.

23

The cordiality between Robert R. Livingston and Thomas Jefferson was remarkable considering the bitter hostility that flourished simultaneously between Robert's brother Edward and the former President. Thanks to Jefferson's exertions, Edward's New Orleans Batture property still lay idle and abandoned after five long and fruitless years. It is not surprising that the war of words between the two grew less restrained as the years went by; or that when Jefferson, in a public pamphlet defending his actions in the Batture case, made use of the pronoun "We" to refer to himself, Edward's rejoinder displayed a certain demonic glee:

"As I do not suppose a republican magistrate could assume the ridiculous expression of royalty . . . I must suppose that he had fallen into it by reflecting on the various capacities in which he was thus [acting in the Batture controversy]. . . . As *legislator*, he was to make a new law to fit the circumstances of the case; as *judge*, he was to apply it to those facts, which, as a *juror*, he was to ascertain, and to pronounce that sentence, which, as *executive officer*, he was himself to carry into effect; as *President*, he was to reclaim the lands of the United States; as *Commander-in-Chief* of the armies, a sufficient military force was to be prepared to overawe opposition; as *Mayor* of the city of New Orleans, he was to enforce its rights against the decrees of the court; as *high constable*, he was to abate nuisances, and as *street commissioner* to remove the putrefying mass that threatened the health of the city. We ought not to be astonished that an officer who thought himself obliged to act in all these capacities should speak as if he were more than one, nor that, having in this instance invested himself with all the characteristics of despotism, he should have assumed its style."

The War of 1812 placed the dispute temporarily on the shelf. During the Battle of New Orleans (which was fought, ironically, two weeks after peace had been officially declared), Edward Livingston served as trusted courier and adviser to the hero of the day, Andrew Jackson. Edward and General Jackson had first become political allies eighteen years earlier in Washington, D.C., during their terms in the House of Representatives. Now, standing shoulder to shoulder on the barricades at New Orleans, their mutual respect and amity were revived and enhanced.

The War of 1812 inflicted disgrace and exile on one of Edward's kinsmen: his brother-in-law, Secretary of War John Armstrong. In August of 1814, when British troops easily broke through the American lines at Bladensburgh, Maryland, and marched on a virtually defenseless Washington, D.C., all of capital officialdom fled (including First Lady Dolley Madison, who managed to remove many of the portraits and other valuables from the President's house before taking to her heels). The British burned Mrs. Madison's residence, the Capitol, and a number of other public buildings before withdrawing.

Secretary of War Armstrong, whose reputation for vanity, arrogance and indolence made him the perfect sacrificial lamb, was blamed entirely for his country's humiliation. "His effigy was drawn on the walls of the Capitol after its conflagration, [and] suspended from a gallows with the superscription of 'Armstrong the Traitor.' " The debacle may well have cost Armstrong the presidency, an office to which he had come to aspire, with some justification.

Like many of his Livingston relatives, both before and since, Armstrong retreated with his battered pride to the Hudson Valley, where he faced the pleasing prospect of elegant retirement in the new mansion which he and Alida were building on their land just south of her brother John's Massena. It was the third Hudson Valley mansion constructed by General Armstrong—a record in the family—and he fervently trusted that it would be the envy of all.

The Armstrongs' new dwelling brought to a total of eleven the number of mansions built along the river by the children of Margaret Beekman Livingston and Judge Robert R. Livingston. Of the eleven—which stretched south from Clermont twelve miles to the Staatsburgh establishment of Gertrude and Morgan Lewis—eight were still owned within the immediate family. Next to Staatsburgh on the north stood the Tillotsons' Linwood, followed by Catherine and Freeborn Garrettsons' Wildercliff. Slightly inland, Grasmere, built by the oldest of the sisters, Janet Montgomery, was now occupied by another sister, Joanna (who was married to their cousin, Peter R. Livingston). Nearby, the Morgan Lewises' daughter Margaret and her husband Maturin Livingston (another cousin) had commissioned the architect Benjamin Latrobe to design their elegant Ellerslie. Three miles farther north came the Armstrongs' new mansion, La Bergerie; and completing the chain were John's Massena, Janet's magnificent Château de Montgomery, and finally Clermont, whose two houses were now occupied by the daughters of the late Robert R. Livingston, Jr., and their Livingston husbands.

Janet Montgomery, the eldest of the siblings, turned seventy the year her brother, the Chancellor, died. She lived alone at the Château, her young Ranelagh kinsman having come to a mysterious end one dark night after hearing the banshee wail under his window three times. (Janet later told a timid visitor who hesitated to sleep in Ranelagh's room, "What are you afraid of, child? You are a Yankee; the Banshee will not come after you. Jones was an Irishman.") Widowed for almost forty years, she lived on the memory of her brief, long-ago happiness with Richard Montgomery. Janet fervently wished before she died to see her husband's remains brought home from Canada, "redeem[ed] . . . from a Public Gateway in a Strange land," and in 1818 her efforts to that end were requited. General Montgomery's ashes were disinterred at Quebec and, with Janet's nephew, twenty-year-old Lewis Livingston (Edward's son by his first wife), as official escort, ceremoniously transported overland to Albany, where they lay in state at the New York State Capitol for several days. On July 6, 1818, the ashes were placed aboard the steamboat *Richmond* for the last leg of their journey down the Hudson to a final resting place at St. Paul's Church, New York.

On that summer day all eyes at Château de Montgomery were glued to the parlor windows overlooking the river. As the *Richmond* came into view Janet, requesting her family and friends to remain inside, stepped alone onto the veranda. Everyone stood silent as the *Richmond* halted opposite the house. A salute was fired from the deck, and the strains of a dirge wafted across the water to the listeners on shore. At length, as the boat resumed its stately progress downriver, Janet's companions emerged from the house to discover her stretched on the terrace in a dead faint.

Three years later young Lewis Livingston—the last surviving child of Edward's early marriage—died during a sea voyage. His heartbroken father was at the time engaged in a return to public life. Edward had become a member of the Louisiana state legislature and, at its behest, was embarked on an extensive revision of the Louisiana Penal Codes—a massive undertaking which was interrupted in 1822 by his election to the United States House of Representatives. Edward, his manuscript and family all removed from New Orleans to Washington, where Louise became a famous hostess, their sixteen-year-old daughter Coralie blossomed into a belle, and "Beau Ned"—back in his element—became the philosopher of the House and wit of the drawing room. He even managed to forge a somewhat tenuous reconciliation with ex-President Jefferson; and the following year partial title to the Batture was granted, enabling him at last to begin paying off his debt to the government, now twenty years in arrears. (He still never made a payment on time.)*

Louisiana was much too far to travel during adjournments of the House, so Edward and his family found themselves spending much of their time with his sister Janet at Château de Montgomery. Despite a twenty-one-year difference in their ages, Janet and Edward were very much alike; both were tough-minded, intelligent and profoundly ambitious. With their brother Robert gone, they stood intellectually alone among their siblings. Edward, Louise and Coralie soon became intimates at the Château, and Edward became Janet's heir.

The year 1824 witnessed the return visit of General Lafayette, the dashing French hero of the American Revolution, to the scenes of his youthful glory. Lafayette's five-day progress up the Hudson River in September, during which he visited no fewer than three Livingston family seats, was an occasion of universal celebration. Mile after mile, the Hudson shore was lined with cheering throngs, among whom stood many aged veterans who had fought at the general's side nearly half a century before.

On the second day of the journey, after lunch at the Staatsburgh house of Governor and Mrs. Morgan Lewis, Lafayette's "steamer was approaching Esopus," an eyewitness recounted, "[when] I observed a small boat pulling out from the west shore with a signal. . . . It proved to be a skiff, with an old gentleman seated in the stern, with his bandana handkerchief fastened to his cane as a signal. As we approached the skiff, the commodore remarked, 'I know him,' and then directed the steamer to be stopped, and the steps lowered. The commodore received the old gentleman, and walked with him to the promenade deck, where General Lafayette, surrounded by old comrades, was seated. No word was spoken. As we approached . . . General Lafayette rose, as did the other officers, but still no word was spoken. The stranger offered both his hands, which the general received, and each looked the other steadily in the face. It was evident that General Lafayette was taxing his memory severely, and, after a profound silence of more than a minute, the general exclaimed, 'My old friend, Colonel Harry Livingston!' and then, after a few words of mutual congratulation, he added, 'Do you remember when I reviewed your regiment of infantry on Rhode Island?' "

Henry Beekman Livingston, seventy-four years old, no doubt did remember that scene from a happier time. Nothing in his intervening life had touched it. Estranged from wife, child, sisters and brothers, he emerged like a wraith to greet his old comrade in arms and then disappeared the way he

* Jefferson died four years later on July 4, 1826, the fiftieth anniversary of the Declaration of Independence. Within hours of his death his ardent friend and political rival, John Adams, also died.

had come—as the *James Kent,* carrying Lafayette and his festive party, continued upriver to another brilliant reception at the place of Colonel Harry's birth, Clermont, a reception to which Henry Beekman Livingston had clearly not been invited.

"Before the boat arrived at the [Clermont] dock, it was discovered that the groves were literally alive with people. . . . But while the rocks and glens, and even trees to their topmost branches, presented this animated spectacle, the General, his suite, and friends, were still more surprised by the appearance upon the lawn of this romantic and secluded place, of a regiment of well-disciplined troops, drawn up to receive him. There were several vessels at anchor in the stream, one of which (a large sloop) was decorated with flags, and a streamer floated from her mast, with the motto of 'Welcome Lafayette,' in large letters. On landing, a salute was fired from this vessel, which was unexpectedly returned from a field piece planted in a thick copse of trees upon the shore."

Lafayette reviewed the troops, "by whom he was honoured with a *feu de joie,*" and greeted the assembled dignitaries who included, in addition to multitudinous Livingstons and their friends, "a long procession of the ancient and honourable fraternity of Freemasons, consisting of a Chapter of Royal Arch Masons, the members of 'Widow's Son Lodge,' of Redhook" (their leader, Palmer Cook, Esq., delivered the general "an appropriate address") and the mayor of Hudson, who was accompanied by the town band.

In the evening, Chancellor Livingston's mansion—now presided over by his daughter and son-in-law, Mr. and Mrs. Robert L. Livingston—was "brilliantly lit up, and an elegant ball was given in honour of the General's company. . . . A sumptuous supper was served up in a style of magnificence rarely, if ever equalled in this country. The room selected for this part of the *fête,* was an extensive Greenhouse, or Orangery . . . the tables . . . were spread beneath a large grove of Orange and Lemon trees, with bending branches of fruit, and many other species of exotic shrubs and plants. . . . The beholder stood gazing, as if bound by the wizard spell of the Magician. The night was dark and rainy; but this contributed to the general effect of the *fête,* inasmuch as the darkness heightened the effect of the thousand lamps by which the surrounding groves were illuminated."

At ten o'clock, after the fireworks, General Lafayette returned to his stateroom aboard the *James Kent,* and next morning proceeded to Albany. Three days later, on the return journey downriver, he stopped at Château de Montgomery for lunch with Janet and the Edward Livingstons.

After the festivities Edward and his family also traveled to New York, where he was on the verge of completing his "four codes of crimes & punishment, of criminal procedure, of Prison discipline, & of Evidence" for the state of Louisiana. Shortly after midnight on November 17 he penned the final words of his tome and retired to bed. During the night, fire broke out in his writing room and the manuscript was consumed, "except about fifty or sixty pages which were at the printer's." Edward's distress was tempered by his habitual fortitude: ". . . instead of repining, [I] work all night & correct the [proofs] all day to repair the loss & get the work ready by the time I had promised it to the Legislature." He presented to the Louisiana lawmakers—on time—a code of such clarity, liberality and enlightened humanity that it was rejected at once: no slaveholding society could reasonably be expected to give individual rights precedence over property rights. The codes received wide acclaim elsewhere, however: Jeremy Bentham praised them and entered into a protracted correspondence with Edward; the government of Guatemala adopted portions of them; and the King of the Netherlands awarded Edward a gold medal—after which the Louisiana legislature, belatedly and somewhat grudgingly, vouchsafed him a medal, too.

(Another Livingston author barely beat Edward into the public print, if the Poughkeepsie branch of the family is to be believed. On December 23, 1823, the Troy (N.Y.) *Sentinel* published anonymously a seasonal poem which began:

> 'Twas the night before Christmas,
> And all through the house . . .

Authorship was attributed to—and claimed by—Clement Moore, a professor of Greek literature at a New York theological seminary; but the Poughkeepsie Livingstons, producing an array of circumstantial evidence, claimed authorship for their paterfamilias, Major Henry Livingston, Jr. Mr. Moore's turgid and stilted poetic style clearly was not as close as Major Livingston's to the style of the contested opus; furthermore, he had acquired a reputation for literary light-fingeredness. But in this case nothing could be proved, and Moore's name remains on the poem and in the grateful prayers of millions of American children—all those whose last name is not Livingston and who do not come from Poughkeepsie.)

In 1828, Edward Livingston, by declining to return to Louisiana to campaign for reelection, lost his seat in the House of Representatives, whereupon the Louisiana legislature appointed him instead to the Senate. Janet Montgomery died a few months later, and Edward inherited Montgomery Place (as the Château was coming to be known). Louise Livingston became very attached to the estate and often remained there while her husband traveled to Washington for sessions of the Senate. Edward's marriage, like that of his father and mother, remained extremely affectionate after a quarter of a century. He and Louise wrote each other every day when separated; and one evening in Washington, Edward, having "finished my solitary ride" and entering "my more solitary chamber," spied on the desk one of Louise's gloves. "I surely did not want anything to remind me of you, yet this little circumstance has brought tears to my eyes! Is it folly? Romance it cannot be at my age. No, dear Louise! they are tears of the tenderest affection that I am obliged to stop and wipe off, that I may see to write to you."

In 1831 Edward was appointed by his old friend, President Andrew Jackson, to "the second place in the United States, some say the first . . . the place filled by Jefferson, Madison, and Monroe, and by him who filled it before any of them, my brother." Fifty years before, Robert R. Livingston, Jr., had accepted the honor of becoming his country's first Secretary for Foreign Affairs with considerable qualms and hesitancy. Edward, too, had grounds for wishing to refuse the office of Secretary of State—particularly now that he owned Montgomery Place. Edward felt the strong pull of life on the river; but, unlike his brother, he knew that true fulfillment lay else-where: "Here I am," he wrote Louise from Washington, "and here I have been for a month. I now know what it is, am I happier than I was? The question is not easily answered; had the bait never been thrown in my way; had I been suffered to finished the [tree] graft I had begun . . . had I been permitted to stay and watch its growth until the fall; to wander all the summer through the walks you had planned . . . now and then to plan a pic-nic, or plague myself in the vain attempt to catch a trout . . . could I have passed my summer thus, and taken my independent seat in the Senate in the winter, I could then have answered the question readily. But the temptation was thrown my way; the prize for which so many were contend-ing was offered to me; . . . :ʳ I had rejected it I think it would have been a source of regret that would have made me undervalue the real enjoyments for which I refused it—such is human nature."

Two years later Edward was invited to step into still another pair of his older brother's shoes: in 1833, at the age of sixty-nine, he accepted the post of minister to France. His new son-in-law, Thomas Barton (a straitlaced, antisocial Philadelphia Quaker, who refused to attend church with Coralie because there were candles on the altar), was appointed secretary to the legation, so the whole family—Edward, Louise, Coralie and Barton—sailed to Paris. Edward remained two years, just long enough to accomplish his primary mission of exacting French reparations for American property losses during the French Revolution. On his return he was widely lionized as a grand brahmin of American politics. It was a role in which he delighted; for, unlike his brother Robert, Edward was intellectually enraptured with the idea of democracy, and his single-minded faith in the goodness and intelli-gence of the human race bore him aloft:

"No! republics are not ungrateful! The charge is made by the sordid and the vain, who think nothing valuable but gold, nothing honorable but titles, and that gaudy ribbons are the proper recompense for merit. No, Gentlemen, republics are not ungrateful, but they are judicious in their choice of rewards. They do not give hereditary honors to virtue and wis-dom, which may descend to folly and vice. They do not wring its earnings from the hard hand of labor, that they may be poured out in pensions on the idle and unworthy. They do not decorate with stars and spangled garters, with ribbons and crosses and gewgaws, men who, if they have done anything that may seem to have deserved these childish toys, may afterwards prove unworthy of the decoration. But they give a nobler, a higher recompense for services,—they give their confidence; and the seal of their approbation is a prouder distinction than any that dangles from the button-hole, or is embroidered on the breast of the titled courtier; and I feel myself more honored as well as gratified by the applauding voice of my fellow-citizens, by the grasp of their friendly hands, some of them hard with honest labor, by their countenances, beaming with the fire of patriotism,—infinitely more honored, than I could be by any titular appendage to my name that a monarch could bestow."

Edward was no less patrician than his brother Robert: he did not expect to actually grasp many of those hands so "hard with honest labor." But when called upon to do so, he did not flinch. Edward had gone searching in the new America for El Dorado—a quest his brother could neither understand nor undertake—and it had panned out. But he could not pass it on. When Edward died, very suddenly, at Montgomery Place on May 23, 1836, a one-hundred-and-fifty-year cycle of Livingston family public leadership came abruptly to an end. For four generations the family had served; often from compulsion, but always with commendable devotion and courage. Edward was the first in that long line to *choose* public service, rather than having it forced on him as a matter of family survival; and he was also virtually the last.

Twelve years before Edward's death the Hudson Valley, having turned out the previous autumn to drink a toast to General Lafayette and America's glorious past, raised another glass in celebration of the future. On the morning of October 26, 1825, a flotilla of steamboats, led by the *Chancellor Livingston,* assembled at Buffalo on Lake Erie for the inaugural passage through the newly constructed Erie Canal. After pausing in Albany a few days later for overnight festivities, the fleet turned south for its final passage down the Hudson River to New York City. The cortege, which included the *Seneca Chief,* the *Constitution, Lion of the West, Olive Branch* and *Chief Justice Marshall,* decked with flags and streamers, was greeted by cheering crowds which lined the Hudson shore for a hundred and fifty miles. The squadron traveled through the night, with lanterns outlining its decks and rockets fired astern to mark progress, while bonfires flared ashore and all the river mansions showed their lights. Next morning New York Harbor gave the flotilla an all-out welcome. The Erie Canal was in business—and the American Midwest was suddenly in New York's lap.

It was the second major transportation revolution in the Hudson Valley in less than twenty years; and, like the steamboat, it would change profoundly the lives of the valley celebrants. Until now, wheat had been the

Hudson Valley's principal commodity; Livingston Manor alone operated eleven gristmills. But the relatively modest acreage of the valley could not compete with the vast wheatfields of the Midwest,† and within twenty years most of the valley mills would be defunct. Hudson Valley landlords and farmers had to adapt themselves and their acres to unfamiliar uses: the dairy, the sheepfold and the orchard. It would be a slow and painful process.

For the Livingston clan, these economic consequences of the nascent Industrial Revolution were less traumatic than its political and social effects. As in the aftermath of the recent democratic revolution, the family's manorial mentality seemed to inhibit its ability to adapt to changing times. After Edward's death, with the emergence of a new set of economic and social rules, the Livingston public spirit seemed to recoil. It turned inward, narrowed its focus, lowered its sights. New preoccupations replaced the family tradition of public service: bluebloodedness, exclusivity and money. One notion did survive from the past: the notion of The Family—a more rarefied notion than the practical version espoused by the original Robert and Alida, but still its legitimate offspring.

What did not survive, however, was the seigneurial basis on which the notion of Family rested—thanks once again to those "pests of society," the tenants of Livingston Manor.

† The canal cut the Buffalo–New York City freight rate from $100 to $5.00 a ton, and the transit time from twenty days to eight.

PART SIX

1808 – 1916

"PESTS OF SOCIETY"

24

The latest round of tenant troubles had begun in 1808 (the year after the maiden voyage of the *North River Steam Boat)*, when the proprietor of the old Hardenbergh Patent on the Hudson's west bank, Gerard ("Gross") Hardenbergh, took the unprecedented step of evicting a few of his tenants for nonpayment of rent—and was promptly murdered. The Hardenbergh heirs quickly came to terms with their tenants and the trouble subsided. The Livingston proprietors across the river were apparently unruffled by this unexpected bolt of lightning from the small black cloud that had always lurked on their horizon. The Tillotsons and Lewises, Garrettsons and Armstrongs, Robert R. Livingston, Jr., of Clermont, John Livingston of Oak Hill and Henry Walter Livingston of The Hill, snug and comfortable in their estate, continued to look westward at the end of every day to admire without a qualm the brilliant setting of the sun behind the dark mass of the distant Catskills.

But a few years later, in 1811, Mrs. Henry Walter Livingston, whose husband had died the year before, leaving her to manage The Hill and raise their seven young children alone, was presented with a formal petition challenging her title to the estate. The petition contended that the original 1686 title to the whole of Livingston Manor was fraudulent—Robert the Founder's real estate shenanigans come again to haunt his descendants—and requested that the portion of it referring to The Hill be vacated. This petition was not signed with X's and delivered by a delegation of sheepish tenants tugging at their forelocks; this time the tenants had hired lawyers to draw their document and to submit it, *pro forma*, to the state of New York for judicial review.

But Mrs. Henry Walter Livingston was not to be cowed. Mastering her grief over the recent "dreadfull event which deprived me of my Friend, my Protector, my Guide—which left me for the first time in my life to my own direction, & which presented [me] unto my own view as a Child unable from weakness to go alone," she hired lawyers of her own, filed counter-suits against her tenantry and got in touch with her friends in high places. (Little wonder that Mrs. Henry Walter has come down in family lore as "Lady Mary." Livingston men have always had a weakness for strong-minded women.)

There was an additional new factor in the equation: the tenants now had friends in high places, too, state politicians whom Lady Mary scorned as "Emmet the irish renegade and Van Buren* a Hudson Democrat." When the tenants "published a violent advertisement, accusing the Owners of the Manor of fraud, falsehood, treachery and every crime which can be mentioned," Lady Mary instituted ejectment proceedings against the ringleaders. Meanwhile, however, she predicted correctly that "the hopes of the tenants [will be kept alive] till the election is over and induce them to vote for their friends the Democrats. . . . They threaten violently and the terms 'Murder and Bloodshed' are frequently made use of among them."

This was more than idle rhetoric: on July 3, 1812, The Hill was set afire by a band of tenants using "some chemical preparation." Lady Mary managed to save her family, her furniture and portraits, and even the main body of the house. Learning later that the perpetrators had planned "to guard the doors, and consume my Children and myself," she was nevertheless relieved that the death sentence was not imposed, declaring, ". . . had they been hung I should have been much shocked."

The following year, as her countrymen fought the War of 1812 against Great Britain, Lady Mary Livingston stood her ground in a courtroom in the town of Hudson presided over by her good friend, Judge Van Ness, a man of unambiguous sympathies who felt "the strongest indignation . . . [against] the ringleaders in this impious enterprise." As the trial neared its end the judge's tone became increasingly apocalyptic—". . . the moment of virtuous exultation is fast approaching!—Glory to God!"—and in his charge to the jury he identified "any man" who challenged the title of Livingston Manor "as a rebel against his Country & its Government." The jury discerned its duty clearly and ruled in Lady Mary's favor without ever leaving the courtroom. The tenants of Livingston Manor subsided once again—but only to regroup and await their own moment of virtuous exultation.

* Martin Van Buren, later President of the United States.

This penultimate round in the tenant wars coincided with the death in 1813 of Chancellor Robert R. Livingston. Between that time and the death of the Chancellor's brother Edward in 1836, the Livingston family's inexorable withdrawal from the public arena—so vividly dramatized in Robert's own career—accelerated. A refocusing of energies began to occur, and a new set of family preoccupations appeared. One was an infatuation with the past, specifically with the noble Scottish ancestry of the American Livingston family.

It may be remembered that the first genealogy written by an American Livingston—the 1769 opus of Peter Van Brugh Livingston—referred only in passing to the family's aristocratic Scottish forebears. Half a century later Peter Van Brugh's grandson and namesake, on a Grand Tour of Europe, fell head over heels in love with his own pedigree.

For three intoxicating years, between 1816 and 1819, this elegant young man toured the capitals, viewed the sights and waltzed with the royal princesses of France, England, Italy, Poland, Russia and Austria. He was introduced to Madame de Staël, the Duke of Wellington and Sir Walter Scott and was painted (twice) by Raeburn. But the high point of his trip was a visit to the ruins of the Livingston castle near Callendar in Scotland, where "the pensive eye imperceptibly moistened with the tear of gloomy sensibility, while my bosom heaved with many a sigh, at the sad contrast of the present with that of former days."

He looked up Sir Thomas Livingston, "the only connection of our family in this country, and the nearest male representative of the noble houses of Linlithgow and Callendar." (Sir Thomas' direct ancestor had had the good luck to be out of the country in 1715, so Sir Thomas himself still resided on a portion of the original Linlithgow estate.) Evening after evening, the Scotsman and his American cousin pored over the family genealogical charts, the older man pointing out "the precise ancestor from which the Livingstons of New York are descended, and also the degree of relationship in which they stand allied to him." They visited the old family castle of Linlithgow, "purchased a few years since, by a person of obscure birth, but who by some happy accident of fortune suddenly rose to great wealth and affluence." The obscure person's cordial wife took Van Brugh on a tour, after which he and Sir Thomas spent the journey home musing "in a tone of unusually interesting melancholy." Van Brugh's deepest surges of emotion were reserved for Sir Thomas himself, who, with unfailing condescension, "always drank, at dinner, the health of 'our relations and friends on the other side of the water.'"

At that very moment the "relations on the other side of the water" were shoring up the fortunes of the family of Livingston in a manner of which Sir Thomas would probably not have approved. On May 20, 1818, General John and Alida Livingston Armstrong's daughter, Margaret Rebecca—a great-great-great-great-great-great-great-granddaughter of Alexander, Fifth Lord Livingston of Callendar—was married at her parents' Hudson River mansion to William Backhouse Astor, the grandson of a German butcher.

Astor's father, John Jacob, had landed in New York from Waldorf, Germany, in the spring of 1784, only months after the city was freed from British wartime occupation. Astor was launched by his American wife into the fur trade, where he made his first fortune. His second came from the China trade, his third from New York City real estate, which he entered in 1789 by buying two lots on Bowery Lane. He later revealed the secret of his success in real estate: "Buy de acre, sell de lot"; adding somewhat wistfully, "If I had only known, I'd have bought de whole island."

John Jacob, who turned fifty-five the year of his son's marriage, was not so overwhelmed by the alliance with the elegant Hudson River Livingstons that he lost his head. Before the wedding took place the nineteen-year-old Miss Armstrong was required to sign a waiver of dower rights to the Astor fortune in exchange for a lump sum made over to her personally. It was John Jacob's own idea, and he liked it so well he imposed it on subsequent Astor brides and grooms through several generations.

The new Mrs. Astor—whose doting husband called her "Peachy"—was a devotee of the Gothic novel, so her first daughter, born the following year, was named Emily, after the heroine in Mrs. Radcliffe's *Mysteries of Udolpho*. Peachy also persuaded her father to change the name of his Hudson Valley estate—formerly La Bergerie—to Rokeby, after the Sir Walter Scott poem of that name, in which is described a mysterious and romantic river gorge that reminded her of the wooded ravine at La Bergerie:

> The cliffs, that rear the haughty head
> High o'er the river's darksome bed,
> Were now all naked, wild, and grey,
> Now waving all with greenwood spray;
> Here trees to every crevice clung,
> And o'er the dell their branches hung;
> And there, all splintered and uneven,
> The shivered rocks ascend to heaven.

Unfortunately for Mrs. Astor's Gothic sensibilities, Scott's river was named the Greta, while Rokeby's was the Mudderkill.

Preoccupation with the past was only one token of the spirit of insularity that began to permeate the early nineteenth-century Livingstons. Another was the increasing incidence of family intermarriage, which reached epidemic proportions during this period. Unfortunately the attempt to cement family ties by dynastic marriage usually failed: in spite of it (or perhaps because of it), cracks in the Livingston family solidarity, like the cracks in

Clermont's dining-room ceiling, widened and spread and became increasingly apparent to the naked eye. In response, the family developed a new set of strategies for living with them—partly cosmetic, partly dismissive. The cracks were patched and painted over; but never was the plaster removed, the beams laid bare, the damage assessed and repaired.

Even Clermont, Margaret Beekman Livingston's "house of peace and love," became a warring camp in opposition to its immediate neighbor across the lawn, Chancellor Robert R. Livingston, Jr.'s elegant H-shaped villa.

Property divisions are never easy, particularly when the beneficiaries take up residence afterward, cheek by jowl, each on his own appointed legacy. The Chancellor's will had divided Clermont between his two daughters and their husbands (both cousins from the manor who bore the surname Livingston): Betsey and Edward P. Livingston inherited the main house, Margaret Maria and Robert L. Livingston the Chancellor's newer mansion.† The two men, whose antithetical personalities would have kept them apart in any case, soon found plenty of occasion for open conflict.

Their principal battle was waged over the North River Steam Boat Company. Within months of the Chancellor's death, Edward P. and Robert L. Livingston were quarreling with Robert Fulton—whom they accused of "rancor and malignity, of false propositions & indelicate conclusions"—and then with each other. After the death of the Chancellor's widow Polly (which occurred, in typically ··nassuming fashion, little more than a year after her husband's demise), the rancor and malignity began to attack Clermont itself, and in 1820 the controversy went public when Edward P., in the name of the shareholders of the North River Steam Boat Company, sued Robert L. Livingston, its president, over company management policies.

It is little wonder that Robert L. Livingston was not a successful president. Only a financial wizard could have unsnarled the tangled finances of the North River Steam Boat Company—and Robert L. Livingston was no financial wizard. On the contrary, he was an amiable, easygoing gentleman of cultivated tastes and sensibilities who was very compatible with his wife, Margaret Maria, and with her conceived not only a flock of heirs but a number of pleasant and civilized ways of spending their mutual fortune, including their favorite pastime, European travel.

Margaret Maria's untimely death in 1818 at the age of thirty-five left her husband with eight children, the youngest only four months old. Robert L. shouldered his burden with considerable grace, becoming an attentive

† Edward P. had been born in Jamaica, to which his father, Philip Philip Livingston, had emigrated before the War of Independence. Robert L. was a son of Walter Livingston of Teviotdale. This made Robert L. and Edward P. second cousins to each other, as well as third cousins to their wives. In addition, one of Edward P.'s brothers, Philip Henry Livingston, was married to Robert L.'s sister Maria.

and indulgent father who turned his back on transatlantic travel for the quieter pleasures of the Chancellor's extensive library. But Robert L. had no more talent for proprietorship than he had for finance; and as he pored over his leather-bound volumes of Plutarch, the Chancellor's elegant villa began, slowly but surely, to slide into disrepair.

To the north, at the other end of the acacia *allée,* Margaret Maria's sister Betsey and her husband, Edward P. Livingston, lived in the parent house at Clermont. Both husband and wife had a very Livingston look: widely spaced eyes, straight brows, a long neck and the disastrously prominent Livingston nose. Edward P.—cold, "dull, and heavy-minded"—lived a life apparently unleavened by imagination, warmth or humor. After his wife's death in 1829 he ran successfully for lieutenant governor of New York and then married—to the horror of his five grown children—a young woman from a respectable but undistinguished Hyde Park family. Mary Broome was in her early twenties when she married the middle-aged Edward P. Only slightly older than her oldest stepdaughter, she posed an authentic procreative threat (an idle one, as it turned out; Mary Broome never had a child), and her stepchildren viewed her existence with alarm and repugnance.

After Edward P.'s death ten years later, in 1843, the reading of his will more than justified all his children's antagonism toward their stepmother: the former Miss Broome received not only the $20,000 cash allowed for in what one of her stepchildren called her "anti-nuptial agreement," she was also—appallingly—to receive Clermont itself. The five siblings (three sisters and two brothers, ranging in age from thirty-five to twenty) filed a suit in which they accused their stepmother, among other things, of tampering with the will. Even after the charges were dismissed and the will recorded, they refused to back down. Under threat of further litigation, the widow let it be known that she "would take her 20,000 and leave the house," an offer which her adversaries found acceptable. She removed herself from Clermont forever, and a few years later became the wife of Charles H. Ruggles, a justice of the New York State Court of Appeals (of whom we shall hear more).

With Clermont safely theirs, the five Livingston brothers and sisters fell to quarreling among themselves over its division. First, two of the girls and their brothers ganged up on their sister, Elizabeth Ludlow (Mrs. Edward H.), scoffing at her "pretended rights" and gossiping unmercifully about her marriage: "He manufactures stories and she believes them so the[y] get along sometimes bitter sometimes sweet."‡ The two brothers then sued their three sisters (Mrs. Ludlow, Mrs. David A. Clarkson and the youngest, Miss Mary Livingston) in chancery court over the validity of a map dividing the property—both its riverfront acreage and the large number of inland tenant farms—more or less equally among them. Eventually a settlement

‡ The Ludlows became the great-grandparents of Eleanor Roosevelt.

was reached whereby each sibling received a suitable extent of farmland and a portion of the riverfront. The oldest brother, Clermont Livingston, took the house and grounds for which he was named, while his brother and sisters each took a plot to the north—along the stretch of breathtaking river shore whose possession, a contemporary visitor remarked, "ought to make a man devout, if any of the gifts of Providence can do so. To hold in one's hand that which melts all strangers' hearts is to be a steward in a very serious sense of the term."

Across the lawn from Clermont, in the Chancellor's house, stewardship was also on the rocks. The widowed Robert L. Livingston, an affectionate but improvident father, was paying for his daughters' winters in town and his sons' tours of Europe by selling off land. Generous to a fault, he loaned money to friends and relatives with no prospects and invested in abortive business ventures. Meanwhile, the Chancellor's magnificent mansion was becoming decidedly shabby.

The oldest daughter, Maria, was married to her cousin, John Tillotson; and Adelaide became the bride of William Bayard Clarkson, which Mrs. Astor (Peachy) said she would forgive "if Clarkson could only speak English—but he says 'we was.'"

The girls' brothers were sent in the early 1830s on an extended sojourn in Europe where the youngest, Montgomery Livingston, refused at fifteen to submit to the chaperonage of his older brothers or the discipline of his painting instructors and became intrigued instead with Europe's more voluptuous possibilities. His father was appalled: "Morals are of more importance even than Education." When he threatened to bring the young man home, Montgomery promptly settled down to his primary objective, the serious study of painting, and was soon referring to it as his profession by which he expected to become "independent."

The Wall Street panic of 1837 hit "like the shock of an earthquake." Robert L. Livingston, on the verge of ruin, brought his boys home. His older son, Eugene, a hardheaded realist, took one look at his potential patrimony and began courting an heiress. Montgomery also fell in love, with the seventeen-year-old daughter of the Collector of the Port of New York, Samuel Swartwout, whom we last met in the company of Aaron Burr. Shortly after his daughter's engagement to Montgomery Livingston was announced, Sam was caught in the act of embezzling over a million dollars from his office (the same office, under another name, in which Edward Livingston had come to similar grief forty years before). Managing to slip out of the country just ahead of the police, Sam left his wife and daughter behind to face the music and the loss of his entire property, which was forfeit to the United States Government. Montgomery Livingston, having about as much financial prudence as his father, did not fall out of love. His marriage to Mary Swartwout shocked many members of the family including his cousin from Staatsburgh, Mrs. Maturin Livingston, whose character judgments often depended on credit ratings and who therefore pronounced Miss Swartwout "not a ladylike girl in her conduct."

(Mrs. Maturin Livingston also moved decisively to spike the romance between her own son Lewis and Robert L. Livingston's daughter Margaret, accusing Robert L. of trying to "get rid of his children, he cares not how." Margaret was later married instead to her first cousin Schuyler Livingston, a grandson of Walter of Teviotdale. All of which prompted the chatelaine of Montgomery Place, Madame Louise D'Avezac de Castera Moreau de Lassy Livingston, to observe that "the Livingstons have none of them sufficient moral courage to marry wealth.")

Mary and Montgomery Livingston moved into the Chancellor's house to take care of the failing Robert L., whose rather endearing fecklessness was slowly sliding into incompetence and senility. He died in 1843, the same year as the death of his contentious cousin, Edward P. Livingston of Clermont. There was little to dispose of in his will; most of the property had been sold. His older son Eugene—who by now lived an independent, urbane life in New York City—was horrified to learn that his entire inheritance consisted of the dilapidated old Chancellor's house with its adjacent acreage and some of his father's personal effects. Montgomery, the younger son, would receive an unimproved parcel of riverfront land to the south. Eugene, obviously in a state of shock, lashed out at his brother, accusing him of a series of manufactured petty crimes: drinking up their father's whiskey, stealing a cameo portrait of their mother. Perhaps he was mollified by Montgomery's willingness to exchange patrimonies. Eugene swapped the tumbledown wreck of a Chancellor's house for his brother's empty tract —its river view enhanced by the charming boat basin at the mouth of the Esopus Creek, nearly a mile away on the opposite shore. Eugene soon built himself an elegant house on the property which he christened Eversleigh and used for weekend and holiday respite from his busy life in the city.

Eugene's urbanity was matched by that of the Maturin Livingstons of Staatsburgh,* although the latters' social sophistication was well disguised in garments of Hudson Valley rural domesticity. New York City society's increasing exclusivity (which will be explored more fully in a later chapter) was making some of its members uncomfortable. The solution for many Livingstons—from that day to this—was the adoption of a mildly eccentric farmer pose: overalls and pitchforks in extenuation of snobbery. Mrs. Maturin Livingston's father, ex-Governor Morgan Lewis, set the tone at Staatsburgh one summer by ordering "a moderate-sized basin put in the lawn in

---

* Mrs. Maturin (Margaret) Livingston was the daughter of Gertrude (née Livingston) and Morgan Lewis, who had built the Staatsburgh house in 1792. Her husband was descended from Robert Livingston, the nephew of the first proprietor of Livingston Manor. His brother, Peter R. Livingston, and Gertrude's sister, Joanna Livingston, were married to each other and lived nearby at Grasmere.

sight of the piazza, and filled with water, for the accommodation of a pet goose."

His son-in-law, Maturin Livingston, took the process a step further. Finding the lure of Staatsburgh irresistible, but at the same time "incompatible with [his] business as a lawyer," Maturin chose to abandon his profession. He established residency with his wife's family at Staatsburgh, where he spent his days nursing a mild hypochondria, watching his twelve children grow, and pottering about the small cloth factory which he established in the village nearby to give him something to do.

During the winter months the Staatsburgh ménage repaired to General Lewis' large double house on Leonard Street, Manhattan, where Mrs. Maturin Livingston—who came to be known in the family as "Grandma Grundy"—assumed the mantle of hostess and arbiter of her children's social lives. She assiduously reviewed every aspect of their activities; and when they were old enough to marry, predictably none of their choices satisfied. One son's wife she deemed too cold, another too long-suffering. Her daughter Julia's groom, Major Joseph Delafield, she condemned as lazy and prone to stare. The Lowndes brothers from North Carolina, who successfully courted her two daughters Gertrude and Mary, had the effrontery to remove their brides from under her wing and take them south to live in Lowndes territory. (Grandma tried to get them back, employing all known devices from emotional blackmail to outright bribery, without success.)

Grandma Grundy's greatest scorn, however, was reserved for her daughter-in-law, the former Sylvia deGrasse Depau, daughter of the wealthy New York merchant and shipowner, Francis Depau, and his French wife.† The Depau family's high stylishness, extravagance and European manners made Mrs. Maturin Livingston quiver with reprobation. But at the same time she had to admit that Sylvia was always "beautifully dressed—everything in such perfect keeping. She looked," said Grandma Grundy after a family gathering, "like a being of a different class among the black Delafields."

Mrs. Maturin Livingston's sedulous devotion to her children's affairs was nothing less than the old Livingston matriarchal energy gone awry. Inheritor of the tradition—and the genes—of Alida Schuyler and Margaret Beekman Livingston, Grandma Grundy had no productive outlet for her formidable powers. Her generation had turned its back on the public arena to enter a private enclosure; it had begun to ignore the interests of society in favor of a Society of exclusiveness. The shift occurred almost overnight: Grandma Grundy's own father, Morgan Lewis, a contemporary of Chancellor Robert R. Livingston, had fought a revolution and served as governor of his home state; her husband, Maturin Livingston, a generation later, retired from active life at the age of forty in order to avoid a summertime commute.

† Sylvia's sister Caroline was the wife of Henry Walter Livingston II, Lady Mary's son.

After the Livingstons exchanged active involvement in the public life of their country for self-involvement with personal comfort and the *beau monde,* Mrs. Maturin Livingston was left with no socially redeeming field of activity in which to expend her matriarchal energy. So she turned it inward; and in the process transmogrified from matriarch—ruler and supporter—into unconscious predator. She was the first in a long line of Livingston mothers who are still known within the family as The Dragons.

The principal victim of Grandma Grundy's zealotry would appear to have been her favorite son, Alfred, who, in the face of his mother's strong control and his father's weak example, became an alcoholic. "I often reproach myself," Grandma confessed, "for feeling so much stronger an interest in [Alfred] than in my poor Morgan [her oldest son]. It ought not to be so and I cannot account for it." But Alfred broke her heart; and perhaps she broke his. At the age of thirty-five Alfred asked his mother for funds to buy a piece of property near Staatsburgh in order to live there quietly and become a farmer. She did not approve and sent him off instead to visit his sisters in North Carolina. When he returned he took to his room, never coming downstairs except for meals. Alfred was never redeemed; and five years later his mother wrote to one of his sisters, "Had my poor Alfred been taken from us in childhood, how much misery would we all have been spared."

25

ANTIRENTERS! AWAKE! AROUSE!
Let the opponents of Patroonery rally in their strength.
A great crisis is approaching. Now is the time to strike.
The minions of Patroonery are at work.
Arouse! Awake!
and
Strike till the last armed foe expires,
Strike for your altars and your fires,
Strike for the green graves of your sires,
God and your happy homes!

In the early 1840s the tenants of Livingston Manor once again took the field. Dressed in their grandfathers' Indian disguises, the protesters of this new generation were infinitely more sophisticated than their Palatine and Tory forebears. The rhetoric of their Declaration of Independence recalled the spirit of '76:

We . . . publicly, solemnly, unifiedly declare
ourselves free and independent from and not
under the control of Patroonery;

but their goals, organization, and methods were strikingly modern:

Lay down the murderous musket,
Put by the glittering steel,

> We ask the rights of freemen
> And to freemen we appeal.
>
> A weapon far more potent
> The ballot box shall yield,
> It is the only weapon
> A yeoman's hand should wield.

The movement was called Anti-Rent, and its goal was nothing less than the statutory overturn of the rent system in New York State.

At the heart of the transformation was universal manhood suffrage, which had been instituted in New York in 1821.* With thousands of tenant votes to command, Anti-Rent could take direct aim at the legislature, bypassing the lords of the manors in its drive to eradicate their titles.

The manor proprietors failed at first to appreciate the authenticity of the threat. Dismissing Anti-Rent as just one more outbreak of petulance on the part of "those Pests of Society," they made the single gesture of raising $5000 to lobby in the legislature (the Clermont family contributed generously) and then sat back while their representatives and the local sheriffs did their jobs.

But this time the Pests of Society were not to be deflected. After two years of legislative and legal frustration the tenants took the field in the spring of 1844 and proved conclusively that Anti-Rent was more than just a reprise of former rebellions. The tenant army, led by a Columbia County physician, Dr. Smith Boughton, was organized into a tight structure of secret, independent cells. Its discipline and efficiency were formidable, as was its intelligence. Local sheriffs, riding the manor with eviction papers, soon learned to tremble at the sound of a tin dinner horn, Anti-Rent's call to arms. (The movement became affectionately known as the Tin Horn Rebellion, and its women, in addition to donating their dinner horns, took the secret oath "that they might be honored dressmakers and ornamenters of masks for their husbands, sons or lovers—the brave heroes.") A masked troop of "Indians" would inevitably materialize from the forest, and the hapless constable might receive a tarring and feathering or, if the Indians were in a good mood, a trip to the nearest saloon and the pleasure of buying a round of drinks for the whole tribe. Anti-Rent was not without a sense of humor. To prevent the auctioning off of one dispossessed tenant's property, the crowd deliberately kept bidding for the entire day on the opening item, a milk cow. When, at sunset, the exhausted auctioneer declared the animal sold, the banging of his gavel was echoed by a shot from the woods, and the thousand-dollar cow fell dead at his feet.

Lightheartedness aside, Anti-Rent was an idea whose time had come—a fact recognized by practically everyone except the manor proprietors.

---

* Peter R. Livingston of Grasmere, an "ultra-Democrat," served on the Committee on Suffrage at the state Constitutional Convention of 1821.

In December of 1844, Dr. Smith Boughton was arrested and brought to trial in the town of Hudson on a charge of stealing legal documents (i.e., eviction papers). The first trial resulted in a hung jury; but the second convicted him, and the judge pronounced the maximum sentence allowed by law: life imprisonment.

The excessive harshness of the penalty was immediately condemned, both publicly and privately, throughout New York State. But the Livingston family of Clermont exulted, "The storm is past, the danger is over, the blast that blows loudest is soonest overblown. Hudson . . . has done its duty." The criminal Boughton had dared to challenge everything the Livingstons held most sacred: property and status. The rent system meant more to the Livingstons than just the ownership of farms; it meant the stature that derives from presiding over a vassal class. Anti-Rent was an attack not only on the Livingston pocket book but on the Livingston dignity and amour propre, and its leader deserved the severest penalty the law would allow.

But there was still another aspect of Anti-Rent that the Livingstons failed to recognize—its human aspect. Many of the tenant families who wished to buy their farms had lived on them nearly as long as the Livingstons had lived on their manor, and feeling ran deep:

> When up our mountain streamlets
> And o'er these hills we rove,
> We trace our father's footsteps
> Amid the scenes we love.
>
> 'Tis here their graves are scattered,
> How were they wont to toil,
> And by these sacred memories
> We are wedded to the soil. . . .
>
> We ask no princely favors—
> We ask for this alone—
> The rightful boon of freemen,
> A spot to call our own.

Dr. Boughton's harsh sentence gave Anti-Rent a martyr. Within months of his incarceration opposition in the state legislature crumbled and a new state constitutional convention was called, which—with a single-mindedness and efficiency remarkable in the state—composed in four months a new constitution incorporating all the legal groundwork for the dismantling of the rent system.

The actual changeover took a few years, as lawsuits based on the new constitution wended their ways through the state courts. Meanwhile, Dr. Boughton was pardoned and freed by the new governor, John Young. In a climactic case in 1852 the state Court of Appeals ruled that perpetual leases were actually estates in fee; in other words, that the holders of perpetual leases held title to the land. It was a crucial decision, which effectively abolished the rent system in the state of New York.

It would be difficult to decide whether the Livingstons of Livingston Manor were hurt more in their purse or in their pride. True, they were now forced to sell many acres of farmland to their former tenants, whose servitude was no longer theirs to command. But this was of minor significance: the financial benefits of the rent system had waned drastically over the years. It was the loss of dignity that cut more deeply. The elevation of a vassal class to yeoman status removed one solid affirmation of the superiority of the landlords. For generations the Livingstons had seen themselves reflected in the eyes of their tenants. Now that lens had shifted focus and they would never again see themselves as clear. It is not coincidental that about this time, in the mid-nineteenth century, family genealogists and historians ceased to refer to their ancestors by the designation those gentlemen themselves had used, "manor proprietor," and began styling them instead "Lords of the Manor."

The mortification was perhaps felt more deeply than anywhere at Clermont, where Clermont Livingston and his brothers and sisters had only recently possessed themselves of the house and land: the judge who ruled in the perpetual lease case was Justice Charles H. Ruggles, who, only a short time before, had become the happy bridegroom of their former stepmother, Mary Broome Livingston.

As Clermont's dining-room ceiling continued to sag and creak, Clermont Livingston's siblings and cousins indulged in a new family building boom. Between the years 1843 and 1865 a dozen new Livingston mansions were constructed on the river between Oak Hill and Staatsburgh, bringing the total to nearly forty. All four of Clermont Livingston's brothers and sisters (the Ludlows, the Robert E. Livingstons and two sets of Clarksons) built houses on their acres north of Clermont, so that the stretch of river shore that had once accommodated a single house now made room for nine.

Immediately south of Clermont, Eugene Livingston was established in his charming new Eversleigh, while the Chancellor's house next door continued to fall down around the ears of his brother Montgomery. Montgomery Livingston was a fine painter of landscapes but, like his father, a poor custodian. When he died in 1855—childless, broke and intestate—his cash supply was found in a top hat at the top of the closet, and his debts were deemed so overwhelming that the house would have to be sold. Two of his cousins were appointed executors, and his widow, Mary née Swartwout, was left quite in the cold.

The auction of the Chancellor's house took place on July 10, 1857. Nearly a hundred people, including members of the press, braved a steady rain and the muddy, rutted driveway to attend the sale of this "perfect castle Rack Rent." The company was greeted in the Chancellor's oak-paneled library by auctioneer Edward Ludlow (husband of Elizabeth Livingston of Clermont) and invited to bid on the two thousand volumes. The paintings were offered next, "none," our correspondent reported, "of considerable value, unless I except an original portrait by Sully of General Jackson in uniform with one arm supported on his horse. It brought $500."†

Auctioneer Ludlow did what he could to drum up interest in an enormous "Gobelein" tapestry in the front hall, but no one was fooled: "When I mention the extent of it, no well informed person need be told that it is no more Gobelein work than it is Egyptian papyrus. It covered nearly all the walls of a room 25 × 30 feet, and there could not have been less than two hundred yards of it. Such a piece of Gobelein was never owned except by a crowned head. The pattern and work were very pretty, or had been, but the whole was so soiled and moth-eaten that I wonder anyone would be found willing to admit it into their house upon any terms." The tapestry went for $90.

The real drama of the day occurred after lunch on the veranda, when bidding on the house itself commenced. The opening offer of $27,000 was quickly bid up to $50,000, at which point all but two of the competitors dropped out. Those remaining were a Mr. Magoon, representing the Clarkson sisters (four maiden sisters-in-law of Clermont Livingston's sister), and a mysterious personage who concealed his identity by remaining inside the drawing room behind the draperies. The bidding continued to $61,250— the precise figure at which Mr. Magoon had been secretly instructed to stop —whereupon the unidentified gentleman in the drawing room fell silent. "After a long pause the place was finally knocked down to the Misses Clarkson." The mystery man now emerged; he was Eugene Livingston of Eversleigh, brother of the late Montgomery. The Misses Clarkson were appalled, although not for the reason one might expect. Protesting that they would never have bid against "one of the connection," they offered the house to Eugene, who naturally refused. Our reporter discreetly explained, ". . . he has a beautiful place of some four hundred acres adjoining the Chancellor's place south, which, if I may judge by its tillage and condition, is quite as much as he cares to be troubled with at present." In fact Eugene had no intention of saddling himself with "Castle Rack Rent"; he simply wanted to drive up the price so that his brother's estate would cover the debts. He succeeded with two of the same techniques which his ancestor, Robert the first manor proprietor, had always employed so effectively: thorough preparation (who, I wonder, told him what the Clarksons' limit was?) and deft footwork.

"With this," our correspondent tells us, "terminated the sale of a place second to no other in the country for its combination of natural beauties and

† The portrait had come to the house with Mary Swartwout, presumably a gift from General Jackson to her father. It now hangs at Clermont State Historic Site.

interesting associations. During the lifetime of the Chancellor . . . all that was most distinguished in the world of politics or letters in this country used to be gathered under its shades. . . . Since that period, however, the house has occupied but limited space in the public eye; enough, however, with its past associations to justify this account of the last crisis in its history."

Mary Swartwout Livingston, having lost her husband, her portrait and her house, soon found solace elsewhere. Gazing north that summer of 1857, across the lawn and through the acacia trees toward the old mansion at Clermont, she could see her late husband's cousin, Clermont Livingston, planting muskmelons in his garden. Clermont had been a widower for five years (his late wife was also his cousin, Cornelia Livingston of Oak Hill) and was the father of two young children. By the end of summer he and Mary were married—Clermont, in the words of his sister-in-law, Susan, having been "in a hurry to secure the jolly widow." Baby John Henry Livingston and his sister Mary got a stepmother; and the jolly, if resourceful, widow exchanged the Chancellor's house for Clermont—both the mansion and the man.

26

As the luster of the Chancellor's house faded and it slipped from crown jewel into bargaining chip, its cousins to the south, Montgomery Place and Rokeby, were being burnished and given new settings.

Montgomery Place and Rokeby had not been part of the original Livingston Manor, and their proprietors had never depended on the rent system, either financially or psychologically. Both the Edward Livingstons and the William Backhouse Astors had made their fortunes and established their dignity outside the Hudson Valley, in the worlds of national politics and finance. They had not defined themselves against a background of tenant servitude. Being Livingston was still important to them—very important. But it did not constitute the core of their self-respect.

Edward Livingston's widow, Louise, who lived at Montgomery Place with her daughter and son-in-law, Mr. and Mrs. Barton, did not receive clear title to the remainder of her husband's Batture property until seventeen years after his death, in 1853. She spent a considerable portion of her new income making additions to the house—an enlarged veranda on the river side, an elegant open pavilion to the north—and hiring the renowned landscape architect, Andrew Jackson Downing, to design the grounds, with results that changed forever Hudson Valley notions about the functions and value of land.

Under Mr. Downing's influence, productivity now took second place to adornment. He designed a "Wilderness . . . a richly wooded and highly picturesque valley, filled with the richest growth of trees, and threaded with dark, intricate, and mazy walks, along which are placed a variety of rustic seats. This valley is musical with the sound of waterfalls, of which there are several fine ones in the bold impetuous stream which finds its course through the lower part of the wilderness. . . . [The flower garden,] one of the most perfect in the country . . . is laid out in the arabesque manner . . . glowing with masses of the gayest colors—each bed being composed wholly of a single hue. . . . [Five miles] of highly varied and picturesque private roads and walks [compose] the pleasure-grounds of Montgomery Place." A conservatory, an arboretum and acres of untouched "natural wood" rounded out this "home landscape of dignified and elegant seclusion, rarely surpassed in any country." The only cloud on this highly embellished horizon was Louise's lack of heirs: Coralie Barton, now in her forties, was childless.*

General Armstrong's problem at Rokeby was quite the opposite: too many heirs. When he sold the estate to his son-in-law, William Backhouse Astor, in 1836, his two sons (aptly named for two American Revolutionary sons of Mars, Horatio Gates Armstrong and James Kosciuszko Armstrong) were furious and insisted on stripping the mansion of all its furniture and portraits before the sale was consummated.† After the Astors took possession, feisty old General Armstrong still retained the right to sit at the head of Rokeby's dining-room table during his annual summer sojourn.

The emptying of the house gave William B. and Peachy Astor the chance to redecorate from top to bottom, a project carried out with even greater expense than might have been expected after William B. made a killing in the Panic of 1837—the same panic that had sounded the death knell for the Chancellor's house. Mr. and Mrs. Astor also rearranged the Rokeby landscape, transforming an old wagon track into a romantic "Poets' Walk" and trimming off the top of a hill to open up the view.

At Rokeby, and at the Astor mansion in New York City, strict rules of social decorum prevailed. Children were brought up never to laugh out loud; never to wear bright colors; never to speak at meals; and, when saying good night to their parents, to back respectfully out of the room.

In 1837 the oldest Astor daughter, nineteen-year-old Emily, became engaged to Samuel Ward, a young man with a distinguished colonial pedigree and a cultured, sophisticated turn of mind which he had acquired during extensive travel and study in Europe. Sam's irrepressibly gay spirits appeared in stark contrast to Emily's Astor background. His effect was certainly vivid: Grandma Grundy found him "very clever, highly cultivated,

* After Coralie's death in 1873, three of her New Orleans cousins became life tenants of Montgomery Place. After their deaths the estate passed to Edward Livingston's great-great-nephew, Maturin Livingston Delafield, the grandson of Grandma Grundy.
† Horatio's Rokeby possessions were all destroyed a few years later in a fire in his house in Baltimore.

speaks half a dozen languages, has high spirits, full of fun and frolic; has the bad taste occasionally to appear vain of his escapades; has evidently been much spoiled . . . talks incessantly, tells a story admirably. You cannot help being amused although you are often tempted to say, 'Damn your impudence.' "

Sam's marriage to Emily took place in January of 1838, after he had signed the standard waiver of claim to the Astor fortune. Their first child was born within the year: a daughter named for her grandmother, Margaret Astor Ward, called "Maddie." Three years later Emily Ward died in childbirth, as did her infant son; and little Maddie immediately became the major focus of attention, both sentimental and testamentary, of her Astor grandparents. She spent much of her time at Rokeby, absorbing its unique flavor —an uneasy mixture of material luxury and moral austerity. It was at Rokeby that Maddie learned, when she was five, that her father had committed the unpardonable social sin of marrying again, too quickly and to the wrong woman.

Sam had unquestionably been deeply in love with Emily, but he also had what one of his descendants called a "roving personality," together with a capacity for very poor judgment. Swept away by the sultry beauty of his Creole bride, Medora Grimes (of a New Orleans family and reputation that did not invite close scrutiny), he bestowed on her as a wedding present the house on Bond Street, New York, where he and Emily had lived. It was this, as much as the marriage itself, that touched the Astor nerve center. When news of the marriage reached Rokeby, little Maddie's Aunt Louisa, Sam's sister, was there on an extended visit. Abruptly summoned downstairs, she stood silent in the hall while William B. Astor ordered up the carriage, turned to the butler and announced simply, "Miss Ward is leaving." He spoke no other word; Louisa was whisked away and never saw Rokeby again.

Her little niece Maddie remained behind. Sam dropped his custody suit after the Astors threatened to cut off Maddie's inheritance if he persisted. Maddie grew up with her grandparents, who slowly but surely over the years managed to quash in her every vestige of Sam's gregarious, fun-loving personality. Swallowing whole the Astors' rigid conventionality, Maddie learned to disapprove of her father, and on the few occasions when they met she was unremittingly cold and judgmental.

In Maddie was distilled one pure, single strand of the Astor/Livingston genetic strain: social conformity and moral conservatism. It was a strong element in the total package of family characteristics, but contending with it were the romanticism of an Edward Livingston, the flamboyance of a William ("Don Quixote of the Jersies") Livingston, the juvenile improvidence of a Peter R., the licentiousness of a John and the ambivalence of a Chancellor—not to mention the certifiable craziness of John Jacob Astor, Jr., William B.'s brother. Maddie's personality remained, to the end of her life, simple and coherent; but after her marriage into a family of equally pronounced temperamental eccentricities she produced a flock of children whose variations on their genetic theme would without question have shocked and embarrassed her.‡

In the late 1850s the Astors added on to Rokeby a new third floor with mansard roof, a five-story octagonal tower and a new service wing. The house now had forty-eight rooms, making it the largest of all the Livingston river mansions. General Armstrong would have been pleased.

Rokeby and Montgomery Place—standing in their manicured parks, with lofty French windows overlooking formal gardens and shaded walks— were a far cry from the rustic utility and simplicity of the original Livingston Hudson Valley dwelling: Alida and Robert's 1700 "homestead" on the Roeliff Jansen Kill. But all of these establishments were extensions of their owners' lives. Alida and Robert had built a working manor headquarters with accessibility to the water for commercial reasons; but it was also a fort, to protect them from attack. Their descendants found protection instead in the land, and they sited their mansions at the end of mile-long drives with manned stone gatehouses to keep away the curious. The concept of land was thus transformed from producer and provider to insulator and adorner. The estate became a refuge, the house a pleasure palace.

Of these splendid nineteenth-century Livingston riverfront establishments, Rokeby and Montgomery Place were the grandest of all (too grand, some of their owners' cousins might say, preferring simpler pleasures). But at the moment of their greatest glory many of their cousins' estates were tumbling into degradation and ruin, most notably the once preeminent Chancellor's house. The Livingston mansions on their narrow shelf of the Hudson's east bank—having lost, as it were, their ballast: the vast inland acres of Livingston Manor—seemed more in danger than ever of tipping into the river. It may have been emblematic that the ironworks at Ancram, once the cornerstone of the family's financial edifice, was sold in 1845 on foreclosure.

Or perhaps the Livingston estates should be viewed as jewels on a chain that was wearing thin. Some of the owners of the jewels could afford to make repairs; but others could not, and a chain, as we all know, is only as strong as its weakest link.

‡ Maddie's own uncle, Henry Astor (Emily's brother), cut off by his father for running off with a Dutchess County farmer's daughter, shrugged, "Money counts for little in this world compared with love and life." He could afford to shrug, being one-quarter owner of the Eden Farm, which covered New York City from Broadway to the Hudson River between Fortieth and Forty-second streets. Happy-go-lucky Henry (some say he was certifiably insane) and his bride purchased a farm in the Berkshires where they built a racetrack and paved the dining room with silver dollars.

27

The excision of the rent system from the body of New York State law, so excruciating to the old manor landlords, was scarcely noticed by the rest of the state. The economic life of young America had long since passed the valley by. The Hudson River itself was still an important waterway for Midwestern grain barges out of the Erie Canal, and the shoreline seemed a good place to lay a railroad track. But most of the trains and ships rushed through; very few stopped to do business in the valley itself.

Society was also hurtling along at a faster clip, picking up along the way some strange appendages that drastically altered its shape. New people with new values swept away the old alliances and customs. Janet Livingston Montgomery had remarked a number of years before that "the Livingston family have branched out so widely that the People of Israel can only equal them." Now the rest of society was branching out, too, to the point of explosion. Grandma Grundy, under siege, invited to her New Year's Day "soirée" in 1841 "about 80 persons and nearly one half were Livingstons or had been Livingstons or were descended from them. We had but two foreigners, not one parvenue or nouveaux riche. . . . I was really rejoiced to find I could assemble a company of ladies and gentlemen, for really at our ball I felt myself a little en canaille (if there is such a word; if not I must coin it)."

In the face of society's expansion and fragmentation, Grandma Grundy could always retreat to "Livingston Valley," where her Livingston identity and status were confirmed and proclaimed—loud and clear—by the elegant situation and historical associations of her Staatsburgh mansion. It is not surprising that some of her cousins, "People of Israel" who had wandered and strayed from the Hudson Valley, began at this period to return.

In 1815 two such displaced members of the Livingston family purchased elegant properties on the east bank: the brothers Robert Swift Livingston and John Swift Livingston, grandsons of Robert, the third proprietor of Livingston Manor. The boys' father, Robert Cambridge Livingston, alone among the third proprietor's sons, had chosen not to settle on his portion of the old Livingston Manor. Instead, Robert Cambridge had lived in New York City, engaging in international trade and becoming one of the town's richest and most respected citizens. He left a generous fortune; and after his death Robert Swift and John Swift, both in their mid-thirties, used it to finance a stylish return to the valley.

Robert Swift Livingston, the older brother, purchased the grander property: Almont, originally called The Meadows by its builder, General John Armstrong. Almont had experienced a rousing intervening history under the ownership of one Colonel de Veaux, a "man of mystery . . . a fire eater [with] a reputation as a duellist." De Veaux, whose exploits as a soldier of fortune in the Caribbean had brought him enormous wealth, kept not only a menagerie of monkeys and kangaroos on the property but also a sizable army of black slaves, who mounted guard on the approaches to the deep bay below the house whenever the colonel's fleet pulled in after dark to unload its secret cargo. De Veaux paid his bills sporadically but lavishly, riding around the countryside in his carriage tossing handfuls of silver coins at the feet of the astonished tradesmen.

Under de Veaux's extravagant stewardship Almont had become a showplace. Its landscape design included "waterfalls, picturesque bridges, romantic glens, groves, a magnificent park, [and] one of the most beautiful ornamental gardens in this country." The house, too, had been given a new profile with the addition of porticos, piazzas and a set of imposing marble steps. Inside, stone mantelpieces in every room were carved to depict scenes of Colonel de Veaux's military victories; and in the dining salon "ships of solid silver were set into the wall in such a way as to represent the waves of the sea, and when lighted up either by the sun or from the huge log fire in the stone fireplace resembled the setting sun on the ocean. The walls and ceilings were studded with silver buttons."

Colonel de Veaux died of lockjaw after a tumble down Almont's marble steps; but the estate's succeeding proprietor, Robert Swift Livingston, more than lived up to the colonel's extravagant standards. Where de Veaux had collected kangaroos, Robert Swift collected chambermaids; where de Veaux scattered silver coins, Robert Swift sowed wild oats. Freed by "his ample fortune, derived from his ancestors, [from] the necessity of labor of any kind . . . his life," the New York *Times* blandly assures us, "passed in pursuits rural and agricultural, congenial to his tastes." Robert Swift's taste for laundresses and housekeepers became legendary—as did his devotion to Almont's gardens, orchards, park and trotting track, which he preserved and protected in "the grand old style of years agone."

Robert Swift Livingston had little in common with his younger brother, John Swift Livingston, except a mutual desire to return to their family's ancient stamping ground. In 1815, John Swift and his wife purchased Green Hill, one of the two Livingston mansions near the village of Tivoli that had been built in the 1790s by descendants of the first manor proprietor's son, Gilbert Livingston. The Gilberts' commitment had faded along with Pierre Delabigarre's grandiose schemes for Tivoli; and the two mansions, Green Hill and Sunning Hill, subsequently passed through a number of owners, several of them Livingston kin.

John Swift Livingston, the new owner of Green Hill, harbored "something akin to a contempt for business life." Nevertheless, he found idleness equally abhorrent, and—inspired perhaps by the negative example of his older brother—he instilled in his sons a spirit of enterprise and furnished them with the training and education to satisfy it. John Swift's nine children, all raised at Green Hill, were a refreshingly affectionate brood. The two older sons, Cambridge and Johnston Livingston, both graduated from Union College, Schenectady, after which Cambridge embarked on a legal apprenticeship in New York City and Johnston went to work as a surveyor for the Erie Railroad—well placed, at the age of eighteen, to make his mark in a business of the future.

But two years later Johnston seemed to suffer a crisis of confidence, or at least of resolve. After his sister Sarah's traumatic elopement brought him home for a family council, a mysterious eye ailment persuaded him to resign his job and linger in the valley. His mother's death the following year prolonged the sojourn, and soon the days and weeks had stretched into eight years. At twenty-seven, Johnston Livingston was still in residence at Green Hill.

In 1844—the year of Anti-Rent's great crisis, while his Livingston cousins at nearby Clermont exulted over the conviction of Dr. Smith Boughton—Johnston was roused from his sleep, perhaps by the noise beneath Green Hill's windows where the new Hudson River Railroad track was being laid; perhaps by the presence next door of the president of the railroad, James Borman, the new owner of Sunning Hill; or perhaps most poignantly by his brother, Cambridge Livingston, who wrote from New York, "In this community there is a universal feeling of disrespect—I may almost say contempt, for young men who, not being very wealthy—yet do nothing." Cambridge was a man with his eye on the future: he had recently abandoned the law and was involved in the financing of Samuel Morse's newly patented telegraph. He urged his brother to accept a position that had just become available in the Philadelphia railroad freight office of their cousin, William Livingston, "a first rate man for business."

William Livingston and his brother Crawford* were pioneers in the express freight business, one of the fastest-growing of all the new, free-wheeling ventures spawned by the railroad. Literally hundreds of little express companies had begun to sprout wherever the tracks penetrated. Forty operated at one time out of Boston alone, most of them one-man operations known as "coat pocket expresses."

Johnston Livingston, his mysterious eye ailment inexplicably vanished, went to work in the Philadelphia office of William Livingston in 1845. The following year he was made a partner; and by the end of the decade he had purchased stock and become a partner in a number of other freight companies. The 1850s witnessed the consolidation of the express business into a smaller number of much larger companies, and Johnston Livingston proved particularly adept at financing and reorganization. He served as an officer of virtually every major express company that came into being during this period: Wells Fargo, National Express, Adams Express, Overland Mail, and finally American Express.

In 1852—the year the rent system in the state of New York was given the coup de grâce by Appeals Court Justice Charles H. Ruggles—Johnston Livingston accepted the position of treasurer of the new California company, Wells Fargo. But instead of moving to California, the new frontier, Johnston turned back to the Hudson Valley: he married his cousin, Sylvie Livingston of The Hill (a granddaughter of Lady Mary) and purchased Sunning Hill, the old Livingston mansion right next door to Green Hill, his childhood home.

In his Commonplace Book, Johnston once wrote a lengthy sketch of the life of Friedrich Schiller, commenting, "if . . . happiness consisted in surrounding the imagination with ideal beauty a literary life would be the most enviable which the lot of this world affords. But the truth is far otherwise. . . . The delights of literature are too ethereal and transient to furnish [a] perennial flow of satisfaction." Following the Schiller sketch in Johnston's notebook is a detailed treatment of the life of Meyer Rothschild.

On a later page Johnston carefully computed the cost to His Majesty of maintaining the royal castles at Windsor and Pimlico and the Pavilion at Brighton—a matter of concern to the proprietary side of his nature. Johnston took extremely good care of his Tivoli estate, with money he himself had earned. He was a major purchaser at the auction of the Chancellor's house in 1857, coming away with various works of art and books (including

---

* It is worth noting that the enterprising William and Crawford Livingston sprang from the unlikely loins of the "Fourth Lord of Livingston Manor," the feckless Peter R. Livingston. They were the offspring of his fourth son, Moncrief, a prosperous citizen of the town of Hudson, New York, who managed to instill in his sons the wisdom and initiative to break free of the manor and bustle profitably in the outside world.

what the New York *Evening Post* identified as "a choice edition of Decameron's Boccaccio"). Johnston's acuity and enterprise thus profited from his Clermont cousins' imprudence.

Hardworking Johnston was unlike some of his cousins in still another way: he was not a bit fussy about the pedigrees of the men he worked with, providing they were energetic, ambitious and good at their jobs. But despite this egalitarianism in the marketplace—or perhaps because of it, as a counterpoise for the inner Livingston—one of his first acts on acquiring Sunning Hill was to change its name to Callendar House after the lapsed Livingston Scottish earldom, and, a few years later, to institute a search for what he perceived as the "missing link" between the American Livingstons and the noble branch of the family in Scotland. His genealogical quest was focused entirely on heraldry and titles. The moral and intellectual powers of the untitled Reverend John Livingston became secondary to his function as a conduit of noble blood. Johnston pursued every clue devotedly, spending considerable time (and presumably money) in correspondence with a Scottish genealogist, who finally rewarded him in 1868 with a chart showing the direct descent of the Reverend John Livingston from the erstwhile Earls of Callendar and Linlithgow.

A student of the Livingston family wrote in 1864: "What a change has the intervening half-century wrought, not merely in the affairs of this house, but in those of all like establishments in this country! . . . The strength of combination is gone from them. Our democracy divides every clan, minces every estate, individualizes everybody, disintegrates everything. Each man is the head of his own family; no man can be the head of the family of his ancestors . . ."—to which Johnston Livingston might have answered, Perhaps not, but he can try.

28

No Livingston was in a better position than Johnston to appreciate that American society and business were undergoing a process of fragmentation. Old business alliances, formed over generations of kinship and mutual trust, were being replaced with short-term arrangements of simple expediency; and dynastic marriage, based on communal interest and mutual affection, disappeared in favor of the *mariage de convenance*. In short, the values of family were giving way to the demands of the profit motive. New people and new wealth rubbed at society's old outlines until they threatened to disappear. Because Johnston was himself a part of this new world and in many ways a participant in the process, his appreciation for what was being lost was all the more poignant—and he was prepared to defend his place in the old order, tooth, nail and pedigree.

Johnston Livingston existed, reasonably successfully, in two worlds. First and foremost, he was a Livingston of Livingston Manor (the fact that the manor no longer existed was, in the social context, irrelevant). Secondly, he was a realist, who sensed much more clearly than his Clermont cousins the way the economic winds were blowing. He launched himself into the business world *outside* "Livingston Valley" in order to maintain his estate and his position *in* Livingston Valley.

But Johnston's talent for bridging gaps did not lead him across the Chancellor's old Bridge of Sighs into politics or public service—a span now firmly closed off to members of society by their own decree. The chasm had widened since the Chancellor's day. Democracy had not proved congenial to the sensibilities or responsive to the needs of those who upheld the aristocratic ideal: "Hudson," in the final analysis, had not "done its duty." American aristocracy, therefore, deliberately turned its back on politics. Unwilling to either fight or join with men elected by the common herd, they abdicated entirely. This group withdrawal (to which there were, of course, individual exceptions) is perhaps the ultimate measure of their insecurity as a class.

It also explains why American society during this period acquired a reputation for exclusiveness greater even than that of England or France. Where aristocrats rule by tradition, the worlds of politics and society are identical: but "in America the two systems are totally unconnected. . . . There is perfect freedom of political privilege . . . but this equality does not extend to the drawing room."

Tradition smooths the path of change; without it, differences between people and factions often develop into irreconcilable antagonisms. America was short on tradition; so the marriage between American society and politics had had no time to mellow before society perceived a threat and sued for divorce. Each party flew to its own defense, the issues became lost in clouds of personal vituperation, and settlement was impossible. The disengagement, once effected, was ever after poisoned by perpetual hatred and distrust.

A biographer of Edward Livingston, attempting in 1860 to express the aristocratic viewpoint, came up with a queasy mixture of sound misgivings with sheer snobbery: "We are certainly making some progress in bridging the gulf which once generally separated low manners from high positions. Such progress is one of the worst of our present evils; it threatens us with the most palpable of our future dangers. How far the effrontery of ill-bred ignorance and incapacity will carry itself towards monopolizing places of dignity, power, and trust, is truly a question of moment. It is frightful to contemplate the possibility that the entire government in all its branches of so great and prosperous a country may, some day, be given permanently over to unlettered and unmannered statesmen . . . individuals whom many an obscure, well-bred person would not meet in the same drawing-room for all the world."

One cannot disagree that literacy and good manners will always be desirable in a statesman. But if the most literate and well-mannered elements of society choose to withdraw from public life, politics must learn to do without them.

Johnston Livingston was no doubt well aware that threats to the survival of the Livingston clan did not come entirely from without. He knew his family's weaknesses; he could calculate its dwindling acreage, assess its lack of resolve and estimate its capacity for disunity. Johnston was largely instrumental in providing his family with a new rallying point, an issue on which all his cousins could agree, something they all had in common: an illustrious pedigree. Genealogy is the tie that binds. It resists all challenge and reconciles all differences. It is immutable and forever. And it works better still if—as in the case of the descendants of Callendar and Linlithgow —the tie turns out to be gilded.

The railroad, which had proven so profitable for Johnston, also ironically provided him and his cousins in the valley with their most intrusive reminder of what the world was coming to. The Hudson River Railroad track ran right along the river shore, cutting off the family's mansions from the water, interfering with the view and shattering peace of mind. Fortunately most of the Livingston mansions were set somewhat back from water's edge. Still, every time a train went by chandeliers swayed, porcelain rattled and conversation came to a stop. Even worse, sparks from the engine stacks posed extreme danger on dry, windy days.

Some members of the family were better situated than others. At Grandma Grundy's estate in Staatsburgh the track ran through in a deep gully *inland* of the house, sparing the river view. Least fortunate was a niece of the Chancellor, Mrs. Lowndes Brown,* in her exquisite Greek Revival mansion, Edgewater, at Barrytown. Edgewater's drawing-room windows were only a few feet from the track. Mrs. Brown, a widow by the time this depredation occurred, was so incensed that she sold Edgewater and moved to Europe, declaring she would no longer live in a country where such a monstrous thing could happen.

The Civil War claimed a number of lives from the valley, including that of the oldest son of Eugene Livingston of Eversleigh. The seventeen-year-old had enlisted as a private soldier against his father's wishes (it is difficult to tell whether Eugene objected because of the danger or because his son would face it without benefit of commission) and died—as so many did—of typhoid contracted in training camp. His sacrifice, and that of his local neighbors from nearby Tivoli, was immortalized in an ode penned by a village poet, which names each man (some thirty in all) and pronounces their mutual epitaph:

> Now blest be their mem'ry forever,
> We're proud such defenders to own,
> How firm is the arch of our Union
> When built of the true Living-stone.

The disruptive effect of the Civil War on American society was not limited to the Southern states. In New York a postwar influx of new people and new money threatened to challenge the social security of even so domi-

* Her North Carolina husband was cousin to Grandma Grundy's sons-in-law.

nant a lion as Eugene Livingston. This "new and larger class of people . . . as different from the previous aristocracy of talent and wealth as Grant was from Jefferson" naturally tried to parlay its wealth into social position. When the older group, whose insecurity now verged on paranoia, fought back, new battle lines were drawn and social climbing became a popular spectator sport.

According to the old story, social eminence is determined by three criteria: pedigree, property and cash.

> If there are three people on an island, one of them will say he got there first— and so he is Society. Pretty soon another one will climb up a hill and build a big house and say *he* is Society. And finally, the third one will climb up a tree and corner all the coconuts and claim *he* is Society. Who is Society? Obviously all of them are: The first has family, the second has prominence, and the third has money.

The old society—that small nucleus of families linked by kinship, tradition and mutuality of taste—was weakest in the third category, wealth (except for those of its members who had married Astors or become directors of American Express). The Livingston family also had a weakness in the first category: Robert Livingston the First had stepped ashore on Manhattan Island a number of years *after* the founders of two of the most objectionable of the *nouveaux riches* families, the Vanderbilts and the Goulds.† Robert himself had considered pedigree irrelevant. Everyone in New York in 1680 was an *arriviste;* and besides, he had other ways of getting what he wanted. Marshall Junot's motto fit him perfectly: "I am my own ancestor."

But Robert's nineteenth-century progeny, beleaguered by a new generation of *arrivistes,* wielded their pedigree as a weapon of defense. Clad in the armor of Lords of the Manor, they trumpeted to the world that their founder's date of arrival was less important than his being Somebody before he came.

The increased pressure from social adventurists also gave renewed impetus to the Livingston propensity toward intermarriage. Johnston Livingston himself married a cousin, Sylvie Livingston‡ of The Hill; Johnston's sister Estelle married a de Peyster cousin; and their younger sister Mary, the day after Clermont Livingston of Clermont wed Cornelia Livingston of Oak Hill, became the bride of Grandma Grundy's son Henry. (What a lot of wedding presents.) Intermarriage—once a method of consolidating business

---

† Just for the record, of the families we have mentioned, the Delanos arrived in America the earliest, about 1621; the Vanderbilts, Beekmans, Goulds, Swartwouts, de Peysters and Schuylers came in mid-century; the Jays, Clarksons and Livingstons a decade or two later; and the Astors and Delafields last by a long shot, the year after the Revolution.

‡ Johnston taught his grandson a simple way to remember his descent: from the third son of the Third Lord. What he did not tell him was that Sylvie's descent was "better," from the *second* son.

and political interests—had now become a way of consolidating socially. It was another aspect of retrenchment and retreat.

The Livingston family's most solid claim to status lay, of course, in the second of the above categories: property. Nobody had more extensive or more exquisite acreage than the eastern shore of the upper Hudson River. If the "Lords of Livingston Manor" had lost their economic preeminence, at least there was nobody called "Lord of Gould Manor." If the family finances were in disrepair and the family pedigree less than perfect, the old manor lands made their point simply by existing. Without comment or apology, the string of Livingston mansions could be displayed along the east bank for all the world to see—from a distance. They were there to be glimpsed from the opposite shore or a boat in the river, daunting but unapproachable.

Holding on to the land became an obsession with some members of the Livingston family—at about the same time that the land itself became less valuable commercially. The Hudson Valley was no longer New York City's breadbasket, thanks to the Erie Canal. But the very uselessness of the land was transformed by the family into a virtue: cornfields next to the house became *déclassés*, broad lawns *à la mode*.

In society at large, work itself was becoming the object of disdain, no longer a fit subject for the drawing room. As for money, a "gentleman" never talked about it; he was supposed to be "rich enough to take it for granted or else poor enough to ignore it"—a dangerous attitude unless you can afford it, which many Livingstons could not. It was also at this time that a "lady" became known by the fact that she did precisely nothing. Like her country estate, she appeared precious in proportion to her uselessness. In this role—which Alida Schuyler and Margaret Beekman would have found distasteful—some of the more energetic and ambitious ladies became restless and transmogrified into "dragons." The most prominent amazon in the wars of the new society was a Livingston by marriage: *the* Mrs. Astor, William B. and Peachy's daughter-in-law Caroline, who, with her consort, Ward McAllister,* drew the boundary lines of society around the Four Hundred and then defended them with every weapon at their command.

One of Mrs. Astor's big guns was sheer territorial display: Harry Lahr, watching her walk into a ballroom, dripping diamonds, said she looked like a walking chandelier. Another was her rigid code of social behavior, derived in part from that of her legendary in-laws. She was not alone in her obsession with decorum; between 1830 and 1860 over a hundred books on

---

* A first cousin of Sam Ward's, and therefore Mrs. Astor's relation by marriage. Cleveland Amory disposes of McAllister as follows: "Without the slightest hint of a sense of humor, he imparted such seriousness to his ideas, as well as to himself, that in the socially insecure times in which he lived he was soon taken extremely seriously even by people who should have known better." One of McAllister's innovations was the Patriarchs, a select group of society men who sponsored the most exclusive balls in New York City. Eugene Livingston (of Eversleigh), Maturin Livingston (Grandma Grundy's son) and Johnston Livingston were all members.

social etiquette were published in America, another sign of society's insecurity. Mrs. Astor just took it further than anybody else, as she did so many things. What is amazing, looking back, is that all of society followed her like sheep. The ambitious newcomers could not afford to ignore her, and the old guard was apparently scared to.

Rigidity, exclusiveness, withdrawal: watchwords of society in the most democratic country the world had ever known. The irony is tinged by a sense of inevitability. The very "stress on equality and opportunity" in business and politics "made people class-conscious. Those with claims to a higher status felt a necessity to assert those claims for fear of losing the right to it." Austin O'Malley said that "exclusiveness is characteristic of recent riches, high Society and the skunk." But recent riches and high society in old New York in the latter half of the nineteenth century learned their exclusivity only by imitating the old society they were trying to penetrate.

An English visitor to New York in the 1830s, the delightful, gimlet-eyed Harriet Martineau, concluded that American aristocracy, unlike the European, "must be perpetuated, not by hereditary transmission, but by accessions from below. . . . This little cloud will always overhang the republic, like the perpetual vapour which hovers over Niagara, thrown up by the force and regularity of the movement below." American society lacked the suppleness to take Miss Martineau's advice. Far from welcoming "accessions from below," those at the top did everything they could to block the route. Eventually they found themselves teetering alone in the fog at the top of the ladder, discernible to almost nobody except themselves.

The low visibility made many uncomfortable. Julia Delafield, Grandma Grundy's daughter, tried to see her way clear in an essay entitled "The Upper Ten" and succeeded only in rendering the pea soup thicker. At the outset Mrs. Delafield had trouble identifying the Upper Ten and giving its field marks—an exercise in which she ended by chasing her own tail. A member of the Upper Ten, she affirmed, is one who has a "single-minded, inbred conviction of his position," which results in his never offering "any apology or explanation for being found among its ranks." In other words, he is secure in his position because of the position he is in. (Or, to turn it inside out, the only thing he has to fear is fear itself.)

But how does one achieve the position in the first place? Mrs. Delafield patriotically averred that "the line of separation [between the Upper Ten and the rest of society] is more easily passed in our republic than in the empires of the old world"; but then turned around to declaim that membership is "an advantage which the wealth of the Indies can not purchase, which an Emperor can not bestow, and to which genius may not hope to soar."

Where, then, should genius apply? Nowhere: those who aspire to invade the Upper Ten are "a fidgety, comfortless race, who deserve our sincerest commiseration. . . . They dare not be themselves, and they can not forget themselves. Like the novice of the dancing-school, they are intent upon their toes, their elbows, their positions. Their courtesy wants dignity, and whenever they dare, they are impertinent. . . . Like the mixed multitude who followed Moses out of Egypt, they go in and out of the camp, but they are not the children of Israel."

Mrs. Delafield's description may be apt, but her attempt to rationalize an American Upper Ten was doomed to failure. At the end she gave up and concluded, with a small sigh of relief, that though "Birth is losing its privileges: it never can lose its prestige."

In the same year as Mrs. Delafield's manifesto, 1857, Oliver Wendell Holmes (the writer, father of the Chief Justice) published another on the same subject. Holmes recalled a Boston matron's inquiry as to when she should begin her son's upbringing, to which he replied, "About a hundred years, Madam, before he was born." In *The Autocrat of the Breakfast-Table,* he described in detail the accoutrements of aristocracy, including family portraits, books, old silver, and a coat of arms. But he was uncomfortable, as Mrs. Delafield was, with the implications of an American aristocracy based on heredity, and he proclaimed that "one . . . may have all the antecedents I have spoken of, and yet be a boor or a shabby fellow. One may have none of them, and yet be fit for councils and courts. Then let them change places." But Mr. Holmes insisted on his own personal "democratic liberty of choice. . . . I go for the man with the gallery of family portraits against the one with the twenty-five cent daguerreotype, unless I find out that the latter is the better of the two."

In other words, all things being equal (which they never are), breeding has its benefits.

Samuel Johnson, from the vantage point of an earlier and simpler time, neatly defined "gentleman" as *"homo gentilis,* a man of ancestry. All other derivations seem to be whimsical."

29

Julia Delafield died in 1882, a quarter of a century after writing "The Upper Ten." That same year her niece, Ruth Livingston, was married to a specimen of the "fidgety, comfortless race," the newest and richest of the new rich, Ogden Mills of California. Mills's father, Darius, had been a forty-niner, one of the lucky ones. The Mills family's wealth was immense but its social credentials were nil, a fact which the new Mrs. Mills set out to extinguish.

What Ruth Livingston Mills lacked in charm and subtlety she made up for in determination and audacity. Disdaining her cousin Caroline Astor's Four Hundred—and hedging only slightly on her Aunt Julia Delafield's Upper Ten—she announced that society consisted of exactly twenty families. The Four Hundred naturally demurred; and their queen, Mrs. Astor, was able to beat off the challenge from her younger kinswoman. Ruth Mills, "defeated . . . by her own exclusiveness," retreated, Livingston-like, into the Hudson Valley to lick her wounds and plan her next campaign.

The Millses inherited the Staatsburgh estate from Ruth's father in the 1890s (Grandma Grundy, her grandmother, had died in 1860); and they engaged the distinguished society architect, Stanford White, to revamp the house in conformity with their social designs. White added enormous wings to the relatively modest structure and gave the monolithic facade a Grecian look, with pilasters, statuary and marble balustrades. Inside, the Millses reinvented the French eighteenth century with furnishings, marble fireplaces, oak paneling and universal gilt. Mrs. Mills's incessant house parties soon acquired a reputation for luxury, social intrigue and inflated stakes at the bridge table.*

Most of Mrs. Mills's cousins up and down the valley—at Clermont, Oak Hill, Pine Lawn, Callendar House and Montgomery Place—attended her parties infrequently and felt no temptation to adopt her style of country living. Simpler pleasures were the rule at these establishments: winter afternoons tobogganing with the children or racing the family iceboat; summer days spent riding, sailing and swimming in the river. The cousins rarely went out of the family circle, but they called on one another constantly, traveling by foot or carriage along the private road that had been cleared through the woods between their houses or, in summer, by rowboat or canoe on the river. Children drove their pony carts back and forth to visit their cousins, with baby brothers and sisters jogging along behind in elegant little wicker seats strapped to the backs of donkeys. The public road, about a mile inland, was sealed off from the houses by deep woods and stone walls with iron gates.

Swimming parties by the river were a favorite family entertainment, as was the game of tennis. Two of the Hall boys at Oak Lawn (their mother, a Ludlow daughter, had built Oak Lawn next door to her parents' Pine Lawn) held the national doubles championship, and down in Hyde Park a pair of Roosevelt girls were U.S. champions. Everyone played on weekends at the private court of one cousin or another, the gentlemen dressed in long white trousers, stiff collars and neckties, the ladies in full, ankle-length skirts and wide-brimmed hats. Between games "iced tea and barley water and sandwiches [were served] in the shade under the trees."

In 1884 the family decided to institutionalize the combat by founding its own tennis club, the Edgewood Club of Tivoli. An organizational meeting was held at Oak Lawn,† and sixty-odd people signed on as charter members, all of them Livingstons, Livingston cousins or close neighbors. Edgewood's definition as a "family club" did not mean, in the usual sense, a club for all the family but rather a club for The Family and its closest friends. Annual dues were set at $10, and a committee composed of two Livingstons, two Clarksons and a de Peyster was commissioned to oversee construction of the clubhouse and five tennis courts on land donated by family members just across the public road from Clermont and Eversleigh. The unpretentious clubhouse, which opened the following summer, consisted of a main room, its walls covered in fashionable mauve burlap; a small kitchen; two dressing rooms; and a wide front porch overlooking the courts, where tea was served each Saturday at four o'clock by one of the lady members.

* Ruth and Ogden Mills were said to be the models for Judy and Gus Trenor in Edith Wharton's *The House of Mirth.*
† A few weeks after the meeting at their house the Halls celebrated the birth of a new granddaughter, Eleanor Roosevelt, who later married her cousin Franklin of Hyde Park.

The game of tennis was taken very seriously, as it frequently is by otherwise benign and rational human beings. Edgewood naturally subscribed to the rules of the National Lawn Tennis Association; but it refused to join, because the Association held its national tournament on Labor Day weekend, when the Edgewood Club wished to hold *its* tournament, and the tennis committee did not wish any "possible conflict" to occur. But even tennis bowed to God: for the first quarter-century of the club's existence, no play was permitted on Sunday. (Golf was allowed, because from the golf course, situated in a remote field, "the language of the players off their game does not carry to the road.")

Edgewood was founded in an era of clubs—country clubs, city clubs and residential clubs (Tuxedo Park, for example, established the year after Edgewood) sprang up throughout American society, thus confirming its commitment to exclusivity. It is not surprising, in a world which increasingly presented members of the old guard with situations and people that made them feel uncomfortable, that they should have resorted to what Ralph Waldo Emerson called "the good invention whereby everybody is provided with some one who is glad to see him."

The founding of the Edgewood Club was also a gesture in the direction of Livingston family unity, that precious commodity which appeared to be slipping away so swiftly. Like pedigree, the club was something all members of the family could hold in common—neutral territory, if you like. It didn't work out that way, of course; the ritual combat of the tennis court reduced family tension no better than Saturday afternoon tea on the club porch engendered family affection. The intended neutral ground came to resemble a battlefield, with one possibly constructive aspect: the feuds that year after year rattled the teacups were frequently fought over club issues instead of personal issues, which may in some small way have reduced the level of carnage.

The Edgewood Club claims to be the oldest country club in the civilized United States. What it forgets is that the very earliest exclusive club on Livingston Manor, the "Club of Claverack Manor and the Roeliff Jansen Kill," was established by a group of tenants some one hundred and thirty years previously, before the Revolutionary War, and that its rules of decorum, the Sabbath notwithstanding, were a good deal stricter.

The Livingston family of Clermont was well represented on Edgewood's list of charter members, although its family structure—like its dining-room ceiling—was on the verge of collapsing from within. Clermont Livingston and his wife attended the meeting at Oak Lawn, as did his son John Henry, with his wife. The two men rarely spoke to each other, after John Henry's second marriage to a woman of whom his father did not approve. Clermont's displeasure was so palpable that John Henry, his wife and baby daughter (by his late first-wife-and-cousin, Catherine Livingston

Hamersley) had moved to Philadelphia, returning to Clermont during the summer months to oversee John Henry's patrimony. The patrimony, however, was no longer his: Clermont Livingston, no doubt unbeknownst to his son, had altered his will to leave the estate directly to his granddaughter, Catharine, with John Henry receiving life tenancy only.

When Clermont died eleven years later, in 1895, Catharine Livingston was twenty-two years old. No one knows what passed between the girl and her father that led to her deeding the estate over to him. But within a few years she had burned a fair number of other bridges as well: she changed the spelling of her name to Katharine and, after marrying, moved herself and her family permanently to England.

John Henry, at fifty-eight, was undisputed master of Clermont; but his second wife had died in the meantime, and he was very much alone. It did not take the slender, handsome, landed bachelor long to find a wife (or, as some of the family have speculated, for a wife to find him). His new bride was thirty-four-year-old Alice Delafield Clarkson, a distant cousin for whose father John Henry had served as best man, forty years before. Alice was a Livingston to her fingertips, being descended from the Reverend John Livingston of Scotland through no fewer than three different lines. Her husband was probably the only man in the world to whom she had to defer in this regard (Alice was not in the habit of deferring): his descent came down through four lines.‡

John Henry's English daughter, Katharine Timpson, was profoundly shaken by her father's marriage. Perhaps she feared the prospect of rival siblings. Had her father promised to leave Clermont to her when he died? No one seems to know. Or perhaps she simply disliked having a stepmother only one year older than herself. In any case, Katharine severed all remaining ties with her father and for the next fifteen years there was no communication between them.

Meanwhile the new Mrs. John Henry Livingston was busy producing two daughters, Honoria Alice* and Janet. The couple also purchased from the heirs of the "Clarkson aunties" the tumbledown old Chancellor's house across the lawn and renamed it Arryl House (an acronym for R.R.L., the Chancellor's initials), thus reuniting the estate of Clermont for the first time since the Chancellor's death in 1813. But Arryl House burned a few months later, under somewhat muddled circumstances. John Henry fought through the night with a crew of men; but in the morning only the blackened shell remained and he appeared inconsolable. Nevertheless it was decided to let the ruin stand as it was. Alice's imagination was beginning to be fired by the gardening possibilities at Clermont, and the blackened brick fingers of the

‡ Which makes their children Livingstons-times-seven. Only one other present-day member of the family outdoes them, with eight lines.
* "Honor to Alice," a mother for the first time at age thirty-seven.

Chancellor's walls furnished an extremely picturesque, modishly Gothic addition to the landscape.

John Henry devoted much of the rest of his life (he died in 1927) to the study and commemoration of his ancestry. In 1911 he founded and became first president of an organization known as the Order of Colonial Lords of Manors in America—only one of a number of genealogical societies which, like private clubs, were being born in vast numbers at this period. In one decade alone (1887–97) were established the Daughters of the Cincinnati, the Sons of the Revolution, the Daughters of the American Revolution, the Colonial Dames, the Society of Mayflower Descendants, the Baronial Order of Runnymede, and the Aryan Order of St. George of the Holy Roman Empire in the Colonies of America.†

John Henry's cousin, Charles L. Livingston, a devoted and diligent acolyte, served as secretary to the Order of Colonial Lords, a responsibility he took extremely seriously. Charles L. became highly indignant when some of his cousins failed to treat the enterprise with sufficient gravity. After receiving the genealogical papers of a Van Rensselaer connection, he complained to John Henry that the young man had "only carried his claim back to the *last* Patroon, not to the one who had the grant, nor the first Lord of the Manor. Then he took up his Mother's line, giving her descent from a New *Jersey Judge*. . . . He signed without any notary, and as for his duplicate paper, he sent that perfectly *blank*. It is very odd how they all leave so much for me to do."

Another of John Henry's cousins, Edwin Brockholst Livingston, brought forth the same year as the founding of the Colonial Lords a family history entitled *The Livingstons of Callendar and Their Principal Cadets.* This privately published, tenderly inaccurate family chronicle reserves its only harsh words for those family members who "through a false idea of modesty, or through ignorance, repudiate that nobility to which [they] are fully and legally entitled." One of the book's chapter headings sets the tone for the entire opus, a quotation from Shakespeare's *King Richard II:*

O, call back yesterday, bid time return!

Another feuding father and son attended the Edgewood Club meeting at the Halls' in the summer of 1884: General John Watts de Peyster and his son, Johnston Livingston de Peyster. General de Peyster, a descendant of the original Gilbert Livingston, was married to his distant cousin, Johnston Livingston's sister Estelle. After the de Peysters built their elegant villa, Rose Hill, next door to Estelle's childhood home, Green Hill, the environs

† If the latter seems to be stretching a bit, consider the claim of the twentieth-century French aristocrat who, chancing to overhear a question pertaining to the length and shape of his very distinctive profile—to wit, "How long do you suppose it took to make that nose?"—responded, "Ever since Clovis was crowned at Rheims by St. Remy," an event which took place in about the year 500 A.D.

of Tivoli, New York, became firmly established as the haven of choice for repatriated branches of the Livingston family.

General de Peyster was, by all accounts, a holy terror. Invariably hostile, always colorful, his outbursts achieved the force of legend. He kept loaded a Civil War cannon in the front hall at Rose Hill, trained at the front door, and signed his various literary masterpieces "John Watts de Peyster, Brigadier-General (M.F.S.N.Y.) and Brevet Major-General (N.G.S.N.Y.)." The library at Rose Hill, its shelf space devoted largely to multiple copies of the general's own works, had a conspicuous sign over the door that read simply, SHUT UP. The general was an ardent Republican. During one campaign he "ran the photographs of the Presidential and Vice-Presidential candidates up the spire of the Episcopal Church . . . the Democrats came and pulled them down and put up the Democratic candidates and then the Republican candidates went up again—this continued until Mass was out in the Roman Catholic Church when the Democrats triumphed on top."

General de Peyster's influence at St. Paul's Episcopal Church in Tivoli was considerable, particularly after he donated the land for a new building in 1868. But, assuming that his largesse gave him license to "indulge in his penchant for erecting monuments," he was furious when the minister gently suggested that the growing accumulation of marble threatened to close off the aisles. De Peyster stalked out of St. Paul's, converted on the spot to Methodism and donated the money for a splendid new brick Methodist church designed to dominate the village's main street.‡

It is not surprising that General de Peyster did not get on well with his family, particularly his sons. One of these hapless fellows, Frederic, married John Henry Livingston's sister, Mary, and became an alcoholic. The youngest, Johnston Livingston de Peyster, carried on a prolonged feud with his father which spilled over into the politics of the village of Tivoli. General de Peyster had financed the building of a fine brick fire house in the village, which housed the John Watts de Peyster Hook and Ladder Company and also provided a meeting hall for the village trustees. When his son Johnston was elected president of the village in 1900, the general not only demanded that the trustees stop using the fire house but declared that the fire company itself could stay only "so long as they not admit one Johnston Livingston de Peyster or . . . the Trustees . . . to any part of the building. . . . If any damage is done to my building," the general continued ominously, "I hold the Village responsible; and if through any untoward accident it burns down it will not be rebuilt nor will my church if that burns down be rebuilt by me nor will I insure it again."

‡ Another version of General de Peyster's conversion to Methodism attributes it to his dog, who always accompanied his master to church and during one Sunday sermon jumped up and bit the minister. When the pastor requested de Peyster to leave the animal home in future, the general was inspired to take his spiritual business elsewhere.

General de Peyster never made peace with the trustees or with his son. When Johnston joined the Edgewood Club, the general did not; and when the younger man came to Rose Hill to see his mother on her deathbed, "his father is supposed to have laid hands upon him and dragged him around the bed and tried to put him out of the house."

The old man had the last word on all of them: having survived his sons, he left Rose Hill in his will to the Leake & Watts Orphan Home of New York City. It was a fine thumb of the nose to any relations who might have expected to inherit, as well as to the village of Tivoli, which lost a prime piece of property from its tax rolls. It was also a portent of the future for all the general's kin who lived in the neighborhood, although they may not have realized it. Rose Hill became the first Livingston riverfront mansion to be occupied by an institution—an innovation that altered forever the private, cloistered, clannish character of "Livingston Valley."

30

About twenty miles south of Rose Hill, a new estate was being created that also changed forever the character of "Livingston Valley." In 1896, Frederick William Vanderbilt purchased the magnificent old Bard property near the village of Hyde Park, demolished the existing house and hired Stanford White's architectural firm to design a mansion "like the Trianon, only larger." Vanderbilt, having not had the grace to marry a Livingston before invading the family turf, presumably wanted to be sure his presence would be noted. It was. As a neighboring Livingston mother advised her son regarding the Vanderbilts, "You may be nice to them, but don't get involved."

Not to be outdone, William Backhouse Astor, Jr., son of the Rokeby Astors and husband of *the* Mrs. Astor, promptly hired the same architects to design a large and elegant tennis building at Ferncliff, his estate near Rhinebeck; and at Rokeby itself a new generation of Astors hired the firm to build a new stable. Rokeby's gardens, walks and vistas were also revamped by the eminent landscaping firm of Olmsted Brothers, whose founder had been a designer of Central Park.

Rokeby now belonged to William B. and Peachy Astor's great-grandchildren, the eight young "Astor orphans" as they were known after the untimely deaths of their mother, Maddie Astor Ward, and her husband, John Chanler. Maddie and John Chanler had been married in 1862. They were fourth cousins once removed, Chanler's mother having been descended from the first proprietor of Livingston Manor.

In John Chanler's paternal heritage ran rich veins of contradiction and idiosyncrasy. The first Chanler in America—John's great-grandfather—was a Baptist minister in Charleston, South Carolina, and distinguished author of a treatise on the subject of "Glorious Grace and Eternal Damnation." The minister's son also became an author in the field of medicine, his best-known title being *De Hysteria*. In addition to eloquence and erudition, Dr. Chanler had personified several other strong family traits: social prudence—he quit the Baptists for the Church of England—and an exuberant eccentricity—his favorite recreation, which he pursued in the streets of Charleston in broad daylight, was to jump out from behind trees to grab pretty girls and kiss them.

The doctor's son, in his turn, furthered the family's social advancement by moving to New York, becoming an Episcopal minister and marrying a daughter of the Massachusetts Winthrop family. His daguerreotype depicts a handsome man, with a globe in one hand, a Bible in the other and the bust of John Calhoun peering over his shoulder, indicating (as a later Chanler put it) his interests in "Religion, the World, and the Democratic Party."*

This gentleman was the father of the John Winthrop Chanler who married Maddie Ward. The new Mrs. Chanler, like her husband, boasted a rich mixture of traditional family personality quirks, ranging from extreme social conformity to certifiable insanity. (As one of John and Maddie's children remarked later, "The Chanlers were a very respectable lot of people in Charleston until the yellow splotch of the Astors stained their escutcheon. But you never would have heard of the Chanlers if it hadn't been for that yaller stain"; and he wasn't talking just about money.) The predictable explosion was delayed, however, for one more generation. Maddie had fully absorbed her Astor grandparents' rigid, straitlaced rules of decorum; and in her husband she found an equally devout social conformist.

But both Maddie and John Chanler died before their oldest child was fourteen. Their ten children (the youngest only three) were installed at Rokeby, which they inherited jointly from their mother. Their vast fortune was administered by a panel of trustees, and their persons were catered to by a staff of governesses, tutors, nurses, cooks, laundresses, seamstresses, maids, butlers, grooms and gardeners, all under the supervision of a distant cousin of their late father, Miss Mary Marshall.

Miss Marshall, a gentle Southern maiden lady, was no match for the

---

* A slightly different slant on the Chanler personality comes from seventeenth-century England, when three members of the family, sitting in the Long Parliament, were required to pass judgment in the trial of Charles I. It was a dicey business; Cromwell had the votes, but regicide could prove extremely hazardous in the long run. The Chanlers found an elegant solution: one voted for conviction, another for acquittal and the third stayed home—thus illustrating the premise that, for every Chanler who puts all his eggs into one basket, another always hedges his bets.

rambunctious brood of "Astor orphans." The eight survivors (two brothers died young) were a restless, energetic lot, impatient with the strictures of their society but never totally able to break free. Each was at war within himself and, when necessary, with his siblings. Deprived of parents, the eight Chanlers developed a fierce loyalty to one another; yet at the same time their greatest fear as individuals was of being smothered by the group. They adored each other and they quarreled, violently and incessantly. In their youth, disputation became the family recreation, and "voices resounded everywhere in the great house, children talking on all floors, at all hours, and all at once. Each child was prepared pugnaciously to challenge anything said, and to back up the challenge with arguments. Since the disputants seldom allowed an antagonist to finish a sentence, in these noisy debates pro and con could be heard simultaneously. The participants enjoyed their verbal battles with sensual satisfaction. There were rules, one being that there should be no hitting ('take it out in words'), and another forbade 'showing off.' A third provided that 'a bore must shut up.' " It is not surprising that stuttering became a family problem, at least among several of the boys.

Since the children were only sporadically educated, these disorderly debates were usually stronger on form—the Chanler verbal agility was staggering—than substance, a fact which inhibited the disputants not at all. Miss Marshall, though kindly, was helpless to control her charges, who grew up utterly undisciplined intellectually or emotionally, except by each other and the demands of their society.

By the year of the founding of the Edgewood Club, 1884, the Chanler brood ranged in age from twenty-two to eleven.† The first to marry was Wintie, who wrote to his sisters from Rome in 1886 that he was engaged to their cousin (Sam Ward's niece), Margaret ("Daisy") Terry, who had lived most of her life in Italy and become a Catholic convert. It was the latter that sent a "shudder of revulsion" through the female population of Rokeby, where New York society's prejudice against the Church of Rome was absolute. Miss Marshall, "feeling sure that [her charges] could only speak ill" of Wintie's bride, simply "issued orders that [she] should never be mentioned."

The bride and groom visited Rokeby the following summer to await the birth of their first child; and it soon became apparent that the antipathy of Wintie's two older sisters toward Daisy was fueled by something stronger than theological conviction. Both Elizabeth and Margaret Chanler were exorbitantly possessive, and Daisy's expropriation of their brother and intrusion into their Chanler-Rokeby universe, trailing whiffs of popery, was deeply resented.

† Two of the older boys, Winthrop (Wintie) and William (Willie), attended the Edgewood meeting, although apparently only Willie joined. They weren't really the club type.

Margaret, in particular, fought a bitter and prolonged internal tug-of-war between loyalty to her brother and animosity against his wife. Margaret's internal battles were always fought to the death; she was a black-and-white, all-or-nothing kind of person. Of all the eight siblings, Margaret always had the strongest will, the greatest pride. At the age of five she had defied her older brothers and sisters, who taunted her, on returning from church one Sunday, for having spent the morning shut in the sewing room as a punishment and thereby missing the christening of a pair of twins. "I did not know," Margaret wrote later, "what twins were. I spoke scornfully of them; expressed my pleasure in lonely tranquillity, and experienced joy of overhearing [the curate's wife] say to Mary Maroney [the governess] 'She is not penitent at all.' 'Not she,' replied Mary, 'her heart is too hard.' With a sense of triumph I brushed out into the sunshine delighted to have been of so much importance."

But Margaret's warring spirit could not be entirely pacified. Try as she might, for the rest of her very long life, to clothe her behavior in garments of pride and principle, her contradictory, chaotic nature almost invariably betrayed her.

Margaret's seventeen-year-old response to the theological and personal conundrum posed by her brother's popish infant was typically disorganized and absolutely unique. Margaret was convinced, once little Laura had been baptized by the local Catholic priest, that "the kindest thing one could do to the infant would be to kill it in its innocence." At the same time, she confessed, "she loved the child better than anything on earth, and had even gone into the nursery one night to kiss it in its sleep." But during the day, when the baby was brought into the room, Margaret "rose and fled, as at the approach of a leper." Her problem, it appeared, was with appearances. She could kiss the baby secretly and love her devoutly, but "could not acknowledge it *in the presence of others*" [italics added].

Margaret and her sisters, after being presented to New York society under the watchful eye of their aunt, Caroline Astor, spent two seasons in London. Both Elizabeth and Alida were presented at court; but Margaret refused the honor because she would not curtsey to the Queen of England when "White House etiquette . . . made no provision for curtseying to the President." Her patriotic zeal in refusing to "pay greater deference to [a] foreign sovereign than she was expected to pay to the head of her own nation" was perhaps admirable—but the curtsey gives her away. The year before, her sister Elizabeth had forgotten to curtsey at her presentation, an omission which the Queen graciously ignored but the press did not. The word "trepidation" was not, of course, in Margaret Chanler's vocabulary; so her refusal to undergo the ceremony had to be couched in terms of high morality. It was a stylistic touch that was to become her hallmark.

Margaret's five brothers all made a mark on the world, in vastly diverting and divergent ways. Archie, the eldest, was committed by his brothers to an insane asylum at the age of thirty-four.‡ He managed to escape and flee to Virginia, where he spent the remainder of his life eating three meals a week—mostly duck and ice cream—and cultivating what he called his "X-faculty," a visionary state in which he claimed to be able to change the color of his hair and eyes, communicate with the dead and relive (literally) the death of Napoleon Bonaparte.

The second brother, Wintie, became an international sportsman and master of the *beau geste.* Gallant, witty, stylish and utterly self-indulgent, Wintie succeeded at nearly everything he tried, including his long and remarkably satisfactory marriage with Daisy.

Willie Chanler, the third brother, was an African explorer and dabbler in international intrigue. Like all the family, he was casual about money. A safari outfitter in London, with whom Willie had placed an enormous order, inquired somewhat timidly at the American Embassy concerning the fate of the account should Mr. Chanler fail to return from the expedition. He was informed that in that melancholy event the account would be promptly paid by Willie's bank; it was only if Mr. Chanler *did* return that he might have to worry. Toward the end of his life Willie lost a leg and wore thereafter a wooden peg leg, in honor of his ancestor, Peter Stuyvesant. He once removed it in a restaurant and hurled it across the room at an inattentive waiter, after which he received prompt service wherever he dined.

The fourth and fifth brothers were as different as two men could be, except that both went in for Democratic politics. Lewis, the most diligent and conventional of the clan (and his sister Margaret's favorite), became lieutenant governor of New York State. His brother Bob, known in the precincts of Rokeby as "Sheriff Bob," was a wildly talented painter and a formidable drunk—another Chanler at war with himself.

Rokeby—the "Astor orphans' " joint inheritance and childhood home —became the sole property of Margaret after all of her brothers and sisters had married. Margaret's affection has fastened itself on Rokeby from the first moment she saw it, at the age of six. Her siblings perhaps donated their shares to give their spinster sister a home; on the other hand, at least one of Margaret's descendants swears that she "forced" them out of the estate— "she was very tough." In any case Margaret, at twenty-eight, became sole mistress of Rokeby. After a stint as a Red Cross nurse during the Spanish-American War, in which she earned a reputation for executive efficiency and physical courage, she served as her brother Willie's hostess in Washington, D.C., during his term in Congress, and subsequently traveled to the Philippines on a personal inspection trip in support of her effort to convince Congress to establish an army nursing corps. The voyage took her not only

‡ Archie later wrote a book of sonnets condemning his siblings, published under the title *Scorpio.* One critic called it "the anchovy paste on the buttered toast of our literature."

to Manila but on to China, where she arrived just in time for the Boxer Rebellion.

By 1906 Margaret had returned home and settled into Rokeby, where, at the age of thirty-six, she startled everybody, including possibly herself, by marrying. (It was a good year for Livingston spinsters; Alice Delafield Clarkson was also married in 1906 to John Henry Livingston.) Her groom was Richard Aldrich, the distinguished music critic of the New York *Times* and scion of a highly respectable but impecunious family. Richard was gentle, kindly, erudite—and he stuttered badly. Nothing in his situation or makeup enabled him to stand up to his assertive and very rich wife.

Like her cousin Alice of Clermont, Margaret sensibly lost no time in having children: Richard Chanler Aldrich was born in 1909, and Margaret Astor Chanler Aldrich (another "Maddie") the year after. But the joy of little Maddie's birth was somewhat dampened by an apostasy in the ranks of Margaret's siblings: her youngest sister, Alida, that year became a convert to the Roman Catholic Church. Overnight Alida's presence, even the mention of her name, became taboo at Rokeby. Margaret's rules admitted no exception and brooked no appeal.

The ban on converted Catholics was only one of Margaret's rules. Two other prohibitions were by now etched in the marble of her soul: the use of alcohol and "plural marriage" (i.e., remarrying after a divorce). Not surprisingly, perhaps, all of her ˙blings except Archie and Elizabeth eventually fell under one or more of these interdicts: at least two of the men were alcoholics, one married a converted Catholic and two were guilty of plural marriage. All were expunged from their sister's life and from Rokeby forever.

Margaret had painted herself into a corner. When even her beloved Lewis, her greatest joy and hope for the family, let her down, it nearly broke her heart. No doubt she never ceased to love Lewis, as fiercely and possessively as ever; but after he defied her injunction against plural marriage, she would never again acknowledge him "in the presence of others," nor would she permit him to cross the threshold of his childhood home. Rokeby, her citadel, was not to be defiled.

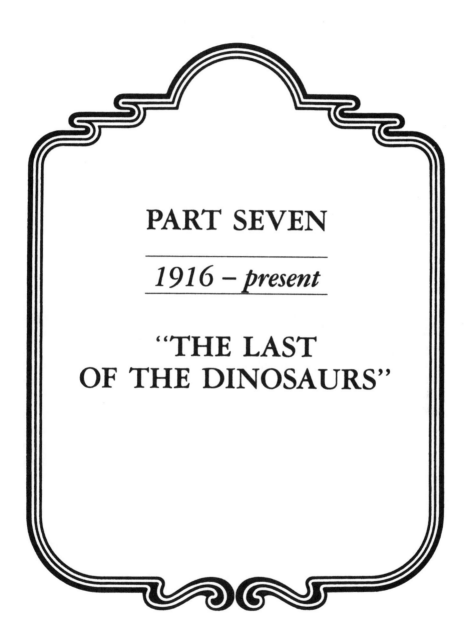

PART SEVEN

1916 – present

"THE LAST OF THE DINOSAURS"

31

As the great-granddaughter of William Backhouse Astor, Margaret Livingston Chanler Aldrich could easily afford to subscribe to the contemporary view that "money-getting . . . comes from rather a low instinct . . . it is scarcely met with in combination with the finer or more interesting traits of character." Her society—old New York society—had begun to look down its nose at "money-getting" a generation before, when the post-Civil War influx of new wealth first threatened to overwhelm its traditional structures and alliances. By the outbreak of the First World War, this ripple of disparagement had grown into a tidal wave: social New York, equating earning power with vulgarity, looked down on " 'successful' men" as incapable of "humor, thought or refinement. A set of mere money-getters and traders, they [are] essentially unattractive."

Unfortunately this attitudinal wave crested about the same time that the graduated income tax became the law of the land. After passage of the Sixteenth Amendment in 1913, followed three years later by a progressive estate tax, many of the belittlers of "money-getting" had to reassess their position. A number of Livingston proprietors on the Hudson's east bank, for example, changed their tune and emulated their ancestors: they went to work, and in the process reinvigorated the Livingston family tradition of accomplishment in the worlds of American finance, trade and the professions.

Some of their cousins, on the other hand, were incapable of adapting to the new economic realities. Transfixed by prejudice—against "mere money-getters"—and fear—of being considered "essentially unattractive"—they clung instead to their notion of lordship over a phantom manor. In 1929, when Wall Street crumbled, they were found posing for posterity with their heads firmly stuck in the sand.

Ironically, many of these same cousins were devoted students of the Livingston family history, although they failed to profit from its lessons. Beguiled by the tenuous, bygone connection to Scottish nobility, they ignored the fact that the American Livingstons' financial and personal equilibrium had always depended on having one foot firmly planted outside of "Livingston Valley."

Evolution demonstrates that survival depends on adaptation. Those who fail to adapt are often consumed, at the hour of their death, with nostalgia about the good old days. If the past is a textbook, one focuses at one's peril on the pretty colored pictures. Castles in the clouds, the Elysian Fields and even El Dorado are always out of reach, and those who pursue them exclusively are bound for disappointment and sorrow, along the road to extinction.

In 1920, John Henry Livingston, now seventy-two and sporting an enormous silver ear trumpet, took his wife and daughters for a postwar sojourn in Europe. A Florentine villa became their principal home for the next five years, during which Alice devoted herself to a study of Italian gardens, the little girls practiced their languages and attended the opera, and John Henry forged a reconciliation with his English daughter, Katharine Timpson. Katharine, who had become a British citizen in 1919, was much engaged in the latest literary effort of their cousin, Edwin Brockholst Livingston: a revised edition of the first half of his earlier family history, published in Edinburgh in 1920 under the title *The Livingstons of Callendar* and dedicated to Katharine in recognition of her interest and financial backing.

What Katharine may not have known was that just before leaving home her father had rewritten his will a final time. When he died, six years later in America, she professed complete surprise to learn that Clermont had been left to her stepmother, Alice, free and clear—together with John Henry's express approval if at some future date she chose to either sell or give it away. Nevertheless, within six months of her father's death, Katharine executed a legal document assigning to Alice her interest in the estate, thereby turning her back on Clermont forever.

Proprietorship affected Alice Clarkson Livingston as profoundly as it had Margaret Chanler Aldrich. But without an Astor fortune to command, her plans for leaving her mark on Clermont necessarily remained more modest. Whereas Margaret had hired Stanford White and the Olmsted Brothers to enhance her *mise-en-scène,* Alice followed her own design.

She cared little for the house itself, and the cracks in Clermont's dining-room ceiling beams extended into their fifth generation. Her lasting impact was on the landscape. Between the time of her husband's death and the late 1950s, this experienced and knowledgeable gardener transformed the grounds of Clermont into an elegant tapestry of borders, rockeries, walks, spaces and views inspired by the European establishments she knew so well. *Allées* of trees were planted, fieldstone paths installed, retaining walls constructed. A cozy spring garden nestled in a sheltered corner, and a formal walled garden was juxtaposed against an English "Wilderness." East of the house a lilac walk was set, while to the south the "Long View," leading down a broad sweep of lawn past the blackened brick ruins of the Chancellor's house, ended with the Shawangunk Mountains rising in the hazy distance.

The wedding reception of Alice's older daughter, Honoria, was held in 1931 on Clermont's east lawn, with all of river society in attendance. Honoria had inherited the great physical beauty of both her parents. Her sister Janet's legacy was more in the area of personality: imperiousness derived from her mother and, from her father, John Henry, infatuation with the past glories of the family of Livingston.

Janet also had an inchoate grasp of sober economic truth, and over her mother's strenuous protests went to night school for financial training and then took a job in a New York City bank. Her weekend energies were divided between the grounds of Clermont—where she wielded hedge clippers and sickle bar in furtherance of her mother's landscaping schemes— and the Edgewood Club, where she wielded the verbal clippers in defense of the eternal family verities. Janet was never outfaced and on only one recorded occasion nonplussed. Introduced at a large summer gathering to an affable young man, she was momentarily taken aback when he calmly— innocently—informed her that he lived across the river on the west bank. The west bank, Janet had learned in her cradle, was "Wrongside" (all one word); one simply did not meet people from the west bank. She recovered quickly, though—breeding will tell—and politely observed how very nice it must be for him to look out his living-room windows and be able to see all the Livingston mansions across the water.

In 1930, Janet received from her kinsman and kindred spirit, John Ross Delafield of Montgomery Place, "Brigadier General, D.S.M.," a copy of a statement which constituted "the only proof we have that our ancestor Alexander Livingston was the son of Master James Livingston, who was in turn the son of William, fourth Lord Livingston." General Delafield, who served as president of the Order of Colonial Lords of Manors in America, deemed the statement "so valuable from a family history point of view that I am sending you a copy thinking you may wish to lay it, or fasten it, at page 66, in your copy of *The Livingstons of Callendar,* 2nd edition."

It appears that even Lords of Manors in America need constant reassurance.

W. Stewart Woodfill remarked in the 1920s that "three things killed Society—the automobile and bad manners and no sense of history." "Livingston Valley" remained immune to all three between the world wars, according to members of the family who were growing up there. These men and women, now grandparents, look back with great affection on childhoods of vast security and serenity. Life in their east-bank mansions was slow-paced, old-fashioned and elegant. The children were surrounded by plenty of servants, cousins and mile after mile of the family property, with the mighty Hudson as a private moat in front.

They remember the beauty of the out-of-doors. Winter vacations were organized around skating, iceboating, and sledding down favorite runs whose every curve, bump and patch of ice is still etched in memory half a century later: down a steep bank, around the porch, "down across the field, up over the bank and straight for the railroad track—and then you'd fall off." At Northwood, Mrs. Robert R. Livingston's parlormaid placed sofa cushions along the porch steps, in case one of the little ones didn't make the curve.

In summer, while their parents were occupied at the Edgewood Club (where children were not welcome), the youngsters spent day after golden day riding horses, building tree houses, inventing games, fishing, chasing fireflies, or stealing down to the kitchen for cookies and a stint at the butter churn. Dressing up was rarely called for except for family weddings and dancing class, when the organdy dresses and white mohair suits came out of the drawer. Dancing class was held regularly at one cousin's estate or another, with supper afterward; and the children traveled back and forth on the train, which made special stops for them, house by house. Their instructor, Mr. Rutherford, who had "a fat tummy and white waistcoat and white gloves," taught a ladies' class as well, and the children used to sneak away from supper to spy on their mothers, taking particular delight in the spectacle of Mrs. Ogden Mills prancing through a fast polka with her bright red hair and red high heels, "just like Queen Elizabeth."

With the children fully occupied, and increasing numbers of the men working in the city during the week, the Livingston wives, mothers, grandmothers and aunts had plenty of time to engage in their own favorite summer recreation: family feuding. The crowning age of the Dragons had arrived: a generation of commanding females who dominated Livingston family life for half a century. In a staggering display of vitality, authoritativeness and stamina, these ladies fought over everything, from the style of the candlesticks on the altar of St. Paul's Church to the responsibility for canine birth control (who was to blame for an unwanted litter of puppies, the unfenced bitch in heat or the roving male from next door?). With energy, ingenuity and remarkable tenacity, the Dragons elevated the slightest disagreement into a major family feud, often resulting in one party not speaking to the other for a summer, a year, or even longer. "It was," a bystander recollects, "exhausting."

Much of the feuding was territorial in origin, and it is no coincidence that the two with the most to defend—Alice Clarkson Livingston and Margaret Chanler Aldrich—were fire breathers par excellence. Clermont and Rokeby provided the ideal settings for the magisterial behavior that came so naturally to both their mistresses.

Many of the Dragons are said to have had charm; but while some of their contemporaries look back on their beauty, grace and wit, others recall only the knife in the ribs. Attractive or not, they ruled the roost. They have also been called "the last of the dinosaurs"—a felicitous metaphor indicating both their scale and their fate. Nearly half of these formidable matriarchs spawned generations of children who did not reproduce, with the result that many of their family lines have become, or are about to become, extinct.

Deeply suspicious and warmly jealous of one another, the Dragons nevertheless "took a lively interest in each other" and maintained an intimacy that was utterly lacking in cordiality. Mrs. Aldrich, for instance, frequently dropped in unannounced for tea at Clermont, where she and her hostess, Mrs. John Henry Livingston, would sit on the sofa for the prescribed hour, arguing about "some moot point of family history . . . they'd be there with their tea cups, looking at each other eyeball to eyeball, and neither one would give an inch."

There was no disagreement, of course, on the overriding values: family tradition and solidarity. Intrusion or innovation—from a new bride to a new idea—was viewed with suspicion until it could be assimilated. One young Livingston male, proud father of a new baby boy named Thomas Johnston Livingston Redmond, entered an elevator in New York one day and found himself face to face with his formidable aunt who, forgoing both salutation and felicitation, simply barked, "Why *Thomas?*"

Only a few of the Dragons' daughters attempted to replicate their mothers' modes. One who did was Laura née Livingston, daughter of the Robert R. Livingstons of Northwood, who with her husband purchased in 1927 the old Eugene Livingston property, Eversleigh. Laura immediately rechristened the estate Teviot, after the seventeenth-century Scottish parish served by her ancestor, the Rev. John Livingston. Perhaps she heard that Elizabeth Chanler (Margaret Chanler Aldrich's older sister) considered the renaming of houses "vulgar"; or perhaps she simply wished to compensate for the fact that Teviot was neither as large nor as ancient as some of her rivals' estates. In any case she successfully expanded her hegemony to include the Edgewood Club, just across the road.

In a way Laura inherited the club from her mother, who had been a fixture on the House Committee for over fifty years. Within a very short time Laura managed to bring the club so entirely under her control that both Mrs. Aldrich and Mrs. John Henry Livingston—each of them old enough to be her mother—found reasons to stop coming. Mrs. Aldrich resigned from the club when one of Laura's candidates, a plurally married woman, was admitted to membership; Alice Livingston stayed away for reasons that are obscure but probably had more to do with dogs than divorce.

Laura and her tennis partner always won the mixed doubles tournament on Labor Day; so one year, taking responsibility as usual for selecting the tournament prizes, she ordered up a set of sheets with her monogram and paid for it with club funds. That year two young players of championship caliber unexpectedly turned up—the son and houseguest of another member—and triumphed in the finals. At the award presentation, with neither apology nor explanation, the victors were handed, to their utter astonishment, a handsome set of matching sheets and pillowcases embroidered with the initial L.

The Edgewood Club facilities, which had never been grand at the best of times, were pretty run down by the mid-1930s. Nevertheless, each Saturday afternoon at four o'clock, tea was served on the porch by one of the lady members, and strict rules of decorum were followed. Tea itself was always delicious, with the hostess—and her cook at home—trying to outvictual the previous week's hostess. Serving tea was like playing house; and the ladies of the club, like little girls, derived amusement from performing chores they would never have done at home. But there was no playing around about the rules: no children on the porch, and proper attire required for all—ties and jackets for the gentlemen, dresses, hats and gloves for the ladies, and tennis clothes, if they were clean, for the athletes. The overall effect was formidable. Strangers to the club, houseguests and particularly new brides, felt that in mounting the steps at teatime they were running a gauntlet of female Livingston eyes, ever alert to any lapse in demeanor that signified the newcomer would not do.

In the early twenties, the Edgewood Club had almost been lost. The land on which the club stood had been donated, quite informally, by members of the Livingston family, and "every time an estate was being settled . . . a hole would disappear off the golf course." Incorporation in 1925 was followed by formal deeding of the remaining property, and the club marked its golden anniversary in relative peace and security, with many of the original members still on board. The club history, written in 1937 by James Livingston Freeborn, celebrated this lack of change. For example, the author apologized for the fact that the mauve burlap had finally been stripped from the walls of the front room: "between us members, you know that burlap would still be there were it not that age and use had withered and torn it to a disreputable extent." The front steps had been upgraded from stone to concrete only because "snakes made their home in the [stone] foundations and sunned themselves in the path. One day the Countess de Laugier Villars* got out of her carriage and Mr. [Edward de Peyster] Livingston with great presence and quickness of mind, lifted a snake casually on his boot and cast it far away before she noticed. We could not afford to lose members in those days, and the Countess had a fear of snakes." In summary, our author stressed, "the changes [that have occurred] were due to necessity . . . and not from the wish to change . . . [and] I feel the happiest and most significant fact about [the club] is the very few changes that have occurred in its fifty-three years of existence."

In fact, the frumpier the Edgewood Club became the more it suited the family mood—the dinosaur mood. Modernization and enhancement of property became unacceptable in the face of economic and social change, and certain petrified emblems of the family's past glory were held inviolate. Meanwhile, not only the Edgewood Club but many other of the Livingston family structures in the Hudson Valley followed the Chancellor's house, Clermont and even Rokeby in an inexorable downhill slide.

---

* Johnston Livingston's daughter—Johnston himself had served as president of the club from 1900 until his death in 1911.

32

No one along the river, lord or vassal, escaped the effects of the Depression, although many responded with considerable ingenuity and fortitude. Alice Clarkson Livingston's spinster sister Nellie at neighboring Holcroft* was determined to pull her estate through. She closed off most of the house, to the delight of her great-nieces and -nephews who played spooky games of sardines on rainy days in the darkened, dust-sheeted upstairs rooms. She also named her two new horses Banker and Broker, perhaps as a talisman against further disaster.

Depression hoboes traveled the trains into the valley, begging food from Livingston kitchens and sleeping in the estate boathouses, where the charred remains of cooking fires roused fears of arson and theft. At Midwood,* every night after dinner, Mr. and Mrs. Robert L. Clarkson packed up the family silver in a laundry basket, carried it upstairs and put it under their bed for the night.

Next door at Southwood, Edward Clarkson, Robert L.'s brother (both were great-grandsons of the Chancellor), precipitated a family crisis by being married late in life to Rachel Coons, the young daughter of the Southwood cook. His expulsion from river society was instantaneous and absolute: invitations stopped arriving at Southwood, and Clarkson was tactful enough to stay away from the Edgewood Club. Instead he took to entertain-

* Holcroft was formerly the Ludlows' Pine Lawn, rebuilt after a fire in the 1870s. Midwood, two doors down, was built in the 1890s by a son of the Southwood Clarksons.

ing at large picnics, to which were invited Rachel's village friends: the chauffeurs, housemaids, cooks and laundresses from his cousins' river mansions. Eddie and his brother Robert never gave each other up, however, although the impossibility of Robert's meeting Rachel made things awkward. Robert would drive over to Southwood every morning, rain or shine, to sit with his brother on the front porch for one hour and then get up and go home. He never again entered the house where he had been born, nor was he ever introduced to his brother's wife.

Robert L. Clarkson was one of a select group of Livingston river squires who found the atmosphere of Morey's Tavern congenial. Morey's was the local Tivoli saloon, and alcohol can be a social leveler. Robert's cousins and neighbors, the Hall boys of Oak Lawn, also did a lot of their drinking at Morey's. The onetime elegant tennis champions, now drowned in booze, learned to rely on the fact that at the end of a long evening the bartender could load them into their carriage, give the horse a slap on its rump, and the animal would be able to find its way home without guidance.

Vallie (Valentine) Hall lived to a great age at Oak Lawn. His alcoholism was a source of great distress to his niece, Eleanor Roosevelt, who visited often from the Albany governor's mansion (and, after 1932, the White House) to try to bring a little order into his life. Among other things, Vallie kept hurting himself, badly. Leaning over the upstairs balustrade to look at the time one day, he fell into the grandfather's clock in the hall below. On another occasion he dashed out of an upstairs window in pursuit of an imagined intruder, utterly disregarding the fact that the balcony outside the window had been removed a number of years before ("I thought I was going to grab him," explained Vallie, "but . . . all I grabbed was air"). He also took target practice almost every afternoon from his bedroom window, blasting off at passing trains, phantasmic trespassers and anything else he thought needed shooting. He never hurt anyone; and his young nieces and nephews from the neighboring houses invented a thrilling, uniquely Livingston version of the game of chicken which consisted of stalking through the tall summer grass "just like the Jungle Boy" toward Oak Lawn, to see who dared get closest to Uncle Vallie's window.

The high incidence of alcoholism in the Livingston male population at this period tempts speculation about the inner lives of men from a prominent family that has passed its zenith. As little boys their noses have been rubbed unmercifully into their progenitors' glorious attainments; yet for one reason or another they lack both the will and opportunity to measure up. It is particularly difficult, perhaps, when the family females are in the ascendancy. The epidemic of alcoholism among the Livingston men was countered, as already noted, by the emergence of a female generation of remarkable strength. Perhaps the Dragons simply drained off the family's entire ration of vitality, ambition and assurance, leaving the men to submit to service in their trains, as gentlemen-in-waiting, troubadours and court jesters.

In 1936, Franklin Delano Roosevelt, the renegade patroon, was running for reelection as President of the United States. His campaign theme that "the most serious threat to our institutions comes from those who refuse to face the need for change" was anathema to his wife's cousins at the Edgewood Club, who regarded Roosevelt as "a drip" and "a silly young man." The few exceptions included Margaret Chanler Aldrich of Rokeby, upholding her Chanler Democratic heritage, and Eleanor Roosevelt's cousin, Margaret ("Daisy") Suckley.

Daisy Suckley lived at Wilderstein, a magnificent river mansion near Rhinebeck, with her widowed mother and two bachelor brothers. Daisy was a Livingston several times over, being descended through her father from the first manor proprietor's son, Gilbert, and through her mother from the Clermont branch of the family. The Suckleys had staged their comeback to the Hudson Valley in the mid-nineteenth century, when Daisy's grandfather purchased "the north field of Wildercliff" from his Garrettson cousins and built Wilderstein. Daisy's father enlarged the house in Queen Anne magnificence, landscaped the surrounding property, constructed a greenhouse to grow prize chrysanthemums, and kept the whole thing afloat on real estate investments—which, understandably, were never quite sufficient.

Daisy's mother was a member in good standing of the dinosaur generation, with all the requisite bloodlines and property, together with the self-assurance that comes from always being right. Her husband, in renovating Wilderstein, built a little private office for himself where he retreated frequently for hours on end behind the locked door. Little Daisy would be sent by her mother to fetch him for meals, but her timid knockings went unanswered although she knew he was there. Daisy became a master at accommodation. When her parents could not agree about her education (Mr. Suckley wished her to get a college degree, Mrs. Suckley did not), she effected a compromise by attending Bryn Mawr for two years and then returning home. No one, including probably Daisy herself, ever thought to ask what *she* might want: girls of her generation were expected to be dutiful and ameliorative, not to harbor independent opinions or pursue personal desires.

Daisy was forty-one years old when "Cousin Franklin" was first elected President, in 1932. By this time her bachelor brothers, Robert ("Robin") and Arthur, had become known in the family as "the upstairs and downstairs Suckleys," because after a quarrel Robin had moved to the basement and the two men never spoke to one another. Daisy lived between, keeping the peace among them and her mother.

Robin was silent and antisocial. He always wore a necktie, even when plowing the fields of Wilderstein on his giant tractor. The tractor had a

piece of old clothesline in place of a fan belt, and every few minutes Robin
would have to stop and dismount to tighten the knot. Arthur, on the other
hand, was gregarious. He frequented the Edgewood Club, where he was
noted for his dandified attire (he had a pair of pin-striped trousers that
looked as if they had been "bought . . . for McKinley's inauguration")
and his tennis game: holding the racket like a baseball bat, he executed a
devastating repertoire of cuts, spins and slices. At teatime Arthur would
repair to the porch to munch on handfuls of homegrown bean sprouts,
which he always carried in his pocket, and regale his cousins with long-
winded accounts of how, for example, he had been inspired to invent the
tennis backboard.

Arthur was unpredictable. At Wilderstein one day, offering to show a
visitor the horses, he led her through the kitchen, out the back door and
into a fenced yard of wooden hobby horses. On another occasion he disappeared from a luncheon party at the Delanos', and Mrs. Delano, becoming
alarmed, sent the butler to find him. Arthur's presence was detected in the
powder room, but he failed to respond to the butler's knock. When Mrs.
Delano knocked and called out, however, Arthur deigned to answer, invit-
ing airily, "Come in, Leila." She opened the door to discover her guest
standing in the bathtub in an inch of water in order, he said, to remove the
squeak from his new shoes.

Arthur Suckley was one of a group of Livingston males who threw off
the weight of their vanished neritage by flipping it on its head. Their flam-
boyant eccentricity is an assertion of status, a behavioral hallmark that says,
"Look at me, I am a Livingston, and nobody but a Livingston would *dare* to
behave this way." At the same time it is a thumb of the nose: "I will survive
joyfully, taking rich delight in the invention of my own legend." Whatever
one thinks of this—and many Americans, in the best puritan tradition,
would neither dare nor care to indulge themselves in this manner—one
must admit that it has more to recommend it than taking to the bottle.

After their mother's death in 1953, Arthur, Robin and Daisy Suckley
lived on at Wilderstein together. The family had been short of funds for a
number of years, and rising costs caused the deterioration of Wilderstein's
magnificent gardens and the house itself to accelerate alarmingly. Only
Daisy had a job, at the presidential library in Hyde Park where she served
as archivist on Cousin Franklin Roosevelt's pet project, the local history
section. She was utterly devoted to the President and all his causes, occasionally traveling to serve him in Washington and Warm Springs, where she
was on the day he died.

Daisy, Robin and Arthur Suckley had two other sisters and a brother,
only one of whom married. There are no surviving Suckleys in the next
generation. Daisy is the last of the line, in more than one way. She is one of
a vanishing breed of gently reared women who developed to perfection a
faculty that is no longer in the human repertoire: authentic naiveté. Many

daughters of Livingston Dragons had it. One of its chief advantages is the refusal to recognize the defeated, the outlandish, the dissolute, the unspeakable. In these women's memory, for instance, the drunken, destructive Hall brothers become "absolutely enchanting . . . gay and fun." A female cousin has too many affairs because she "fell on her head." And a dear one's twenty-year hegira in the attic is gently explained by a fall from his baby carriage which rendered him "delicate"—despite the fact that the gentleman in question lived without illness to a ripe old age. By refusing to see, they survive—and they serve to paper over, to prop up, to hold together. They are very strong; although their kind of strength is perhaps not apparent to modern young people, who take pride in calling a spade a spade and then actively trying to make it over into a heart. To them, naiveté may appear weak, a withdrawal in the same category as alcoholism. But it is far less pernicious; and it often performs a vital social, and family, function.

Relentless naiveté does, however, have one thing in common with the alcoholism, degeneracy and inveterate fecklessness to which it was a response: none is the hallmark of a family on the way up.

Postscript: On Monday, February 18, 1985, Daisy, "the last of the Suckleys," was taken at the age of ninety-three on her first iceboat ride on the Hudson. Lying flat on the deck of the *Vixen,* grasping the railing in front as instructed, she and the boat's owner skimmed the surface of the ice at unmeasurable speeds, down to the Kingston-Rhinecliff Bridge and back. She adored it. Asked afterward if, like most neophyte iceboaters, she had been frightened, she declared confidently, "Oh no. They wouldn't have taken me out if they thought it was dangerous." When somebody handed her a Polaroid picture of her ride she announced with delight, "Now, that's the proof. I have to show that to the family."

Margaret Chanler Aldrich remembered that when she was very small, the family honors for raucous insobriety went to James and Louis Livingston of Grasmere (grandsons of Grandma Grundy). Jim's most memorable exploit led to his defeat as a candidate for the state Assembly: at a political rally on election eve he fell, dead drunk, off the edge of the speakers' platform into the bass drum. He and Louis lived with their aged, long-suffering parents; and when they drove past in their buggy, Margaret recalled her brothers shouting excitedly, "There go Jim an' Lou and I thought Jim an' Lou was an animal and sorry I had not seen it."

At least two of Margaret's own brothers eventually joined Jim an' Lou in the family pantheon of dipsomaniacs, and Margaret herself developed a phobia about drinking which translated into a rigid ban on alcohol. Her unassailable rectitude was not perhaps as attractive as Daisy Suckley's steadfast denial, but it was a response to the same set of facts: the "animals" of childhood kept at bay through sheer strength of will.

Margaret, with Rokeby and plenty of money of her own, could afford
not to compromise on anything, including her three principles: no alcohol,
no plural marriage and no conversion to the Catholic religion. But over the
years, as greater and greater numbers of her kin transgressed her bans—
including, eventually, her own son—she became increasingly isolated.
Rokeby itself became her Valhalla, the stronghold of dead family heroes
who one day would issue forth, under her command, to counter the forces
of evil and change. The less the world lived up to her expectations, the
more she retreated into the "Rokeby mystique" (as some of the family call
it). Rokeby was the only object of Margaret's devotion that never broke a
rule and never talked back.

Margaret's three principles, like marble goddesses on a pedestal, had
dozens of lesser little principles draped around their ankles. Her daughter
Maddie remembers that as a teenager she and her friends were not permitted to wear blue jeans downstairs because "we don't do that at Rokeby."
The bedrooms were infested with mosquitoes because "we don't have
screens at Rokeby." Maddie remembers finally getting a screen for her
bedroom window, but allows, "I must have made a scene."

The children's upbringing was rife with contradictions. Maddie, having
been taught to scorn the conventions of New York society, was suddenly at
age eighteen subjected to a full-scale formal debut at the Ritz. She and her
brother Dick "were brought up like the children of British aristocrats . . .
we didn't have any manners." *Surface* manners were emphasized: the courtly
gesture performed with style, which had always been a Chanler trademark.
Maddie realized after many years of fearsome battle with her mother that
she could get away with almost anything if she did it with style. ("My
mother would have adored my coming to Africa," she said recently in
Nairobi, where she works for the Flying Doctor Service; "that's the kind of
thing she understood.") But a deeper kind of bad manners was a traditional
element of the Chanler style, too, expressed in a brazen disregard for the
feelings, situation and property of others. Young Maddie was embarrassed
by her family's lack of that kind of manners and took care to learn hers
elsewhere.

Margaret's policies toward Rokeby were paradoxical as well. In her
eyes the house and all its objects were valuable chiefly by virtue of their
historical associations. Any other value—aesthetic, utilitarian or monetary—
was irrelevant. This led her into a highly convoluted, often counterproduc-
tive theory of historic preservation. She refused, for example, to have new
upholstery made for a French Empire divan in the drawing room, because
during General John Armstrong's Paris embassy days in the early nineteenth century the divan had been sat on by the great Monsieur de Talleyrand. Margaret apparently preferred shabbiness, even deterioration, to
any interference with the locus of the great man's posterior. Perhaps she
was simply once again clothing her real motive—thrift—in garments of high

principle; but if so, she was wearing the costume inside out. At the same time that she was letting the divan—and also Rokeby's roof, plumbing and exterior walls—deteriorate, she was losing a great deal of money on an expensive certified dairy operation, which she entered into in replication of the eighteenth-century scientific agrarian idealism of her ancestor, General Armstrong. As the house spiraled downhill the cows operated in the red— for over fifty years. If, as one of her grandsons says, she thereby "intensified her relationship to the place," she seems to have done so at the place's expense. The Armstrong legend lived on at Rokeby; but stewardship was turned on its head.

During Dick and Maddie Aldrich's youth—in the 1920s and early '30s —the family spent the winters in New York City where Richard Aldrich served as music critic of the *Times* and the children attended school. During holidays Rokeby was full of houseguests. Friends of Richard Aldrich, distinguished musicians, came for weekends; and each Labor Day and New Year's a large house party of young people played in the Edgewood Club tennis tournament (until Margaret resigned, when they retreated to the Rokeby court) or challenged the Roosevelt house party at Hyde Park to an annual ice hockey match. Margaret's nephews and nieces, the children of her errant siblings, were welcome at Rokeby so long as they remained innocent of the three transgressions; in fact Margaret encouraged their visits, attempting to infect them with her mystical vision of the estate and its central role in the family history. But this generation was quick to note the discrepancy between her fondness for them (or perhaps for their supposed malleability) and her treatment of their parents, and Aunt Margaret's Rules became a kind of joke. When one of her grown nephews wrote to inform her of his marriage to a divorcée, he expressed mock relief at finally becoming "one of the boys" by being exiled from Rokeby.

Margaret's own son, Dick Aldrich, did not fare so well. After his best friend, Warren Delano of Steen Valetje,† was barred from Rokeby for spiking the punch at one of Mrs. Aldrich's parties, the boys found ways of carrying on elsewhere. By the time Dick Aldrich reached his early twenties he was an alcoholic. His mother refused to recognize his condition openly, although she began to adopt a posture of extreme overprotectiveness. Rokeby was offered—and accepted, by Dick—as a refuge. By the time of his marriage in 1939 he was as much in the thrall of the estate as he was of the bottle.

Dick's situation only increased his mother's isolation. She had no real friends, only people in the neighborhood who, while obliged to call on her periodically, were put off by her manner and her manners. One young

† Steen Valetje, which stood next door to Rokeby, had been built by Margaret's great-aunt, Laura Astor Delano, on land given her as a wedding present by her father, William B. Astor. Like Rokeby, Steen Valetje had no window screens, and the boys spent rainy summer afternoons chasing bats in the attic with tennis rackets.

bride, reluctant to return Mrs. Aldrich's formal call, waited until she saw Margaret drive past in her car and then rushed to Rokeby to leave a card before she could return. Looking back, the woman observed, not without sympathy, that "the people who would have come to see her were the people she wouldn't see, and the ones she would see didn't want to come."

Margaret prided herself on being self-sufficient; but after her husband's death in 1937 she had no one except her son, his wife and their two sons born in 1940 and 1942. (Maddie was married by this time to Christopher Rand, having expressed her wish not to become joint legatee with her brother of Rokeby.) From the beginning Margaret was a major figure in her grandsons' lives. She spent time with them, read to them, entertained them and took pains to inoculate them with the Rokeby strain.

In 1942, when Margaret was seventy-two, she attended the funeral in New York of her beloved but long-estranged "nursery twin," Lewis Chanler. Sitting alone in the front pew at St. Mark's in the Bouwerie waiting for the service to begin, she became aware that the lady who had been placed next to her by the usher was none other than her sister Alida, to whom she had not spoken for thirty years. The two women shared a hymn-book throughout the service without speaking or acknowledging one another. But a few weeks later, when Alida became ill at her house in New York, Margaret rang the doorbell one day and marched, unannounced, into the house and upstairs to her sister's room. Pronouncing Alida's illness pure nonsense, she demanded that her sister get up, get dressed and join her for a ride in the park—which Alida did. As far as anyone knows, the two women chatted for the length of the ride and never mentioned the thirty-year hiatus. They continued to see each other regularly, just as if nothing had happened. It appears that Margaret's principles were not compromised as long as nothing was *said*. She had not changed her rules; she had simply paid a call on her sister on a lovely afternoon and invited her for a ride. What could be more normal and natural than that?

In 1943, the year after Lewis Chanler's death, his son and namesake built a house on the east bank of the Hudson River, just south of Rokeby. The land for Orlot had been willed to him by his Uncle Archie (of X-faculty fame), who expressed his hope that the name of Chanler would thus be perpetuated on the river. Since so many of that name were by now banned from Rokeby, his point was well taken. Orlot, completed just before World War II construction restrictions were imposed, was the last in a very long line. For nearly two hundred years, since before the War of Independence, a new Livingston house had been constructed in the valley on an average of every five years. Orlot was, and is, the last.

33

After World War II the siege of "Livingston Valley" entered a grim phase. The besiegers without—forces of time and change, strengthened by new postwar social and financial realities—increased the pressure on the Livingston defenders within, who reacted in a variety of ways: some dug in, others cut and ran; many averted their eyes; and a few, sinking into hysterics, crumbled with the castle walls. A notable number, however, remained calm and managed to salvage something of the old way of life, including their own dignity.

Alice Clarkson Livingston, having moved out of the mansion at Clermont and into a gardener's cottage at the beginning of the war, never moved back. In a postwar world where good servants were unavailable or unaffordable, she preferred, in her seventy-third year, to remain in her little cottage and conserve her energy and resources for the Clermont gardens, which she never ceased to enlarge, modify and refine.

Everywhere around her, Livingston family estates were being sold, many to institutions which razed the old mansions and replaced them with modern, functional chapter houses, nursing facilities or school buildings. Sometimes the destruction was subtler: right next door to Alice at Ridgely,* the Order of Carmelite Sisters preserved the charming white stucco house, with its graceful wrought-iron balconies and delicate tracery windows, but

* Built around 1865 by one of Chancellor Livingston's great-granddaughters.

tacked on an awkward, outsized red brick extension and wavy green plastic sunshading. The Sisters manicured the woods and blacktopped the drive. Elegant, ethereal Ridgely was depersonalized, sterilized, institutionalized.

Private ownership was no guarantee of protection. At Teviotdale during the 1950s the owner (who was not a family member) sheltered his goats and pigs in Walter Livingston's classic eighteenth-century drawing room. Next door, Lady Mary's magnificent The Hill stood empty and abandoned, its tall white columns still dominating the valley below, its balustrades and doorframes, windows and fittings victimized by incessant scavenging. One group of vandals finally set the place afire, finishing the job that Lady Mary's rebellious tenants had started a hundred and fifty years before.

Saddest of all was the fate of The Hermitage, built just before the outbreak of the Revolutionary War by Robert Livingston, the third manor proprietor, for his son Peter R. Livingston. When the estate was purchased in the early 1980s by a wealthy outsider as a horse farm, the house had been derelict for years and was virtually uninhabitable. The new owner tried to sell the old mansion with a few acres attached; but after a short time, with no prospective purchaser forthcoming, she simply hired a bulldozer and knocked The Hermitage down.

A number of the old Livingston houses have endured roller-coaster existences in recent years. Grasmere, near Rhinebeck, originally built in 1774 by Janet and Richard Montgomery and subsequently owned by various Livingston sisters and cousins, eventually passed out of the family and survived the Depression by becoming a boarding school for girls. Twenty years later, in the 1950s, Grasmere became the setting for another family comeback, when Robert Clermont Livingston Timpson, grandson of John Henry Livingston of Clermont, purchased the estate and moved into river society with his wife, the former Duchess of Argyll. Ten years later Grasmere was put on the market again by Mrs. Timpson's son. By this time it was not so easy to find purchasers for large, drafty houses with whopping tax assessments, and Grasmere remained empty for a number of years. The caretaker's daughter camped out in the mansion with her children, husband and cats. The husband ran his motorcycle into the drawing room for an overhaul, leaving as his legacy a large black oil stain in the center of the parquet floor; and the cats deposited generations of droppings throughout Grasmere's elegant parlors, libraries, vestibules, boudoirs and stair landings.

Then, in 1972, Grasmere was purchased by an informal consortium of six New York City couples who began, slowly but surely, to bring the house back to life. Relying almost solely on their own man and woman power, they have restored the elegant marble porch, the graceful colonnaded foyer and the high-ceilinged drawing room (except for the oil stain, which will never disappear). More than ten years later they are still at it; and with luck and perseverance, Grasmere and they will prosper.

Teviotdale also has been redeemed by the cash, labor and devotion of newcomers from the city, as have Wildercliff, Edgewater and a number of other Livingston mansions. Fifteen of the original forty family houses are now the property of non-Livingston private owners. Nine belong to institutions. Seven are still in the family, occupied by descendants of their original builders—most of whom have to work extremely hard at various professions in order to earn the money to maintain their estates. One Livingston runs her late brother's mansion as a bed-and-breakfast establishment. Daisy Suckley's Wilderstein has not had a fresh coat of paint since 1910. (A recently formed nonprofit preservation group hopes to remedy that soon.) At Montgomery Place, raw two-by-fours brace the pillars on the front portico, and in the drawing room gold museum ropes are stretched across sofas and chairs, lest anyone should sit in them.

One contemporary Livingston proprietor puts it bluntly: "These monsters just aren't feasible for living. If you have one, you do nothing else. . . . You're always living poor, worried about things that nobody should worry about." Why, then, do they do it? Because, when all else fails, the land endures. Proprietorship has always furnished the Livingstons with their best demonstration of authenticity as aristocrats. Longevity in place—their continued suzerainty in "Livingston Valley"—defines the Livingston essence and tells them who they are.

It is not surprising, therefore, that the interest in "Livingston Valley" recently evidenced among conservationists, preservationists and architectural historians has prompted members of the family to react in a variety of ways that range from ecstasy to outrage. For every Livingston proprietor who looks to public concern as the salvation of his property, another sees it as rank invasion of privacy. The family simply cannot get together to either encourage or fight the trend. When, in 1979, most of the Livingston river frontage was placed on the National Register of Historic Places, virtually all the Livingston owners attended the ceremony at Clermont, except the owner of Montgomery Place, who deliberately boycotted it. Perhaps he was trying to avoid having to listen to quips like the one made by a valley newcomer who, after receiving his National Register plaque, laughingly dubbed his brand-new, modest summer cabin on the river an "instant landmark."

Given their history, Livingston heirs who choose to sell their estates face a unique set of problems, and letting go becomes an art form. Developers are anathema, of course, although the type of development that would be permitted has been somewhat restricted by the National Register designation. Nobody likes to see the estates go to charitable or religious institutions, neither the landed neighbors along the river nor the local villagers with their eyes on the tax rolls. Selling to a private individual or family is the most desirable course, especially if the buyers look like congenial prospects for the Edgewood Club. But even this can be painful, particularly if the sellers remain in the neighborhood. One former owner bemoans the "desecration" of the family seat by the new owners (or rather, by their decorator); and there are dispossessed Livingstons who consistently refuse invitations from the proprietors of their childhood homes.

In 1962, Alice Clarkson Livingston at the age of eighty-nine sold Clermont to the state of New York as a public historic site. Five years later, after a potentially disastrous false start, the state, in a rare display of bureaucratic competence, began gathering a group of talented, sensitive and knowledgeable conservators to supervise and carry out the restoration and preservation of the house and grounds. The dining-room ceiling beams were at long last laid bare, raised gingerly upward an inch at a time, reinforced and replastered. Clermont's roof was restored, tile by tile; its plumbing and heating systems modernized to museum standards; and the house and grounds opened to the public on a regular basis. Clermont, "disposed of to a Stranger," was saved for posterity.

Since the 1970s, Clermont State Historic Site has celebrated Independence Day with a fireworks display. Thousands of people come to the park for the whole day, to picnic and play frisbee on the lawn, to listen to patriotic airs played by a local band and witness a hot-air balloon ascension on the east lawn. After dark skyrockets and Roman candles shoot up from the dock where the *North River Steam Boat* stopped on its maiden voyage in 1807. They may also serve as reminders, to the romantics in the crowd, of General Vaughn's cannon balls and bombs fired from the warship *Friendship* off that same point of land in 1777, the day that Clermont burned.

Nobody has a better time at Clermont on the Fourth than Alice and John Henry Livingston's surviving daughter, Honoria, whose husband once said, with a twinkle in his eye, that after Clermont was open to the public "everybody [could] enjoy the privilege of a Hudson River estate without having to pay the taxes." But Honoria's satisfaction goes much deeper than that. Prepared by her parents to accept the loss of her childhood home, she now derives genuine pleasure from its use and enjoyment by the people of New York. Any poignancy one might feel at the thought of the former Miss Livingston bearing witness to the public takeover of her estate is quickly squelched by her own delighted response to the spectacle—living proof that the old public spirit of her Livingston forebears is not entirely dead and buried in the Hudson Valley.

34

In the late 1950s, Mrs. Robert Clermont Livingston Timpson gave a party at Grasmere that presented postwar Rhinebeck society with its moment of truth. The occasion was the coming of age of Mrs. Timpson's son, the future Duke of Argyll, and she decided to hold festivities in the Scottish manner with bagpipers, sword dancers and a whole black Angus steer turning on a spit. In true manorial style Mrs. Timpson invited the whole community, both her friends from the "river set" and the village people of Rhinebeck, not realizing that the manorial mentality of the village of Rhinebeck had gone with the wind of World War II.

When the guests arrived they were divided into two groups. The "river folk" were ushered up to the house to drink champagne on the veranda and gaze down at the entertainment in the field below. In that same field, behind a rope barricade at the far end, stood the villagers of Rhinebeck, dressed in their Sunday best. Druggists, postal clerks, housewives and telephone operators—whose children were contemplating Ph.D.s and high-paying jobs with IBM—were not amused at being asked to stand in a cow pasture and watch the Livingstons go to a party to which they thought they had been invited; and to a man and woman they walked out. The middle class of the Hudson Valley finally performed its revolution, barricades and all, in the sixth decade of the twentieth century.*

* Mrs. Timpson was genuinely puzzled by the walkout. Afterward, when it was explained to her, she apologized publicly for her miscalculation and, at the request of the town fathers of

Mrs. Timpson's party was only one turning point for the antimanorial forces abroad in the Hudson Valley. Much more harrowing was the controversy that nearly tore apart the village of Tivoli. Tivoli had two Episcopal churches, Trinity, the village church, and St. Paul's, which stood nearer the river. Both parishes had been in existence for over a hundred years. Trinity's tradition was democratic: its founder did not permit individual families to buy pews, and he frowned on the "elitism" of a choir. St. Paul's, on the other hand, stood on land donated by members of the Livingston family and was universally regarded as a "family church," in much the same spirit that Edgewood was the "family club." In fact the St. Paul's vestry and the Edgewood Club greens committee were usually composed of the same people, who frequently disposed of the business of both bodies at one sitting.

Even before World War II, hard times in the village of Tivoli had forced the two parishes to share a minister. By the early 1950s, Tivoli's economy had shrunk further. The new agricultural areas of Florida and California were taking over the Hudson Valley's fruit markets, and the young people of Tivoli, with no jobs and no future, were leaving in droves. In 1960 the Tivoli stop was taken off the railroad timetable, and the station closed down.

The first formal attempt at a merger between Trinity Parish and St. Paul's was made by the St. Paul's rector, the Reverend Lever Bates (large and redheaded, he was known in some circles as "The Lord's Lever"), who proposed, naturally, to close down Trinity. This aroused a "great controversy" in the community. The grandsons and great-grandsons of manor tenant farmers—Trinity-ites to a man—demanded to know why the larger number of Episcopalians should have to walk the extra distance to "the manor church." Let the manor come to Trinity—which was precisely what the manor could not conceive of doing. All the centuries-old antipathies on both sides came rushing to the surface. Lines were drawn, positions hardened, friendships ended. It was, in the words of an eyewitness, "a very nasty fight, completely un-Christian in every respect."

Finally, after long and bloody battle, Trinity Church was closed. Since then the Episcopalians of the village and Episcopalians of the manor have been rubbing elbows every Sunday at St. Paul's, whose minister has his work cut out for him, socially speaking.

That other family institution down the road, the Edgewood Club, also changed after the war, although its ambience remained remarkably antique. To this day tea is served every Saturday on the porch by one of the members, with the older ladies, dressed in their flowery frocks, perched on wicker furniture that is into its umpteenth coat of dark green paint. Children

---

Rhinebeck, became the founding patroness of the Rhinebeck Historical Society and an honorary colonel of the village Fife and Drum Corps. After her death her ashes were divided at her request, half being buried in Scotland and half in the Rhinebeck cemetery.

are permitted on the porch now—their parents have no nannies to leave them with—but there is little for them to do at the club except climb on a weathered jungle gym that sits in the middle of a poison ivy patch. Clubhouse and grounds are just as down at heels as ever. There is no carpetiny or bridge table in the ladies' locker room, no bar and no swimming poo nobody wants them. The chipped teacups are hand-me-downs from members' defunct servants' halls, and the locker-room towels are threadbare and mismatched. A garden committee weeds and plants the flower beds witl marigolds, petunias, and dusty miller. The chicken wire fencing around the tennis courts is in shreds, and on a recent Sunday morning the president of the club, arriving early for his match dressed in impeccable whites, took from his tennis bag a pair of heavy gloves and some clippers to trim back the poison ivy running rampant through the fence behind the center court.

The last of the great Edgewood/family feuds occurred in the early 1950s between the serious tennis faction, which wanted to cut back some oak limbs overhanging the far court, and Laura née Livingston of Teviot, who announced that the trees stood on her land and were not to be touched. The tennis faction took to literary pamphleteering:

Elegy in a Country Club

> Full many a shot of purest skill serene
> the dark unfathom'd caves of oak do shade;
> Full many a lob is born to blush unseen
> and waste itself within the forest glade.

and:

The Crime of the Ancient Shadower

> It was an ancient oaktree
> and it stoppeth all of four;
> "By my long gray branch and glimmering leaf
> ye shall play here no more."
>
> The sun came up upon the left
> out of the sky came he,
> and he shone bright, and on the right
> into the oaks went he.
>
> Higher and higher every day
> till over the net at noon
> the Hopeful guest here beat his breast,
> for his match was coming soon.
>
> And through the shots, the sunny spots
> did send a dismal sheen
> nor shapes of lines nor balls we ken,
> the oaks were all between.

> The oaks were here, the oaks were there
> the oaks were all around.
> They dropped a bit of this and that
> all over on the ground.
>
> The fair breezes blew, the white ball flew,
> the racquets followed free.
> We were the first that ever durst
> sever those ——— oak trees.

But Laura stood her ground, as did the oaks, and the tennis faction continued to grumble. Years later, after Laura's son inherited Teviot and proposed to donate the debated strip of woodland to the club, a surveyor informed him that it wasn't his to give: most of it had belonged to Edgewood all along.

This was the last of the good old family feuds. The next major fracas at the club concerned membership policy; and it was not a family feud because the club was no longer a family club, at least not on paper. By the mid-1970s the family simply couldn't support Edgewood. The countryside was suddenly full of new people—summer people from New York, who could not only afford the club's modest dues but who were even rather nice, in a nonfamily way. The membership began to expand, slowly and cautiously. New owners of Livingston mansions were automatically invited to join, although after one lady and gentleman in that category actually said no, thank you, they preferred not to join, the membership committee, in shock, realized that it was time to begin asking in advance.

It was then, and still is, easier for New York City summer people to be accepted by the club than for people from the local villages. But after a couple of lamentable incidents and some badly hurt feelings, the names of former Livingston tenants may be found on the club roster; and at Saturday afternoon tea the decorous daughter of a Livingston Dragon rubs elbows with an international corporation chairman on one side and a local plumber on the other. Tea costumes range from Peck & Peck to Indian cotton to country chic. Culinary standards remain high, with old faithfuls like watercress sandwiches offered alongside fancy cookies from a Madison Avenue pâtisserie or a cake made from a Midwestern high school Home Ec. recipe.

Without a kitchen staff at home, giving a tea is a lot of work. One recent Saturday hostess—the wife of a local Germantown youth who made a fine career in New York and now commutes in the summer to a renovated tenant cottage near his childhood home—rested from her dishwashing chores by chatting with a member of the old guard. When the daughter of the manor chanced to remark with a satisfied sigh that "the heart of this club is still the old river families" the younger woman responded, somewhat tartly, "The heart of this club is the people who do the work."

In fact, there is still considerable subsurface tension between the "left-over Livingstons" and the newer elements. Most of the membership ignores it; but every once in a while a flash of the old Livingston arrogance gives ample demonstration that the lords of "Livingston Valley," like the Bourbons of France, learn nothing and forget nothing. The Edgewood Club dances cheerfully around the edge of its social and financial quicksand. Distinctly frayed around the edges, like its towels, it is absolutely unique and seldom boring.

Myths endure: one of the river folk, trying to make sense of the new membership policies, inquired, "But we don't just let *anybody* in, do we?" And a latter-day Dragon, on being introduced to a woman who had lived in the valley for only six years but whose husband had nevertheless just been elected president of the Edgewood Club, sniffed and said, "Well, if you've only lived here six years, I don't see how he's going to do *that.*" (He did, of course, very nicely.)

The club used to be the focus of summer life for family members up and down the river. Now a number of them never come, although they still keep up their memberships from a sense of "social obligation" and "civic duty." One river scion, who usually shows up only for the two annual luncheons on Labor Day and the Fourth of July, recently remarked that he didn't know if he could afford these hundred-dollar lunches any more.

Perhaps lack of homogeneity explains why people don't spend as much time at the club as they once did; but a more operative reason may be that they simply don't have the leisure. Maintaining a house in the country, whether Livingston mansion or renovated tenant cottage, is a lot of work, and help is hard to come by. A lady who weeds her own garden and washes her own dishes doesn't come over to the club to play house; nor does her husband arrive with his chain saw after a morning's work in his own woods. People nowadays paint their own living rooms and clear their own power lines. The blue jeans at teatime are not an affectation. (Usually, only the old guard wears them; it takes considerable social security to appear on the porch in overalls.)

Do-it-yourself has also brought many property owners back into the intimate relationship with their land that was so assiduously avoided during the latter part of the nineteenth and early twentieth centuries. Gentleman farming—where the gentleman, unlike his eighteenth-century counterpart, actually gets his hands dirty—is once again a socially acceptable topic of conversation. Even men and women who can afford to hire outdoor help do much of their work themselves and are endlessly proud of their cleared vistas, prolific vegetable gardens and heavily laden fruit trees. These activities ground them in older, more solid values. They are also more predictable and secure than the job of serving on the Edgewood Club membership committee. The latter may lead to anything; but plant a carrot, you get a carrot.

Even in back-to-the-land there is socially treacherous footing. A member of the club who arrives for tea in his work shirt and jeans will not be embarrassed on the porch; but he may be nonplussed in the parking lot when he meets the man who takes care of the club tennis courts—a village man, great-grandson of a Livingston tenant—who is dressed exactly the same way. Members of the old guard have no trouble with this; their ancestors and Mr. Frey's drew a fine, precise line generations ago, and each still stays on his side of it quite cheerfully, no matter how they are dressed. Greeting one another respectfully as "Mr. Livingston" and "Mr. Frey," they confer on the state of the weather and the net cords with perfect serenity.

It is some of the newcomers—the less socially adept ones—who have difficulty. They tend, no matter how they are dressed, to call Mr. Frey by his Christian name. The question is, are they trying to treat him like a friend or put him in his place? If the latter, it fails; he calls them by their first names right back. But occasionally he will ask one of the newer members what his first name is. This is a precious moment, for then that person knows that he may call Mr. Frey "Adolph," and he also knows that he's arrived.

"Livingston Valley" is more prosperous now than in the late 1940s. IBM has spread its corporate cloak over its towns and villages, bringing new employment, a new vocabulary and a new set of expectations. It has also brought about a more shifting population. With faster cars, wider highways and three cross-Hudson bridges, "Wrongside" is suddenly right at the front door.

The old families—both the Livingstons and their former tenants—feel that they are different from the newcomers, sharing an attachment to the valley that is as powerful as it is ancient, as exacting as it is honorable. No newcomer, even the most admiring, can feel as they do. Coming and going is too easy nowadays, too taken for granted. In the old days traveling to the valley by sloop or steamboat or local train took time and, once there, people stayed longer. Now they come by car or express train, and they tend not to linger long. The sloops and carriage horses are gone; the train doesn't stop at Tivoli or Clermont anymore; and dancing class is over.

35

The postwar social growing pains of Edgewood Club society were of little interest in the withdrawn society of Rokeby. Dick Aldrich's wife tried to break out, joining the club "in the hope that [her children] would find friends and play games and do what other children do. . . . This place [Rokeby] does seal you off"; but her efforts were doomed. Margaret Chanler Aldrich had an iron grip on her grandchildren's hearts and minds, and by the time they were teenagers they not only knew they were different from other children but gloried in the difference. "Rokeby," Winty Aldrich remembers, "wasn't the way the rest of my friends lived"; but if it made him feel—still makes him feel—out of step with the times, "there is something wrong with the times." From the lofty world their grandmother created for them, the Aldrich children glanced coolly down at the tea drinkers and tennis players and kept their distance.

They were far from unhappy in their feudal enclave. Although they had no television because their grandmother, for reasons of principle and thrift, refused to buy one, they could always sneak over to the caretaker's cottage to watch. (The caretaker also had a speedboat, which the Aldriches couldn't afford.) The house might be falling down around their ears, but the greenhouses and flower beds thrived under the ministrations of two full-time gardeners. If their father existed in a perpetual haze, their grandmother was ever attentive. They vividly recall her reading aloud to them every night before dinner and, at the Rokeby Christmas party, giving out presents and checks to the staff, who lined up with their families, one at a time, at the door of her small reception room off the parlor.

Mrs. Aldrich took tea in a different room each day, in order to possess them all in turn. Yet she never spent enough money to preserve their magnificence, and over the years her mansion slid inexorably into dereliction. Her obsession with Rokeby's historical associations led her from time to time to bestow on a favored niece or nephew a small object from the house —a book or a vase—as a concrete embodiment of Rokeby's living spirit. It was, her grandson recalls, "like an apostolic laying-on of hands"; although other close observers have likened it more to the deliberate transmission of a fatal disease.

Margaret never faltered in her three principles, but she was capable of blinking when they got in her way. On the New York train one day she happened to sit across the aisle from a Livingston cousin's wife, a divorcée whom she had always refused to meet. The woman was reading a musical score, and Margaret, who prided herself on musical erudition, could not resist striking up a conversation. She did not introduce herself nor did her companion, although each knew perfectly well who the other was. For the length of the two-hour trip they had a delightful and stimulating conversation. They parted at the end of the journey with extreme cordiality and never spoke to each other again.

When guests came to Rokeby for tea, Mrs. Aldrich always dictated the topic of conversation. One afternoon's discussion with a distinguished professor of literature commenced, "Now, Mr. ———, what do you think of the French novel?" When he politely inquired which French novel she had in mind, Margaret countered, "Never mind, they're all pederasts," and that was the end of that.

After her daughter Maddie's marriage to Christopher Rand came to an end and Maddie married again, Mrs. Aldrich refused to see her or to recognize her new husband's existence. She wrote to Maddie occasionally, addressing her envelopes to "The Mother of the Rand Children" with the correct street address in California. When Maddie and her husband came east for a visit, Dick invited them to Rokeby. Enthusiastically he ushered his new brother-in-law into every room of the house he loved so well—except the prize of them all, the octagonal library. Mrs. Aldrich had closed herself in the library for the duration of her daughter's visit, and she did not emerge until it was over.

Dick Aldrich's pattern remained the same. "Utterly devoted" to Rokeby, his refuge from the world, he farmed his mother's acres, lived in her dilapidated house and quietly, sweetly and persistently drank himself to death. He never inherited the estate, dying the year before his mother, in 1961.

Margaret rewrote her will to leave Rokeby jointly to Dick's three children, in a trust without funds. After her death the trustees declared that the estate would have to be sold to pay the taxes. The new owners refused to permit it. Joined by their mother, the three children borrowed money from their cousins to pay the first year's property taxes and then scraped together the cash to purchase Rokeby from their own trust, in a maneuver that left their resources depleted and their financial advisers flabbergasted.

Today Margaret's grandsons spin out their lives in thrall to their estate. They are bound to Rokeby, defined by Rokeby, and sure that somehow Rokeby will be preserved to them and their children, although they have no idea how. Their grandmother has left them in a classic psychological and financial bind: she instilled in them a deeply felt obligation to cling to the estate at all costs, but at the same time enjoined them never to lower themselves to "mere money-getting" in order to maintain it. Neither brother has ever considered taking up a career or profession that would bring in some real money; and philosophically speaking, their great-great-great-great-grandfather, John Jacob Astor, the founder of the Rokeby fortune, is not part of its mythological pantheon because he was "in trade." One of their cousins describes the Rokeby family, with its "phobia about the middle class," as "one of the most spectacularly downwardly mobile families I've ever seen." They will tolerate "poverty, *Tobacco Road,* yes; but not middle class."

Chekhov may be a more apt literary analogy than *Tobacco Road.* A few summers ago *Three Sisters* was staged in the Rokeby drawing room by a local theater company, attended among others by Margaret Chanler Aldrich's three little granddaughters. The faded French wallpaper and threadbare gilt sofas provided the perfect setting, and the view from the large double doors led into a glorious landscape whose distance from Moscow was palpably just as great as ever. A distant Chanler cousin predicts that the Aldrich quixotism will eventually cost them Rokeby, adding rather ruefully that perhaps this is just "Nature's way of recycling wealth . . . the great F.D.R. in the sky."

The divan on which Monsieur de Talleyrand sat has been stashed in an attic. It will never be sold, although it might fetch a handsome price; enough to restucco some walls, stop a leak or fix the furnace. Ricky Aldrich isn't even sure that his grandmother told the truth about the sofa; she made things up, he says. She did promise, however, to haunt Rokeby after her death, and perhaps her spirit finds the divan a congenial place to sit and contemplate her posterity.

In 1978 the Pulepocken Historical Society of Womelsdorf, Pennsylvania, joined with a group of residents of Germantown, New York, to sponsor a reunion of descendants of the original Palatine families who had come to the Hudson Valley in 1710 to make naval stores under the supervision of Alida and Robert Livingston, the first manor proprietors. The Pennsylvanians, who traveled to Germantown for the reunion in a chartered bus, were descended from the Palatine families who had left the valley in 1712 after their food supplies were cut off. They met with their Germantown counterparts—the ones who had stayed—at the Stagecoach Inn on Route 9 to compare genealogies, search out long-lost cousins and share a catered lunch at banquet tables decorated with boughs from the infamous pine trees. The lunch was also attended by the man acknowledged (informally, but quite seriously) as the current Lord of Livingston Manor. Henry Livingston of Oak Hill is a genial soul; and his opening remark to the group was along the lines of "We may have parted badly in 1712, but welcome back; all is forgiven." After a split second of stunned silence, he was rewarded with a hearty laugh.

Three years later, in 1981, the Livingston family also held a reunion at Clermont State Historic Site (once again, lagging a little behind their former tenants, socially speaking: remember the Private Club of Claverack Manor and Roeliff Jansen's Kill and the Edgewood Club). At lunch, under the huge striped tent, there were gathered over five hundred Livingstons and Livingston kin from as far away as Hong Kong: painters and corporation lawyers; mining engineers and members of the State Department; a governor and a congressman (both from other states); genealogy buffs and genealogical fakes (only a couple); the rich and famous, the poor and obscure, the respectable and the debatable. What they all had in common was curiosity: about each other, about The Family, and about "Livingston Valley." On bus tours after lunch, many of these displaced cousins saw for the first time the point of land where Robert and Alida Livingston had raised their fortified "homestead" and the vast, breathtakingly beautiful fields and woods and streams and farms of the eastern manor. Though many were amazed, few were really surprised: the pull of the place, as well as curiosity about their cousins, was what had brought them. They came, as much as anything, for confirmation.

A number of their spouses may have felt the need for confirmation as well. Marrying into this family has always posed the threat of being swallowed whole. In the eighteenth century, for example, *all* of Chancellor Robert R. Livingston's six married sisters settled in the neighborhood of Clermont rather than on their husbands' home territory. That generation seems to have rather enjoyed being expropriated by its in-laws; but a number of latter-day Livingston sons- and daughters-in-law have found the experience less agreeable. Many decide to join rather than fight, becoming "more Livingston than the Livingstons." They acquaint themselves with Livingston history and genealogy more intimately and devotedly than many of the blood. They become overly jealous of family privacy and inappropriately solicitous of family prerogatives. Like all devotees, they exhibit a high-minded disregard for the facts: I was earnestly informed, for example, that the "crazy Chanlers . . . have some Astor blood, but I don't think they have any Livingston blood." The inaccuracy of these spouses' zeal is less interesting than the fact that they felt it was called for in the first place.

At the opening ceremonies of the Sixteen-Mile Historic District, Winty Aldrich, during his slide presentation of the houses that were being included, said of the Reverend Freeborn Garrettson, the builder of Wildercliff, that "because this Methodist minister married a Livingston, he became the most important Methodist minister in America." Winty's smile was mischievous, and he got his laugh; but somehow he also managed to convey the impression that it wasn't entirely a joke.

In the twentieth century, family solidarity seems to demand the acceptance of new in-laws even when they are not acceptable personally. The goal of unity overrides personal antipathy and social mortification. The clan sticks together; it takes care of its own, often with considerable grace and courtesy. But every once in a while an outsider may detect a note of strain. At these rare moments, when the politesse wears thin, the observer begins to appreciate the effort that goes into keeping the family image intact.

Apparently it is worth it, to hold together a family deeply rooted in both time and place. This sense of continuity and support is rare in America. Those of us who lack the sense of connectedness to a clan and to a specific territory may be missing something. If we feel ambivalent, as good democrats, in the presence of what passes for an aristocracy—as close to one as our culture will ever get—and if we chastise them as "the goddam Livingstons" for their exclusiveness and the "dreadful Livingstons" for their genealogical pretensions, we must also acknowledge their solid identification with the political heroism of our mutual past and their continued stewardship of the magnificent piece of turf from which it rose.

Besides, in the best of all possible worlds, wouldn't we all like to have a three-hundred-year-old home and family to call our own (while remaining, of course, immaculately elevated above snobbery and hubris)? In other words, some of the name-calling may be sour grapes.

American culture has never appreciated "the sere, the yellow leaf." We like our roses fresh and dewy and discard the faded blossoms, even though their colors achieve the softest, richest and subtlest tones just before the petals drop. We are uneasy in the presence of decline—except on the east bank of the Hudson River, where every day progress rubs elbows with decrepitude and the signs of an aristocracy on the decline are not only taken for granted but often prized.

In what other society, for example, would guests at a wedding reception *not* turn away in embarrassment when an offshoot of the local gentry, in the course of explicating Spanish culture to a new acquaintance, burst into a full-throated rendition of a lengthy flamenco lament? As it was, those who noticed just smiled and remarked, "There goes ——— again," and the recipient of the song, though nonplussed for a moment, was soon mesmerized and finally delighted. The view westward toward the Catskills makes a person realize that the setting of the sun may rival and often surpass its rising.

In America at large, however, the spectacle of aristocracy on the decline is unacceptable because the notion of aristocracy itself is unacceptable. A good twentieth-century republican hears the latter-day Livingston eccentrics ululating to the heavens, or sees them prancing joyfully to the bold, ingenious rhythms of their ancestors, and scorn is mixed with his pity. He is no more comfortable with their assumptions of self-importance than with their symptoms of decay.

Most Americans have never come to terms with a fact which Alexander Hamilton pointed out in 1788 to the Poughkeepsie Constitutional Convention, that it is "human nature . . . to depart from the republican standard." Alexis de Tocqueville put it differently: "The taste which men have for liberty, and that which they feel for equality, are in fact two different things." Class is a fact of life; aristocracy, in one form or another, is always with us. But America, as one would-be escapee from "Livingston Valley" puts it, is "a country that pretends it doesn't have [an aristocracy] but at the same time wishes it did"—and when faced with the genuine, indigenous article "doesn't recognize or appreciate it." We are awash in ambivalence—and so are our aristocrats.

They are also awash in insecurity. The American experience has been utterly unconducive to the solid development of a landed aristocracy based on the British model—powerful, cultivated and impregnable. From the marginal, wilderness existence of Robert, the first proprietor, through the political storms of the world's first successful democratic revolution, to the rise of the new rich and then of the middle class, there has been neither time nor leisure for the aristocratic ethos to mature and the behavior to become established. The horticultural comparison stands: shallow-rooted plants develop spindly stalks that are topheavy and vulnerable to every wind that blows.

Or consider the Boeuf Bourguignon: in order to taste like anything at all, to develop a flavor that really stays with you, it has to simmer over a very slow flame for a very long time.

In the summer of 1984 the first annual Clermont Croquet Tournament was played on the east lawn at Clermont State Historic Site. Entries, for which a small fee was charged, were open to the public; and the teams were assembled more or less at random by the volunteer tournament director. One team was composed of Honoria née Livingston, daughter of John Henry and Alice, and a young man temporarily transplanted to the valley by his employer, IBM. Honoria played in a flowered dress and wide-brimmed straw hat, holding the mallet to the side, knees together. She played—as she always does—like a demon; and when, at the end of the fourth round, she struck the final post with her ball to win the tournament, she and her young partner gave a mutual whoop of delight, embraced one another warmly, and then marched arm in arm across the lawn, through the applauding crowd, to receive their prizes.

The mouth of the Roeliff Jansen Kill has silted up; shallow water and little islands, blanketed in summer with wild loosestrife, stand where Robert and Alida Livingston once had their commercial boatyard. No trace of their "homestead" remains; nobody is even sure precisely where on the point it stood. Oil tankers and cement barges have replaced the Hudson River sloop; and up in Albany, at the foot of the long, steep State Street hill, an arterial highway cuts the river off from the town.

But pollution levels are down in the Hudson, and the shad have returned to spawn. The river itself and the Catskill Mountains are as thunderous and brilliant as ever, rising above the fact that their valley has proved to be a backwater. In winter "The River That Flows Two Ways" still freezes over in steely magnificence; and on sparkling April days the mammoth, broken ice floes are a grand sight, floating upstream and down on the tidal currents in a stately saraband. Unable, it seems, to make up their minds which way to go—and never, of course, getting anywhere—they still present a grand brontosaurian spectacle as, drifting back and forth, crashing and rubbing against one another, they begin imperceptibly but inevitably to melt away.

SOURCE NOTES

I am indebted to the following institutions, individuals and publications for permission to quote from original materials:

Adriance Memorial Library, Poughkeepsie, N.Y. (Local History Department), Livingston Family Correspondence

Clermont State Historic Site, Germantown, N.Y., Livingston Family Papers

Columbia County Historical Society, Kinderhook, N.Y., Diary of Mary Livingston

Drew University Library, Madison, N.J., Garrettson Papers

Dutchess County Historical Society Yearbook, Poughkeepsie, N.Y., "Dutchess County Men of the Revolutionary Period: Henry Livingston"; "Events on Hudson's River in 1777"; and "The Reminiscences of Mrs. Richard Montgomery"

East Hampton Free Library, East Hampton, N.Y., Long Island Collection

Jan Gehorsam, Poughkeepsie *Journal,* Poughkeepsie, N.Y., "River Estates Struggle to Survive"

Library of Congress, Washington, D.C., Shippen Family Papers

Museum of the City of New York, Livingston Family Papers

New-York Historical Society, New York, N.Y., Duane Papers, Livingston Family Correspondence, Robert R. Livingston Papers

New-York Historical Society Quarterly, New York, N.Y., "The Tenant Rising at Livingston Manor, May, 1777"

New York Public Library, New York, N.Y., Emmet Collection, Livingston-Bancroft Transcriptions, Livingston Family Papers, Philip and Peter Van Brugh Letters and Documents

J. Woodward Redmond, Livingston-Redmond Papers

Donna Seelbach, *Gazette-Advertiser,* Rhinebeck, N.Y., "Miss Suckley Skims the Hudson River"

Vassar College Library, Poughkeepsie, N.Y., Mrs. Maturin Livingston Letters

Full publishing information for all sources is given in the Bibliography.

In cases where the identity of a contemporary interview subject is not germane, I have quoted without attribution.

Abbreviations:

Adriance	Adriance Memorial Library, Poughkeepsie, N.Y.
LFP	Livingston Family Papers
Lieurance	Kathryn Lieurance Translations of Livingston-Redmond Papers, Roosevelt Library, Hyde Park, N.Y.
Liv-Bancroft	Livingston-Bancroft Transcriptions, New York Public Library
Liv-Redmond	Livingston-Redmond Papers, Roosevelt Library, Hyde Park
MCNY	Museum of the City of New York
NYHS	New-York Historical Society
NYPL	New York Public Library
RRLP	Robert R. Livingston Papers, New-York Historical Society

PROLOGUE

p 5   "Inequality is as dear": quoted in Amory, *Who Killed Society?*, p. 9.

CHAPTER 1

p 10   "if seen in England": Harriet Martineau, *Retrospect of Western Travel*, Vol. I, p. 52.

pp 10f   "Here bee not many": Governor Thomas Dongan, "Report on the State of the Province," in O'Callaghan, *Documents Relative to the Colonial History of the State of New-York*, Vol. III, p. 415.

p 11   "wealth and disposition": John Miller, "A Description of the Province and City of New York" (1695), p. 31.

p 11   "awful solitudes": Washington Irving, *A Book of the Hudson*, p. 31.

p 13   "in a strain": Rev. John H. Livingston, *Memoirs*.

p 14   "Emblem of what": Rev. John Livingston, Autobiographical Notes, in Philip Livingston and his son Peter Van Brugh Livingston: Letters and Documents, NYPL.

p 14   "God be gracious": E. B. Livingston, *The Livingstons of Livingston Manor*, p. 44.

CHAPTER 2

p 16   "Broad acres are a patent": Charles Dudley Warner, *My Summer in a Garden*, quoted in Bartlett's *Familiar Quotations*, 14th ed. p. 733a.

p 20   "upon matter of some dubious words": O'Callaghan, *The Documentary History of the State of New-York*, Vol. II, p. 875.

p 20   "have some regard": John Hull to Robert Livingston, January 30, 1678, Liv-Redmond.

p 21   "Whether this prediction": Mrs. Richard Montgomery, "The Reminiscences of Mrs. Richard Montgomery," p. 54.

p 21   Footnote: Rev. John Henry Livingston, *Incestuous Marriage: A Dissertation on the Marriage of a Man with his Sister in Law.*

p 21   "Now you are come": Captain Thomas De Lavalle to Robert Livingston, August 22, 1679, Liv-Redmond.

p 22   "my worthy helpmeet": E. B. Livingston, p. 58.

p 23   "Secretary Livingston" and "He cannot be induced": Maria Van Rensselaer, *Correspondence of Maria Van Rensselaer 1669–1689,* p. 128.

p 24   "Tract or Parcell": O'Callaghan, *Documentary History,* Vol. III, p. 616.

p 24   "Three hundred guilders": Ibid., p. 612.

pp 24f   "in the territory" and "about 600": Ibid., p. 617.

p 25   My argument concerning chronology and the motives of the parties is suggested in Kim, *Landlord and Tenant.*

CHAPTER 3

p 26   "wholly upon trade": Governor Dongan's "Report to the Committee of Trade on the Province of New-York," 22nd February, 1687, in O'Callaghan, *Documentary History,* Vol. I, p. 160.

p 28   "in very easy circumstances": Mrs. Anne Grant, *Memoirs of an American Lady,* p. 31.

p 29   "in such abundance": Daniel Denton, "A Brief Description of New York, formerly called New Netherlands," (1670), *Gowans's Bibliotheca Americana,* No. I, pp. 3f.

CHAPTER 4

p 30   "I do not mean": quoted in G. M. Waller, *Samuel Vetch, Colonial Enterpriser,* p. 257.

p 31   "ye vulgar sort": Letter from Robert Livingston, Boston, November 27, 1690, Liv-Redmond.

p 32   "Dutch boor": quoted in Holgate, *American Genealogy,* p. 158.

p 33   "Ro. Livingston towld me": in O'Callaghan, *Documents Relative,* Vol. III, p. 747.

p 33   "the instigation of the Devill": in O'Callaghan, *Documentary History,* Vol. II, p. 179.

p 33   "a case belonging": Ibid., Vol. II, p. 228.

pp 33f   "We have all Leisler's": Ibid., Vol. I, p. 312.

CHAPTER 5

p 38   "the enemy finds," "the homesteads" and "I long for you to come up": Alida Livingston to Robert Livingston, April 7, 1692, Lieurance.

pp 39, 40 "having perished," "O, what is there," "as a true Christian" and "the Spanish are": Robert Livingston's Journal of his voyage to England, 1694–95, Liv-Redmond.

p 40   "[Livingston] has made": Fletcher to the Board of Trade, December 20, 1696, in O'Callaghan, *Documents Relative,* Vol. IV, p. 251.

p 41   "My Lords this hard": Petition of Robert Livingston to the Lords of Trade, September 19, 1695, ibid., p. 131.

p 41   "mighty man": Dictionary of American Biography, 1933 ed., sv "Kidd, William," by Frank Monaghan.

p 43   "aliene born": Provincial Council Minutes, September 1696, New York Colonial Manuscripts, New York State Library, Albany.

CHAPTER 6

p 44   "courting after Jacob Rutsen's": Alida Livingston to Robert Livingston, June 6, 1698, Lieurance.

p 45   "a sword and cane": same to same, January 12, 1697/8, ibid.

p 45   "your loving and lonesome": same to same, June 6, 1698, ibid.

p 46   "a good Judge": Bellomont to Board of Trade, May 1699, in O'Callaghan, *Documents Relative,* Vol. IV.

p 46   "His Lordship has beene kind": John Riggs to Robert Livingston, September 23, 1699, Liv-Redmond.

p 47   "perswaded by Mr. Livingston": Bellomont to Secretary Vernon, October 18, 1700, in O'Callaghan, *Documents Relative,* Vol. IV, p. 760.

p 47   "at Albany": Bellomont to Lords of Trade, October 17, 1700, in O'Callaghan, *Documents Relative,* Vol. IV, p. 720.

p 47   "without a nickel": Alida Livingston to Robert Livingston, March 14, 1700, Lieurance.

p 48   "ashamed to let any": Jannet Miller to Robert Livingston, December 1700, Liv-Redmond.

p 48   Kidd's testimony in House of Commons: quoted in Harold W. Thompson, *Body, Boots and Britches,* p. 27.

CHAPTER 7

p 53   "very like" and "comely": quoted in Julia Delafield, *Biographies of Francis Lewis and Morgan Lewis,* Vol. I, p. 121.

p 53   "to be parted asunder": John Livingston to Robert Livingston, New London, December 10, 1700, Liv-Redmond.

p 54   "Miss Mary" and "need not screwple": Duncan Campbell to Robert Livingston, New London, December, 1700, Liv-Redmond.

p 54   "good humor" and "extremely taken": Robert Livingston to Fitz-John Winthrop, April 14, 1701, *Collections of the Massachusetts Historical Society,* Sixth Series, Vol. III.

p 54   "I hope that wee": John Livingston to Alida Livingston, December 22, 1701, Liv-Redmond.

p 55   "great frauds": Lieutenant Governor Nanfan's Reasons for Suspending Robert Livingston from the Council, April 27, 1702, in O'Callaghan, *Documentary History,* Vol. III, p. 629.

p 55   "borrowed coats": Mrs. Richard Montgomery, "Memoir by Janet Livingston Montgomery," Liv-Bancroft.

p 56   "Sitt down quietly": Robert Livingston to Lord High Treasurer, Liv-Redmond.

p 56   "Now, my love": Robert Livingston to Alida Livingston, April 29, 1704, Liv-Redmond.

pp 56f "chest with provisions": same to same, May 10, 1706, Liv-Redmond.

p 57   "Now, my dear sweetheart": same to same, ibid.

p 58   "fall on us": Philip Livingston to Robert Livingston, June 13, 1712, Liv-Redmond.

p 58   "senecas and coyouges": Alida Livingston to Robert Livingston, November 22, 1711, Lieurance.

p 58   "Your daughter Mary": Robert to Alida, New York, September 7, 1711, Lieurance.

CHAPTER 8

p 60   "I think it is unhappy": O'Callaghan, *Documentary History*, Vol. III, p. 656.

p 61   "at Aryaentje Verplanck": Alida to Robert, July 25, 1711, Lieurance.

p 61   "intrepidity," "the lower end" and "attention was attracted": Julia Delafield, *Biographies*, Vol. I, pp. 122f.

p 61   "the melancholy news": Robert to Alida, July 12, 1711, Lieurance.

p 61   "for money at this time": George Clarke to Robert Livingston, March 5, 1711, Liv-Redmond.

p 61   "I can not stand": Alida to Robert, August 7, 1711, Lieurance.

p 61   "My love": Robert to Alida, July 23, 1711, Lieurance.

p 61   "You won't do": Alida to Robert, July 18, 1711, Lieurance.

p 62   "base and Villainous" and "ye most selfish": Hunter to Robert Nicholson, October 22, 1711, in O'Callaghan, *Documentary History*, Vol. III, p. 676.

CHAPTER 9

p 63fn   "a good garment": Alida to Robert [Autumn, 1711], Lieurance.

p 64   "a woman of . . . Stained Character": Joanna Livingston to Robert Livingston, June 22, 1713, Liv-Redmond.

p 64   "abhorrance," "unlawfull familiarityes" and "told mee hee Vallues": Margaret Vetch to Robert Livingston, June 19, 1713, Liv-Redmond.

p 64   "decency and good manors": Sarah Knight to Robert Livingston, June 22, 1713, Liv-Redmond.

p 64   "past ye years": John Livingston to Robert Livingston, Liv-Redmond.

pp 64f   "be sorry if she": Philip Livingston to Robert Livingston, June 18, 1717, Liv-Redmond.

p 65   "disfigured": Robert Livingston [Jr.] to Robert Livingston, July 18, 1717, Liv-Redmond.

p 65   "the Gratious God": Henry Beekman to Robert Livingston, July 3, 1717, Liv-Redmond.

p 65   "As regards the Palatines": Robert to Alida, May 31, 1713, Lieurance.

p 66   "I wish you heartily Joy": Philip Livingston to Robert Livingston, April 22, 1717, Liv-Redmond.

CHAPTER 10

p 68   "your shoes": Alida to Robert, May 5, 1717, Lieurance.

p 69   "a likely negro": Philip Livingston to Robert Livingston, Liv-Redmond.

p 69   "A veil": Robert to Alida, June 11, 1719, Lieurance.

p 69   "My body": same to same, May 13, 1717, Lieurance.

p 69   "My longing": Alida to Robert, December 3, 1717, Lieurance.

p 69   "seiz'd with an extreme pain": Robert Livingston (Jr.) to Philip Livingston, May 30, 1716, Liv-Redmond.

p 69   "had to be carried": Robert to Alida, October 18, 1720, Lieurance.

p 69   "I want you to come home": Alida to Robert, October 19, 1720, Lieurance.

p 69   "You sent me a doctor": same to same, June 23, 1722, Lieurance.

p 69   "tea from the": Robert to Alida, November 9, 1720, Lieurance.

p 69   "Please do not take": Alida to Robert, June 8, 1722, Lieurance.

p 69   "You know, don't you": same to same, June 13, 1722, Lieurance.

p 69   "It seems we": same to same, April 30, 1726, Lieurance.

p 70   "He is less worried," "for as soon as" and "in my intended resolution": Robert to Alida, October 18, 1720, May 19, 1722, and June 8, 1722, Lieurance.

pp 70, 71   "Our son has cost" and "It's a shame": same to same, April 9, 1713, Lieurance.

p 71   "I always walk": same to same, June 27, 1724, quoted in Lawrence H. Leder, *Robert Livingston*, p. 273.

p 71   "beautiful daughter": same to same, June 9, 1724, Lieurance.

CHAPTER 11

p 73   "heirs male": Will of Robert Livingston, August 2, 1728, RRLP.

p 74   "a good warm room": Philip Livingston to a Van Rensselaer cousin, LFP, NYPL.

pp 74f   "Myndt must not think" and all quotes same paragraph and following paragraph: Robert Livingston (Jr.) to Robert Livingston, January 25, 1714, Liv-Redmond.

p 75   "if that is how": Alida to Robert, September 15, 1717, Lieurance.

p 75   "a melancholy but a sensible": Mrs. Richard Montgomery, "The Reminiscences," p. 50.

p 76   "Callendar was an historical": Julia Delafield, *Biographies*, Vol. I, p. 123.

p 76   "bring any of my Sons": Philip Livingston to Jacob Wendell, May 23, 1738, Livingston Papers, MCNY.

p 76   "to keep an Estate": Robert R. Livingston to Robert Livingston (of Clermont), March 19, 1766, RRLP.

p 77   "obstrepolous" and all quotes same paragraph: Robert Gilbert Livingston to Henry Livingston, July 4, 1752, Livingston Family Correspondence, Adriance.

pp 77f   "Love laughs at bolts": J. Wilson Poucher, "Dutchess County Men of the Revolutionary Period: Henry Livingston."

p 78   "Dear brother": Samuel Livingston to Henry Livingston, June 1, 1745, Livingston Family Correspondence, Adriance.

CHAPTER 12

pp 79f   My description of the Livingston-DeLancey rivalry is based on detailed analyses in Launitz-Schurer and Bonomi.

p 80   "We Change Sides": Philip Livingston to Jacob Wendell, October 17, 1737, Livingston Papers, MCNY.

p 80   "Regulations of the Private Club of Claverack Manor and the Roeliff Jansen Kill," Claverack Papers, NYHS.

p 81   "Our people are hoggish": Philip Livingston to Robert Livingston, Jr., June 1, 1745, Liv-Redmond.

p 82   "Women of the upper class": Mary Gay Humphreys, *Catherine Schuyler,* p. 72. [Please see Bibliography annotation regarding this book.]

p 83   "seemed resolved to assume": Mrs. Anne Grant, *Memoirs of an American Lady,* pp. 155f.

p 83   "[but] what, alas": Ibid., p. 159.

p 83   "if the French knew": Henry Livingston to Jacob Wendell, March 26, 1747, Livingston Papers, MCNY.

CHAPTER 13

p 86   "If trade continues": Peter Van Brugh Livingston to Robert Livingston, September 7, 1751, Liv-Redmond.

p 87   "wisely orders a perpetual": William Livingston to Robert Livingston, November 25, 1751, Liv-Redmond.

p 87   "I find myself Obliged": Robert Livingston to Lieutenant Governor De-Lancey, February 12, 1754, O'Callaghan, *Documentary History,* Vol. III, p. 767.

p 88   "You are not unacquainted": Robert Noble to Oliver Partridge, March 25, 1755, Mass. Archives, Vol. VI, p. 188.

p 88   "Dad or Alife": O'Callaghan, *Documentary History,* Vol. III, p. 753.

p 88   "Robert Livingston": Ibid.

p 89   "Ulcer in his Bladder": Peter R. Livingston to Oliver Wendell, April 15, 1756, Livingston Papers, MCNY.

p 89   "prepared for this very great": Livingston Rutherfurd, *Family Records and Events,* p. 54.

p 89   "dear Remains": John Livingston to Robert Livingston, March 23, 1756, Liv-Redmond.

p 89   "in which one man was killed": Governor Hardy to Sir William Johnson, May 16, 1757, in O'Callaghan, *Documentary History,* Vol. II, p. 744.

p 90   "get the least encouragement": Robert Livingston to James Duane, February 15, 1762, James Duane Papers, NYHS.

p 90   "We have heard lately from Detroit": Robert R. Livingston to Robert Livingston, August 4, 1763, Liv-Bancroft.

p 90   Account of prisoner exchange: Mrs. Anne Grant, *Memoirs of an American Lady,* p. 231.

CHAPTER 14

p 91   "my kitchen wore out": Robert Livingston to Robert R. Livingston, March 14, 1760, LFP, NYPL.

p 92   "the flowing well powdered wig": Julia Delafield, *Biographies,* Vol. I, pp. 133f.

p 92   "to oblige Persons to sell": quoted in Beverly McAnear, "Mr. Robert
         R. Livingston's Reasons Against a Land Tax," p. 84.

p 92   "[His expression] was dignified": Catherine Garrettson to George Ban-
         croft, September 22, 1843, Liv-Bancroft.

pp 92f   "If I were to be placed": Catherine Garrettson, conversation with
         George Bancroft, August 1863, Liv-Bancroft.

p 93   "I do not believe": Joseph Livingston Delafield, *Chancellor Robert R.
         Livingston of New York and his Family,* p. 314.

p 93   "in Pope's words": Mrs. Richard Montgomery, "The Reminiscences,"
         p. 60.

p 93   "was made the happy wife": Margaret Beekman Livingston to Adr. Van
         de Kemp, January 31, 1790, Liv-Bancroft.

p 93   "[If] upon reading": Robert R. Livingston to Margaret Beekman Liv-
         ingston, May 1755, LFP, NYPL.

p 93   "bring me back to": same to same, 1771, ibid.

p 93   "hot, tedious & disagreeable": same to same, July 1755, Liv-Bancroft.

p 94   "natural and moral philosophy": George Dangerfield, *Chancellor Robert
         R. Livingston of New York 1746–1813,* p. 45.

p 94   "a very Proteus": Nathaniel Du Bois to Robert R. Livingston, February
         19, 1763, RRLP.

p 94   Press report of RRL, Jr.'s graduation oration: New York *Gazette,* Num-
         ber 1169, May 30, 1765, Liv-Bancroft.

p 94   "Nouvelle Rochelle": Margaret Livingston to Robert Livingston, Octo-
         ber 27, 1761, RRLP.

p 94   "a house [of] peace and love": Margaret Beekman Livingston to Nancy
         Shippen Livingston, Shippen Family Papers, Library of Congress.

CHAPTER 15

p 96   "The ministry appears": Robert R. Livingston to Robert Livingston,
         June 1764, RRLP.

p 97   "Every man amongst us": Robert R. Livingston to Moses Franks, May 2,
         1766, Liv-Bancroft.

p 98   "If any Person or persons": Kempe Papers, Unsorted Legal MSS.,
         NYHS.

p 98   "The [New York City] Sons of Liberty": Montresor Journals, p. 363.

p 98   "give up nothing": Robert R. Livingston to Robert Livingston, May 14,
         1766, Liv-Redmond.

p 99   "those Pests of Society": Walter Livingston to Robert Livingston, De-
         cember 29, 1766, Liv-Redmond.

p 99   "some little time of calm": Robert R. Livingston to John Sargent, May
         2, 1766, Liv-Bancroft.

p 99   "intense thinking": Robert R. Livingston to Margaret Beekman Living-
         ston, December 27, 1767, LFP, NYPL.

p 100   "Beware my good Friends" and "[He] dances with": Broadside Collec-
         tion, NYPL.

p 101   "Madness seems to prevail": Robert R. Livingston to Robert Livingston,
         September 18, 1767, Liv-Bancroft.

CHAPTER 16

pp 103f "You have a parcel of People": Robert R. Livingston to Robert Livingston, April 12, 1766, RRLP.

p 104 "so that he might have": Julia Delafield, *Biographies*, Vol. I, p. 132.

p 104 "We are hott and pepper": Peter R. Livingston to Philip Schuyler, January 16, 1769, Philip Schuyler Papers, NYPL.

p 104 "As to the Old Chariot": Peter R. Livingston to Robert Livingston, April 1766, Liv-Redmond.

p 105fn "We are at a loss": Peter R. Livingston to Robert Livingston, Liv-Redmond.

p 105 "very quiet in her manner": Letter from Clermont Livingston, LFP, Clermont State Historic Site, #1979.196.

p 106 "You are now in the Country": John Jay to Robert R. Livingston, Jr., March 4, 1766, RRLP.

p 106 "I hardly know whether": Robert R. Livingston, Jr., to Catherine Livingston, February 10, 1775, LFP, NYPL.

p 106 Account of New York tea party: *New York Gazette and Weekly Mercury,* April 25, 1774.

CHAPTER 17

p 110 "in a continual Bustle": Robert R. Livingston to Margaret Beekman Livingston, April 27, 1775, LFP, NYPL.

p 111 "turn the hearts": Robert Livingston to James Duane, March 1775, James Duane Papers, NYHS.

p 111 "I sincerely join with you": James Duane to Robert Livingston, October 23, 1775, Liv-Redmond.
Duane's conservatism was more conspicuous than that of his Livingston in-laws, and later in the war he was formally charged with Loyalism. His exoneration was due in part to testimonials on his behalf by Philip Livingston and John Jay.

p 111 "Every good man wishes": Robert R. Livingston to Robert R. Livingston, Jr., May 5, 1775, Liv-Bancroft.

p 111 "in disgust": Mrs. Richard Montgomery, "The Reminiscences," p. 67.

p 112 "melancholy honor": Richard Montgomery to Robert R. Livingston, Emmet Collection, NYPL, #8773.

p 112 "first person he would shoot": Staughton Lynd, "The Tenant Rising at Livingston Manor, May 1777," p. 169.

p 112 "the most Tory-ridden": Edward Countryman, *A People in Revolution*, p. 173.

p 112 "many of our Tenants": Robert R. Livingston, Jr. to John Jay, quoted in Lynd, "The Tenant Rising," p. 167.

p 112 "they boast that": Margaret Beekman Livingston to Robert R. Livingston, Jr., June 27, 1775, LFP, Clermont, #1978.223.

p 112 Account of Robert of Clermont's death: Mrs. Richard Montgomery, "The Reminiscences," p. 69.

p 112 "What I feared": Ibid., p. 75.

p 113 "All the militia": Ibid., pp. 74f.

p 113 "I will if possible": Richard Montgomery to Robert R. Livingston, Emmet Collection, NYPL, #8773.

p 113   "His consequence in the province": Richard Montgomery to Robert R.
             Livingston, Jr., June 3, 1775, Liv-Bancroft.

pp 113f   "Be contented, Janet" and "Janet, how would you like": Katherine M.
             Babbitt, *Janet Montgomery: Hudson River Squire,* p. 10.

p 114   " 'Tis a mad world" and "You shall never have cause": Mrs. Richard
             Montgomery, *Biographical Notes Concerning General Richard Montgom-
             ery,* p. 10.

p 114   "He is very active": Richard Montgomery to Robert L. Livingston, Jr.,
             December 17, 1775, Liv-Bancroft.

p 114   "O fortunate Agricolae!": same to same, Liv-Bancroft.

pp 114f   Margaret Beekman Livingston's account of her husband's death: Letter
             to Unknown, February 16, 1776, LFP, NYPL.

p 115   "I weep, my Dear Sir": Philip Schuyler to Robert R. Livingston, Jr.,
             January 13, 1776, Liv-Redmond.

p 115   "As, Sir, I have not the pleasure": Robert R. Livingston, Jr., to Alexan-
             der Montgomery, Liv-Bancroft.

CHAPTER 18

p 118   "to expose your self needlessly": Margaret Beekman Livingston to Rob-
             ert R. Livingston, Jr., August 15, 1776, RRLP.

p 118   "massacreed about 20": Walter Livingston to Robert Livingston, June
             12, 1776, Liv-Redmond.

p 118   "Some say their number": Margaret Beekman Livingston to Robert R.
             Livingston, Jr., July 6, 1776, LFP, NYPL.

p 118   "his contempt": Olin Dows, "The Murals" in *Murals in the Rhinebeck
             Post Office.*

p 119   "in order to Harrass": Henry Beekman Livingston to Margaret Beek-
             man Livingston, September 13, 1776, transcription in Long Island
             Collection, East Hampton [Long Island] Free Library.

p 119   "He is brave": Richard Montgomery to Robert R. Livingston, Decem-
             ber 16, 1775, Liv-Bancroft.

p 119   "Cowardice has rendered him unworthy": Henry Beekman Livingston
             to Robert R. Livingston, Jr., June 30, 1777, RRLP.

p 119   "lodge [your] complaint": George Washington to Henry Beekman Liv-
             ingston, RRLP.

p 119   "though the colonel": quoted in E. B. Livingston, p. 244.

p 120   "In this state": Robert R. Livingston, Jr., to Edward Rutledge, October
             10, 1776, Liv-Bancroft.

p 120   "[one must swim] with a stream": Robert R. Livingston, Jr., to William
             Duer, June 12, 1777, RRLP.

pp 121f   "We are hellishly frightened": Gouverneur Morris to Robert R. Living-
             ston, Jr., October 8, 1777, RRLP.

p 122   "a Nursery for almost": "Events on Hudson's River in 1777," p. 118.

p 122   "two acres adjoining": Robert R. Livingston, Jr., to John Alsop, Decem-
             ber 19, 1777, RRLP.

p 123   Gouverneur Morris' inscription for Belevedere: Letter to Robert R. Liv-
             ingston, Jr., December 1, 1777, RRLP.

CHAPTER 19

p 124   "God bless him": Robert Livingston to Peter Van Brugh Livingston, April 4, 1780, Philip Livingston and his son Peter Van Brugh Livingston: Letters and Documents, NYPL.

p 125   "flutter in rum": Dangerfield, p. 97.

p 125   "Robert R. Livingston" and "the Consequences of a War": William Smith, *Historical Memoirs from 12 July 1776 to 25 July 1778*, p. 277.

p 125   "a disaffection of [the] tenants": Robert R. Livingston, Jr., to Trustees of the Town of Kingston, March 1, 1778, RRLP.

p 126   "I well know" and "We must defend ourselves": Robert Livingston to Peter Van Brugh Livingston, April 4, 1780, Philip and Peter Van Brugh Livingston: Letters and Documents, NYPL.

p 126   "I would not have you think": Margaret Beekman Livingston to Robert R. Livingston, Jr., April 4, 1780, RRLP.

p 126   "which surely cannot be construed": Robert Livingston to Robert R. Livingston, Jr., October 16, 1779, Liv-Redmond.

p 127   "from habit & passion": Robert R. Livingston, Jr., to John Jay, February 2, 1779, RRLP.

p 127   "dirty village": same to same, March 4, 1779, RRLP.

p 127   "I have found myself sometimes": Robert R. Livingston, Jr., to Gouverneur Morris, September 10, 1778, Liv-Bancroft.

p 127   "your Tempers are so different": Gouverneur Morris to Robert R. Livingston, Jr., September 22, 1778, Liv-Bancroft.

p 127   "drawn . . . from domestick peace": Robert R. Livingston, Jr., to John R. Livingston, November 5, 1779, RRLP.

p 128   "May the Almighty pour": Margaret Beekman Livingston to Robert R. Livingston, Jr., December 30, 1779, RRLP.

p 128   "As you have neither purling": Hannah Arnold to Benedict Arnold, September 4, 1780, Tomlinson Collection, NYPL.

p 129   "Had Arnold's treachery": Margaret Beekman Livingston to John R. Livingston, January 21, 1781, RRLP.

pp 129f   "The Office of Secretary": Thomas McKean to Robert R. Livingston, Jr., September 6, 1781, Liv-Bancroft.

p 130   "I have heard of the gay life": Margaret Beekman Livingston to Robert R. Livingston, Jr., December 22, 1781, RRLP.

p 130   "I hope to repair": Robert R. Livingston, Jr., to John Jay, May 1, 1783, Liv-Bancroft.

PART FIVE

p 131   "My son Robert": Robert R. Livingston to Margaret Beekman Livingston, January 11, 1768, quoted in E. B. Livingston, *The Livingstons of Livingston Manor Supplement*, p. 14.

CHAPTER 20

p 132   "insupportably dull": Catherine Livingston to Robert R. Livingston, Jr., November 12, 1782, RRLP.

p 132fn	*"not* of any distinguished": Gouverneur Morris to Robert R. Livingston, Jr., RRLP.
p 133	"the race of Tories": Quoted in E. B. Livingston, p. 470.
p 133	"I send you a box": John Jay to Robert R. Livingston, Jr., July 19, 1783, Liv-Bancroft.
p 134	"I was so unsuccessful": Margaret Beekman Livingston to Robert R. Livingston, Jr., April 1789, RRLP.
p 134	"Long live George Washington": quoted in Rufus Wilmot Griswold, *The Republican Court,* p. 141.
pp 134f	George Washington's letter to Robert R. Livingston, Jr.: May 31, 1789, RRLP.
p 135	"very formal": Janet Montgomery to Robert R. Livingston, Jr., June 1789, RRLP.
p 135	"I should be very warm": John Livingston to Walter Livingston, March 23, 1792, RRLP.
p 135	"Not being able": quoted from Thomas Allen Glenn, ed., *Some Colonial Mansions and Those Who Lived in Them* (Philadelphia, 1898), LFP, Clermont, #1978.277.
p 136	"ravages of luxury" and cigars "which come from": Brissot de Warville, quoted in Griswold, p. 87.
p 136	Descriptions of the Chancellor's sisters: Julia Delafield, *Biographies,* pp. 183 and 199.
p 136	"I don't like stupid people": Louise Livingston Hunt, *Memoir of Mrs. Edward Livingston,* p. 71.
p 137	Janet Montgomery letter to Viscountess Ranelagh, RRLP.
p 137	"large, dark, expressive eyes": Julia Delafield, *Biographies,* p. 202.
p 137	"I'm too poor": Armstrong to Horatio Gates, May 30, 1788, Gates Papers, NYHS.
p 137fn	"Better English has seldom": John Fiske, *The Critical Period of American History, 1783–1789,* quoted in C. Edward Skeen, *John Armstrong, Jr., 1758–1843,* p. 11.
p 137	"By thine agony": "Autobiography of Catherine Livingston Garrettson," Garrettson Papers, MSS Collections, Drew University Library, Madison, N.J., p. 11.
p 138	Catherine Livingston's letter to Freeborn Garrettson: December 23, 1791, Garrettson Papers.
p 138	"reserve the Ladies": John Jay to Robert R. Livingston, Jr., July 19, 1783, Liv-Bancroft.
p 139	"my inferiors": Henry Beekman Livingston to Henry Laurens, November 19, 1778, RRLP.
p 139	"rather low": John R. Livingston to Robert R. Livingston, Jr., March 29, 1780, RRLP.
p 139	"On Monday she likes L": William Shippen to Thomas Lee Shippen, January 27, 1781, Shippen Family Papers, Library of Congress.
p 139	"to divert myself": Henry Beekman Livingston to Nancy Shippen, ibid.
p 140	"friend and favorite": Arthur Lee to Nancy Shippen Livingston, September 22, 1784, ibid.
p 140	"fogs in the moral": Nancy Shippen Livingston Journal, January 23, 1784, ibid.
pp 140f	"I have seen him": Margaret Beekman Livingston to Nancy Shippen Livingston [probably 1787 or 1788], ibid.
p 141	"Were I to take her": same to same, December 15 [1789?], ibid.

p 141   "refused. They wished": same to same, date unknown, ibid.
p 141   "I will find out" Peggy Livingston to Nancy Shippen Livingston, ibid.
pp 141f "heart [was] sore," "Y^e next day," "was safe" and "impossible to per-
         mit": Margaret Beekman Livingston to Nancy Shippen Livingston,
         ibid.
p 142   "Is the subject of Genealogy": Margaret Beekman Livingston to Mr.
         Vanderkemp, April 17, 1790, LFP, NYPL.

CHAPTER 21

p 143   "Staten Island rose gradually": Grant, pp. 272f.
p 143   Description of Chancellor's house: Horatio Gates Spofford, *A Gazetteer
         of the State of New-York*, p. 119.
p 144   Robert R. Livingston, Jr.'s letter to Arthur Young: January 10, 1794,
         RRLP.
p 145   "Maecenas": Pierre Delabigarre to Robert R. Livingston, Jr., June 30,
         1794, RRLP.
pp 145   "There was not one of them" and "a capacious brick": Julia Delafield,
and 146 *Biographies,* Vol. I, pp. 192 and 193.
p 147   "Permit a distant relative": Unknown to Philip Van Brugh Livingston,
         June 20, 1797, Philip Livingston and Peter Van Brugh Livingston
         Letters and Documents, NYPL.
p 148   "one of the chastest": Andrew Jackson Downing, *Landscape Gardening,*
         p. 13.
p 148   "It is impossible": Peter R. Livingston to Walter Livingston, February
         22, 1790, RRLP.
pp 148f "untenantable old house" and "heaven has preserved": Margaret Beek-
         man Livingston to Robert R. Livingston, Jr., December 15, 1790,
         RRLP.
p 149   "All is not well": Henry Livingston to Walter Livingston, December 13,
         1790, RRLP.
p 149   "in going away": same to same, December 23, 1790, RRLP.
p 149   "who after dinner" and "our late *Frolic*": same to same, January 16,
         1791, RRLP.
p 149   "all the expressions": Henry Livingston to Peter R. Livingston, [Janu-
         ary] 30, 1791, Liv-Redmond.
p 149   "by word or act": Henry Livingston to Walter Livingston, February 7,
         1791, RRLP.
p 150   "in a very gross manner": same to same, January 23, 1790, RRLP.
p 150   "sent [Walter] his things": Peter R. Livingston to Walter Livingston,
         February 22, 1790, RRLP.
p 150   "Was not so much startled": Peter Schuyler Livingston to Walter Living-
         ston, February 14, 1790, RRLP.
p 151   "I acknowledge that you": Walter T. Livingston to Walter Livingston,
         March 1797, RRLP.
p 151   "did falsely and fraudulently" and "upon terms & conditions": Tenant
         petition, January 7, 1795, LFP, Clermont, #1978.22.

CHAPTER 22

p 153   "The old Lady of Clermont": Walter Rutherfurd to John Rutherfurd, July 14, 1800, quoted in Rutherfurd.

p 155   "paid [Robert], through an interpreter": Madame de Staël, *Oeuvres,* quoted in Dangerfield, p. 311.

p 155   "Wary Corsican": Janet Montgomery to General Horatio Gates, December 4, 1803, Emmet Collection, NYPL.

p 155   "Nothing is done here": Robert R. Livingston, Jr., to John Armstrong, January 18, 1803, RRLP.

p 155   "intimate acquaintance with this people": same to General Horatio Gates, May 12, 1802, LFP, NYPL.

p 155   "I cannot say much": Robert L. Livingston to Cornelia Livingston, December 1802, RRLP.

p 156   "I fear you will laugh": Robert R. Livingston, Jr., to Thomas Tillotson, November 12, 1802, LFP, NYPL.

p 157   "a malignant Sore Throat": John R. Livingston to Robert R. Livingston, Jr., March 17, 1801, RRLP.

p 158   "You are not formed": Robert R. Livingston, Jr., to Edward Livingston, April 25, 1804, RRLP.

p 161   "The Next president": Robert Fulton to Robert R. Livingston, Jr., November 23, 1807, LFP, Clermont, #1978.160.

p 161   "involved in the horrible sin": Harriet Livingston Fulton to Robert R. Livingston, Jr., July 29, 1812, RRLP.

p 162   "With respect to Bugs": Captain Andrew Bartholomew to Robert R. Livingston, Jr., August 17, 1811, RRLP.

p 162   "That we are not": Robert R. Livingston, Jr., "Essay on Sheep," p. 20.

p 162   "Being a farmer": Thomas Jefferson to Robert R. Livingston, Jr., April 20, 1812, RRLP.

p 162   "I have always shared": Catherine Livingston Garrettson to Edward Livingston, March 3, 1813, Wainwright Autograph Collection, Princeton.

CHAPTER 23

pp 164f   "As I do not suppose": quoted in Charles Havens Hunt, *Life of Edward Livingston,* pp. 171f.

p 165   "His effigy": William Stewart to Thomas L. McKenney, January 15, 1847, quoted in Skeen, p. 199.

p 166   "What are you afraid of": quoted in Julia Delafield, *Biographies,* Vol. I, p. 220.

p 166   "redeem[ed] . . . from a Public Gateway": Janet Montgomery to Stephen Van Rensselaer, January 20, 1818, Emmet Collection, NYPL.

p 167   "steamer was approaching Esopus": *Autobiography of Thurlow Weed,* quoted in Roland Van Zandt, *Chronicles of the Hudson,* p. 327, fn 20.

p 168   Lafayette at Clermont: Frederick Butler, *Memoirs of the Marquis de Lafayette* (1826), quoted in Van Zandt, *Chronicles,* pp. 161ff.

p 169   "except about fifty or sixty": Edward Livingston to Mr. Duponceau, November 18, 1824, Liv-Bancroft.

p 169   "finished my solitary ride": quoted in Louise Livingston Hunt, *Memoir of Mrs. Edward Livingston,* pp. 89f.

p 170   "the second place" and "Here I am": Edward Livingston to Louise Livingston, quoted in L. L. Hunt, pp. 100f.

pp 170f   "No! republics are not": Speech by Edward Livingston in Philadelphia, 1835, quoted in C. H. Hunt, pp. 421f.

CHAPTER 24

p 175   "dreadfull event which": Mrs. Henry Walter Livingston's Diary, December 1, 1811, Columbia County Historical Society, Kinderhook, N.Y.

p 175   "Emmet the irish renegade": Ibid., March 20, 1812.

p 175   "published a violent": Ibid., May 1814.

p 175   "the hopes of the tenants": Ibid., April 1, 1814.

p 175   "some chemical" and "to guard the doors": Ibid., June 1815.

p 175   "the strongest indignation" and "the moment of virtuous": Ibid., October 6, 1813.

p 176   "the pensive eye imperceptibly": Peter Van Brugh Livingston to Mrs. Philip Livingston, December 28, 1818, Philip Livingston and Peter Van Brugh Livingston Letters and Documents, NYPL.

p 176   "the only connection of" and all quotes this paragraph: same to same, January 16, 1819, ibid.

p 177   "Buy de acre": Quoted in Lately Thomas, *Sam Ward, "King of the Lobby,"* p. 75.

p 178   "house of peace and love": see source note for p. 94.

p 178   "rancor and malignity": Robert L. Livingston to Robert Fulton, December 29, 1813, RRLP.

p 179   "dull, and heavy-minded": Jabez D. Hammond, *The History of Political Parties in the State of New York,* Vol. II, p. 335.

p 179   "anti-nuptial agreement" and "would take her 20,000": Mary Livingston Clarkson to Robert E. Livingston, December 4, 1843, LFP, Clermont, #1977.135.

p 179   "pretended rights": David Augustus Clarkson to Robert E. Livingston, September 5, 1844, LFP, Clermont, #1977.90.

p 179   "He manufactures stories": Margaret Livingston Clarkson to Robert E. Livingston, February 2, 1844, LFP, Clermont, #1977.157.

p 180   "ought to make a man devout": Martineau, Vol. I, p. 75.

p 180   "if Clarkson could only": Mrs. Maturin Livingston Letters, December 31, 1826, Vassar College Library, Poughkeepsie, N.Y.

p 180   "Morals are of more importance": Robert L. Livingston to Robert Livingston, October 29, 1833, Livingston Family Correspondence, NYHS.

p 180   "independent": quoted in Ruth Piwonka, *The Landscape Art of Montgomery Livingston,* p. 4.

p 180   "like the shock of": Mrs. Maturin Livingston Letters, April 13, 1837.

p 181   "not a ladylike": Ibid., March 9, 1838.

p 181   "get rid of his children": Ibid., September 24, 1838.

p 181   "the Livingstons have none of them": Ibid.

pp 181f   "a moderate-sized basin": Julia Delafield, *Biographies,* Vol. II, p. 129.

p 182   "incompatible with [his] business": Ibid., Vol. II, p. 63.

p 182   "beautifully dressed": Mrs. Maturin Livingston Letters, January 13, 1839.

p 183   "I often reproach myself": Ibid., November 28, 1834.
p 183   "Had my poor Alfred": Ibid., May 14, 1840.

CHAPTER 25

p 184   "ANTIRENTERS! AWAKE!": Broadside, reproduced in Henry
             Christman, *Tin Horns and Calico*, p. 80.
p 184   "We . . . publicly, solemnly": quoted ibid., p. 65.
pp 184f   "Lay down the murderous musket": quoted ibid., pp. 342f.
p 185   "those Pests": see source note for p. 99.
p 185   "that they might be honored": The Albany *Argus,* quoted in Christman.
p 186   "The storm is past": David Augustus Clarkson to Robert E. Livingston,
             December 26, 1844, LFP, Clermont, #1977.91.
p 186   "When up our mountain streamlets": quoted in Christman, pp. 342f.
pp 187ff   "perfect castle Rack Rent" and account of auction following: "Sale of
             the Estate of the Late Chancellor Livingston," New York *Evening Post,*
             July 10, 1857.
p 189   "in a hurry": Susan Livingston to Robert E. Livingston, September 6,
             1857, LFP, Clermont, #1977.100.

CHAPTER 26

pp 190f   Description of Montgomery Place: Downing, p. 327.
pp 191f   "very clever, highly cultivated": Mrs. Maturin Livingston Letters, Janu-
             ary 26, 1837.
p 192   "roving personality": Recollections of Margaret Chanler Aldrich (inter-
             view with John Ross Delafield, 1952).
p 193fn   "Money counts for little": quoted in Virginia Cowles, *The Astors,* p. 68.

CHAPTER 27

p 194   "the Livingston family have": Mrs. Richard Montgomery, "The Remi-
             niscences, p. 56.
p 194   "about 80 persons": Mrs. Maturin Livingston Letters, January 11, 1841.
p 195   "a man of mystery": "The Romance of Almont" (Xerox copy of hand-
             written ms.), p. 1.
p 195   "waterfalls, picturesque bridges": Poughkeepsie *Daily Eagle,* January 1,
             1878, p. 3.
p 195   "ships of solid silver": "Romance of Almont," p. 2.
p 195   "his ample fortune": Obituary of Robert Swift Livingston, New York
             Times, March 1, 1867, p. 4, col. 6.
p 196   "the grand old style": Poughkeepsie *Daily Eagle,* January 1, 1878, p. 3.
p 196   "something akin to a contempt": Obituary of Cambridge Livingston,
             New York *Times,* September 19, 1879, p. 5, col. 6.
p 196   "In this community": Cambridge Livingston to Johnston Livingston,
             July 20, 1844, Liv-Redmond.
p 197   "coat pocket expresses": Sylvie R. Griffiths, "Johnston Livingston: The
             California Connection," p. 7.

p 197	"if . . . happiness consisted": Johnston Livingston's Commonplace Book, Liv-Redmond.
p 198	"a choice edition of": "Sale of the Estate of the Late Chancellor Livingston."
p 198	"What a change has": C. H. Hunt, pp. 12f.

CHAPTER 28

p 200	"Hudson . . . its duty": see source note for p. 186.
p 200	"in America the two systems": *The Laws of Etiquette* (1836), quoted in Douglas T. Miller, *Jacksonian Aristocracy: Class and Democracy in New York, 1830–1860,* p. 56.
p 200	"We are certainly making": C. H. Hunt, p. 14.
p 201	"Now blest be their mem'ry": Dr. Thomas Barton, *Ode,* 1866.
p 202	"new and larger class of people": Roland Van Zandt, *The Catskill Mountain House,* p. 222.
p 202	"If there are three people": Gardner Cowles, quoted in Amory, p. 67.
p 202	"I am my own ancestor": quoted ibid.
p 203	"rich enough to take": Dixon Wecter, *The Saga of American Society,* p. 7.
p 203fn	"Without the slightest hint": Amory, p. 118.
p 204	"stress on equality and": D. T. Miller, p. 60.
p 204	"exclusiveness is characteristic": quoted in Amory, p. 39.
p 204	"must be perpetuated, not by": Martineau, Vol. III, pp. 36f.
pp 204f	"The Upper Ten": Julia Delafield, 1857 Appendix to *Biographies,* pp. 230f, 232, 236f.
p 205	Holmes, *The Autocrat of the Breakfast-Table,* quoted in Amory, pp. 250f.
p 205	*"homo gentilis":* quoted in Edwin Harrison Cady, *The Gentleman in America,* p. 9.

CHAPTER 29

p 206	"defeated . . . by": Wecter, p. 336.
p 207	"iced tea and": Olin Dows, *Franklin Roosevelt at Hyde Park,* p. 57.
p 208	"possible conflict": James Livingston Freeborn, *The Edgewood Club,* p. 6.
p 208	"the language of the players": Ibid., p. 5.
p 208	"the good invention whereby": quoted in Stephen Henry Olin, *Occasional Addresses,* p. 7.
p 210	"only carried his claim back": Charles L. Livingston to John Henry Livingston, June 11, 1912, LFP, Clermont, #1978.288.
p 210	"through a false idea of modesty": E. B. Livingston, p. 507.
p 211	"ran the photographs of": Margaret Chanler Aldrich, Recollections, p. 18.
p 211	"indulge in his penchant": Richard C. Wiles, *Tivoli Revisited: A Social History,* p. 17.
p 211	"so long as they not admit": quoted in Wiles, p. 26.
p 212	"his father is supposed": Aldrich, Recollections, p. 18.

CHAPTER 30

p 213   "like the Trianon": quoted in Henry Noble MacCracken, *Blithe Dutch-ess*, p. 357.

p 213   "You may be nice": quoted in Amory, p. 50.

p 214   "Religion, the World": Winthrop Chanler, *Winthrop Chanler's Letters*, p. iii.

p 214   "The Chanlers were": Winthrop Chanler to Amos Tuck French, quoted in Lately Thomas, *A Pride of Lions*, p. 53.

p 215   "voices resounded everywhere": Thomas, *Pride*, pp. 34f.
           This book and its privately printed sequel tell the whole Chanler saga in splendid detail.

p 215   "shudder of revulsion": Thomas, *Pride*, p. 59.

p 215   "feeling sure that": Mrs. Winthrop Chanler, *Roman Spring*, p. 59.

p 216   "I did not know": Margaret Chanler Aldrich, "Rokeby Room by Room."

p 216   "the kindest thing one could do" and all quotes same paragraph: Mrs. Winthrop Chanler, *Roman Spring*, p. 190.

p 216   "White House etiquette": Thomas, *Pride*, p. 181.

p 217fn   "the anchovy paste": quoted in J. Bryan III, "Johnny Jackanapes, the Merry-Andrew of the Merry Mills," p. 14.

CHAPTER 31

p 220   "money-getting . . . comes from" and " 'successful' men": *Charles Francis Adams 1835–1915; an autobiography*, quoted in Matthew Josephson, *The Robber Barons*, p. 338.

p 222   "the only proof we have": John Ross Delafield to Janet Livingston, November 5, 1930, LFP, Clermont, #1978.286.
           General Delafield sent copies of the genealogical statement to a number of other family members beside Janet, with an identical covering letter.

p 223   "three things killed": quoted in Amory, p. 16.

p 225f   "between us members," "snakes made their home" and "the changes": Freeborn, pp. 3 and 5.

CHAPTER 32

p 229   "the most serious threat": quoted in E. Digby Baltzell, *The Protestant Establishment*, p. 235.

p 231   Daisy Suckley's iceboat ride: "Miss Suckley skims the Hudson River," Rhinebeck, N.Y. *Gazette Advertiser*, February 21, 1985, p. 3.

p 231   "There go Jim an' Lou": Margaret Chanler Aldrich, *Recollections*, p. 15.

p 232   "we don't do that," "I must have made," "were brought up like" and "My mother would have adored": Interview, August 12, 1982.

p 233   "intensified her relationship": Interview with J. Winthrop Aldrich, June 2, 1984.

CHAPTER 35

p 245   "in the hope that": Interview with Susan Cutler Aldrich, August 27, 1979.

p 245   "Rokeby wasn't the way": quoted in Jan Gehorsam, "River Estates Struggle to Survive," Poughkeepsie *Journal,* November 13, 1983, p. 2B.

p 246   "like an apostolic": Interview with J. Winthrop Aldrich.

p 250   "human nature . . . to depart": Francis Childs, *The Debates and Proceedings of the Convention of the State of New-York,* quoted in Dangerfield, p. 226.

p 250   "The taste which men have": quoted in Walter L. Arnstein, "The Survival of the Victorian Aristocracy," p. 255.

BIBLIOGRAPHY

Albany, N.Y. Albany Institute of History and Art, McKinney Library. Ludlow-Livingston Papers.

Albany, N.Y. New York State Library, Manuscripts and Special Collections. S. Hedding Fitch, "Lady Mary's Place," 1925.

———. Miscellaneous original mss.

Aldrich, Margaret Chanler. "Memoirs of Rokeby." (Written in Washington, D.C., 1900.)

———. "Rokeby Room by Room." (Written prob. 1930s.)

———. Recollections (transcription of taped interview with John Ross Delafield, Autumn, 1952).

———. *Sonnets for Choice.* New York: Moffat, Yard and Company, 1910.

"An American Moralist." *Times Literary Supplement* (London), No. 1, 489, August 14, 1930, p. 645.

Amory, Cleveland. *Who Killed Society?* New York: Harper & Brothers, 1960.

Ann Arbor, Mich. University of Michigan, William L. Clements Library. Papers of Dr. William Wilson.

Anthony, Rev. Robert Warren. "Philip Livingston." Address delivered at the annual dinner of the Philip Livingston Chapter, Sons of the Revolution in the State of New York, January 22, 1924. Albany: Fort Orange Press, 1924.

Arnstein, Walter L. "The Survival of the Victorian Aristocracy," in Jaher, *The Rich, the Well Born, and the Powerful,* pp. 203–57.

Babbitt, Katherine M. *Janet Montgomery: Hudson River Squire.* Monroe, N.Y.: Library Research Associates, 1975.

Baltzell, E. Digby. *The Protestant Establishment.* New York: Random House, 1964.

Barton, Dr. Thomas J. *Ode.* 1866.

Beekman, Mrs. William B. "The Beekman Family." Address read before the New

York Branch of the Order of Colonial Lords of Manors in America. Baltimore: 1925.

Bonomi, Patricia U. *A Factious People, Politics and Society in Colonial New York*. New York: Columbia University Press, 1971.

Boston, Mass. Massachusetts Historical Society. *Collections of the Massachusetts Historical Society*, Sixth Series, Vol. III, published by the Society, 1889.

————. H. H. Edes Papers.

————. Public Record Office transcriptions (Parkman), Vols. 36 and 37, 1693–1725.

————. Winthrop Papers.

Boston, Mass. State House. Mass. Archives, Vol. VI.

Boyle, Robert H. *The Hudson River*. New York: W. W. Norton & Company, 1969.

————. "Step in and Enjoy the Turmoil." *Sports Illustrated*, Vol. 46, No. 25, June 13, 1977.

Brandt, Clare, and Arthur Kelly, compilers. *A Livingston Genealogy*. Rhinebeck, N.Y., 1982.

Bryan, J. III. "Johnny Jackanapes, the Merry-Andrew of the Merry Mills." *Virginia Magazine of History and Biography*, Vol. 73, No. 1, January 1965, pp. 3–21. Richmond: Virginia Historical Society.

Cady, Edwin Harrison. *The Gentleman in America*. Syracuse, N.Y.: Syracuse University Press, 1949.

Carmer, Carl. *The Hudson*. New York: Holt, Rinehart and Winston, 1939.

Chanler, Julie. *From Gaslight to Dawn*. Privately printed, 1956.

Chanler, Winthrop. *Winthrop Chanler's Letters*. Collected by Margaret Terry Chanler. New York: privately printed. 1951.

Chanler, Winthrop Astor. *Some Letters from "Chan" 1886–1926*. Edited and with introduction by Amos Tucker French. Chester, N.H.: privately printed by Amos Tucker French, 1939.

Chanler, Mrs. Winthrop. *Roman Spring*. Boston: Little, Brown & Company, 1934.

————. *Autumn in the Valley*. Boston: Little, Brown & Company, 1936.

Chastellux, Marquis de. *Travels in North America*. Trans. from the French by an English Gentleman. 2 vols. London: G. G. J. and J. Robinson, 1787.

Christman, Henry. *Tin Horns and Calico*. New York: Henry Holt & Company, 1945.

Claflin, John C. Letter to Clare Brandt regarding the Lowndes family, September 23, 1981.

Countryman, Edward. *A People in Revolution*. Baltimore and London: The Johns Hopkins University Press, 1981.

Cowles, Virginia. *The Astors*. New York: Alfred A. Knopf, 1979.

Crowninshield, Frank. "The House of Vanderbilt," *Vogue*, November 15, 1941.

Dangerfield, George. *Chancellor Robert R. Livingston of New York 1746–1813*. New York: Harcourt, Brace & Company, 1960.

Delafield, John Ross. "The Hill," *Dutchess County Historical Society Yearbook*, Vol. 26 (1941), pp. 23ff.

————. "Montgomery Place," *New York History*, Vol. XX, No. 4, October 1939, pp. 445–62.

————. *A Short Account of St. Paul's Church, Tivoli*. Address delivered at St. Paul's Church, September 16, 1936.

————. "The Stories of Linwood, Wildercliff and Ellerslie," *Dutchess County Historical Society Yearbook*, Vol. 17 (1932), pp. 33–55.

————. "The Story of the Hermitage," *Dutchess County Historical Society Yearbook*, Vol. 24 (1939), pp. 30–39.

————. "The Story of Teviotdale," *Dutchess County Historical Society Yearbook,* Vol. 24 (1939), pp. 40–46.

Delafield, Joseph Livingston. *Chancellor Robert R. Livingston of New York and His Family.* American Scenic and Historic Preservation Society, Sixteenth Annual Report, 1910.

Delafield, Julia. *Biographies of Francis Lewis and Morgan Lewis.* 2 vols. New York: Anson D. F. Randolph & Company, 1877.

Denton, Daniel. "A Brief Description of New York, formerly called New Netherlands," *Gowans's Bibliotheca Americana,* No. I. New York: William Gowans, 1845 [originally published 1670].

Dictionary of American Biography. 1933 ed. Sv "Armstrong, John," by Julius W. Pratt.

————. Sv "Duane, James," by Sarah H. J. Simpson.

————. Sv "Duer, William," by H. W. Howard Knott.

————. Sv "Hull, John," by Katharine H. Amend.

————. Sv "Kidd, William," by Frank Monaghan.

————. Sv "Livingston, Henry Brockholst," by Robert E. Cushman.

————. Sv "Livingston, James," by Katharine Elizabeth Crane.

————. Sv "Livingston, John Henry," by William H. S. Demarest.

————. Sv "Livingston, Peter Van Brugh," by John A. Krout.

————. Sv "Livingston, Philip," by John A. Krout.

————. Sv "Smith, William," by Richard B. Morris.

————. Sv "Swartwout, Samuel," by Isaac J. Cox.

Downing, Andrew Jackson. *Landscape Gardening.* 10th ed. revised by Frank A. Waugh. New York: John Wiley & Sons, 1921.

Dows, Olin. *Franklin Roosevelt at Hyde Park.* New York: American Artists Group, 1949.

————. "The Murals," *Murals in the Rhinebeck Post Office.* Rhinebeck, N.Y.: The Civic Club, 1940.

Earle, Alice Morse. *Colonial Days in Old New York.* New York: Charles Scribner's Sons, 1896.

East Hampton, N.Y. East Hampton Free Library. Long Island Collection. Transcription of letter from Henry Beekman Livingston to Margaret Beekman Livingston, Say Brook [Conn.], September 13, 1776.

Eberlein, Harold Donaldson. *The Manors and Historic Homes of the Hudson Valley.* Philadelphia and London: J. B. Lippincott Company, 1924.

"Edgewater in Review," Hudson River Heritage *News,* May 1982, p. 2.

Ellis, David Maldwyn. *Landlords and Farmers in the Hudson-Mohawk Valley Region 1790–1850.* New York: Octagon Books, 1967.

"Events on Hudson's River in 1777." From reports of British officers on file in the Public Records Office, London. *Dutchess County Historical Society Yearbook,* Vol. 20 (1935), pp. 88–105; and Vol. 21 (1936), pp. 105–20; and Vol. 23 (1938), pp. 34–38. Author listed, for the last installment only, as J. Wilson Poucher.

Evers, Alf. *The Catskills from Wilderness to Woodstock.* Garden City, N.Y.: Doubleday & Company, 1972.

Fowler, Dorothy Canfield. *A City Church: The First Presbyterian Church in the City of New York, 1716–1976.* The First Presbyterian Church in the City of New York, 1981.

Fox, Dixon Ryan. *The Decline of Aristocracy in the Politics of New York 1801–1840.* New York: Harper & Row, 1965.

Fredriksen, Beatrice. *The Role of Dutchess County During the American Revolution.* A Dutchess County American Revolution Bicentennial Project, 1976.

Freeborn, James Livingston. *The Edgewood Club.* Privately printed, 1937.

Gardner, John W., and Francesca Gardner Reese, eds. *Know or Listen to Those Who Know.* New York: W. W. Norton & Company, 1975.

Gebhard, Elizabeth L. *The Life and Ventures of the Original John Jacob Astor.* Hudson, N.Y.: Bryan Printing Company, 1915.

Gehorsam, Jan. "River Estates Struggle to Survive," Poughkeepsie *Journal,* November 13, 1983, pp. 1A and 1B.

Gekle, William. *A Hudson Riverbook.* Poughkeepsie, N.Y.: Wyvern House, 1978.

Germantown, N.Y. Clermont State Historic Site (New York State Bureau of Parks, Recreation and Historic Preservation, Bureau of Historic Sites, Taconic Region). Livingston Family Papers.

————. Notebook of Louis Livingston, 1852–66.

Girouard, Mark. *Life in the English Country House.* New York: Penguin Books, 1980.

Goebel, Julius Jr. "Some Legal and Political Aspects of the Manors in New York." Address delivered at the annual meeting of the New York Branch of the Order of Colonial Lords of Manors in America, April 11, 1928. Baltimore: 1928.

Gordon, Patricia Joan. *The Livingstons of New York 1675–1860: Kinship and Class.* Ph.D. dissertation, Columbia University, 1959. Ann Arbor, Mich.: Xerox University Microfilms, authorized facsimile, 1975.

Grant, Mrs. Anne. *Memoirs of an American Lady.* New York: D. Appleton & Co., 1846 [originally published in London, 1808].

Griffiths, Sylvie R. "Johnston Livingston: The California Connection." Draft of unpublished biographical sketch, supplied by the author.

Griswold, Rufus Wilmot. *The Republican Court.* New York: D. Appleton & Company, 1854.

Gross, Mark. "Tivoli, New York," *Bard Papers,* Fall 1968.

Grund, Francis J. *Aristocracy in America.* New York: Harper & Row, 1959 [written 1839].

Hall, Mrs. Basil. *The Aristocratic Journey.* New York: G. P. Putnam's Sons, 1931.

Hammond, Jabez D. *The History of Political Parties in the State of New York.* 2 vols. Albany: C. Van Benthuysen, 1842.

Hardenbrook, Louise. "Something of the Livingston Family," *Columbia County Historical Society Bulletin,* No. XXXIV, April 1936, pp. 17–19. Kinderhook, N.Y.

Hatcher, William B. *Edward Livingston, Jeffersonian Republican and Jacksonian Democrat.* University, La.: Louisiana State University Press, 1940.

Historic American Buildings Survey. Rhinebeck Project, 1975.

"The History of the Old Red Church." Red Hook *Times,* November 19, 1921.

History of the Reformed Dutch Church of Rhinebeck Flatts, N.Y. by the Minister, Elders and Deacons. Rhinebeck: Frank D. Blanchard, 1931.

Holgate, Jerome B. *American Genealogy.* Albany: printed by Joel Munsell, 1848.

Humphreys, Mary Gay. *Catherine Schuyler.* New York: Charles Scribner's Sons, 1897. [N.B.: Large sections of this book are lifted verbatim from Mrs. Grant's *Memoirs of an American Lady.*]

Hunt, Charles Havens. *Life of Edward Livingston.* New York: D. Appleton & Company, 1864.

Hunt, Louise Livingston. *Memoir of Mrs. Edward Livingston.* New York: Harper & Brothers, 1886.

Hunt, Thomas. *A Historical Sketch of the Town of Clermont.* Hudson, N.Y.: The Hudson Press, 1928.

Hyde Park, N.Y. Franklin Delano Roosevelt Library. Livingston-Redmond Papers.

————. Lieurance translations of Livingston-Redmond Manuscripts.

Irving, Washington. *A Book of the Hudson.* New York: G. P. Putnam, 1849.

————. *Journal, 1803.* New York: Oxford University Press, 1934.

Jaher, Frederic Cople, ed. *The Rich, the Well Born, and the Powerful.* Urbana: University of Illinois Press, 1973.

Josephson, Matthew. *The Robber Barons.* New York: Harcourt, Brace & Company, 1934.

Judd, Jacob, and Irwin H. Polishook, eds. *Aspects of Early New York Society and Politics.* Tarrytown, N.Y.: Sleepy Hollow Restorations, 1974.

Kavaler, Lucy. *The Astors.* New York: Dodd, Mead & Company, 1966.

Kim, Sung Bok. *Landlord and Tenant in Colonial New York.* Chapel Hill: University of North Carolina Press, 1978.

Kinderhook, N.Y. House of History (Columbia County Historical Society). Mrs. Henry Walter Livingston's Diary, December 1811 to April 1820.

Kinkead, Rev. George B. "Gilbert Livingston and Some of His Descendants," *New York Genealogical and Biographical Record,* Vol. LXXXIV, 1953, pp. 4–15.

Klein, Milton M. *The American Whig: William Livingston of New York.* Dissertation, Columbia University, 1954. Ann Arbor, Mich.: University Microfilms.

———. "Politics and Personalities in Colonial New York," *New York History,* Vol. XLVII, No. 1, January 1966, pp. 3–16.

Krout, John A. "Behind the Coat of Arms: A Phase of Prestige in Colonial New York," *New York History,* Vol. XVI, No. 1, January 1935, pp. 45–52.

Lamb, Mrs. Martha J. *History of the City of New York.* 2 vols. New York and Chicago: A. S. Barnes and Company, 1877.

Langdon, William Chauncy. *Everyday Things in American Life 1607–1776.* New York: Charles Scribner's Sons, 1937.

Launitz-Schurer, Leopold S. Jr. *Loyal Whigs and Revolutionaries.* New York: New York University Press, 1980.

Leach, Douglas Edward. *The Northern Colonial Frontier 1607–1763.* New York: Holt, Rinehart & Winston, 1966.

Leder, Lawrence H. " '. . . Like Madmen Through the Streets,' the New York City Riot of June 1690." *New-York Historical Society Quarterly,* Vol. XXXIX, No. 4, October 1955, pp. 405–15.

———. "The Politics of Upheaval in New York, 1689–1709," *New-York Historical Society Quarterly,* Vol. XLIV, No. 4, October 1960, pp. 413–27.

———. *Robert Livingston 1654–1728 and the Politics of Colonial New York.* Chapel Hill: University of North Carolina Press, 1961.

———. "Robert Livingston: A New View of New York Politics," *New York History,* Vol. XL, No. 4, October 1959, pp. 358–67.

———. "Robert Livingston's Sons: Preparation for Futurity," *New York History,* Vol. L, No. 3, July 1969, pp. 235–49.

———. "Robert Livingston's Voyage to England, 1695," *New York History,* Vol. XXXVI, No. 1, January 1955, pp. 16–38.

———. "The Unorthodox Dominie: Nicholas Van Rensselaer," *New York History,* Vol. XXXV, No. 2, April 1954, pp. 166–76.

Lewis, John A. "Reminiscences of Annandale." Lecture at St. Stephen's College, Annandale, N.Y., February 12, 1895.

Livingston, Cambridge, obituary, New York *Times,* September 19, 1879, p. 5, col. 6.

Livingston, Edwin Brockholst. *The Livingstons of Livingston Manor.* New York: The Knickerbocker Press, 1910.

———. *"The Livingstons of Livingston Manor* Supplement." Handwritten manuscript. Clermont State Historic Site.

Livingston, Gracia B. Letter to Rev. Elliott Lindsley, February 15, 1973.

Livingston, J. H. "The Clermont Estate," *Tivoli Times,* September 12, 1902.

Livingston, Rev. John H. *Memoirs of the Rev. John H. Livingston.* New York: Rutgers Press, 1829.

Livingston, John Henry. "The Livingston Manor." Address written for the New York Branch of the Order of Colonial Lords of Manors in America.

Livingston, Rev. John Henry. *Incestuous Marriage: A Dissertation on the Marriage of a Man with his Sister in Law.* New Brunswick: Deare & Myer, 1816.

Livingston, John Swift, obituary. New York *Times,* May 31, 1867, p. 2, col. 2.

Livingston, Robert Swift, obituary. New York *Times,* March 1, 1867, p. 4, col. 6.

Livingston Memorial Church, One Hundredth Anniversary. Linlithgow, N.Y., 1970.

Livingston, Robert R. *Essay on Sheep.* New York: T. and J. Swords, 1809.

Lynch, Mary C. " 'Glenburn' 50th Anniversary." Handwritten notebook, 1906.

Lynd, Staughton. *Anti-Federalism in Dutchess County, New York.* Chicago: Loyola University Press, 1962.

―――. "The Tenant Rising at Livingston Manor, May 1777," *New-York Historical Society Quarterly,* Vol. XLVIII, No. 2, April 1964, pp. 163–77.

MacCracken, Henry Noble. *Blithe Dutchess.* New York: Hastings House, 1958.

―――. *Old Dutchess Forever!* New York: Hastings House, 1956.

Mackesy, Piers. *The War for America 1775–1783.* Cambridge, Mass.: Harvard University Press, 1964.

Madison, N.J. Drew University Library. Garrettson Papers.

Mark, Irving. *Agrarian Conflicts in Colonial New York 1711–1775.* New York: Columbia University Press, 1940.

Martineau, Harriet. *Retrospect of Western Travel.* 3 vols. London: Saunders and Otley, 1838.

Mason, Bernard. "Aspects of the New York Revolt of 1689," *New York History,* Vol. XXX, No. 2, April 1949, ρp. 165–80.

McAllister, Ward. *Society As I Have Found It.* New York: Cassell Publishing Company, 1890.

McAnear, Beverly. "Mr. Robert R. Livingston's Reasons Against a Land Tax," *Journal of Political Economy,* Vol. XLVIII, No. 1, February 1940, pp. 63–90.

Miller, Douglas T. *Jacksonian Aristocracy: Class and Democracy in New York, 1830–1860.* New York: Oxford University Press, 1967.

Miller, Ethel. "A Short History of the Ancram Paper Mill." Paper presented to a meeting of the Historical Society of the Town of Ancram, July 17, 1981.

Miller, John. "A Description of the Province and City of New York," *Gowans's Bibliotheca Americana,* No. III. New York: William Gowans, 1862 [originally published 1695].

"Miss Suckley Skims the Hudson River." *Gazette-Advertiser* (Rhinebeck, N.Y.), February 21, 1985, p. 3.

Monaghan, Frank. "An Examination of the Reputation of Captain Kidd," *New York History,* Vol. XIV, No. 3, July 1933, pp. 250–57.

Montgomery, Mrs. Richard. *Biographical Notes Concerning General Richard Montgomery.* Poughkeepsie: "News" Book and Job Printing House, 1876. [Purportedly the complete, original notes of Janet Montgomery, with prefatory notes and filler by "L.L.H."]

―――. Extracts from Janet Montgomery's Diary. Rhinebeck *Gazette,* August 9, August 16, August 23, September 6 and September 13, 1930.

―――. "Memoir by Janet Livingston Montgomery." Livingston-Bancroft Transcriptions, New York Public Library.

―――. "The Reminiscences of Mrs. Richard Montgomery." Introduction and editorial notes by John Ross Delafield. *Dutchess County Historical Society Yearbook,* Vol. 15 (1930), pp. 45–76.

Moore, Lela. *A Brief History of Tivoli.* Privately printed, 1921.

Morse, Howard H. *Historic Old Rhinebeck.* Rhinebeck, N.Y.: published by the author, 1908.

Mylod, John. *Biography of a River.* New York: Hawthorn Books, 1969.

Naramore, Bruce. *Master Plan for Clermont State Historic Park.* Waterford, N.Y.: New York State Park, Recreation and Historic Preservation Bureau of Historic Sites, 1982.

Navins, Joan. "Tivoli: A Historical Sketch," *Tivoli 1872–1972.* Rhinebeck, N.Y., 1972.

Neu, Irene D. "The Iron Plantations of Colonial New York," *New York History,* Vol. XXXIII, No. 1, January 1952, pp. 3–24.

Nevins, Allan, and Henry Steele Commager. *A Pocket History of the United States.* New York: Washington Square Press, 1942.

New York, N.Y. Museum of the City of New York. Livingston Papers.

New York, N.Y. The New-York Historical Society. Alida Livingston Papers.

———. Claverack Papers.

———. *Collections,* Vol. XIV, The Montresor Journals.

———. Duane Papers.

———. Kempe Papers.

———. Livingston Family Correspondence.

———. Robert R. Livingston Papers.

———. Winthrop Papers.

New York, N.Y. New York Public Library. Broadside Collection.

———. Emmet Collection.

———. Livingston-Bancroft Transcriptions.

———. Livingston Family Papers.

———. Gilbert Livingston Papers.

———. Philip Livingston and his son Peter Van Brugh Livingston: Letters and Documents.

———. Tomlinson Collection.

Nissenson, S. G. *The Patroon's Domain.* New York: Octagon Books, 1973.

O'Callaghan, E. B., ed. *The Documentary History of the State of New-York.* 4 vols. Albany: Weed, Parson & Company, 1849–51.

———. *Documents Relative to the Colonial History of the State of New-York.* 15 vols. Albany: Weed, Parson & Company, 1853–87.

Olin, Julia M. *The Perfect Light.* New York: Anson D. F. Randolph, 1866.

Olin, Stephen Henry. *Occasional Addresses by Stephen Henry Olin.* The DeVinne Press.

"A Packet of Old Letters," *Dutchess County Historical Society Yearbook,* Vol. VI (1921), pp. 26–61.

Palmer, R. R., and Joel Colton. *A History of the Modern World.* 4th ed. (1971), 2 vols. New York: Alfred A. Knopf, 1950.

Pearson, Edmund. "The Great Chowder Murder," *The New Yorker,* April 6, 1935, pp. 53–57.

Piwonka, Ruth. *The Landscape Art of Montgomery Livingston.* Kinderhook, N.Y.: Columbia County Historical Society, 1979.

Polk, Julia Branli, and Jean Schroeder Settin. *A History of the Roeliff Jansen Area.* Roeliff-Jansen Historical Society Publication No. 1. Lakeville, Conn.: The Lakeville Journal Press, 1975.

Poucher, J. Wilson. "Dutchess County Men of the Revolutionary Period: Henry Livingston," *Dutchess County Historical Society Yearbook,* Vol. 23 (1938), pp. 39–51.

Poughkeepsie, N.Y. Adriance Memorial Library. Livingston Family Correspondence 1732–99. Transcribed by Kevin Gallagher.
————. Uncatalogued correspondence of the Livingston Family.
Poughkeepsie, N.Y. Vassar College Library. Mrs. Maturin Livingston Letters.
Princeton, N.J. Princeton University Library. Wainwright Autograph Collection.
"Profile of an Historic District Property: Edgewater," *HRH News,* July 1979, pp. 4f.
Reed, John. *The Hudson River Valley.* New York: Bonanza Books, 1960.
Register of Properties on the Upper Hudson to be Sold or Let. New York: Frothingham & Timpson, 1896.
Reich, Jerome R. *Leisler's Rebellion.* Chicago: University of Chicago Press, 1953.
Reynolds, Helen Wilkinson. *Dutchess County Doorways.* New York: William Farquhar Payson, 1931.
————. "A Lady of the Victorian Era," *Dutchess County Historical Society Yearbook,* Vol. IX (1924), pp. 51–53.
Roach, George W. "Colonial Highways in the Upper Hudson Valley," *New York History,* Vol. XL, No. 2, April 1959, pp. 93–116.
"The Romance of Almont." Xerox copy of handwritten ms.
Rutherfurd, Livingston, ed. *Family Records and Events.* Compiled principally from the original manuscripts in the Rutherfurd Collection. New York: The DeVinne Press, 1894.
"Sale of the Estate of the Late Chancellor Livingston," New York *Evening Post,* July 1, 1857.
Schuyler, Montgomery. *Notes on the Patroonships, Manors and Seigneuries in Colonial Times.* New York: John B. Watkins Company for the Order of Colonial Lords of Manors in America, 1953.
————. *The Patroons and Lords of Manors of the Hudson.* New York: Publication of the Order of Colonial Lords of Manors in America, 1932.
Seager, Robin. "Elitism and Democracy in Classical Athens," in Jaher, *The Rich, the Well Born, and the Powerful,* pp. 7–26.
Shippen, Nancy (Mrs. Anne Hume Livingston). *Nancy Shippen, Her Journal Book.* Compiled and edited by Ethel Armes. Philadelphia: J. B. Lippincott Company, 1935.
A Short Account of the Winthrop Family. Privately printed. Cambridge: John Wilson and Son, 1887.
Singleton, Esther. *Social New York Under the Georges.* New York: D. Appleton & Company, 1902.
Skeen, C. Edward. *John Armstrong, Jr., 1758–1843.* Syracuse, N.Y.: Syracuse University Press, 1981.
Smith, Helen Evertson. *Colonial Days & Ways.* New York: The Century Company, 1901.
Smith, William. *Historical Memoirs from 12 July 1776 to 25 July 1778.* Edited and with introduction by William H. W. Sabine. New York: 1958.
Spofford, Horatio Gates. *A Gazetteer of the State of New-York.* Albany: B. D. Packard, 1824.
Steele, F. M. Sketch of Moncrief Livingston. Excerpted by Mrs. Laurence Barrington, in a letter to the author.
Strickland, William. *Journal of a Tour in the United States of America, 1794–1795.* New York: The New-York Historical Society, 1971.
Thomas, Lately. *A Pride of Lions.* New York: William Morrow & Company, 1971.
————. *Sam Ward, "King of the Lobby."* Boston: Houghton Mifflin Company, 1965.
Thompson, Harold W. *Body, Boots and Britches.* Philadelphia: J. B. Lippincott Company, 1940.

Titus, Rev. Anson. "Madam Sarah Knight, Her Diary and Her Times, 1666–1726."
The Bostonian Society Publications, Vol. 9. (1912), pp. 101–26.

"Tivoli, A Historical Sketch." Rhinebeck: Jator Printing Company, 1972.

Van Rensselaer, Florence, compiler. *The Livingston Family in America.* New York:
1949.

Van Rensselaer, Kiliaen. *The Van Rensselaer Manor.* Address delivered to the Order
of Colonial Lords of Manors in America, New York, April 24, 1915.

Van Rensselaer, Maria. *Correspondence of Maria van Rensselaer 1669–1689.* Trans. and
ed. by A. J. F. van Laer. Albany: The University of the State of New York,
1935.

Van Zandt, Roland. *The Catskill Mountain House.* New Brunswick, N.J.: Rutgers
University Press, 1966.

———. *Chronicles of the Hudson.* New Brunswick, N.J.: Rutgers University Press,
1971.

Waller, G. M. *Samuel Vetch, Colonial Enterpriser.* Chapel Hill: University of North
Carolina Press, 1960.

Walworth, Reuben Hyde. *Livingston Genealogy.* Rhinebeck, N.Y.: Friends of Clermont, Inc., 1982 [reprint edition; originally written in the 1860s].

Washington, D.C. Library of Congress. Shippen Family Papers.

Wecter, Dixon. *The Saga of American Society.* New York: Charles Scribner's Sons,
1937.

White, Philip L. *The Beekmans of New York.* New York: The New-York Historical
Society, 1956.

Wiles, Richard C. *Tivoli Revisited: A Social History.* Rhinebeck, N.Y.: Moran Printing,
Inc., 1981.

Wilkins, Harold T. *Captain Kidd and His Skeleton Island.* New York: Liveright Publishing Corporation, 1937.

Wilstach, Paul. *Hudson River Landings.* New York: Tudor Publishing Co., 1933.

Wood, Gordon S. "This Land Is Our Land," *New York Review of Books,* Vol. XXX,
No. 1, February 3, 1983.

Wooley, Charles. *A Two Years Journal in New-York: and part of its Territories in America.*
Gowans's Bibliotheca Americana, No. II. New York: William Gowans, 1860
[originally written 1678].

INDEX

Arryl House, 209–10
  See also Clermont
Articles of Association, 112
Articles of Confederation, 129
Aryan Order of St. George of the Holy
    Roman Empire in the Colonies of
    America, 210
Assembly, colonial
  Livingston men in, 66–67, 73, 78, 101
    Robert the Founder, 68, 71
    Robert the Judge, 92
  at start of Revolution, 110
Astor, Caroline, 203–4, 206
  and Astor orphans, 216
Astor, Emily, 177, 191, 192
Astor, Henry, 193n
Astor, John Jacob, 177, 247
Astor, John Jacob, Jr., 192
Astor, Margaret Rebecca Armstrong
    "Peachy," 176–77, 180, 191
Astor, William Backhouse, 4, 177, 191
Astor, William Backhouse, Jr., 213
Astor children, proper behavior of, 191
Astor family, 202n
Astor orphans, 213, 214–18
Autocrat of the Breakfast-Table, Holmes, 205

Bartholomew, Andrew, 162
Barton, Coralie Livingston, 170, 190–91
  See also Livingston, Coralie
Barton, Thomas, 170, 190
Bates, Lever, 240
Battle of Bunker Hill, 112
Battle of New Orleans, 165
Battle of Saratoga, 122
Batture project, 159–60, 164, 167, 190
Beekman, Cornelia, 63n
Beekman, Gertrude Van Cortlandt, 93
Beekman, Henry, 63n
Beekman, Henry, Jr., 64–65, 70, 82
Beekman, Janet Livingston, 65, 82
Beekman, Margaret, 65, 82
  See also Livingston, Margaret Beekman
Beekman family, 202n
Beekman Patent, 82
Bellomont, Richard Coote, Earl of, 41, 42,
    45
  and Robert Livingston, 55
  and William Kidd, 46–47, 48
Belvedere, 106, 122
Bentham, Jeremy, 169
Blackham, Richard, 42, 57
Bonaparte, Napoleon, Robert the
    Chancellor and, 155
Border dispute, between Massachusetts and
    New York, 87, 88, 90
Borman, James, 196
Boston Tea Party, 106

Boughton, Smith, 185–86, 196
Broadway house, Manhattan, 136
Broek, Mr., 45
Broome, Mary, 179, 187
Brown, Mrs. Lowndes, 201
Bunker Hill, Battle of, 112
Burgoyne, John, 121, 122
Burnet, William, 71
Burr, Aaron, 154, 158–60

Callendar, Earl of, 13
Callendar (Scotland), 75–76
Callendar House, 198
  See also Sunning Hill
Campbell, Duncan, 54
Canada, conflict with, 17, 32, 57–58
  1740s, 83
  1754, 88
  1760, 90
Catskill Mountains, 8
  Robert of Clermont's purchase, 81, 82
Chain across Hudson River, 126–27
Chancellor Livingston, 171
Chancellor of New York, Robert R.
    Livingston, Jr., as, 120
Chanler, Alida, 216, 218, 234
Chanler, Archie, 216–17, 234
Chanler, Bob "Sheriff Bob," 8, 217
Chanler, Elizabeth, 215, 216, 224
Chanler, John, 213–14
Chanler, Laura, 216
Chanler, Lewis, 217, 218, 234
Chanler, Margaret Livingston, 215–18
  See also Aldrich, Margaret Livingston
    Chanler
Chanler, Margaret Terry "Daisy," 215, 217
Chanler, William "Willie," 215n, 217
Chanler, Winthrop "Wintie," 215, 217
Character traits
  of Astor family, 192, 214
  of Livingston men, 2, 15, 52, 86, 116
    Edward "Beau Ned," 170–71
    Philip, son of the founder, 73–74
    Robert of Clermont, 74
    Robert the Chancellor, 145, 154, 162–
      63
    Robert the Founder, 12
    second generation, 95
  of Livingston women, 231
Charity, 39–40
Charles I, King of England, 14
Charles II, King of England, 14, 19
Charlestown, Masachusetts, Robert
    Livingston in, 17
Château de Montgomery, 146, 166, 169
  Lafayette's visit, 168
  See also Montgomery Place
Childhood activities

Oak Hill, 147
Oak Lawn, 207, 228
Olmsted brothers, 213
O'Malley, Austin, 204
Order of Colonial Lords of Manors in
    America, 210, 222
Orford, Edward Russell, Earl of, 42
Orlot, 234
Orphanage at Rose Hill, 212
Oswego French-and-Indian attack, 83
Otto, Eliza Livingston, 141
Otto, Louis, 139, 141, 142
Ownership of land, 24

Palatines, 59–62
    descendants of, 247–48
    as Livingston Manor tenants, 65–66
Paper-making project, 145
Patent for Livingston Manor, 1, 24–25, 66
Paterson, Catherine, 105
Paterson, John, 105
Patience, William, 57
Patriarchs, 203n
Patroon, 2
Patroonships, 18
Paulding (Revolutionary soldier), 129
Pearl Street house, Manhattan, 136
Personality traits of Livingston men, 2, 15,
    52
    of John (the Reverend), 13
    of Robert the Chancellor, 145
    of Robert the Founder, 12, 62
    of Robert the Judge, 92–93
Philipse Manor, tenants' uprising, 98
Pine Lawn, 207
    See also Holcroft
Pirates, colonial, 38
    William Kidd as, 45–47
Political office, and social position, 200
Political power, in colonial New York, 100–
    1
Politics
    in colonial New York, 79–80, 100–2,
        106–7, 110
    of Robert the Chancellor, 116
Poughkeepsie
    British attack, 121
    New York state legislature, 127
Prendergast, William, 98, 99
    pardon of, 100
Presidential election
    of George Washington, 134
    1800, 154
Pretty, Richard, 33
Primogeniture, abolishment of, 133
Private Club of Claverack Manor and the
    Roeliff Jansen Kill, 80, 208
Privateers, 38

William Kidd as a, 42
Livingston men as, 83
Proprietorship, 24
Pulepocken Historical Society, 247

Quartering Act, 99
Quebec, Montgomery's attack on, 114

Railroads, development of, 196–97, 201
Rand, Christopher, 234
Rand, Margaret Aldrich "Maddie," 234,
    246
Ranelagh, Viscountess, 136–37
Reade, Catharine Livingston, 147
Rebellion of Livingston Manor tenants, 88–
    89
Recreation in colonial Albany, 28–29
Redmond, Thomas Johnston Livingston,
    224
Refugees, German Palatine, in New York,
    59–62
Religion of Catherine Livingston, 137–38
Rensselaerwyck, 18–19, 66
    Livingston claims on, 22–23
    Robert the Founder as secretary, 20
    royal patent, 25
Rent strike, 1794, 151
Rent system, overthrow of, 184–87
Revolutionary War, 3
    beginning of, 110
    Canadian expedition, 113–15
    close of, 130
    roots of, 96, 99, 106–7
Rhinebeck, 239–40
    baptism of baby, 133
    British attack, 122
Richmond, 166
Ridgely, 235–36
Riots
    at Livingston Manor, 89
    Stamp Act Riots, 97
Roeliff Jansen Kill, 23, 47, 251
    harbor, 69
    water rights to, 81–82, 126, 151, 152
Rokeby, 177, 190, 191, 193, 213, 217–18,
    232–33, 245–47
    See also La Bergerie
Romeyn, Dominie, 133
Romney, Henry Sidney, Earl of, 42
Roosevelt, Eleanor, 4, 179n, 207n, 228
Roosevelt, Franklin Delano, 4, 229, 230
Rose Hill, 210–12
Rothschild, Meyer, 197
Roundout Creek, 11
Royal patent of Livingston Manor, 1, 24–
    26, 66
Ruggles, Charles H., 179, 187
Rum trade, 2